THE LEGAL
PROCESS
from a
BEHAVIORAL
PERSPECTIVE

THE DORSEY SERIES IN POLITICAL SCIENCE

EDITOR   NORTON E. LONG   *Brandeis University*

THE LEGAL
PROCESS
from a
BEHAVIORAL
PERSPECTIVE

STUART S. NAGEL, Ph.D., LL.B.
Professor of Political Science
University of Illinois

1969
The Dorsey Press, Homewood, Illinois
Irwin-Dorsey Limited, Georgetown, Ontario

Library of Congress Catalog Card No. 69–19988
Printed in the United States of America

1/20/72 Bm-Sect 9.50

To
my wife Joyce,
my parents,
and my children

Introduction

The purpose of this book is to bring together a series of studies dealing with various aspects of the legal process which were all written by a single author from a common behavioral perspective. Most of the studies included have previously appeared in diverse law and social science journals, but only by making them accessible between two covers can their integrated nature be perceived. When each study was originally being written, its role in such an integrated volume was taken into consideration. It has thus been unnecessary to do a large amount of editing in order to provide a coherent whole.

In the context of this book, a behavioral perspective toward law refers to a specific conceptual and methodological orientation. The conceptual orientation views law not as a set of rules and decisions to be read by law students, applied by lawyers, and evaluated by law professors. Instead, law is viewed mainly as the responses of lawmakers to prior stimuli, and as stimuli to the subsequent responses of law appliers and law recipients. This orientation thus involves viewing legal policies and decisions in their total context as both effects and causes.

With regard to methodology, a behavioral orientation toward law tends to emphasize the quantitative testing of generalizations about the relations between various legal phenomena and other phenomena. The quantitative testing generally involves determining (1) some hypotheses to test; (2) a sample of persons, places, or things on which to make the tests; (3) measurements for the relevant characteristics of the entities; and (4) a tabulation of the relations between the measured characteristics.

The cause-and-effect or stimulus-and-response conceptualism of the behavioral perspective can be contrasted with a more legalistic approach which tends to view legal policies and decisions mainly as objects of study in themselves. Likewise, the quantitative or scientific methodology of the behavioral perspective can be contrasted with a more verbal approach which avoids the precision of quantification. One can thus have (1) a legalistic-verbal approach, which is present in much law review writing; (2) a legalistic-quantitative approach, which is present in those works that quantify judicial votes without considering the causes or effects of decisional variations external to the court reports in which the votes are found; (3) a causal-verbal approach, which is interested in external causes and effects such as the impact of pressure groups on Supreme Court decision making, but in a descriptive, nonquantitative way; or (4) a causal-quantitative approach, which combines both the conceptualism and methodology of the behavioral perspective. It is the fourth kind of perspective that this book attempts to achieve.

Further elaboration on the nature of the concepts and methods associated with the behavioral perspective is given in Chapters 1 and 2. Chapter 3 then discusses the utility of behavioral and social science to the practicing lawyer, the legal policy maker, and the legal scholar. The studies referred to as examples in that discussion are mainly behavioral studies although some represent the causal-verbal or legalistic-quantitative approaches. All three approaches might be considered to come within the general scope of social science as contrasted to the legalistic-verbal approach which represents legal scholarship in its non–social-science form.

Part Two of the book presents 10 studies that view lawmaking and adjudication as responses to prior stimuli as perceived by the lawmakers and adjudicators. The prior stimuli include legal norms such as constitutional principles (Chapter 4), procedural rules (5), and judicial precedents (6). The prior stimuli also include factual stimuli such as the cultural context (7), the contestants (8 and 9), and the evidentiary and other facts (10 through 13). When read together, the four items in Chapters 10 through 13 provide a simple but meaningful system for predicting and understanding judicial outcomes. They particularly illustrate the need for bringing together the articles on which this book is based.

Part Three is devoted to the role of legal decision makers in determining lawmaking and adjudication responses. The emphasis is particularly on testing relations between their characteristics and their decision-making propensities (Chapter 14). Their characteristics especially include methods of recruitment (15), attitudes (16), and political party affiliation (17). Their decisions emphasize criminal cases (18) and regulatory agency decisions (19), although other characteristics and decisions are discussed as well. This part also deals with the interaction between legislators and judges, particularly at the federal level where the politics of judicial review (20) and congressional reaction (21) are discussed.

Part Four presents four studies that view lawmaking and adjudication as stimuli. Chapter 22 deals with the differential impact of the church and state cases on newspaper editorials. Twenty-three deals with the effects of excluding illegally seized evidence on the behavior of police, judges, criminals, prosecuting attorneys, and defense attorneys. Chapter 24 demonstrates how a computer can quickly determine what effect alternative redistricting policies will have on the equality, compactness, and partisan composition of the districts involved. It also demonstrates how a computer can suggest a redistricting policy or plan that will be close to ideal in light of the criteria specified by those responsible for the computer redistricting. The notion of an ideal policy leads to the last study whose title "Optimizing Legal Policy" sets the theme for a future book on which the author is working. Like some of the prior studies, this last chapter places a heavy emphasis on explaining matters of quantitative methodology in terms that law-oriented readers should be able to understand, particularly after having read the prior chapters (e.g., Chapter 12) where some of the methods are first introduced.

The audiences to which this book is directed include persons with interests in sociology, political science, law, and psychology. Thus the chapters which deal with the role of societal variables in the legal process (like Chapters 7 and 8) might be particularly relevant to sociologists, whereas chapters which deal with political parties as key variables (like Chapters 17 and 19) might be particularly relevant to political scientists. Likewise the chapters that emphasize the role of legal rules and evidence (like 4 and 11) might be considered more worthwhile to law professors, as contrasted to psychologists or those concerned with psychology who might find the attitudinal chapters (like 16 and 23) to be more interesting. With regard to methodological audiences, the book is designed to be readable by those who are behaviorally oriented or nonbehaviorally oriented and by undergraduates, graduate students, professors, lawyers, and laymen so long as they are interested in a scientific approach to studying the inputs and outputs of the legal process.

The contributions of various people to specific chapters are acknowledged in the footnotes, but there are some people and institutions who have contributed substantially to the whole book and to whom I am extremely grateful. These include: my research assistants—Marsha Dickinson and George Forgie; my formal and informal teachers—Victor Rosenblum, Richard Snyder, Glendon Schubert, Harold Guetzkow, and Lester Milbrath; my sources of research funds—the Social Science Research Council, the American Council of Learned Societies, the Center for Advanced Study in the Behavioral Sciences, the East-West Center, and the University Research Board of the University of Illinois; and especially my helpful wife and patient family.

I am also indebted to those University of Illinois students who collaborated with me in writing certain chapters, especially Constantine Curris (Chapter 15), Robert Erikson (22), Felix Gagliano (9), and Martin Lubin (19). I also acknowledge the generosity of the following journals for allowing me to reprint portions of my articles: *American Behavioral Scientist, Journal of Legal Education, American Bar Association Journal, Administrative Law Review, Southwestern Social Science Quarterly, Vanderbilt Law Review, UCLA Law Review, Nebraska Law Review, Practical Lawyer, Texas Law Review, Michigan Law Review, Indiana Law Journal, Western Political Quarterly, American Political*

Science Review, Journal of the American Judicature Society, Journal of Criminal Law, Criminology and Police Science, Journal of Public Law, Public Opinion Quarterly, Wisconsin Law Review, Stanford Law Review, Florida Law Review, Law and Society Newsletter, and the Free Press Publishers.

March, 1969   STUART S. NAGEL

Table of Contents

Part One

BASIC CONCEPTS AND METHODS

P̲art One is mainly designed to describe the basic conceptual and methodological orientation that permeates the rest of the book. As mentioned in the Introduction the behavioral conceptual scheme emphasizes that legal policies are responses to prior stimuli and that they are also stimuli to subsequent responses. This is contrasted with a more legalistic approach, which views legal policies or adjudications as doctrines or judicial votes to be analyzed in themselves, irrespective of their external causes or effects.

The language of the conceptual scheme used here is that of stimulus–response psychology, although it could be input–output systems analysis, in which input is substituted for stimuli, output is substituted for responses, and conversion structure is substituted for organism. However, there are several advantages to using the stimulus–response terminology. First, the terminology emphasizes that we are basically dealing with *human beings* who are performing in the roles of policy makers (e.g., judges or legislators), policy appliers (policemen or school superintendents), or policy recipients (contract makers or automobile drivers) rather than with institutions (courts or legislatures), countries, or other abstractions. Second, a body of *empirically tested principles* already exists to describe how various human organisms respond to various stimuli in various circumstances which by analogy can to some extent be applied to the personnel involved in the legal process.[1] Third, the notion of a stimulus emphasizes *cause* more than the notion of an input does, just as response emphasizes *effect*, and social science should encourage a striving to determine what causes differences in behavior and what effects are due to such differences.

Closely related conceptual schemes include those of Glendon Schubert[2] and Walter Murphy.[3] Schubert's input–output scheme, however, views the legal process only in terms of the first half of the conceptual scheme used in this book. Thus, the outputs, whether they are norms (i.e., policies) or decisions (i.e., adjudications), are viewed by Schubert almost exclusively as the end product of the judicial process or as feedback variables on the decision makers, with a resulting neglect of the role of these outputs as stimuli that influence the behavior of those outside the judiciary toward whom they are directed. Like much political science research on the legal process, Walter Murphy's input–output scheme possibly overemphasizes the United States Supreme Court, thereby unduly limiting its applicability.

The methodological as contrasted to the conceptual orientation emphasizes the quantitative testing of hypotheses on a sample of entities after the entities have been measured or positioned on the characteristics or variables involved, and after the researcher has decided what tabulation or analysis tends to confirm or refute the hypotheses. This is really nothing more than the scientific method of distinguishing highly probable generalizations from less probable ones—a method now being increasingly taught at the high school and elementary levels as well as in college science and social science courses. It can be contrasted with case studies and traditional verbal syntheses of cases that abound in the legal literature.

Other descriptions of the scientific method as applied to legal research include essays by Sidney Ulmer[4] and Hans Zeisel.[5] Both essays are excellent, although not so detailed as Chapter 2 of this book, especially

---

[1] Lambert, *Stimulus-Response Contiguity and Reinforcement Theory in Social Psychology,* in G. LINDZEY, 1 HANDBOOK OF SOCIAL PSYCHOLOGY 57 (1954) and Osgood, *Behavior Theory and the Social Sciences,* in R. YOUNG (ed.), APPROACHES TO THE STUDY OF POLITICS 217 (1958).

[2] G. SCHUBERT, *Policy-Making Analysis,* in JUDICIAL POLICY-MAKING 104 (1965).

[3] W. MURPHY, ELEMENTS OF JUDICIAL STRATEGY 31–36 (1964). Also see more recently J. SIGLER, AN INTRODUCTION TO THE LEGAL SYSTEM (1968) whose conceptual scheme avoids some of the truncated impact of Schubert and the Supreme Court emphasis of Murphy.

[4] Ulmer, *Scientific Method and the Judicial Process,* 7 AM. BEHAV. SCI. 21 (1963).

[5] Zeisel, *Social Research on the Law: The Ideal and the Practical,* in W. EVAN (ed.), LAW AND SOCIOLOGY—EXPLORATORY ESSAYS 124 (1962).

when Chapter 2 is considered along with the methodology portions of Chapters 10 through 14 and 22 through 25. To be more clearly understood, methodology should also be put into important substantive contexts as is attempted in most of the chapters.

Chapter 3 of Part One then attempts to show how social science studies, especially those that combine the behavioral conceptual and methodological orientation, can be useful to the practicing lawyer, the legal policymaker, and the legal scholar in a way that has practical, social, and theoretical significance. Other studies that emphasize the actual as well as potential utility of specific behavioral legal research include a recent essay by Hans Zeisel[6] and two more abstract essays by Arthur Miller and Lee Loevinger.[7]

It is interesting to note that all three of these authors express some disappointment with the present as contrasted to the potential contributions of political science and as contrasted to other fields of social science.[8] Unfortunately, political scientists have been overly concerned with analyzing Supreme Court opinions and votes in constitutional law cases to the relative neglect of other courts, external causes, external effects, and other fields of law. Nevertheless, the epilogue to this book does clearly bring out some important contributions that political science is making to a social science of law, and Chapter 3 deals with the utility to law of behavioral science in general.

---

[6] Zeisel, *The Law*, in P. LAZARSFELD, *et al.* (eds.), THE USES OF SOCIOLOGY 81 (1967).

[7] Miller, *Observation on the Interdependence of Law and the Behavioral Sciences,* 43 TEXAS L. REV. 1994 (1965) and Loevinger, *Law and Science as Rival Systems,* 19 FLA. L. REV. 530 (1966–67).

[8] Zeisel says, "The reason why they [Schubert-type studies] are not given more prominence in this essay is that they have proved of little 'use' in the meaning of this book." Zeisel, *The Law*, in P. LAZARSFELD *et al.* (eds.), THE USES OF SOCIOLOGY 86 (1967). Loevinger, *supra* at 543. Miller, *supra* at 1098 and 1100.

CHAPTER 1

A Conceptual Scheme of the
Legal Process

Systematic conceptual schemes have been devised for analyzing psychological,[1] sociological,[2] and political[3] phenomena. These schemes reveal gaps in the literature and thereby generate hypotheses as did Mendelyeev's periodic table of chemical elements. They also provide categories for integrating empirically tested propositions. It is the purpose of this short chapter to present a modest conceptual scheme of the legal process.

I. THE SCHEME

Legal policies represent the heart of the legal process. Such policies may be made by judicial, legislative, or administrative policymakers. They may involve substance or procedure and any field of public law (government-to-citizenship and government-to-government relations) or private law (citizen-to-citizen relations). They may represent a response to prior stimuli, or they may represent stimuli to subsequent responses.

A. Legal Policies as Responses

The prior stimuli that bring about legal policies consist of normative standards of right and wrong and of empirical facts. The normative standards consist of legal norms promulgated by governmental bodies and nonlegal norms that are not so promulgated. The legal norms are embodied in constitutions, statutes, administrative regulations, judge-made law, and administrative adjudications depending on the nature

---

[1] HANDBOOK OF SOCIAL PSYCHOLOGY 257–58 (G. LINDZEY ed. 1954).
[2] THEORIES OF SOCIETY (T. PARSONS et al. eds. 1961).
[3] APPROACHES TO THE STUDY OF POLITICS (R. YOUNG ed. 1958).

of the promulgating governmental body. The nonlegal norms are embodied in customs of the populace, in scholarly commentaries, and in recorded notions of justice and social utility.

The empirical facts, which also serve as stimuli to legal-policy responses, consist of evidentiary facts (which according to the norms can or should be considered in reaching decisions) and nonevidentiary facts (which the norms do not deem relevant but which do empirically correlate with differential outcomes). The evidentiary facts consist of admissible testimony by laymen and experts, and admissible physical evidence. The nonevidentiary facts (some of which may be evidentiary in some instances) consist of the time when the policymaking occurs, the place where it occurs, and the statuses and other normatively irrelevant characteristic of the parties (both formal parties and behind-the-scene parties) and their pleaders (court counsel and legislative lobbyists).

The normative standards and empirical facts are filtered through the policymakers before a policy response results. The policymakers thus correspond to the organisms in stimulus–response theory. Two aspects of the policymakers are particularly relevant in determining how the standards and facts will be perceived and weighed. One is the characteristics of the individual policymakers, and the other is the interaction among the policymakers. Relevant individual characteristics have to do with recruitment (e.g., elected, appointed), education (e.g., preschool socialization, college training), group affiliations (e.g., political party, ethnic) demographic statuses (e.g., age, birthplace), and acquired attitudes (e.g., liberalism, dogmatism). Relevant forms of interaction have to do with relations of attraction–repulsion (e.g., friendship, respect) and relations of leadership–followership (e.g., formal, informal).

The stimuli being channeled through the policymakers lead to a policy, but the policy can also have a feedback effect on the stimuli, since the new policy is likely to become part of the growing, changing body of normative standards for future policymaking.

B. LEGAL POLICIES AS STIMULI

The policy so made also becomes (along with other reinforcing and conflicting policies) a stimulus toward subsequent compliance responses. Degrees of compliance and noncompliance are stimulated not only by the policy and related policies but also by various facilitating and inhibiting factors. These factors may be natural or social. The natural factors relate to physical phenomena such as geological changes (which might effect land ownership) and to biological phenomena such as sexual drives (which might affect compliance to family or criminal laws). The social factors relate to economic, political, religious, educational, familial, linguistic (including communication media), and aesthetic phenomena, each one of which can in some instances influence the impact of legal policies.

The policy and these factors feed through a set of policy appliers and policy recipients. The policy appliers generally consist of administrators and judges, but they may also consist of legislators writing statutes designed to implement a broader policy. Administrators, like judges, in some circumstances also may be important policymakers whose policies are applied by other administrators. The policy recipients consist of the total public, or some segment within it that is ultimately affected by the policy. The characteristics and interaction of the policy appliers and recipients (like those of the policymakers) affect their differential response.

The policy effects represent the response to the stimulus provided by the policy, the facilitating and inhibiting factors, and the filtering of the policy appliers and recipients. The policy effects may manifest themselves in behavioral or attitudinal change, or in lack of change. Sometimes, one can infer attitudes from observed or recorded behavior, but frequently it is necessary to question the attitude holders themselves. The behavioral and attitudinal effects may relate to the goals expressed in the policy or to side effects.

Thus, if the policy is "no admissibility of illegally seized evidence," then the most relevant policy appliers would be police, prosecutors, and trial court judges, while criminals and law-abiding citizens would be the main policy recipients. The desired goals of such a policy would probably be a decrease in illegal searches (a behavioral effect) and thus an increase in public attitudes of security from arbitrary search (an attitudinal effect), without substantially increasing criminality (a behavioral effect) or lowering police morale (an attitudinal effect). Possible side effects (not likely to be mentioned as part of the goals of the policy) might include the simplification of search warrant procedures, the broadening of the concept of legal search, and perhaps increased friction between prosecutors and police over police tactics.

Like the response of the policymakers, the response of the policy appliers and the policy recipients has a feedback effect. It feeds back on the policy in that noncompliance or adverse effects may result in changing the policy, while high compliance and beneficial effects may result in broadening the policy. The policy effects also feed back on the facilitating or inhibiting factors in such a way as to strengthen or weaken them, depending on the circumstances involved.

This scheme can be made clearer with the aid of conceptual boxes, connective horizontal lines, subordinate vertical lines, and causal arrows (see Figure 1–1). What is especially needed in legal research are more empirically tested propositions that provide details on the more specific nature of the interrelations shown by the arrows running among and

FIGURE 1–1

A CONCEPTUAL SCHEME OF THE LEGAL PROCESS

(see the text for concepts beneath the third level of subordination)

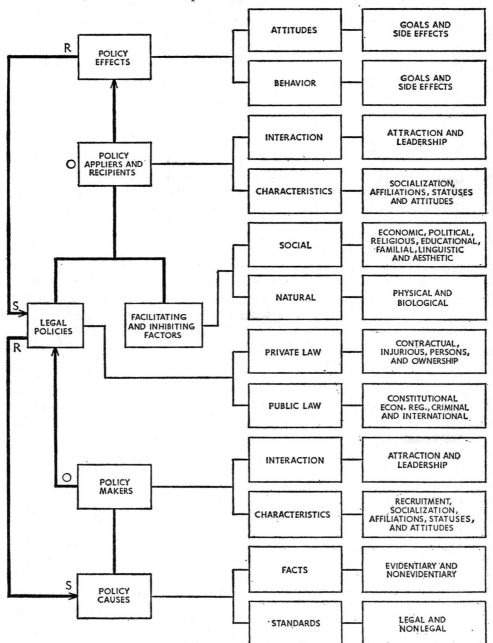

through the primary concepts. A perusal of legal research literature reveals a particular lack of propositions with regard to the relation between (1) the presence or absence of various nonevidentiary facts and (2) alternative policy outcomes, and also between (1) the presence or absence of alternative policies and (2) differential attitudes and behaviors of policy recipients. In addition to empirical testing, there is a need for more hard thinking about the meaning and elaboration of the categories and subcategories which belong in such a conceptual scheme.

II. AN APPLICATION

To illustrate the scheme presented, one may very briefly try to apply it to the legal policy of school desegregation enunciated in *Brown* v. *Board of Education,* 347 U.S. 483 (1954). This policy represented a response to certain normative standards and empirical facts being filtered through the Supreme Court policymakers. The normative standards of a legal nature include the relevant precedents which ordered desegregation on narrower grounds such as *Missouri* ex rel. *Gaines* v. *Canada,* 305 U.S. 337 (1938) (equal protection violated by subsidizing Negroes to attend out-of-state schools), and *Sweatt* v. *Painter,* 339 U.S. 629 (1950) (equal protection violated by the intangible differences between Negro and white law schools). The nonlegal norms include a shift in white public opinion toward a less negative attitude toward Negroes than was present at the time of *Plessy* v. *Ferguson,* 163 U.S. 537 (1896), when the separate but equal doctrine was established.

The evidentiary facts include testimony on the physical differences between the Negro and white schools involved and on the psychological effects of segregation. The nonevidentiary, but probably relevant, facts include such things as the role of the NAACP Legal Defense and Educational Fund, the increased power of Negroes as consumers and as Northern-urban voters, and the attitudes of Afro-Asian countries in the cold war.

The attitudinal and background characteristics of the Supreme Court policymakers were significantly different in 1954 as compared to 1896. These differences can be determined by a content analysis of the off-the-bench comments of the respective judges and by an analysis of their respective group affiliations, prejudicial occupations, and presidential appointers. The leadership of Earl Warren probably also played an important part in the unanimous decision that was reached.

The policy, once made, fed back into the normative standards available to the courts and thus became a source of subsequent expanding cases such as *Bolling* v. *Sharpe,* 347 U.S. 497 (1954) (expanding the

Brown policy to federal territory), and the *Girard College* case, 353 U.S. 922 (1957) (expanding the Brown policy to private schools administered by governmental officials as trustees).

Compliance with the resulting constitutional policies was facilitated by some factors and hindered by others. Facilitating factors included the economic expense of duplicate facilities, the loss of industrial development where violent noncompliance occurred, and the influence of many religious bodies which endorsed the desegregation policy. Inhibiting factors included economic competition between Negroes and whites, fear of the potential political strength of Negroes, and biological differences in skin color.

The characteristics of the policy appliers have affected the impact of the policy. Relevant characteristics include geographical characteristics such as region and urbanism, and political role characteristics such as whether the policy applier is a federal or state official, or whether the policy applier is a local legislator or a local school superintendent. Relations of attraction and repulsion among the policy appliers have affected implementation (e.g., relations between certain northern congressmen and certain southern congressmen), as have relations of leadership and followership (e.g., relations between Senator Byrd and the state officials in the Virginia government. Likewise, the characteristic of the policy recipients have partially determined the differential impact of the policy on them. Characteristics like race, region, urbanism, age, and class account for some people's having been effected differently than other people by the desegregation policy.

The policy enunciated in *Brown* v. *Board of Education* has had many effects. The behavioral goal of the policy was to remove race as a consideration in determining which public school a schoolchild could attend. The degree to which this goal has been achieved can be measured by determining the percent of school districts that are integrated, using as a percentage base only those school districts that have some schoolage Negro children and some schoolage white children. The degree of this type of goal achievement can also be measured by determining the percent of Negro school children who attend schools with whites and the percent of white schoolchildren who attend schools with Negroes, again using only school districts that have biracial populations. Other behavioral side effects that may be attributed to the *Brown* decision include the partial breakdown of the practice of segregation in noneducation activities, such as housing and employment, and the antisegregation demonstrations that *Brown* has indirectly inspired.

The attitudinal goal of the school desegregation policy was to lessen the feelings of Negro inferiority, which common sense and social science evidence tended to indicate was partially a result of school segregation. Psychological depth studies of Negro schoolchildren could be made before and after various communities desegregate their schools, using similar nondesegregating communities as a control group. One may hypothesize that, in the desegregating communities, one will find an increase in optimism and possibly ambition on the part of both the Negroes who go to the white schools and also the Negroes who remain in the Negro schools. Other attitudinal side effects include the changed attitudes one may find on the part of whites toward Negroes and on the part of Afro-Asians toward American foreign policy.

The effects of the desegregation policy have already had some feed-back effects on related policies and on the facilitating and inhibiting factors. Related policies that have been partially stimulated by the effects include the Civil Rights Act of 1957 and 1960, and such court precedents as *Cooper* v. *Aaron,* 358 U.S. 1 (1958) (reaction to the Little Rock violence), and *Watson* v. *City of Memphis,* 373 U.S. 526 (1963) (reaction to the slowness of desegregation). Facilitating factors that have been strengthened by the effects include the attitude of the Catholic church and other religious bodies, and inhibiting factors that have been weak-ened include the resistance of lower federal court judges and other po-litical officials.

The above application could have been elaborated in more detail. As mentioned above, however, what seems to be needed in applying the conceptual scheme to a legal policy or a set of legal policies or decisions is not only further hypothesizing but also systematic empirical testing (through questionnaires, content analysis, and statistical tech-niques) of the explicit and implicit hypotheses that the conceptual scheme may lead one to formulate.

CHAPTER 2

Methods for Testing Empirical
Generalizations in Legal Research

Social scientists for many years have been testing empirical generalizations in their respective disciplines.[1] Some of their techniques are beginning to trickle into the legal journals at an increasing rate.[2] The
legal research that has thus far used such techniques, however, has
largely been done by social scientists rather than by legal scholars.[3]
It is the purpose of this chapter to describe briefly some of the techniques
involved in systematically testing empirical generalizations, in the hope
that increased understanding will stimulate more law school scholars
to apply them.[4]

The writer gratefully thanks Jerry Bonham, Deno Curris, and the other members
of his Public Law Seminar of Autumn 1962 for the constructive suggestions they
made concerning this chapter.
[1] The standard textbooks on general social science methodology include W. GOODE
& P. HATT, METHODS IN SOCIAL RESEARCH (1952); C. SELLTIZ et al., RESEARCH
METHODS IN SOCIAL RELATIONS (1959); T. McCORMICK & R. FRANCIS, METHODS
OF RESEARCH IN THE BEHAVIORAL SCIENCES (1958); and G. LINDZEY (ed.), HAND-
BOOK OF SOCIAL PSYCHOLOGY 259–561 (1954). These textbooks elaborate many of
the points made in this paper.
[2] See, e.g., Tanenhaus, Supreme Court Attitudes toward Federal Administrative
Agencies: Application of Social Science Methods to the Study of the Judicial Process,
14 VAND. L. REV. 473 (1961); Zeisel, Kalven, & Bucholz, Is the Trial Bar a Cause of
Delay?, 43 J. AM. JUD. SOC'Y 17 (1959); Ulmer, An Empirical Analysis of Selected
Aspects of Lawmaking of the United States Supreme Court, 8 J. PUB. L. 414 (1959);
Barton & Mendlovitz, The Experience of Injustice as a Research Problem, 13. J.
LEGAL ED. 24 (1960); and Nagel, Judicial Backgrounds and Criminal Cases, 53
J. CRIM. L., C. & P.S. 333 (1962) (Chap. 18, infra).
[3] See Jones, Some Current Trends in Legal Research, 15 J. LEGAL ED. 121 (1962).
[4] For a defense of the desirability of applying the general scientific method to legal
research (as contrasted to a clarification of some of the techniques involved) see
Loevinger, Jurimetrics: Science and Prediction in the Field of Law, 46 MINN. L. REV.
255 (1961); H. CAIRNS, THE THEORY OF LEGAL SCIENCE (1941); and Cohen, Transcendental Nonsense and the Functional Approach, 35 COLUM. L. REV. 809 (1935).

Basically, the steps involved in empirically testing generalizations are approximately as follows: (1) decide on a general topic; (2) review the relevant prior literature; (3) decide which hypotheses to test; (4) decide on the research design to make the tests; (5) compile the data in accordance with the research design; (6) draw conclusions from the data in accordance with the research design; and (7) offer explanations for one's findings. One can, however, reconsult the relevant literature or reformulate the hypotheses or research design out of the sequence presented.

The most technical step is the research design. It involves determining the sample of entities on which to test the hypotheses, determining the method of measuring the relevant variables, and especially determining what analysis of the data will be used to indicate whether the hypotheses have been confirmed or refuted. In order to clarify what is involved, each of the testing steps and each of the aspects of the research design need to be discussed in more detail and with legal research examples.

I.   THE STEPS

A. Choosing the Topic and Reviewing the Literature

Between alternative topics for research, the better topic is the one that has the greater social or legislative benefit, or at least the greater theoretical significance. Topics that are more likely to lead to findings that will generate other studies are more worthwhile than topics that have less heuristic value. The better topic, of course, is also the one that is more controversial and that has been less adequately researched previously. It is also the one that is more easily researched, given the limited time, expertise, interests, funds, and other resources of the researcher. Ease of research, however, should not be a significant consideration unless the other criteria of social utility, heuristic value, and prior inadequacy are also met.

After a topic has been chosen, one should make an extensive search of the relevant literature in order to avoid wasteful duplication and in order to obtain suggestive ideas for the hypotheses and the research design. In addition to consulting the traditional legal indexing tools (such as the *Index to Legal Periodicals* and the various tools for finding relevant cases), a search should also be made of the indexes likely to reveal relevant social science material, such as the *International Index to Periodical Literature* and the *Cumulative Book Index*.

B. FORMULATING THE HYPOTHESES

After deciding on a general topic and reviewing the literature, at least one hypothesis or tentative conclusion should be formulated. The most interesting kind of hypotheses are those that indicate a relationship between two or more variables. A one-variable hypothesis merely indicates the degree to which one variable is present among a set of entities (e.g., the percent of contested wills among the wills probated before a given court in a given year). A two-variable hypothesis says, in effect, "If I know X is present, then I can *generally* predict that Y will be present." In this context, X is called the independent variable (the thing used to predict), and Y is called the dependent variable (the thing predicted). One usually cannot substitute "always" for "generally" in social science research because, unlike the chemist and physicist, the social scientist cannot consistently eliminate or control other variables that may interfere with the relation. Unless the hypothesis specifies otherwise, no causal relationship is assumed between the variables, although frequently the independent variable is a cause (or something related to a cause) of the dependent variable.

The independent variable of a hypothesis may refer to an element in an adjudication (e.g., an element relating to the evidence, the personnel, the place, or the time period), and the dependent variable may refer to a case outcome (e.g., decision for the defendant, decision within a short time from initiation of the case, or amount of damages awarded). The independent variable may also refer to a type of law (e.g., one that provides for relatively easy divorce, one that provides for a state income tax, or one that provides for capital punishment), and the dependent variable may refer to a characteristic of a geographical area (e.g., the number of divorces per 1,000 population, the state's gross economic product, of the number of murders per 1,000 population). In fact, the variables can refer to almost anything, although in order to keep the hypothesis within the field of law, at least one of the variables must refer to some legal phenomenon.

A meaningful empirical hypothesis is one that is potentially capable of being proved or disproved through observation or through the examination of someone else's observations (e.g., the observations of a court reporter who records judicial voting behavior). A hypothesis that is true or false by definition is not an empirical hypothesis (e.g., "If a society uses the interrogatory system of adjudication, then its judges will take an active part in the trial process."). Likewise, a hypothesis is nonempirical if it is normative or policy-oriented without providing reasonably objective criteria of the goals sought (e.g., "Where X law has been adopted, the results have been good."). If such criteria are provided, however, the hypothesis may be empirically testable (e.g., "Where X law or analogous laws have been adopted, the amount of disparity in sentences for similar crimes from judge to judge has been reduced.").

C. SAMPLING THE ENTITIES

After a hypothesis has been formulated, one must decide which entities to sample in order to test the hypothesis. The nature of the hypothesis will, in part, indicate the entities to be used. The entities may consist of all the northern states that have or have not adopted certain legislation, all the cases heard by the Supreme Court in 1958, or all the justices of the peace serving in Ohio between 1930 and 1935. They may also consist of time periods before and after an event, lawyers, courts, voters, legislators, occurrences, pressure groups, countries, or any other entities relevant to the hypothesis.

In addition to relevancy, the type of entity chosen should be a type on which data is accessible. The study, however, should address itself to how the findings might have differed if a different type of relevant entity were used. This may involve reasoning from analogy or from small unrepresentative samples of alternative entities. Thus, a hypothesis about American judges may be meaningfully tested mainly on appellate judges if one is rationally capable of indicating whether the relations observed between the variables would be stronger, weaker, or about the same with trial court judges, given the relevant differences between trial and appellate court judges.

After the type of entity has been decided, the specific entities on which data will be compiled must be determined. One can sometimes compile data on all the entities within the type. If this number is too large to be manageable, however, and there is no meaningful way to limit the entities to a narrower time period, geographic region, or the like, then random sampling may be used to limit the size of the sample. Random sampling involves giving a numerical designation to all the entities that potentially could come into the sample. For instance, one number might be assigned to each case in a set of 1,000 cases; or each case might be given a number in terms of the page, column, and number of inches from the top of the page on which the case appears if the names are already in some form of a list, such as the cases in one of the decennial digests of the American Digest system. Then one can draw as many random numbers out of a list of random numbers as one needs to fill his sample quota. Lists of random numbers can be found in many textbooks on statistical techniques.[5]

---

[5] For an example of a random numbers table and a description of how to use one in drawing samples, see H. WALKER & J. LEV, STATISTICAL INFERENCE 126, 171-73, 484 (1953).

D. MEASURING THE VARIABLES

The next step in the research design is to determine how the variables are to be measured or, in other words, how the entities are to be positioned on each of the variables. For example, if one has a hypothesis dealing with the political party affiliation of judges, this step will involve deciding whether certain minor parties should be grouped with the Democrats, the Republicans, or neither. It will also involve determining what sources will be consulted to find the party affiliation of the judges.

If one has a hypothesis about the effect of a statute (e.g., a statute establishing a public-defender system) or a judge-made law (e.g., the exclusionary rule as applied to illegally seized evidence), the measurement step may involve preparing a meaningful questionnaire or observation checkoff list and deciding how it is going to be administered. Questions can sometimes be used from standardized questionnaires to determine certain background characteristics, attitudes, and abilities, but most of the questions will probably have to be original.[6] The items can be structured so that the respondent must check off or otherwise choose between the alternative responses that are provided (e.g., agree or disagree); or they can be open-ended, where one seeks more verbose answers or descriptions. The questionnaire can be administered by mail or by competent interviewers. Mailing is less costly, but it generally brings a lower response (although sometimes a more frank response) than personal interviews do. Mailed questionnaires are most effective when accompanied by an explanatory letter and a return envelope, and followed by a reminder letter.[7]

Sometimes, a controlled behavioral index can be used in order to position the entities on a variable instead of, or in addition to, analyzing the subjective views of the participants. For instance, in order to determine how states' rights-oriented various Supreme Court judges are relative to one another, one might give each judge a score representing the difference between (1) the percentage of state statutes he upheld that expanded economic regulation, and (2) the percentage of federal statutes he upheld that also expanded economic regulation. Likewise, one might determine how powerful various pressure groups are before the Supreme Court by giving each pressure group a score that represents the difference between (1) the percentage of victories for the pressure

---

[6] For suggestive questionnaire items, see the relevant questionnaires mentioned in the various editions of O. BUROS (ed.), MENTAL MEASUREMENTS YEARBOOK (1938–59). For ideas on wording original questions, see S. PAYNE, THE ART OF ASKING QUESTIONS (1951).

[7] For further details on conducting a survey, see M. PARTEN, SURVEYS, POLLS, AND SAMPLES—PRACTICAL PROCEDURES (1950).

group when it provided counsel or an amicus curiae brief, and (2) the percentage of victories for the pressure group's position in similar cases in which it did not participate, provided there were at least a few of both types of cases. In a similar manner, one could possibly measure the amount of courtroom discrimination against Negroes from one period to another by giving each period a group of scores, each one of which would represent the difference between (1) the average sentence received by Negro defendants, and (2) the average sentence received by white defendants committing a similar type of crime, with a different such score for each type of crime.[8]

E. PLANNING THE ANALYSIS

The research design should systematically plan how the data compiled will be analyzed to determine whether or not the hypothesis has been confirmed. A basic social science tool for analyzing data relevant to a two-variable hypothesis is the fourfold table. A fourfold table has the form shown in Table 2–1. The cell labeled a should show the *number*

TABLE 2–1

A FOURFOLD TABLE

Independent Variable

		Negative Position	Positive Position	
Dependent Variable	Positive Position	$\left(\dfrac{a}{a+b}\%\right)$	$\left(\dfrac{c}{c+d}\%\right)$	a + c
	Negative Position	$\left(\dfrac{b}{a+b}\%\right)$	$\left(\dfrac{d}{c+d}\%\right)$	b + d
		a + b (100%)	c + d (100%)	a + b + c + d = N (total sample of entities)

of entities that have a negative position on the independent variable and a positive position on the dependent variable. Likewise, cell b should show the number of entities that have a negative position on the independent variable that also had a negative position on the depen-

---

[8] For more complex aspects of measuring variables (including factor analysis and Thurstone, Guttman, and Likert scales), some of which may occasionally be applicable to testing empirical relationships in legal research, see J. GUILFORD, PSYCHOMETRIC METHODS (1954).

dent variable. And so on with cells c and d. If neither of the positions on a variable are negative (less affirmative) or positive (more affirmative), then the positions should be placed in such a way that a concentration of entities in cells b and c confirm rather than refute the hypothesis being tested. Cell a should also show the *percentage* of entities in the negative group on the independent variable that were in the positive group on the dependent variable, and so on with cells b, c, and d. The percentages in cells a and b add down to 100 per cent, as do the percentages in cells c and d. Decimal points should be eliminated from these percentages, since they are unnecessary and confusing in this context.

If the percentage in cell c is *greater* than the percentage in cell a, then there is a direct or positive correlation between the independent variable and the dependent variable. If the percentage in cell c is the *same* as the percentage in cell a, then there is a zero correlation. On the other hand, if the percentage in cell c is *less* than the percentage in cell a, then there is an inverse or negative correlation between the two variables.

A fourfold table provides only two positions for each variable—for example, being high or low on a self-restraint variable, or relatively effective or relatively ineffective on an effectiveness variable. For most empirical legal research, two positions on each variable are adequate. If, however, one of the variables provides for three positions, then one could use a three-by-two or a two-by-three table, with six cells, rather than a two-by-two table, with four cells. In other words, the number of cells in an expanded fourfold table equals the number of positions or intervals provided for on the independent variable times the number of positions or intervals provided for on the dependent variable. The method of calculating percentages downward is still the same as in the basic fourfold table; and just as in fourfold table, one compares the percentages toward the right side of the larger table with those toward the left side to determine the direction of the correlation. If the percentages on the far left are relatively low, however, and the percentages in the middle are high, and the percentages on the far right are also low (or vice versa), then a curvilinear correlation is present.

One can plan to compile the data on index cards, and then sort and count the cards to fill in the cells of the fourfold table. If the number of entities or the number of interrelated variables becomes large, however, this method of transcribing the data from the source material to the fourfold or comparable tables becomes extremely cumbersome. In such circumstances, it is advisable to compile the data on IBM cards. Each IBM card corresponds to a different entity (unless the quantity of variables requires more than one card per entity), and each column of 10 numbers (0 through 9) corresponds to a variable (unless more than 10 positions are provided for on a variable). Thus, a punch in position 1 on column 57 might indicate that the criminal case represented by the card was decided in favor of the prosecution; and a punch in position 2 on column 57 might indicate that the case was decided in favor of the defense.

In using IBM cards to process data, one has to devise a coding key that describes which column corresponds to each variable and which hole on the column corresponds to each position on the variable. One should then transcribe the source data (e.g., scratch notes) onto the coding sheets in light of the coding key. The coding sheets consist simply of a pile of sheets with 80 short lines on each sheet corresponding to the 80 columns available on each IBM card. After the transcribing or coding is complete, one then takes the coding sheets to an IBM key punch and punches a set of IBM cards from the coding sheets as if he were typing from the coding sheets. The next step in using IBM equipment is to feed the set of punched cards into an electric counter-sorter or an electronic computer in order to get the numbers for the cells in the fourfold or comparable tables.[9]

After the fourfold tables have been filled in, one may want to determine the degree of correlation between the variables—not just whether there is a positive, zero, or negative direction. The difference between the percentage in cell c and the percentage in cell a gives a rough measure of the degree of correlation. This difference can be any number from plus 100 percentage points (perfect positive correlation) to 0 percentage points (no correlation) to minus 100 percentage points (perfect inverse correlation). If one wants a more precise measure of the degree of correlation or a measure of correlation in a six-cell or greater table, one can make use of the correlation coefficients described in the standard textbooks on statistical techniques.[10]

In addition to determining the degree of correlation, one might want to determine the probability of arriving at the observed correlation purely by chance, given the sample size involved. A rough way to calculate this chance probability is simply to multiply the sample size for the fourfold table by the square of the difference between the percentage in cell c and the percentage in cell a. One then takes this product

---

[9] For greater detail concerning the key punch, the sorter-counter, and other basic IBM equipment, see B. FRIEDMAN, PUNCHED CARD PRIMER (1965); and IBM CORP., IBM OPERATORS' GUIDE (1959).

[10] On statistical techniques in general, see J. GUILFORD, FUNDAMENTAL STATISTICS IN PSYCHOLOGY AND EDUCATION (1956); and WALKER & LEV, *op. cit. supra* note 5. On statistical techniques especially designed for use with the crude kind of measurement frequently necessary in legal research, see S. SIEGAL, NON-PARAMETRIC STATISTICS FOR THE BEHAVORIAL SCIENCES (1956). For a simplified step-by-step approach to statistics, see H. YUKER, A GUIDE TO STATISTICAL CALCULATIONS (1958).

to the first row of any chi-square probability table and reads off half the chance probability immediately above the place where the product appears in the table. The probability is not halved if one merely hypothesizes that there will be a difference between the two groups or positions on the independent variable without specifying the direction of the difference. Chi-square tables, as well as more complex ways of calculating chance probabilities, can be found in statistical textbooks.[11] If a correlation could occur purely by chance less than 5 times in 100 (i.e., contrary to 19-to-1 odds), then it is conventional among social scientists to say that the correlation was not owing to chance coincidence but, rather, to the presence of a real relationship between the variables.

In planning the analysis, it is productive of useful insights to apply the plan of analysis to a few select hypotheses on a small sample from the total sample before making the full study. Such a pilot study or microcosm of the full study usually proves time-saving in the long run because of the unanticipated defects it tends to reveal in the research design. Pilot studies are also helpful for generating hypotheses.

F. Compiling the Data and Drawing a Conclusion

In accordance with the sampling techniques, the measurement techniques, and the plan of analysis developed in the research design, data should now be compiled for the purpose of testing the hypothesis or hypotheses. The data may be obtained from library materials, interviews, mailed questionnaires, observation, contrived experiments, court records, or from any other relevant sources. This step can be extremely time-consuming, and therefore techniques should be devised to minimize the time involved and to delegate much of the work to competent research assistants.

After the data is compiled and placed in the relevant tables, one should observe the tables and make whatever calculations are needed to determine if the data confirms or fails to confirm the hypothesis.[12] Depending on one's purposes, one might decide to conclude that the hypothesis is confirmed if the correlation goes in the direction hypothesized (1) beyond both a certain intensity and a certain chance probability, (2) merely beyond a certain intensity where one does not seek to generalize beyond the sample involved, or (3) merely beyond a

---

[11] See note 10 *supra*. For a more detailed explanation and justification of the statistical estimation methods given in this paper, see Nagel, *Estimation of Correlation and Statistical Significance in Fourfold Tables,* a mimeographed paper, available from the writer on request.

[12] To simplify the mechanical work involved in making the calculations, see W. Varner, Computing with Desk Calculators (1957); and H. Borko, Computer Applications in the Behavorial Sciences, 1–171 (1962).

certain chance probability where one does not seek a high-intensity relation. A hypothesis is further confirmed if it is consistent with other known relationships and if a repetition of the research design reveals similar findings.

G. EXPLAINING THE CONCLUSION

The testing of empirical generalizations is not complete until a tested or untested explanation is offered for *why* the relationship found exists, or for *why* the relation hypothesized but not found does not exist. One should attempt to account for not only why the relation went in the direction it did, but also why it was not a stronger relationship. For example, the initial hypothesis may have been that a greater percentage of Democratic members rather than Republican members of the independent regulatory agencies are above the average liberalism score of their respective agencies. In positioning the commissioners on the liberalism variable, each commissioner can be given a score equal to the proportion of times he decided in favor of what might be considered the liberal rather than the conservative side in those adjudications where this variable is applicable. If a +.30 correlation were present, one might hypothesize that it was *not weaker* partly because a greater percentage of Democratic commissioners rather than Republican commissioners come from urban areas (a testable hypothesis) and urban commissioners tend to vote more liberally than rural commissioners of the same agency (also a testable hypothesis). Likewise, one might hypothesize that the correlation was *not stronger* because a greater percentage of the Democratic commissioners rather than the Republican commissioners come from the South (a testable hypothesis) and southern commissioners tend to vote more conservatively than northern commissioners of the same agency (also a testable hypothesis).

If an explanation is tested and shown to be true, one might go further and attempt to explain why the explanation is true. For instance, one might attempt to explain why southerners tend to be Democrats in terms of historical reasons and why southerners tend to be conservatives in terms of lack of industrialization. Once the chain of explanations leaves the realm of social science and enters into the realm of natural science, however, the explanation process should end. Thus, one need not go on to indicate that the lack of industrialization in the South may be attributable to its warmer climate, which, in turn, is attributable to the tilt of the Earth's axis, which, in turn, is attributable to certain gravitational factors.

In general, there are four basic kinds of explanations to account for a correlation between an independent and a dependent variable:

(1) the independent may be *a* cause or *the* cause of the dependent variable, or vice versa; (2) the independent and dependent variables may be coeffects of an explanatory variable or set of explanatory variables; (3) the independent may be the cause of an explanatory variable or variables, which, in turn, may be the cause of the dependent variable; or (4) there may be a combination of the above three kinds of explanations operating simultaneously.

Basically, there are two ways of testing an explanatory variable—a positive method and a negative method. The positive method recognizes that if the explanatory variable is responsible for the relation, then when the explanatory variable is present or increased, the relation should generally be present or increased. The negative method recognizes that if the explanatory variable is absent or decreased, the relation should generally be absent or decreased. For example, one might suspect that part of the reason for the liberal voting behavior of Democratic commissioners is that they have liberal attitudes as measured by a liberalism questionnarie. In accordance with the positive method, one would test (1) to see if Democratic commissioners scored higher on the liberalism questionnaire than Republican commissioners, and also (2) to see if high questionnaire scorers tended to vote more liberally than low questionnaire scorers. In accordance with the negative method, one would test (1) to see if liberal Democrats (high questionnaire scorers) distributed themselves on the voting dependent-variable about the same as liberal Republicans, and also (2) to see if conservative Democrats (low questionnaire scores) distributed themselves on the voting dependent-variable about the same as conservative Republicans. This fractionation of the sample into a liberal fourfold and a separate conservative fourfold in effect holds constant the liberalism–conservatism variable, while allowing political party and voting behavior to fluctuate freely. Fractionation of a sample is comparable to a chemist's using a vacuum in order to hold constant the wind resistance that might interfere with the testing of a hypothesis concerning falling objects.

To feel more confident that a *causal* relation is present, one should not only satisfy the positive and negative methods of explanation testing, but one should also find that an increase in the alleged cause is generally followed in time by an increase in the alleged effect. Some would further say that one should also find that an increase in the alleged effect is generally preceded by an increase in the alleged cause, although such a requirement overemphasizes single causes at the expense of multiple causes.

Explaining the conclusion may also involve pointing out conditioning or catalytic variables, which, unlike explanatory variables, do not in themselves cause an increase or decrease in the independent or dependent variables. Instead, a conditioning variable, when it accompanies an independent variable, tends to increase the relation between the independent and dependent variables. Thus, American history seems to show that having substantial difference (the conditioning variable) in the political party affiliations of the Supreme Court and Congress will not in itself bring on court-curbing bills (the dependent variable), but such party differences may be an important or even necessary condition to facilitating court-curbing bills when intense judicial activism (the independent variable) is present. Complete explanations may also point out the relevance of unique variables that may be responsible for another variable or set of variables in a few instances but not as a general matter. Thus, having a close relative who was a murder victim may make a juror prosecution-oriented, but few prosecution-oriented jurors are so oriented for that reason.

In explaining why complex relations exist, it is sometimes helpful to draw a diagram with the variables in boxes or circles connected by arrows to indicate causal direction and dotted lines to indicate non-causal correlations.[13]

II. AN APPLICATION

In order to clarify further the concepts and techniques that have been presented, it may be helpful to go through one application from the topic step through the explanation step.

An interesting topic that potentially could have social or theoretical significance is the broad topic of variables that influence the outcome of litigation. This topic may be narrowed to deal just with variables concerning the attraction and repulsion that certain courts seem to have for each other as sources of authority in certain types of cases. Approached from a different point of view, the topic may be narrowed to deal just with labor law litigation.

A review of the prior literature would reveal little concerning the phenomenon of favorable or unfavorable attitudes among American courts toward each other. A review of the literature would, however, reveal many studies of factors influencing labor litigation. Nearly all of these studies, however, are merely designed to describe and evaluate the rulings laid down in the relevant precedents. Few of them empirically test the extent to which the presence of variables mentioned in the rulings and variables not mentioned in the rulings correlate with whether the union interest wins or loses in a sample of labor law cases.

A pair of hypotheses that the topic and the literature might suggest is that the Supreme Court is more likely to reverse antiunion decisions from southern courts than from northern courts, but is more likely to affirm prounion decisions from southern courts than from northern courts.

These hypotheses logically indicate that the relevant entities are Su-

---

[13] For further detail on causal explanations, see R. MACIVER, SOCIAL CAUSATION (1942).

preme Court opinions (or cases) involving labor law disputes. Professor Harold Spaeth, of the University of Detroit, has compiled for a different purpose a list of 91 such opinions from the 1953 through 1959 terms of the Supreme Court.[14] Labor law disputes in this context refer to formal opinions dealing with the kind of subjects covered in such statutes as the Taft-Hartley Act,[15] the Fair Labor Standards Act,[16] the Railway Labor Act,[17] the Norris-LaGuardia Act,[18] and analogous state statutes, but not workmen's compensation or antitrust statutes. In light of the hypotheses, cases involving disputes between two unions are excluded from the sample, although they are included in Spaeth's list. Two or more cases decided under the same opinion are treated as separate cases if the separate cases differed with regard to the decision of the Supreme Court, the decision of the initial court, or the region of the initial court. In light of these considerations, the original 91 opinions become 94 cases. If the hypothesis is confirmed with this sample of cases, one might try to test on a broader sample of cases whether appellate courts in general in economic regulation cases tend (1) to reverse conservative decisions from relatively conservative lower courts more than those from liberal lower courts while tending (2) to affirm liberal decisions from relatively conservative lower courts more than those from liberal lower courts.

There are three variables involved in the pair of hypotheses. The independent variable relates to region. A southern court can be meaningfully defined as a state or federal court located in one of the states that had legalized slavery as of 1860. A northern court can be defined as any other state or federal court. The federal courts of appeals from the third, sixth, eighth, and tenth circuits cover some southern states and some northern states, but they are classified as northern courts because a check of *Who's Who in America* indicates that more of the judges on each of these courts were appointed from northern rather than southern states. For the same reason, the courts of the District of Columbia are classified as northern courts, although many of their judges are natives of the District of Columbia. The dependent variable simply involves determining whether the Supreme Court affirmed or reversed the initial court's decision. The third variable (called an intervening or constant variable) relates to whether the initial court's decision was favorable or unfavorable to the union interests involved. In his work with these cases, Spaeth sometimes attempts to determine whether the decisions were favorable or unfavorable to the workers' interests, which is a more subjective variable to measure. By initial court in this context is meant the first court in the

---

[14] Spaeth, *An Analysis of Judicial Attitudes in the Labor Relations Decisions of the Warren Court*, 25 J. POL. 290 (1963).
[15] 61 Stat. 136 (1947, 29 U.S.C. §§ 141–44, 151–67, 171–82, 185–87 (1958).
[16] 52 Stat. 1060 (1938), 29 U.S.C. §§ 201–19 (1958).
[17] 44 Stat. 577 (1926), 45 U.S.C. §§ 151–63, 181–88 (1958).
[18] 47 Stat. 70 (1932), 29 U.S.C. §§ 101–15 (1958).

judicial hierarchy that heard the case. The initial court is used rather than the court immediately prior to the Supreme Court in order to have more cases decided by southern courts, and because predictions tend to be more interesting if they are based on data further away from the event being predicted.

Any case that cannot be clearly positioned on all three variables are excluded from the analysis (e.g., an affirmance in part and reversal in part), thereby decreasing the sample of 94 cases to a sample of 91 cases. The findings would probably be strengthened if only those cases are used in which a prounion decision also means a proworker, antimanagement decision (and vice versa with an antiunion decision), but purifying the sample in this manner might unduly decrease the sample size. All three variables are measured dichotomously (i.e., with two positions per variable). There seems to be little purpose in talking about the degree of southernness (border versus deep), the degree of anti- or prounion impact (based on the extent each case is cited in certain labor law treatises), or the degree of affirmance (nine to zero, five to four, zero to nine, and so on), although these kinds of measurement could be used later if they subsequently appeared fruitful.

The plan of analysis calls for positioning each case on each of the three variables in order to obtain the information necessary to fill Table 1–2. Either index-type cards alone or index cards transcribed to IBM cards can be used to record the necessary information from the cases prior to sorting and counting. The pair of hypotheses will be considered confirmed if there is at least a 20 percentage point difference in the direction hypothesized between the affirmance rate of the North and the South for each of the two hypotheses, and if the relevant differences observed could not have occurred more than 5 times out of 100 purely by chance.

Table 2–2 contains the data compiled. Any set of two or more fourfold tables with a common independent or dependent variable, like those in

TABLE 2–2

THE RELATION BETWEEN INITIAL COURT REGION AND SUPREME COURT DECISION IN LABOR LITIGATION

(detailed presentation)

	Region South	North			Region South	North	
Affirmed	3 (18%)	17 (43%)	20	Affirmed	6 (67%)	12 (48%)	18
Supreme Court Reversed	14 (82%)	23 (57%)	37	Reversed	3 (33%)	13 (52%)	16
	17	40	57 cases		9	25	34 cases

(Initial Court Decisions Unfavorable to the Union)   (Initial Court Decisions Favorable to the Union)

Table 2–2, can be converted for easier reading into a table like Table 2–3, which contains all the essential data from Table 2–2. As indicated in rows one and two of Table 2–3, there is more than a 20 percentage point difference in the direction hypothesized between the affirmance rate of the North and the South for only the first of the two hypotheses. Given the group sizes of 17 and 40, the difference of 25 percentage points in Table 2–3 could have occurred purely by chance only 4 times out of 100, which meets the predetermined standard of confirmation. On the other hand, given the groups sizes of 9 and 25, the other difference of 19 percentage points could have occurred purely by chance as many as 15 times out of 100, which does not meet the predetermined standard of confirmation. In view of the interlocking nature of the hypotheses, however, the really important difference is not the isolated difference between

TABLE 2–3

THE RELATION BETWEEN INITIAL COURT REGION AND SUPREME COURT
DECISION IN LABOR LITIGATION

(simplified presentation)

Initial Court Decision	*Number of Southern Cases*	*Number of Northern Cases*	*Percentage of Southern Cases Affirmed*	*Percentage of Northern Cases Affirmed*	*Difference*	*Probability of Difference Being Due to Chance*
Unfavorable to Union 17	40	18	43	+25	about $4/100$
Favorable to Union 9	25	67	48	−19	about $15/100$

18 percent and 43 percent or the one between 67 percent and 48 percent, but rather the overall difference between +25 and −19. This difference of 44 percentage points, given the relevant group sizes of 57 and 34, could not have occurred purely by chance more than about once in 100 times.[19]

A tentative explanation that one might offer to account for the basic phenomenon observed in the difference column of Table 2–3 is that southern courts have a reputation for having a more antiunion bias relative to the northern courts (a testable hypothesis using questionnaires applied to lawyers), and this reputation is valid in light of southern court behavior (a hypothesis testable on a random sample of southern and northern labor cases). Therefore, when a southern court hands down an

---

[19] This combined chance probability was calculated simply by multiplying $4/100$ by $15/100$. The other chance probabilities were calculated by the estimation method described in note 11 *supra* and the accompanying text.

antiunion decision, the Supreme Court is more likely to be suspicious (not so testable, given the reluctance of Supreme Court justices to answer questions about things like this), and the southern court decision is more likely to be erroneous (not so testable, given the subjectivity of the concept of "erroneous," although questionnaires presenting hypothetical cases to lawyers might be feasible), and therefore the southern court decision is more likely to be reversed. On the other hand, for reasons converse to the above explanation, if the southern court decides in favor of a union the southern court is more likely to be upheld than is a northern court similarly deciding in favor of a union. The relations were not stronger because Supreme Court affirmance or reversal in labor union cases obviously is dependent on more variables than just the region and the decision of the initial court. Other relevant variables may relate to the law involved, the evidence introduced, the group interests at stake, and the historical context of each case.

Incidentally, the practicing lawyer (who is usually more interested in bread-and-butter predictions than in theoretical hypotheses) may observe that Table 2–2 indicates that by predicting an affirmance when the Supreme Court takes on a prounion decision and a reversal when the Supreme Court takes on an antiunion decision, he would have predicted accurately 55 times (18 plus 37) and inaccurately only 36 times (16 plus 20). The numbers in parentheses, in effect, represent the entries from a fourfold table deducible from Tables 2–2 and 2–3, in which the independent variable is the initial court's decision and the dependent variable is the Supreme Court's decision.

From the data given in Tables 2–2 and 2–3, one can deduce other interesting tables. For example, if the independent variable is the decider (initial courts versus the U.S. Supreme Court) and the dependent variable is the decision (favorable to the union versus unfavorable to the union), then one finds that 60 percent of the 91 Supreme Court decisions were favorable to the union, whereas only 37 percent of the initial court decisions were favorable to the union. This difference of 23 percentage points in the direction hypothesized with a sample of 182 decisions could occur purely by chance less than 1 in 1,000 times. This table clearly refutes Glendon Schubert's conclusion from the same data that "the evidence is so slight that on the basis of this sample, there is little ground for such an inference . . . that the union bias (i.e., decisional orientation) is opposite to the bias of the trial (i.e., initial) courts."[20]

Findings like those of Tables 2–2 or 2–3 could conceivably have some value to legislators who write labor legislation, to persons responsible for staffing the relevant courts, to judges who want to know their biases

---

[20] G. SCHUBERT, JUDICIAL BEHAVIOR: A READER IN THEORY AND RESEARCH 459 (1964).

better in order to control them better, as well as to the practitioner who seeks additional information about whether to appeal and about what to emphasize or include in an appellate brief.

III. CONCLUSION

In the last few hundred years, the systematic empirical testing of generalizations has become more and more important in one field of knowledge after another. First, it was the physical sciences, including astronomy, physics, chemistry, and geology. Then, the scientific method enveloped the biological sciences. The 20th century has been witnessing a methodological revolution in the social sciences. Psychology, which is partly a biological science, was the first social science affected. Then sociology succumbed. Then economics. Since the end of World War II, political science has been undergoing a methodological rejuvenation. Its close neighbor, the field of law, seems next in line.

Legal scholars have long been concerned almost exclusively with individual case studies, chronologies of precedent development, armchair speculation, statements of author preferences, individual biographies, and especially descriptions of the holdings in sets of judicial opinions. In order to further aid the legislator, administrator, judge, and practitioner, it seems time to supplement traditional scholarship with more testing of empirical generalizations in legal research.

CHAPTER 3

The Utility of the Concepts
and the Methods

It is the purpose of this chapter to offer some tentative answers to the question, "What can social science contribute to law?" It seems logical to answer this question from the point of view of the three main types of personnel within the legal profession: the practicing lawyer, the legal policymaker and the legal scholar. The specific examples given in the footnotes represent a sampling of the relevant literature.[1]

I. THE PRACTICING LAWYER

Social science methodology and substance can be useful to the practicing lawyer mainly by providing him with some materials that he might be able to introduce into evidence to win specific cases or points.[2] With regard to methodology, polling techniques may be valuable in resolving such issues as trademark infringement,[3] change of venue[4] or community standards of fitness for citizenship.[5] Systematic statistical analysis may be relevant to show that an alleged favoritism or discrimination is not readily attributable to chance.[6] Systematic observation or content analysis of documents may reveal patterns of behavior relevant to determining

---

[1] For further dicussion of the relations between social science and law, see LAW AND SOCIOLOGY (EVAN ed. 1962); DAVIS et al., SOCIETY AND THE LAW—NEW MEANINGS FOR AN OLD PROFESSION (1962); and *Frontiers of Legal Research*, 7 AM. BEHAV. SCI. 1 (December, 1963).

[2] Greenberg, *Social Scientists Take the Stand—A Review and Appraisal of Their Testimony in Litigation*, 54 MICH. L. REV. 953 (1956).

[3] Zeisel, *The Uniqueness of Survey Evidence*, 45 CORNELL L. Q. 322 (1960).

[4] Sherman, *Use of Public Opinion Polls in Continuance and Venue Hearings*, 50 A.B.A.J. 357 (1964).

[5] *Repouille* v. *United States*, 165 F. 2d (1947), especially Jerome Frank's dissent.

[6] Ulmer, *Supreme Court Behavior in Racial Exclusion Cases*, 56 AM. POL. SCI. REV. 325 (1962).

what constitutes reasonable care in a negligence case or common usage in a contract dispute.[7]

With regard to substance, psychological information may be crucial in civil or criminal insanity cases[8] or in any case involving the perceptive powers of witnesses.[9] Economic information may be crucial in antitrust, labor–management, or commercial disputes.[10] Information gathered from historical[11] or political science[12] sources may be relevant to interpreting a statute or other legal document; it may also be relevant to a constitutional or administrative law issue. Sociological knowledge may be important in the sentencing aspects of a criminal case or the disposition of a family law case.[13]

Social science methodology and substance, in addition to being of value to the practicing lawyer with regard to the presentation of evidence in specific cases, can also help to improve his techniques as a lawyer in general.

As to trial techniques, social science methods are capable of testing a variety of hypotheses concerning the relative effectiveness of alternative techniques. Professors Kalven and Zeisel of the University of Chicago jury project, for instance, have played tape recordings of trials to many actual juries in order to determine how the juries would react to slight variations in the trials. Among other things, they found that if the plaintiff's lawyer mentions that the defendant has insurance and the defendant's lawyer successfully objects, then the juries will tend to award higher damages to the plaintiff than if the defendant's lawyer did not object at all. They also found that working-class jurors in personal injury cases are more likely to find liability but are less likely to award higher damages than upper-class jurors—a bit of information helpful in picking juries after one has assessed the probability that liability will be found.[14]

Social science potentially can contribute to the skillful handling of clients in one's office. The Jury Verdict Research Corporation of Cleveland, Ohio, for instance, publishes a loose-leaf service indicating the percentage of a wide variety of cases that have been decided in favor of the

---

[7] SELLTIZ *et al.*, RESEARCH METHODS IN SOCIAL RELATIONS 199–234 and 315–42 (1962).

[8] Lassen, *The Psychologist as an Expert Witness in Assessing Mental Disease or Defect*, 50 A.B.A.J. 239 (1964).

[9] McCARTY, LEGAL AND CRIMINAL PSYCHOLOGY (1961).

[10] *Economics in Antitrust Policy and Practice*, 20 A.B.A. ANTITRUST SECTION (1962).

[11] Kelly, *The Fourteenth Amendment Reconsidered*, 54 MICH. L. REV. 1049 (1959).

[12] *Reynolds* v. *Sims*, 377 U.S. 533 (1964), cites numerous political scientists on various aspects of the reapportionment controversies.

[13] Rose, *The Social Scientist as an Expert Witness*, 40 MINN. L. REV. 205, 209 (1956).

[14] Broader, *University of Chicago Jury Project*, 38 NEB. L. REV. 744 (1959).

plaintiff and the average damages awarded. This kind of information, systematically gathered from across the country, can be helpful in advising a client on an out-of-court settlement.[15] A number of social psychologists have made systematic studies of elements affecting bargaining and negotiation. These would also be of value in developing out-of-court settlement techniques.[16]

Linguistic analysis, which is becoming an increasingly important part of social science, can be of value to lawyers interested in drafting legal instruments that are more meaningful and precise.[17] Content analysis by computer, which is being developed by social scientists, shows promise of becoming a useful aid in legal research.[18]

II. THE LEGAL POLICYMAKER

By legal policymaker in this context is meant a legislator, appellate court judge, or upper level administrator. Social science can possibly contribute to improving both the procedure of the policymaker and the substantive materials available to him.

With regard to procedure, social science studies have tested systematically a number of proposals to reduce delay in the courts, such as splitting the liability and damages decision,[19] providing for nonjudicial auditors,[20] and a variety of other techniques.[21] Other procedural reforms have also been subjected to social science analysis, such as providing neutral medical testimony,[22] appointing rather than electing the judiciary,[23] using blue-ribbon juries,[24] providing counsel to the indigent,[25] and releasing indigent criminal defendants without bail pending trial.[26] The last study, for example, showed that a careful screening and noti-

---

[15] Nagel, *Statistical Prediction of Verdicts and Awards*, 63 M.U.L.L. 135 (1963).
[16] Sacks, *Human Relations Training for Law Students and Lawyers*, 11 J. LEGAL ED. 316 (1959).
[17] Allen, *Some Uses of Symbolic Logic in Law Practice*, 8 PRAC. LAW. 51 (1962).
[18] Gurr & Panofsky (eds.), *Information Retrieval in the Social Sciences—Problems, Programs, and Proposals*, 7 AM. BEHAV. SCI. 1 (June, 1964).
[19] Zeisel & Callahan, *Split Trials and Time Saving—A Statistical Analysis*, 76 HARV. L. REV. 1606 (1963).
[20] Rosenberg, *Auditors in Massachusetts as Antidotes for Delayed Civil Courts*, 110 U. PA. L. REV. 27 (1961).
[21] ZEISEL, KALVEN & BUCHOLZ, DELAY IN THE COURT (1959).
[22] Assoc. Bar. N.Y.C., IMPARTIAL MEDICAL TESTIMONY (1956).
[23] Nagel, *Political Party Affiliation and Judicial Decisions*, 55 AM. POL. SCI. REV. 848 (1961) (partly included in Chap. 15 *infra*).
[24] *Fay v. New York*, 332 U.S. 261 (1947).
[25] SILVERSTEIN, DEFENSE OF THE POOR IN CRIMINAL CASES IN AMERICAN STATE COURTS—A PRELIMINARY SUMMARY (1964). This study, made possible by the American Bar Foundation, was presented to the House of Delegates of the American Bar Association in August of 1964. The House of Delegates adopted recommendations for standards for representation of the indigent accused. 50 A.B.A.J. 969 (1964).
[26] Ares, Rankin & Sturz, *Manhattan Bail Project*, 38 N.Y.U. L. REV. 67 (1963).

fying of defendants released without any bond produced a higher percentage of court appearances than the traditional bail bond system.

As to substantive developments in the law, social science has been
helpful in many fields. A revealing study was made, for instance, on the
effects of replacing the contributory negligence rule with the comparative
negligence rule.[27] The effects of capital punishment have also been subjected to social science scrutiny,[28] as have the effects of income taxes on
incentives to work[29] and the $1 minimum wage on the labor market.[30]
Of course, the effects of segregation and desegregation have been studied
extensively.[31] There has recently been a call for more social science
research aimed at improving compliance with international law[32] and
into the effects of prayers and Bible reading in the public schools.[33] At a
more down-to-earth level is the perceptive questionnaire study that was
made to determine the extent to which inheritance laws conform to the
intent of people who die without wills.[34]

III. THE LEGAL SCHOLAR

Legal scholars in this context refers to law professors and to practicing
lawyers and policymakers who are interested in the theoretical aspects of
the legal process. Social science can probably make its greatest contribution to legal theory by investigating the causal forces behind judicial,
legislative and administrative decision making and by probing the general effects of such decisions.

With regard to the causal forces behind the lawmaking and law-applying processes, the anthropologists[35] and historians[36] especially can
broaden the legal scholar's perspective of the cultural roots beneath his
legal field. The impact of public opinion on some aspects of the legal
system also has been scrutinized systematically.[37] Likewise, the interac-

[27] Rosenberg, *Comparative Negligence in Arkansas—A Before and After Survey*, 13 ARK. L. REV. 89 (1959).

[28] SELLIN, THE DEATH PENALTY (1959) (a report for the Model Penal Code project).

[29] Break, *Income Taxes and Incentives To Work—An Empirical Study*, 47 AM. ECON. REV. 529 (1957).

[30] Douty, *Some Effects of the $1.00 Minimum Wage in the U.S.*, 27 ECONOMICA 137 (1960).

[31] MYRDAL, AN AMERICAN DILEMMA (1944).

[32] LARSON, INTERNATIONAL RULE OF LAW (1961).

[33] *Abington Township School District* v. *Schempp*, 374 U.S. 203, 290, 319 (1963).

[34] Dunham, *Method, Process, and Frequency of Wealth Transmission at Death*, 30 U. CHI. L. REV. 1 (1963).

[35] HOEBEL, LAW OF PRIMITIVE MAN (1954).

[36] KEMPIN, LEGAL HISTORY—LAW AND SOCIAL CHANGE (1963).

[37] Rose and Prell, *Does the Punishment Fit the Crime—A Study in Social Valuation*, 61 AM. J. SOC. 247 (1955).

tions between governmental bodies as a factor in determining decisional outcomes has been studied[38] as has the role of pressure groups[39] and political parties.[40] Witnesses,[41] lawyers,[42] and litigants[43] have all been the subject of systematic social science study. Studies have also been made of the relation between the backgrounds and attitudes of judges[44] and legislators[45] and their decisional behavior.

As to the general impact of broad fields of law contrasted to specific laws, a number of studies have been and are under way. One sociologist has been studying the relation of legal impact to informal and formal controls[46] and to negative and positive appeals.[47] Other social scientists have contributed theory and data to the analysis of sanctions and legal compliance in general,[48] in public law[49] and in private law.[50] Using extensive interviewing techniques, one legal scholar analyzed the impact of contract law on business practice.[51] The role of such factors as the mass media, which facilitate or inhibit the impact of the law, has also been studied.[52]

Although this chapter has dealt only with what social science can contribute to law, it should be noted that no social scientist can really understand the American or any other society unless he has a reasonable understanding of its legal system. Nevertheless, there is much that lawyers can learn from social scientists. What is probably needed is a greater awareness by lawyers of the research of interest to them that social scientists and lawyers oriented to social science are doing.

---

[38] Murphy, *Lower Court Checks on Supreme Court Power*, 53 AM. POL. SCI. REV. 1017 (1959).

[39] Vose, *Litigation as a Form of Pressure Group Activity*, 319 ANNALS 20 (1958).

[40] SAYRE & KAUFMAN, GOVERNING NEW YORK (1960).

[41] Fishman & Morris (eds.), *Witnesses and Testimony at Trials and Hearings*, 13 AM. J. SOC. ISSUES 1 (1957).

[42] Ladinsky, *Careers of Lawyers, Law Practice, and Legal Institutions*, 28 AM. SOC. REV. 47 (1963).

[43] HUNTING & NEUWIRTH, WHO SUES IN NEW YORK CITY (1962).

[44] Nagel, *Judicial Backgrounds and Criminal Cases*, 53 J. CRIM. L., C. & P.S. 333 (1962) (Chap. 18 *infra*).

[45] WAHLKE *et al.*, THE LEGISLATIVE SYSTEM—EXPLORATIONS IN LEGISLATIVE BEHAVIOR (1962).

[46] Schwartz, *Social Factors in the Development of Legal Control*, 63 YALE L. J. 471 (1954).

[47] Schwartz, *Field Experimentation in Socio-legal Research*, 13 J. LEGAL ED. 401 (1961).

[48] ARENS & LASSWELL, IN DEFENSE OF THE PUBLIC ORDER—THE EMERGING FIELD OF SANCTION LAW (1961).

[49] Ball, *Social Structure and Rent Control Violations*, 65 AM. J. SOC. 598 (1960).

[50] Litwak, *Three Ways in Which Law Acts as a Means of Social Control—Punishment, Therapy, and Education—Divorce as a Case in Point*, 34 SOC. FORCES 217 (1956).

[51] Macaulay, *Non-Contractual Relations in Business*, 28 AM. SOC. REV. 55 (1963).

[52] Newland, *Press Coverage of the U.S. Supreme Court*, 17 W. POL. Q. 15 (1964).

Part Two

STUDIES THAT VIEW LAW MAKING AND ADJUDICATION AS RESPONSES FROM PRIOR STIMULI

SECTION I
The Normative Stimuli

This section is designed to deal with the role of law and other normative stimuli in shaping legal policies and adjudications. Law norms include constitutions, statutes, administrative regulations, and judicial precedents. Nonlaw norms include popular customs and widely advocated notions of justice that have not yet been incorporated into the law.

Chapter 4 deals with constitutional principles as reciprocal determinants of basic domestic and foreign policies. The constitutional principles relate to federalism, separation of powers, judicial review, the two-party system, and majority rule with minority rights. The policies relate to the regulatory and welfare state at home and the cold war abroad. Some related materials can be found in the growing literature on comparative constitutional law.[1] Unfortunately, however, this literature consists almost completely of constitutional law case studies and loose verbal analysis. What is needed is the systematic positioning of the constitutions of nearly all the members of the United Nations on a number of structural variables, such as national centralization.[2] This data could then be correlated with functional policy variables, while holding constant per capita income level and other intervening variables.[3] A more sophisticated approach would use for each country its behavioral constitution rather than its nominal or written constitution.[4]

---

[1] E.g., T. FRANCK, COMPARATIVE CONSTITUTIONAL PROCESS—CASES AND MATERIALS: FUNDAMENTAL RIGHTS IN THE COMMON LAW NATIONS (1968); and H. GROVES, COMPARATIVE CONSTITUTIONAL LAW—CASES AND MATERIALS (1963).

[2] For copies of constitutions, see L. WOLF-PHILLIPS, CONSTITUTIONS OF MODERN STATES—SELECTED TEXTS AND COMMENTARY (1968).

[3] Many policy variables and intervening socioeconomic variables are included in R. RUMMEL et al., DIMENSIONS OF NATIONS (1966).

[4] See, e.g., Mechan, Latin American Constitutions: Nominal and Real, 21 J. POL. 258 (1959).

Chapter 5 deals with the effects of procedural rules on the behavior of the administrative adjudicators and court judges. It is part of a growing body of literature that applies behavioral science research techniques to determining how alternative procedural rules can increase or decrease the efficiency of the judicial process, particularly with regard to delay in decision making. This literature includes scientific efficiency studies of civil proceedings by Hans Zeisel, Maurice Rosenberg, and Leo Levin.[5] It also includes related studies of criminal and administrative proceedings by Navarro and Nagel.[6] This is a field that has important practical implications and readily lends itself in many ways to the quantitative analysis of recorded data.

Chapter 6 views the influence of judicial precedents on decision making from the viewpoint of how the courts actually do cite one another rather than from the viewpoint of the legal rules about what constitutes an appropriate precedent. This chapter fits into the broader context of studies that have been made of how judges legally justify their decisions.[7] Future studies will more systematically determine the conditions that correlate with various types of justifications. The conditions can refer to such things as the nature of the evidence, the law, the judges, the time, and the place. The justifications can refer to such things as the nature of references to precedents, commentaries, logic, empirical generalizations, and natural law values.

---

[5] H. Zeisel *et al.*, DELAY IN THE COURT (1959); M. ROSENBERG (ed.), DOLLARS, DELAY AND THE AUTOMOBILE VICTIM—STUDIES IN REPARATION FOR HIGHWAY INJURIES AND RELATED COURT PROBLEMS (1968); and L. LEVIN & E. WOOLEY, DISPATCH AND DELAY—A FIELD STUDY OF JUDICIAL ADMINISTRATION IN PENNSYLVANIA (1961).

[6] J. NAVARRO & J. TAYLOR, DATA ANAYLSES AND SIMULATION OF A COURT SYSTEM FOR THE PROCESSING OF CRIMINAL CASES (Institute for Defense Analysis, 1967); and S. NAGEL (ed.), EVALUATION CHARTS AND QUESTIONNAIRE SURVEY ON DELAY IN ADMINISTRATIVE PROCEEDINGS (U.S. Senate Judiciary Committee, 1966).

[7] K. LLEWELLYN, THE COMMON LAW TRADITION: DECIDING APPEALS (1960); J. WETTER, STYLES OF APPELLATE OPINIONS (1963).

CHAPTER 4

Constitutional Principles:
Structure-Function Relations

The purpose of this chapter is to attempt to integrate into a unified conceptual scheme some basic facts about American governmental structures and functions. It represents a further attempt to bridge the gap between law and political science. The separate facts are known and need not be documented, but an integrating causal model has not previously appeared in the political science or legal literature.[1]

I. BASIC ELEMENTS OF STRUCTURE AND OF FUNCTION

To characterize the basic structure of the American national government, it is necessary to look at five somewhat legalistic dimensions or variables. American government is federal in form in that the Constitution delegates some powers to the national government and some powers to the state governments rather than all power to the national government to dole out to the states as it sees fit. American government also provides for a separation of horizontal powers in that the chief executive and the national legislature both are chosen by the electorate rather than either one by the other. It is further characterized by the presence of judicial review, whereby the Supreme Court has the power to declare acts of legislators and administrators unconstitutional. The party system is basically a two-party system with some minor parties, although the ideological difference between the two parties has, at least prior to 1964, been relatively weak in comparison with the British and other two-party systems. Finally, American government has a democratic structure in

---

[1] For a more philosophical and more normative discussion of structure–function analysis in political science than this chapter provides, see FUNCTIONALISM IN THE SOCIAL SCIENCES: THE STRENGTH AND LIMITS OF FUNCTIONALISM IN ANTHROPOLOGY, ECONOMICS, POLITICAL SCIENCE, AND SOCIOLOGY (D. MARTINDALE ed. 1965).

which the law provides for majority rule by universal adult suffrage, with freedom for unpopular viewpoints to make themselves heard.

The functional aspects of American government can probably be characterized best as involving increasing governmental regulation or responsibility for coping with various domestic economic and social problems, and as involving increasing governmental activity in international relations, particularly with regard to competition with the Soviet Union. The tremendous increase that has occurred can be measured by comparing the number of federal employees or the amount of federal funds involved in such activities in 1960, with analogous figures for 1790 after one allows for national population increase and for inflation. A more dramatic way to point up the changed domestic role is to examine the 10 regulatory and welfare changes Karl Marx advocated in his *Communist Manifesto*, and see how many in part now have considerable support from both American political parties (e.g., banking regulation and abolition of child labor).

How have domestic regulation and the cold war affected each of the five structural dimensions? How have each of the five structural dimensions affected increased domestic regulation and foreign policy? Potentially, 5 structural variables and 2 functional variables yield 20 reciprocal relations. Figure 4–1 shows these relations and also mentions the variable of socioeconomic forces. These forces include the growth of large-scale economic units, which has brought a loss of intimate contact between worker and employer and between consumer and producer, and the growth of nuclear missile warfare, which has brought a stalemate of military power between the great powers. Such forces have affected domestic regulation and foreign policy much more than the governmental variables have, and such forces, in turn, have been more affected by regulation and the cold war than by the governmental variables. These socioeconomic forces have also affected the structural variables directly (e.g., the Supreme Court's response to the historical context in which it operates) and indirectly by their effect on domestic regulation and foreign policy. However, in view of the purpose of this chapter, the socioeconomic variables will not be discussed in detail. Also, the role of the policymakers who conceptually stand between the governmental and socioeconomic variables and the functional policies will not be discussed. The rest of this chapter will attempt to clarify the nature of the 20 relations shown in the upper portion of Figure 4–1.

II. RELATIONS BETWEEN STRUCTURE AND DOMESTIC FUNCTIONS

Federalism has had some important effects on government regulation. It has made government regulation more decentralized than would otherwise be so (e.g., telephone company regulation). It has provided testing

FIGURE 4–1

MUTUAL RELATIONS BETWEEN AMERICAN GOVERNMENT STRUCTURES AND FUNCTIONS

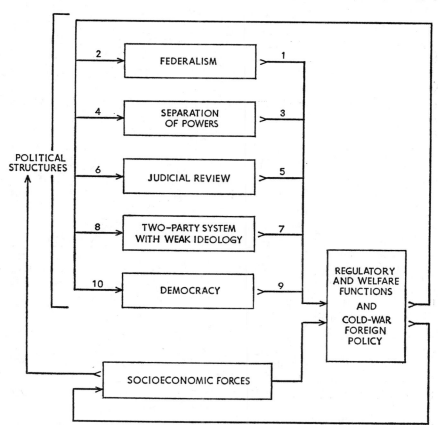

grounds for new forms of government regulation in particular states (e.g., workmen's compensation in Wisconsin). It has also provided a less uniform regulatory program than a unitary governmental system would, with accompanying possibilities of intergovernmental conflict (e.g., trucking regulation) and of intergovernmental vacuums (e.g., union–management regulation). Government regulation also has a feedback effect on federalism. Increased responsibility has tended to increase the power of both the federal and the state governments, but relatively speaking, the increase has been substantially greater at the federal level because to be effective so many regulatory programs require interstate regulation (e.g., programs designed to prevent depression and inflation).

Just as federalism has produced relatively uncoordinated regulatory programs in terms of intergovernmental relations, separation of powers has likewise produced relatively uncoordinated regulatory programs in terms of interbranch relations. Separation of powers makes possible the control of Congress and the Administration by opposed political parties or opposed ideologies, which leads to at least temporary inaction (e.g., the lack of a vigorous relief and recovery program between 1930 and 1932). On the other hand, increased government regulation has tended to weaken separation of powers by concentrating more quasi-legislative and quasi-judicial power in the hands of administrative agencies, where quicker and more expert action can generally be taken than in Congress or the courts (e.g., transportation ratemaking or the adjudication of stock brokerage violations).

Judicial review has had the effect of slowing the increase in governmental regulation (e.g., the child labor cases), but not preventing it. On the other side of the picture, the increase in government regulation has grown so large that this phenomena, along with personnel and social changes, has probably been a major cause of the withdrawal of the federal courts from nullifying economic regulatory legislation since 1937.

The check and balance provided by the two-party system has probably tended to make regulatory programs operate more efficiently than they otherwise would. The out-party is constantly trying to find and reveal to the public examples of waste, corruption, and unresponsiveness on the part of the in-party. However, the two-party system has meant that the planning of regulatory programs must be more short run than would be so with a one-party system. Federal economic programs, for instance, generally cannot be planned for more than one presidential administration ahead because of the possibility of a change in the party occupying the White House. The relatively weak ideological split in the American party system, however, has meant that when the out-party comes in it will not drastically change all the economic programs of the former in-party. It has also meant that campaign disputes over regulatory issues generally tend to be fought along pragmatic lines rather than along ideological lines of socialism versus capitalism.

Viewed from the other side of the conceptual scheme, increased government regulation and regulatory issues have probably sharpened the differences between Democrats and Republicans. In the 1964 Congress, for instance, the sharpest interparty disputes were over Keynesian fiscal policy, medicare for the aged, and President Johnson's incipient anti-poverty program. Upsurges in economic regulation during the Wilson and Roosevelt administrations clearly sharpened interparty differences.

That the United States has a meaningful universal adult suffrage combined with relative freedom for unpopular viewpoints to make themselves heard has enabled substantial economic reforms to be introduced without violent revolution. In both England and the United States, socialistic-reformist philosophies were able to win acceptance without generating reactionary repression.

Probably the most controversial relation shown in Figure 4–1 is the impact of economic regulation on democracy. If one defines democracy so as to include the right to operate a business for profit as the owner sees fit, without being subject to government regulation, then government regulation, by definition, has decreased democracy. If, on the other hand, one defines democracy in terms of universal adult suffrage combined with freedom for unpopular viewpoints to make themselves heard, then most regulatory programs of the 20th century have directly or indirectly helped to increase American democracy. Surely, universal adult suffrage can be more effectively exercised by workers who have the time to familiarize themselves with politics instead of merely working long hours at a bare subsistence wage starting in early childhood. Maximum hour laws, minimum wage laws, and child labor laws have helped to free the worker so that he can gain increased political familiarity, and business regulation legislation has probably helped (along with the mass media and increased education) to decrease the undue power that business concerns exercised over state and federal legislatures in the past.

III. RELATIONS BETWEEN STRUCTURE AND FOREIGN FUNCTIONS

The mutual relations between governmental structure and American foreign policy activities are similar to the relations between structure and domestic functions in some respects and different in other respects. Federalism, for instance, has affected American foreign policy by making it more provincial and isolationist than it would otherwise be if the state governments had less influence on the national government. Federalism has especially served to embarrass the national government on many occasions when state or local governments acted contrary to American foreign policy, such as the Little Rock school desegregation riots, New York's attempt in the 1930's to disrupt the American acceptance of Czarist bank deposits in New York banks in payment of Russian debts, and the New Orleans lynching of Mafia-associated Italians in the 1900's. The cold war and increased American international activity, however, have greatly strengthened the national government relative to the states in that only the national government conducts diplomatic relations and provides for the common defense.

Separation of legislative and executive powers has hampered presidential foreign policymaking in comparison with such countries as Great Britain, where the chief executive is always the leader of the dominant legislative party. A classic example of the lack of coordination occurred in the post-World War I period when Congress and the President could not agree on the role the United States should play in the Versailles Treaty and the League of Nations. The cold war, however, has increased the importance of the President by virtue of his access to secret diplomatic and intelligence information, his ability to make relatively quick decisions combined with the increased need for such decisions, his power to recognize revolutionary governments, and his status, along with the vice president, as the only elected official with a national constituency.

Judicial review has had little, if any, effect on American foreign policy. The Supreme Court has held that American treaties and foreign policy actions must conform to the Constitution, but the Supreme Court has never held a treaty to be unconstitutional. On the other hand, treaty making has had some effect on judicial power because a treaty becomes the law of the land, and it thus gives the courts a weapon by which contrary state laws can be declared illegal. This weapon could become more important if the United States signs the United Nations Declaration on Human Rights, although practically all its provisions have already been incorporated explicitly or by interpretation into the federal Constitution or federal statutes.

The American two-party system lessens the united front that the United States might otherwise maintain in comparison with the one-party communist system. This interparty friction to the extent it exists could have been a factor in Nazi Germany's feeling that the United States could be beaten. On the other hand, the cold war has promoted a substantial quantity of bipartisanship in Congress that might otherwise be absent.

The democratic structure of American government affects American foreign policy by being a partial factor in determining with whom and against whom the United States is allied. It also shapes the process whereby American foreign policy is made by placing more emphasis on debate and consensus. A view of the relation from the other direction, however, shows that the cold war and an intense foreign policy in general do tend to reduce the aspects of democracy that relate to the freedom to disagree. There tends to be a decreased tolerance of political nonconformists, particularly nonconformists whose ideology may be interpreted as leaning in the same direction as the ideology of the enemy powers. Nevertheless, the cold war has strengthened American democracy by encouraging the political and economic upgrading of depressed economic and ethnic groups in order to unify the country and in order to improve the national image. Some of the New Deal activity with regard to providing for the right to join unions and with regard to social insurance programs was probably motivated partly by ideological competiton with the Soviet Union. Likewise, the cold war has provided incentives for the passage of civil rights laws, which have broadened the base of American democracy.

IV.   CONCLUSIONS

It has become fashionable in political science to play up the role of individual policymakers and of informal pressure group activities as determinants of domestic and foreign policy decisions. This development seems laudable, since those variables previously had been underemphasized in political and legal research. This development, however, seems partially undesirable if it now tends to underemphasize the reciprocal role of the largely legalistic structures as policy determinants.

Integration of the separate facts of this chapter shows there is a close mutual relation between governmental structures on the one hand and domestic and foreign functions on the other. If any of the above-mentioned aspects of American governmental structures were substantially different, the domestic and foreign policies of American government would also be substantially different and vice versa.

CHAPTER 5

Procedural Rules: Effects on Behavior

A few years ago, the House Government Operations Committee, under the chairmanship of Representative William L. Dawson of Illinois, undertook a survey of the organization, procedures, and practices of the federal administrative agencies.[1] Eighty-three lengthy questions were sent to all the executive departments and independent agencies. It is the purpose of this chapter to analyze the responses to those questions which asked the chairmen of the independent regulatory agencies what choices their agencies had made with regard to how to exercise the discretion that the Administrative Procedure Act and other relevant statutes had given them over various procedural matters. An attempt is made to determine some of the causes and effects of the variations among the agencies. The agencies involved are the CAB, FCC, FPC, FTC, ICC, NLRB, and SEC.[2]

I. DISCRETION IN RULEMAKING PROCEDURE

Section 4 (a) and (b) of the Administrative Procedure Act indicate the requirements for public notification and participation. These requirements are, however, generally applicable only to substantive rulemaking.

---

[1] STAFF OF HOUSE COMM. ON GOVERNMENT OPERATIONS, 85TH CONG., 1ST SESS., SURVEY AND STUDY OF ADMINISTRATIVE ORGANIZATION, PROCEDURE AND PRACTICE IN THE FEDERAL AGENCIES (Comm. Print 1957) [hereinafter cited as the Dawson Committee Survey]. The writer gratefully thanks Victor Rosenblum, former counsel to the Dawson Committee, for making available to him the unanalyzed data compiled in the survey.

[2] According to data available in ADMINISTRATIVE CONFERENCE OF THE U.S., STATISTICAL DATA RELATING TO ADMINISTRATIVE PROCEEDINGS (1962), these 7 agencies heard approximately 2,781 of the 3,000 ratemaking-rulemaking proceedings of 1961. They heard 2,285 of the 2,621 disciplinary-suspension-revocation adjudications (excluding 951 suspension and revocation of seamen licenses by the Coast Guard), and they heard 5,581 of 5,955 licensing proceedings.

Other forms of rulemaking are excluded from the act's scope by the provision that "except where notice or hearing is required by statute, this subsection shall not apply to interpretive rules, general statements of policy, rules of agency organization, procedure, or practice, or in any situation in which the agency for good cause finds . . . that notice and public procedure thereon are impractical, unnecessary, or contrary to the public interest."[3] This exclusion gives considerable discretion to the agencies to determine their procedures in non-substantive rulemaking.

Table 5–1 shows how the agencies have exercised this discretion with regard to the following types of rulemaking: (I) procedural rules, (II) general statements of policy, (III) interpretive rules, (IV) statements of the general course and method by which functions are channeled and determined, and (V) rules relating to agency management, organization and personnel. Table 5–1 also shows how the agencies have exercised their discretion with regard to the following types of public participation: (A) collection of data from public sources for determination of proposed rulemaking, (B) notice to interested persons, (C) provision for public hearings, and (D) allowance of public participation in the decision-making process through written submission of arguments. The chairman of the NLRB did not respond to this part of the questionnaire, asserting that his agency is only an adjudicative body without rulemaking powers.

The findings can be discussed in terms of comparisons between the five types of rulemaking activity, between the four types of public participation, or between the individual agencies. With regard to the five types of rulemaking activity, Table 5–1 indicates that interpretive rules most frequently involve participation, followed by the formulation of general statements of policy, and then by procedural rules. The absence of participation in the other two categories is initially striking but is probably explainable by the relative disinterest of parties in internal rules that have little effect on their interests. On the other hand, interpretive rules, general statements of policy, and procedural rules have a more important effect on the interests of concerned parties.

An examination of the four types of public participation indicates a strong degree of participation in data collection, lesser amount in provisions for public participation in decision making and in public notice, and still less involvement in public hearings. These findings indicate the amenability of agencies to receive public suggestions, but to restrict public participation in time-consuming hearings.

With regard to the individual agencies, Table 5–1 indicates that the CAB and FPC are relatively low on public participation in the rulemaking activities involved, that the FCC and FTC are in the middle, and that the SEC and ICC are relatively high. Possible explanations might

---

[3] Administrative Procedure Act § 4a, 60 Stat. 243 (1946), 5 U.S.C. § 1005 (1959).

TABLE 5-1

PUBLIC PARTICIPATION IN PROCEDURAL RULEMAKING

(by rulemaking activity, by type of participation, and by agency)

	Type of Rulemaking Activity					Totals by Agency		
	I	II	III	IV	V	Actual Total	Theoretical Maximum	Percent of Actual to Theoretical
A. Collection of Data from Public Sources								
CAB	2	0	2	0	0	4	10	40%
FCC	1	2	2	0	0	5	10	50
FPC	2	-*	0	0	0	2	8	25
FTC	0	2	2	0	0	4	10	40
ICC	1	2	2	0	0	5	10	50
SEC	2	2	2	0	0	6	10	60
B. Notice to Interested Parties								
CAB	0	0	0	0	0	0	10	0%
FCC	0	1	1	0	0	2	10	20
FPC	2	-*	0	0	0	2	8	25
FTC	0	0	2	0	0	2	10	20
ICC	1	2	2	0	0	5	10	50
SEC	1	1	1	0	0	3	10	30
C. Provision for Public Hearings								
CAB	0	0	0	0	0	0	10	0%
FCC	0	1	1	0	0	2	10	20
FPC	0	-*	0	0	0	0	8	0
FTC	0	0	2	0	0	2	10	20
ICC	1	1	1	0	0	3	10	30
SEC	1	1	1	0	0	3	10	30
D. Public Participation in Decision Making								
CAB	0	0	0	0	0	0	10	0%
FCC	0	1	1	0	0	2	10	20
FPC	0	-*	0	0	0	0	8	0
FTC	1	0	2	0	0	3	10	30
ICC	1	1	2	0	0	4	10	40
SEC	1	1	2	0	0	4	10	40
Actual Total	17	18	28	0	0			
Theoretical Maximum	48	40	48	48	48	Totals by Type of Rulemaking Activity		
% of Actual to Theoretical	35%	45	58	0	0			

	Type of Public Participation				Average % per Agency (Total Across ÷ 4 Types)
	A	B	C	D	
CAB	40%	0%	0%	0%	10%
FCC	50	20	20	20	28
FPC	25	20	0	0	13
FTC	40	20	20	30	28
ICC	50	50	30	40	43
SEC	60	30	30	40	40
Avg. % by Type of Public Participation (Total Down ÷ 6 Agencies)	44%	24	17	22	

NOTE: See list of symbols at top of opposite page.

TABLE 5–1—*Cont.*

Symbols used:

Type of rulemaking activity
    I = procedural rules.
    II = general statements of policy.
    III = interpretive rules.
    IV = statements of the general course and method by which functions are channeled and determined.
    V = Rules relating to agency management, organization, and personnel.

Type of questionnaire response
    0 = generally no.
    1 = occasionally.
    2 = generally yes.

Type of public participation
    A = Collection of data from public sources.
    B = Notice to interested persons.
    C = Provision for public hearings.
    D = Written participation in decision making.

    * The FPC does not issue general statements of policy.

emphasize the historical background and development of each agency, the pressures of groups affected by the agency rulings, and the divergent philosophies regarding public involvement held by the various commissioners. The SEC and ICC are possibly more responsive to the groups they are supposed to be regulating than are the other agencies.

Table 5–2 offers data to test the hypothesis offered by some com-

TABLE 5–2

THE RELATION BETWEEN DISCRETIONARY PUBLIC PARTICIPATION AND THE LENGTH OF RULEMAKING PROCEEDINGS

		Extent of Public Participation		
		Low	*Average*	*High*
Average length of rulemaking proceedings	More than one year	FPC	FCC FTC	0
	Less than one year	CAB	0	ICC

mentators that a higher degree of public participation is correlated with more lengthy rulemaking proceedings.[4] Information regarding the length of SEC proceedings was not available. The table indicates that when other relevant variables are not held constant there is a slightly negative correlation between these two variables because the ICC, which allows extensive public participation, averages less than a year for rulemaking proceedings, whereas the FPC, which allows little public participation,

---

[4] E.g., Peck, *The Atrophied Rule-Making Powers of the NLRB*, 70 YALE L. J. 729, 734 (1961).

averages more than a year, although the CAB, which also allows little participation, averages less than a year. The length of rulemaking proceedings is possibly one of the factors that determines whether or not an agency will encourage public participation. Thus, low length of proceedings may cause or facilitate high participation instead of high participation causing high length. Testing this explanation would involve determining agency motives in allowing public participation in each type of rulemaking.

II. DISCRETION IN ADJUDICATION PROCEDURE

The Dawson Committee's questionnaire has many questions dealing with adjudication. While most of these items were constructed to assess agency compliance with statutory requirements, many also explored areas of administrative discretion. The following items represent adjudication activities of a procedural nature that are discretionary with the agencies.

Pleading procedures
1. Use of prehearing or pretrial conferences and agreements.
2. Allowance of voluntary withdrawals or dismissals of proceedings.
3. Use of consent orders.

Hearing procedures
4. Specifications as to nature and form of written submissions.
5. Provision for oral testimony in hearings.
6. Provision for consolidation of proceedings.
7. Issuance of declaratory judgments or orders.

Appeals procedure
8. Use of bureaus or officers who participated in the initial or recommended decision.
9. Use of an independent staff directly responsible to the chief executive officers.
10. Use of other specialized or nonspecialized groups.
11. Use of a general counsel.
12. Use of advisory groups.

Table 5–3 indicates each agency's responses to the questions relating to these items.

Uniform adjudication procedure is generally thought desirable, or at least more so than uniform rulemaking procedure. Table 5–2 does show a high degree of uniformity among the agencies, especially with regard to the discretionary pleading procedures. There is a little more diversity in hearing procedures and still more (but not severely so) in appellate procedures. The FCC and FTC are the most deviant or possibly the most innovative agencies shown in Table 5–3. Of course, there may be some important differences between the existence of uniform rules of proce-

TABLE 5–3

DISCRETION IN ADJUDICATION PROCEDURE

Agency	Pleading			Hearing				Appealing					Percent Yes	Percent of Agreement with Typical Agency
	1	2	3	4	5	6	7	8	9	10	11	12		
CAB	y	y	y	y	y	y	y	n	n	y	y	n	75%	100%
FCC	y	y	y	y	y†	y	y	n	y	n	n	n	67	75
FPC	y	y	y	y	y	y	y	n	n	y	y	n	75	100
FTC	y	y	y	n	y	n	n	n	n	y	y	n	50	75
ICC	y	y	y	y	y	y	y	n	n	y	y	n	75	100
NLRB	y	y	y	−*	y	y	n	n	n	y	y	n	64	91
SEC	y	y	y	y	y	y	y	n	y	n	y	n	75	83
Percent yes	100	100	100	83	100	86	71	0	29	71	86	0	69% = Avg.	
Percent of agreement with typical agency	100	100	100	83	100	86	71	100	71	71	86	100		Avg. = 89%
Mentioned by APA	y	n	y	n	y	n	y	y	n	n	n	n		

Symbols used:
y = yes at least in some circumstances.
n = no.
* The NLRB did not respond to this item.
† The FCC provision for oral testimony is required by statute.

dure and the uniform exercise of such rules. Information on uniform exercise is not available in the questionnaire responses. The bottom row of Table 5–3 reveals that those discretionary procedural items mentioned in the APA are the items on which there is more likely to be 100 percent uniformity, even though the item is mentioned as discretionary in the APA.

Closely related to the question of procedural uniformity in adjudicatory proceedings is the problem of ensuring fairness in such proceedings, since administrative discretion provides opportunities to avoid the requirements that are designed to provide procedural fairness. There is a need for a measure of procedural fairness in administrative adjudication. Such a measure could perhaps be based upon a content analysis of agency opinions, or upon questionnaire responses obtained from lawyers or parties appearing before the agencies, or by checking to see what percent of a sample of each agency's decisions have been reversed by the courts for lack of procedural fairness. When such a measure is used to position the agencies, then hypotheses can be tested concerning the relation between the diverse exercise of agency discretion and the diverse reputations and records that agencies have with regard to procedural fairness.

III. DISCRETION AND CONGESTION

Two factors involved in agency efficiency are (1) the average length of rulemaking and adjudicatory proceedings and (2) the impending backlog of cases. Average length of proceedings can be calculated from data supplied by the agencies to the Dawson committee. The questionnaire also asked about backlog, but only the CAB considered its backlog to be large. The NLRB, however, had 4,110 pending cases on July 1, 1956, which had increased to 7,655 by the end of 1959. It is thus also considered to be a large backlog agency in this study. The present backlog of the FPC began in 1957, subsequent to the 1955–56 questionnaire.

Commentators have been strong in calling for more delegation of decision-making power to initial trial or hearing examiners, rather than merely giving examiners the authority to render an initial or recommended decision to be considered by the commission as a whole.[5] The underlying premise of this proposal is the belief that with more hearing examiner power a significant number of cases presently considered at the commissioner level would be decided with finality at the hearing examiner level because the decision would not be appealed or, if appealed, would not be reviewed by the commission. This hypothesis can be partially tested by examining the number of hearing examiner decisions of each agency reviewed at the commissioner level. Table 5–4 shows the

TABLE 5–4

COMMISSION REVIEW OF EXAMINERS' DECISIONS

	FTC	FCC	ICC	CAB	SEC	FPC	NLRB
Number of cases heard by agency	347	186	6561	124	16	33	735
Number of cases reviewed by commissioners	84	48	3217	70	11	31	708
Percent of cases reviewed	24%	26%	49%	57%	69%	94%	95%
Does agency delegate decision-making power to examiners?	Yes	Yes	Yes	No	No	No	No

extent of agency review of hearing examiner decisions. The last two rows reveal a perfect correlation between (1) the presence of decision-making power at the hearing examiner level and (2) a relatively low percentage of agency review.

---

[5] E.g., Timers & Garfinkel, *Examination of the Security and Exchange Commission's Adjudicatory Process: Some Suggestions*, 45 VA. L. REV. 817, 830 (1959).

It is further hypothesized that delegation of decision-making power, with its concomitant reduction of appeals cases is correlated with having a relatively small backlog. Table 5–5 shows a fairly strong correlation

TABLE 5–5

The Relation between Decision-Making Delegation
and Backlog

| | | Delegation of Decision-Making Power to Trial Examiners | |
		No	Yes
Backlog	Relatively large	CAB NLRB	0
	Relatively small	SEC FPC	FTC FCC ICC

between these variables. The SEC and the FPC, however, do not delegate decision-making power, and yet they have relatively small backlogs. The explanation for this divergence probably is that Table 5–4 had previously shown that these two agencies had relatively few opportunities to utilize hearing examiners and, therefore, few opportunities to review such decisions. The number of instances when power could be delegated is thus so limited for these two agencies that no appreciable effect on their backlog would be felt whether the SEC reviewed none or all of its 16 cases or whether the FPC reviewed none or all of its 33 cases. The finding can thus be reframed to indicate a perfect correlation between the use of delegation and a reduced backlog when there are enough cases to present an opportunity to benefit from such delegation.

Proponents of increased informality in hearings argue that time consumption and administrative delay would be decreased by the abolition of oral testimony in as many stages of the adjudicatory process as possible.[6] While all seven regulatory agencies expressed themselves as preferring written submissions, only the FTC has instituted a procedure of not allowing oral testimony. Contrary to the hypothesis, Table 5–6 reveals an inverse or negative correlation in that five of the six agencies that allow oral evidence had relatively short trial examiner proceedings and the FTC had relatively long examiner proceedings. The admissibility of oral evidence is apparently not an important variable relative to other variables in accounting for the relative length of these proceedings. As with the public participation variable, the agencies that prohibit oral

[6] E.g., Woll, *Administrative Law Reform: Proposals and Prospects,* 41 Neb. L. Rev. 687, 693 (1962).

evidence may do so because other variables have caused these agencies to have lengthy proceedings. Adjudication delay may be explained by the unique nature of hearings in different agencies, by the granting of excessively prolonged recesses and continuances, by the conducting of hearings in several cities rather than in a central locality, or by the absence of incentives or punishments to private parties to expedite hearings.

TABLE 5–6

THE RELATION BETWEEN ORAL PRESENTATION AND LENGTH OF
ADJUDICATION PROCEEDINGS

		Admissibility of Oral Evidence	
		No	Yes
Average length of trial examiner proceedings	More than 6 months	FTC	FCC
	Less than 6 months	0	CAB FPC ICC NLRB SEC

Another aspect of the informality proposals is the advocacy of pre-hearing conferences and agreements. Such conferences and agreements reduce the time involved in adjudication by enhancing the opportunity for settlement by consent agreement and by eliminating the consideration of some arguments during the actual hearing.[7] While all seven regulatory agencies replied affirmatively to the question about the use of prehearing procedures, their responses indicate various degrees of use. The FTC, for example, extensively uses the prehearing conference and disposes of much of its business through consent judgments. The CAB, on the other hand, has encouraged only token activity in this area. Table 5–7 shows an inverse correlation between backlog and agency encouragement of pre-hearing conferences in that backlog tends to be low when encouragement is high. Whether such a finding can be attributed to a causal relation or to coincidence cannot be ascertained, given the small sample of agencies involved in Table 5–7. To go beyond the mere correlation, an intensive analysis of individual prehearing conferences is needed and also a comparative analysis of adjudications that did not involve prehearing conferences.

---

[7] ZEISEL, KALVEN, & BUCHOLZ, DELAY IN THE COURTS (1959).

TABLE 5–7

THE RELATION BETWEEN PREHEARING PROCEDURES AND BACKLOG

| | | Attitude toward Prehearing Procedures | |
		Indifferent	Encouraging
	Relatively large	CAB	NLRB
Backlog			FCC
			FPC
	Relatively small	0	FTC
			ICC
			SEC

IV. CONCLUSIONS

The responses of the Dawson Committee questionnaire reveal varying degrees of participation in procedural rulemaking among the independent regulatory agencies. Participation is highest with regard to interpretive rules and lowest with regard to internal rules. Participation manifests itself most in the collection of data and least in the form of public hearings. The ICC and SEC allow the most public participation, which may indicate a high responsiveness to their clientele groups. There seems to be no significant relation between the allowance of public participation and the length of rulemaking proceedings.

The questionnaire responses also reveal varying degrees of adoption of discretionary adjudication procedures. There is, however, a relatively high degree of uniformity, especially in pleading procedures although less so in appellate procedures.

Relations between fairness and the exercise of discretion were undetermined, but there seem to be some close relations between delay and the exercise of discretion. Delegation of decision-making power to trial examiners correlates highly with having a low percent of cases reviewed and with having relatively small backlog. Encouraging prehearing procedures also correlates highly with having a relatively small backlog. Admitting oral evidence, however, does not correlate with having long proceedings contrary to the proponents of restricted evidentiary rules.

In general, this study and the Dawson questionnaire on which it is based tend to emphasize between-agency comparisons, and the study is thus handicapped by the lack of within-agency detail about different categories of proceedings and by the lack of data from periods both before and after changes in the exercise of discretion. It is hoped that data being compiled for the Administrative Conference will throw more light on the empirical distribution and effects of alternative discretionary procedures among the regulatory agencies.

APPENDIX

RELEVANT QUESTIONS FROM THE DAWSON COMMITTEE QUESTIONNAIRE

I. Rulemaking

3. Describe for each of the categories listed in I through XIII rulemaking process followed as to—

      a. Manner of collection of data for determination.
      b. Extent of notice to interested parties.
      c. Hearing and extent of public participation therein.
  I Procedural rules.
  III General statements of policy.
  IV Interpretive rules.
   V Statements of the general course and method by which functions are channeled and determined.
XIII Rules relating to agency management, organization and personnel.

6. (a) Has your agency afforded public participation in rulemaking when not required by statute to do so? If so, please explain fully, giving reasons for the agency action.

14. As to each rulemaking power, comment on the adequacy—either in statutory language or in legislative history—of the Congressional standards so being implemented:

      e. Where matters are left to agency discretion, are there any areas in which you believe greater statutory specification of standards would be desirable. If so, specify.

II. Adjudication

1. What judicial or quasi-judicial powers—often referred to as adjudication—does your agency exercise?

      b. Who is authorized by statute to exercise it?
      c. If delegated by or within your agency, what office or organization unit is authorized to exercise it?

3. Describe briefly for each category, I through VII, citing pertinent authority therefor, the procedural practices and rules in every class of adjudication by your agency required by statute or the constitution to be determined on the record after opportunity for an agency hearing for:

   g. Prehearing and pretrial conference and agreement.

   h. Voluntary withdrawal or dismissal of proceedings by request of private parties.

5. Describe briefly, citing pertinent authority therefor, the procedures or practice of your agency insofar as they are not covered in your answers to question 3, for:

   a. The forms for written submission.

   c. Oral submissions.

   d. Consolidation of proceedings.

   f. Initial or recommended decisions.

10. (b) Do your rules of procedure designate the type of submission which the agency will consider as relevant?

18. To what extent does your agency encourage the parties to reach a determination of the controversy by consent?

19. Does your agency issue declaratory orders?

23. If the agency has trial examiners, how many examiner decisions were released during 1954, 1955, and the first 9 months of 1956?

25. How many hearings were conducted directly by the agency during 1954, 1955, and the first 9 months of 1956?

26. (c) During the same period, how many decisions were entered by the agency upon review of trial examiner decisions after the filing of exceptions?

27. State the average period of time that the cases which were decided during the calendar year 1955 were pending before the agency.

28. Of the total cases decided during the calendar year 1955, give:

   b. The average time the case was before the trial examiner in hearing and report.

III. *Separation of Functions*

2. Describe the extent to which the powers required to be exercised by the chief executive officials are delegated to subordinates.

7. In reviewing recommended or initial decisions of hearing officers or other officials, does your agency use the advice and services of any of the following:

   a. An independent review staff, directly responsible to the chief executive officials and not part of any subdivision of your agency.

   b. Bureaus, offices, and divisions which have participated in the investigation, prosecution, or formulation of the initial decision.

   c. Any other specialized or non-specialized staff within the agency.

   d. Its General Counsel or chief legal officer.

   e. Advisory groups.

V. Workload and Staffing Patterns

1. Describe the workload and backlog of your agency in the exercise of each of its rulemaking and adjudication powers.
2. List the major steps and state the time required for each step in rulemaking and adjudication powers.

CHAPTER 6

Judicial Precedents: Sociometric Relations[1]

Sociometric relations basically refer to the relations of attraction and repulsion that exist among persons or among social entities.[2] In this regard, courts differ in the extent to which they are cited approvingly by other courts, and they differ in the extent to which they themselves cite other courts approvingly. Likewise, courts differ in the extent to which they are cited disapprovingly by other courts, and in the extent to which they themselves cite other courts disapprovingly. It is the purpose of this chapter to indicate some of these differences and to account at least partially for their existence. While sociometric relations *within* American courts have frequently been studied,[3] sociometric relations *between or among* them have not.[4]

I. THE RESEARCH DESIGN

The courts analyzed consist of all the courts of the 48 state jurisdictions and the one federal jurisdiction whose cases are covered in the 1955–1959 *Shepard's Citations.*[5] This is a multivolumed set of books that

---

[1] The writer gratefully thanks Professors Guetzkow and Rosenblum of Northwestern University for the constructive suggestion they made concerning this chapter.

[2] Lindsey & Borgatta, *Sociometric Measurement,* 1 HANDBOOK OF SOCIAL PSYCHOLOGY 405–48 (1954).

[3] See, for example, C. H. PRITCHETT, THE ROOSEVELT COURT: A STUDY IN JUDICIAL POLITICS AND VALUES, 1937–47 (1948); G. SCHUBERT, QUANTITATIVE ANALYSIS OF JUDICIAL BEHAVIOR 77–172 (1959); and Snyder, *The Supreme Court as a Small Group,* 37 SOC. FORCES 232–38 (1958).

[4] See, however, Mott *et al., Judicial Personnel,* 167 ANNALS 143–55 (1933), in which Mott shows that the state supreme courts most frequently cited by the United States Supreme Court are those courts whose members tend to be better educated and more active in professional organizations. Francis Heller of the University of Kansas is currently working on a trend analysis of whom the United States Supreme Court has been citing during the past 100 years.

[5] SHEPARD'S CITATIONS (1955–1959).

indicates how each case covered has been treated by subsequent cases. It covers practically all the cases of the 20th century that have been decided in published opinions, and it has a high reputation for accuracy.[6] The courts are grouped by the Shepard and the West law book publishing companies into eight regional units.[7] These eight units cover the whole country, and thus taken together they represent a totality, not a sample from a larger population. A citation is a reference by one court (called the citor) to itself or to another court (called the referent). The citations analyzed consist of a stratified random sample of approximately 4,000 citations to 1955 cases made from June, 1955, to April, 1959.[8]

II. APPROVAL RELATIONS

Table 6–1 shows how many times each citor cited each referent approvingly. All citations of an approving nature are indicated in *Shepard's Citations* by a letter f (followed), p (parallel), e (explained), or by the absence of a letter beside the citation. The column totals of Table 6–1 indicate how often each referent was cited by others approvingly. The column totals minus self-citations give a measure of the degree of influence each referent has. The row totals indicate how often each citor cited others approvingly. The row totals minus self-citations give a measure of the degree of extroversion of each citor. Why do some court groupings have more influence as referents than other court groupings? Likewise, why are some court groupings more extroverted as citors than are other court groupings?

The degree of *influence* of a court grouping correlates meaningfully with four variables.[9] First, if a court is on a legal level such that its

---

[6] Arthur Beardsley and Oscar Orman, Legal Bibliography and the Use of Law Books (1947).

[7] The eight regions are as follows: *Atlantic* (Maine, New Hampshire, Vermont, Rhode Island, Connecticut, New Jersey, Pennsylvania, Delaware, Maryland, and District of Columbia); *Northeast* (Massachusetts, New York appellate and trial supplement, Ohio, Indiana, and Illinois); *Northwest* (Michigan, Wisconsin, Minnesota, Iowa, North Dakota, South Dakota, and Nebraska); *Southeast* (West Virginia, Virginia, North Carolina, South Carolina, and Georgia); *Southern* (Florida, Alabama, Mississippi, and Louisiana); *Southwest* (Kentucky, Tennessee, Missouri, Arkansas, and Texas); *Pacific* (Kansas, Oklahoma, Montana, Wyoming, Colorado, New Mexico, Idaho, Utah, Arizona, Nevada, Washington, Oregon, and California); and the *Federal Jurisdiction* (United States Supreme Court, federal intermediate appellate courts, and federal trial courts).

[8] For Table 6–1, the quota of columns of 1955 referents sampled in *Shepard's Citations* for each region equaled 25 times the ratio between the number of columns of 1955 referents for each region and the total number of columns for all the regions. The exact columns used for each region were chosen by giving each half-column a number and then drawing numbers from a random numbers table until the quota of columns for the region had been reached. For Table 6–2, all 234 pages of 1955 referents in *Shepard's* were used.

[9] Between two conflicting precedents, the precedent established by the court with the greater influence is the one more likely to be cited all other variables remaining

TABLE 6–1

How Many Times Each Citor Cited Each Referent Approvingly

Citors	Referents								Times Citing	Times Citing Others
	A	NE	NW	SE	S	SW	P	FJ		
A	338	16	6	4	3	2	4	40	413	75
NE	8	402	8	3	2	0	6	30	459	57
NW	3	9	213	1	2	0	5	23	256	43
SE	3	0	3	211	0	0	3	6	226	15
S	2	1	0	2	302	1	5	4	317	15
SW	3	5	2	1	3	339	1	16	370	31
P	5	14	7	4	0	3	421	46	500	79
FJ	8	17	9	9	7	14	12	1085	1161	76
Times cited	370	464	248	235	319	359	457	1250		
Times cited by others	32	62	35	24	17	20	36	165		

decisions can, in effect, overrule a court beneath it, then the higher court tends to be referred to for authority more than the lower court. Of the eight court groupings used, only the federal jurisdiction has any over-ruling power over any of the other groupings in that the United States Supreme Court can overrule the state supreme courts in cases involving constitutional issues.[10] Second, jurisdictions having a high per capita income are likely to be more heavily cited because they tend to have more money to improve their judicial personnel, their judicial institutions, and their law schools, and thereby gain more respect as a source of judicial authority.[11] Not only do jurisdictions with a higher per capita income generally have a greater ability to achieve these improvements, but they generally also have a greater need for them in order to keep their complex industrial life running smoothly. Third, the more cases a court turns out, the more likely it is to cover a situation that comes up in

---

equal. Other possibly relevant variables include the facts in each of the past cases and their relative similarity to the present case, the majority attitude among other courts toward the precedents, the relative soundness of the reasoning behind each precedent, the past reactions of the present court toward similar precedents, the relatively recency of each precedent, and other aspects of the total context of the two past precedents.

[10] L. Mayers, The American Legal System (1955), 5–54, The point-biserial correlation was +.94 between the influence score of each court grouping (i.e., its column total in Table 6–1) and whether or not it can overrule any of the other court groupings.

[11] The Pearsonian correlation was +.44 between the influence score of each court grouping and its per capita income. The per capita income score, expressed in dollars, for each court grouping in 1955 was determined by consulting Statistical Abstract of the United States 303 (E. Goldfield, 1957). To obtain the per capita income for a court grouping, the per capita incomes of the component states were added together, and the sum was divided by the number of component states.

another court and, therefore, to be cited by the other court for author-ity.[12] Fourth, courts within the same legal system are more likely to cite nearby courts with which they have close cultural contacts and common sectional problems. When dealing with many courts, those closest to the geographical center of all the courts are more likely to be cited than those on the geographical periphery.[13]

The degree of *extroversion* of a court grouping also correlates mean-ingfully with four variables. First, the wealthier jurisdictions tend to cite other jurisdictions more because their lawyers and judges tend to have more comprehensive legal educations and law libraries that deal more with cases of other jurisdictions and place less emphasis on local mate-rials.[14] Second, if a jurisdiction has more new people (including law-yers) coming into it, then the jurisdiction will have more lawyers in it who are familiar with the cases of other jurisdictions and who will cite those other jurisdictions in court.[15] Third, if a court is required by law to cite decisions of other jurisdictions, then such a court will have a higher extroversion score than a court that does not have such an obligation. Of the eight court groupings used, only the federal jurisdiction has a legal obligation to cite any of the other court groupings. This obligation arises

---

[12] The Pearsonian correlation was +.28 between the influence score of each court grouping and its case quantity score. The case quantity score, expressed in numbers of cases, for each court grouping was determined by counting the cases listed in the tables of cases reported, which are located in the front of every 1955 volume of the West Publishing Company series of regional court reports. To obtain the case quantity for a court grouping, the separate case quantities for its component court reports were added together.

[13] The Pearsonian correlation was +.24 between the influence score of each court grouping and its geographical closeness score. The geographical closeness score, ex-pressed in miles, for each court grouping represents the average distance to the geo-graphical centers of the other court groupings. The figures were determined by locating the center of each court grouping, determining how far each center is from the center of each of the other court groupings, adding these amounts, and dividing each of the sums by seven since there are seven other court groupings. The center of a court grouping can be determined by the following steps: (1) cut out the court grouping area from a cardboard map; (2) suspend the cutout from any point on its edge; (3) note where a plumb line from the edge-point crosses the cutout; (4) sus-pend the cutout from any other point on its edge; (5) note where a second plumb line from the second edge-point intersects the first line. This intersection is the physical center of the irregularly shaped cutout and, therefore, the geographical center of the court grouping. C. DULL *et al.*, MODERN PHYSICS 129–30 (1951).

[14] The Pearsonian correlation was +.81 between the extroversion score of each court grouping (i.e., its row total in Table 6–1 and its per capita income).

[15] The Pearsonian correlation was +.71 between the extroversion score of each court grouping and its immigration score. The 1955 immigration score expressed in number of people for each state was determined by consulting GOLDFIELD, STATIS-TICAL ABSTRACT, at 11. To obtain the immigration score for a court grouping, the immigration figures of its component states were added together and the sum divided by the number of component states. Immigration scores represent net immigration (or immigration minus emigration). Gross immigration figures are not compiled by the Bureau of Census, but presumably they would positively correlate with the net immi-gration figures.

when a federal court is hearing a case involving citizens of different states and no federal statute is applicable. The federal court must then use for authority the cases of the state in which the federal court is located.[16] Fourth, the more cases a court turns out, the more likely it is to cover a fact situation that has come up in another court and, therefore, to cite for authority the decision of the other court.[17]

III. DISAPPROVAL RELATIONS

Table 6–2 shows how many times each citor cited each referent disapprovingly. All citations of a disapproving nature are indicated in *Shepard's Citations* by a letter c (criticized), o (overruled), or q (questioned) beside the citation. The column totals of Table 6–2 indicate how

TABLE 6–2

How Many Times Each Citor Cited Each Referent Disapprovingly

Citors	Referents								Times Citing	Times Citing Others
	A	NE	NW	SE	S	SW	P	FJ		
A	20	0	0	0	0	0	0	0	20	0
NE	0	29	0	0	0	0	0	0	29	0
NW	0	0	9	0	0	0	0	0	9	0
SE	0	0	0	4	0	0	0	0	4	0
S	0	0	0	0	16	0	0	0	16	0
SW	0	0	0	0	0	11	0	0	11	0
P	0	0	0	0	0	0	29	0	29	0
FJ	3	4	0	0	0	1	1	76	85	9
Times cited	23	33	9	4	16	12	30	76		
Times cited by others	3	4	0	0	0	1	1	0		

often each referent was cited disapprovingly by others. The column totals minus self-citations give a measure of the degree of disparagement each court is subjected to. The row totals indicate how often each citor cited others disapprovingly. The row totals minus self-citations give a measure of the degree of criticalness of each citor.

Why are some courts more disparaged than others? The data tend to indicate that there are no significant differences between the court groupings with regard to the extent to which each is disparaged by the

---

[16] *Erie* v. *Tompkins,* 304 U.S. 48 (1938). The point-biserial correlation was +.40 between the extroversion score of each court grouping and whether or not it had any legal obligation to cite other court groupings.

[17] The Pearsonian correlation was +.29 between the extroversion score of each court grouping and its case quantity score.

others. Whatever difference may exist between the courts on which are the more disparaged courts is probably associated with which are the more influential courts. Influence increases the likelihood that a court will be cited by opposing lawyers, and the more a court is cited by opposing lawyers, the more times it is likely to be disparaged by the deciding judge, who must decide for one of the opposing lawyers.

Why are some courts more critical than others? The data indicate that except for the federal jurisdiction none of the eight court groupings was critical of anybody but itself. The criticalness of the federal courts can be explained by the federal rule previously described, which, in effect, makes a federal court into a local state court in cases involving parties of different state citizenships but not involving federal statutes.[18] Thus, much, if not all, federal criticism of the state courts can be considered, along with the main diagonal entries, as a kind of self-criticism. Federal criticalness may also be explained by the fact that of all the court groupings involved, only the federal jurisdiction has a hierarchial position that enables it to look down on the other courts.

IV. VARIATIONS AND USES

By varying the courts, the subject matter, and the time period, other sociometric relations among courts can be determined. First, one might analyze sociometric relations between court groupings other than the eight court groupings used here. This can be done through an analysis of the Shepard's volumes that are organized on a state-by-state basis rather than on a regional basis, or through a content analysis of the judicial opinions themselves.[19] Interrelations between courts of national units, such as members of the British Commonwealth or the Soviet Bloc, might also be tallied by consulting their court reports. Second, one might analyze sociometric relations among courts by using cases that only deal with special subject matters instead of the heterogeneous subject matters dealt with by the cases used here. Lists of cases dealing with given subjects can be found in law encyclopedias and similar legal works. Third, one can use time periods other than the one used here. The shorter the time period, the greater the percentage of self-citations, since as time passes, cases are more described in the legal literature, giving other courts greater access to them than they initially had. By controlling the time factors, one can not only determine the sociometric relations among courts, but one might also be able to determine diffusion rates, which

---

[18] *Erie* v. *Tompkins,* 304 U.S. 48 (1938).

[19] Some court reports (e.g., United States Court Reports) have a table of cases cited at the beginning of each volume, thereby facilitating an analysis of whom the court cites.

indicate how long it takes for an average case of a given type from one jurisdiction to be cited approvingly in another jurisdiction.[20]

Studies of the sociometric relations among court systems can aid the judicial reformer who seeks to know why some courts are more influential than others. They can aid the practicing lawyer who seeks further criteria for deciding what citations to use in a legal argument before a court, and such studies can aid the social scientist who seeks further criteria for predicting which way a court will decide a given case where the court has to choose between different judicial precedents.

---

[20] Some possible topics for a quantitative sociometric analysis, which attempts to account for the similarities and differences observed, might include: (1) disapproval relations of various southern courts toward the United States Supreme Court in segregation cases, including the narrowing of Supreme Court decisions; (2) approval relations of the United States Supreme Court toward the various federal circuit courts, including the affirming and reversing of cases on appeal; and (3) disapproval and approval relations of any given state supreme court toward all other courts and possibly toward other forms of referents, such as various periodicals, books, and attorneys' briefs.

SECTION II
The Factual Stimuli

T his section is designed to discuss the role of the main factual stimuli in shaping legal policies and adjudications. These factual stimuli include the cultural context, the competing contestants, and evidence-type facts.

Chapter 7 discusses the role of technological, political, and economic characteristics of societies as determinants of judicial structure and procedure. Five preliterate societies and five literate ones are used as the sample of entities on which the hypotheses are tested. There is elsewhere a growing body of related cross-cultural judicial studies.[1] Unfortunately, however, those studies nearly always deal with only one country per study and generally do not attempt to scientifically test causal or bivariate hypotheses. In order to determine the relation between socioeconomic variables and legal variables, what is needed is a bank of relevant data on nearly all the countries of the world. Such data is already available for the socioeconomic variables.[2] Likewise, data on the legal variables in basic fields such as contracts, torts, property, and criminal law can be found summarized for numerous countries in the international volume of the Martindale-Hubbell legal directory.[3] By correlating the socioeconomic and the legal variables, one can obtain a better appreciation of the restraint and the stimulus that culture has on law reform and legal change, especially if data can be obtained historically as well as cross-culturally.

---

[1] See C. SZLADITS, A BIBLIOGRAPHY ON FOREIGN AND COMPARATIVE LAW BOOKS AND ARTICLES IN ENGLISH (1963); and L. Nader, The Ethnography of Law: A Bibliographical Survey, 1964 (mimeographed paper available from the Behavioral Sciences Center at Stanford).

[2] A. BANKS & R. TEXTOR, A CROSS POLITY SURVEY (1963); B. RUSSETT et al., WORLD HANDBOOK OF POLITICAL AND SOCIAL INDICATORS (1964); and R. RUMMEL et al., DIMENSIONS OF NATIONS (1966).

[3] MARTINDALE-HUBBELL LAW DIRECTORY—LAW DIGESTS (1967).

Chapter 8 deals with the influence that the nature of the defendants, especially their race and indigency, has on the outcomes that occur at various stages of criminal proceedings. The Jury Verdict Research Corporation publishes similar findings on the parties in personal injury cases, which is the most common type of civil case.[4]

Chapter 9 deals with the influence that the nature of the appellant's attorney as compared to the appellee's attorney has on the decision in a variety of appellate cases. The lack of substantial attorney influence this chapter reveals is reinforced by the Kalven-Zeisel jury project studies, which show that if both sides are represented by counsel in criminal cases, then having an imbalance in the quality of the attorneys accounts for the result in only approximately 1 percent of the cases when other variables are held constant.[5] The political pressure group is a type of contestant not discussed in Chapters 8 and 9 partly because it is rarely involved in the average case. Nevertheless, the role of such groups is important in certain United States Supreme Court cases and congressional actions, and these group contestants are often mentioned in the political science literature.[6]

Chapters 10 through 13 deal with a variety of factual elements that can influence judicial outcomes, including how the lower court decided the case, from what region of the country the case came, what the general subject matter is, and whether certain points of evidence were present. The emphasis in these chapters is not on substantive principles but, rather, on a methodological orientation for assessing the importance individually and collectively of a set of variables that are hypothesized as being relevant to judicial outcomes. The methodology can include legal stimuli and the characteristics of the decision makers as well as factual stimuli. Both simplicity and widespread applicability are stressed, unlike other quantitative methods for assessing the influence of a set of variables, which tend to be overly complex and usable only on variables that must be dichotomized or have a high level of measurability.[7] Stress is also placed on applying the methodology in order to arrive at generalizations on *why* certain policies and decisions are reached in contrast to just making mechanical quantitative predictions and in contrast to just quoting the verbal rationalizations given in the cases.

---

[4] JURY VERDICT RESEARCH CORPORATION, STATEWIDE JURY VERDICTS (1961 to present).

[5] H. KALVEN & H. ZEISEL, THE AMERICAN JURY 351–72 (1966).

[6] Hakman, *The Supreme Court's Political Environment,* in J. TANENHAUS & J. GROSSMAN (eds.), FRONTIERS OF JUDICIAL RESEARCH (1969); and *Interest Groups and Litigation* in W. MURPHY & C. PRITCHETT, COURTS, JUDGES, AND POLITICS—AN INTRODUCTION TO THE JUDICIAL PROCESS 274 (1961).

[7] Kort, *A Nonlinear Model for the Analysis of Judicial Decisions,* 62 AM. POL. SCI. REV. 546 (1968); and Grunbaum, *Analytical & Simulation Models for Explaining Judicial Decision-Making,* in J. TANENHAUS & J. GROSSMAN (eds.), FRONTIERS OF JUDICIAL RESEARCH (1969).

A. The Cultural Context

CHAPTER 7

Culture Patterns and Judicial Systems

Comparative law, like comparative government in general,[1] has largely confined itself to unintegrated descriptions of European legal principles.[2] Not only has comparative law traditionally been limited in its subject matter, but it also has rarely, if ever, made use of statistical techniques in accounting for the differences observed. It is the purpose of this chapter to statistically analyze the relations between industrialism, democracy, and collectivism on the one hand and the judicial process on the other in 10 different societies.

I. THE RESEARCH DESIGN

It is hypothesized that statistically significant relations might be found between the following cultural and adjudication characteristics.

I. Cultural characteristics.
    1. Manufacturing versus nonmanufacturing technology.
    2. Mainly dictatorial versus mainly democratic political system.
    3. Collectivistic property system versus individualistic property system.
II. Adjudication characteristics.
    A. Adjudication personnel.
        1. Presence of professional judges or dispute settlers.
        2. Selection of judges mainly by chieftains versus selection mainly by the people as a whole in the society.
        3. Presence of jurors or lay advisers to professional judges.
        4. Frequent presence of lawyers or professional pleaders.

---

[1] MACRIDIS, THE STUDY OF COMPARATIVE GOVERNMENT 1–22 (1955).

[2] See, for example, the methodological discussion and the bibliographic titles in SCHLESSINGER, COMPARATIVE LAW xvii–xxi, 144–51, 499–600 (1959).

B. Sources of decision-making criteria.
1. Presence of vigilantism or informal lay trials accompanied by lynching, blood feuds, or other violence parallel to the formal system.
2. Presence of supernatural divinations, ordeals, judicial duels, effective supernatural oaths, or heavy reliance on religious literature.
3. Mainly rigid precedent-following or norm-following, resulting in considerable judicial restraint, versus mainly case individualization, resulting in considerable judicial discretion.
4. Presence of norms promulgated by councils or judges versus norms stemming only from evolved custom.
C. Adjudication purposes in criminal matters.
1. Mainly defense-oriented versus mainly prosecution-oriented.
2. Primary emphasis on rehabilitation of norm breakers versus primary emphasis on making norm breakers suffer to deter others or satisfy revengefulness.
D. Techniques involved in resolving controversies.
1. Mainly private suits for damages versus mainly public or community handling of norm breakers.
2. Generally more than two months from settlement initiation to completion versus generally less.
3. Presence of frequent provision whereby parties of high classes or ethnic groups have greater chance of winning than parties of low classes or ethnic groups.
4. Frequent or occasional bribery versus seldom if ever any bribery.
5. Judges frequently summon and interrogate witnesses versus system where judges seldom or just occasionally do so.
6. Presence of procedures whereby a losing party can generally apply for another hearing.

To test the hypotheses, 10 societies were analyzed. Of the 10 societies, 5 consisted of the following geographically scattered preliterate societies.

1. Ashanti Confederation as described in Robert Rattray, *Ashanti Law and Constitution* (1929).
2. Cheyenne as described in Karl Llewellyn and E. Adamson Hoebel, *The Cheyenne Way* (1941).
3. Eskimo as described in Knud Rasmussen, *Intellectual Culture of the Iglulik Eskimo* (1929).
4. Ifugao as described in Roy Barton, *Ifugao Law* (1919).
5. Trobriand as described in Bronislaw Malinowski, *Crime and Custom in Savage Society* (1926).

Secondary source material on these preliterate societies is available in
E. Adamson Hoebel's *The Law of Primitive Man* (1954). The other
five societies consisted of the following geographically scattered literate
societies.

1. United States as described in Lewis Mayers, *The American Legal System* (1955), and Jerome Frank, *Courts on Trial* (1949).
2. Pre-Communist China as described in William Burdick, *Bench and Bar of Other Lands* (1939), and John Wigmore, *Panorama of the World's Legal Systems* (1936).
3. Pre-Nasser Egypt as described in the Burdick and Wigmore works listed above.
4. French Fourth Republic as described in Robert Neumann, *European and Comparative Government* (1951), and Rene David, *The French Legal System* (1958).
5. Soviet Union as described in Harold Berman, *Justice in Russia* (1950).

Table 7–1 shows the cultural and adjudication characteristics of the
10 societies according to the sources consulted. The symbols used in
Table 7–1 are defined below the table. The selection of judges, presence
of jurors (lay advisers to judges), bribery of judges, and the interrogatory
role of judges are concepts inapplicable to the Trobriand society, since
it lacks any personages who can be considered judges, professional or
otherwise. The presence of rehabilitation versus deterrence is also inapplicable to the Trobriand society, since the emphasis there is in neither
direction but, rather, in the direction of handling norm breakers so
as to provide compensation to those who have suffered from the violation.
The presence of judges appointed by chieftains versus judges selected
by the people as a whole is inapplicable to the Ifugao society, since
the selector there is the plaintiff, who picks whomever he wants to
judge the dispute.

II. MANUFACTURING AND NONMANUFACTURING COMPARISONS

Table 7–2 shows how the adjudication systems of the manufacturing
societies involved differ from those of the nonmanufacturing societies.
The probabilities in the table represent how many times out of 100
a difference as large as each difference found could have occurred purely
by chance, taking into consideration the size of each difference and
the number of societies involved.[3] If the chance probability is less than

---

[3] The Fisher exact probability test is the appropriate test of chance probability
to use on this data because it takes into consideration the smallness of the samples
and because the societies do not distribute themselves in a bell-shaped manner on the

TABLE 7–1

THE CULTURAL AND ADJUDICATION CHARACTERISTICS OF THE 10 SOCIETIES

	United States	Ashanti Confederation	Cheyenne	Pre-Communist China	Pre-Nasser Egypt	Eskimo	French Fourth Republic	Ifugao	Soviet Union	Trobriand
I. Cultural Characteristics										
Manufacturing	Y	N	N	Y	N	N	Y	N	Y	N
Democratic	Y	E	Y	N	N	Y	N	Y	N	N
Collectivistic	N	E	Y	N	N	Y	Y	N	Y	N
II. Adjudication Characteristics										
A. Personnel										
Professional judges	Y	Y	N	Y	Y	N	Y	N	Y	N
Appointive judges	N	E	Y	Y	Y	N	Y	I	N	I
Jurors	Y	N	N	N	N	N	Y	N	Y	I
Lawyers	Y	Y	N	Y	E	N	Y	N	Y	N
B. Sources of criteria										
Vigilantism	E	N	N	N	N	Y	N	Y	N	Y
Supernaturalism	N	Y	Y	N	Y	Y	N	N	N	N
Little discretion	Y	N	N	N	N	Y	Y	N	N	E
Promulgation	Y	N	Y	Y	Y	N	Y	N	Y	N
C. Purposes										
Defense-oriented	Y	N	Y	N	N	E	Y	N	N	N
Rehabilitation	E	N	Y	N	N	Y	N	N	Y	I
D. Techniques										
Private emphasis	N	N	N	Y	N	Y	N	Y	N	Y
Only short delays	N	Y	Y	N	N	N	N	Y	Y	Y
Discrimination	Y	Y	N	Y	Y	N	E	N	N	Y
Frequent bribery	Y	Y	N	Y	Y	N	N	N	N	I
Adversary system	Y	N	N	N	N	N	N	N	N	I
Rehearings	Y	Y	N	Y	Y	N	Y	N	Y	N

Symbols used:

Y (yes) = has the mentioned characteristic to the extent specified in the hypothesis.

N (no) = has the obverse characteristic to the extent specified in the hypothesis.

E = approximately evenly balanced between Y and N.

I = inapplicable in light of other characteristics of the society (e.g., method of judicial selection is a question inapplicable to a society that has neither professional nor nonprofessional judges).

U = unrevealed in the sources consulted.

5 out of 100, it is conventional to attribute the difference found to a real difference rather than to chance. If the chance probability is greater than 20 out of 100, it is conventional to attribute the difference to chance. A finding with a chance probability between 5 and 20 out of 100 can be treated, where small samples are involved, as being worthy

---

characteristics being measured. See SIEGEL, NONPARAMETRIC STATISTICS FOR THE BEHAVIORAL SCIENCES 95–104 (1956). The probability of attributing each difference found to chance has been doubled because the hypotheses did not specify the direction of the difference. *Id.* at 13–14.

TABLE 7–2

Adjudication Factor	Number of Societies Involved (Mfg. & Non- mfg.)	% of Mfg. Societies Having the Adj. Factor	% of Non- mfg. Societies Having the Adj. Factor	Differ- ence (in per- centage points)	Probability of the Difference Being Due to Chance
A. Personnel					
Professional judges	4 & 6	100%	33%	+67	.05 to .20
Appointive judges	4 & 3	50	67	−17	Above .20
Jurors	4 & 5	75	0	+75	.05 to .20
Lawyers	4 & 5	100	20	+80	.05 to .20
B. Sources of criteria					
Vigilantism	3 & 6	0	50	−70	Above .20
Supernaturalism	4 & 6	0	67	−67	.05 to .20
Little discretion	4 & 5	50	20	+30	Above .20
Promulgation	4 & 6	100	33	+67	.05 to .20
C. Purposes					
Defense-oriented	4 & 5	50	20	+30	Above .20
Rehabilitation	3 & 5	33	40	−07	Above .20
D. Techniques					
Private emphasis	4 & 6	25	50	−25	Above .20
Only short delays	4 & 6	25	67	−42	Above .20
Discrimination	3 & 6	67	50	+17	Above .20
Frequent bribery	4 & 5	50	40	+10	Above .20
Adversary system	4 & 5	25	0	+25	Above .20
Rehearings	4 & 6	100	33	+67	.05 to .20

of further consideration and analysis, although not worthy of acceptance as a proven relationship.

In Table 7–2 there are no relationships that have a chance probability of less than 5 out of 100. There are, however, 6 relationships that involve differences greater than 60 percentage points and chance probabilities between .05 and .20, in spite of the small samples. Thus, Table 7–2 tends to show that manufacturing societies are more likely than non-manufacturing societies to have adjudication systems in which professional judges, jurors, lawyers, promulgating bodies, and appellate courts are present and in which supernaturalism is relatively absent. Table 7–3 shows the specific societies that illustrate these relations, excluding those societies for which the positions used are inapplicable or evenly balanced. The disproportionate presence of professional judges, jurors, lawyers, promulgating bodies, and appellate courts among manufacturing societies can probably be partially explained by the fact that increased industrialization brings increased specialization within the economic system of a society, which carries over into the political and adjudicative systems. The relationships can also be partially explained by the fact

TABLE 7–3

THE SOCIETIES WHICH ILLUSTRATE THE MORE STATISTICALLY SIGNIFICANT
FINDINGS WITH REGARD TO INDUSTRIALISM AS A DETERMINANT OF
ADJUDICATION SYSTEMS

	Nonmanu-facturing	Manufacturing		Nonmanu-facturing	Manufacturing
Professional judges	Ashanti Egyptian	American Chinese French Soviet	Much super-naturalism	Ashanti Cheyenne Egyptian Eskimo	
No professional judges	Cheyenne Eskimo Ifugao Trobriand		Little super-naturalism	Ifugao Trobriand	American Chinese French Soviet
Jurors		American French Soviet	Promulgation of law	Cheyenne Egyptian	American Chinese French Soviet
No jurors	Ashanti Cheyenne Egyptian Eskimo Ifugao	Chinese	Law by evolved custom only	Ashanti Eskimo Ifugao Trobriand	
Lawyers	Ashanti	American Chinese French Soviet	Rehearings	Ashanti Egyptian	American Chinese French Soviet
No lawyers	Cheyenne Eskimo Ifugao Trobriand		No rehearings	Cheyenne Eskimo Ifugao Trobriand	

that increased industrialization better enables a society to have enough economic surplus to support political and judicial officials who are not directly producing food, shelter, or clothing for the society.

The disproportionate presence in nonmanufacturing societies of divination, trial by ordeal, and judicially supervised duels (in all of which divine intervention is presumed to enable the truth to win out) can possibly be explained by the fact that with increased industrialization there comes a greater emphasis on materialistic explanation of phenomena rather than on supernaturalistic explanation. Both industrialization and a naturalistic or materialistic orientation seems to be coeffects of increased acquisition of knowledge and improved scientific techniques in the physical and biological sciences.

III.   DEMOCRATIC AND DICTATORIAL COMPARISONS

Table 7–4 shows how the adjudication systems of democratic societies differ from those of dictatorial societies. Two of the relationships associ-

TABLE 7–4

HOW THE ADJUDICATION SYSTEMS OF DEMOCRATIC SOCIETIES
DIFFER FROM THOSE OF DICTATORIAL SOCIETIES

Adjudication Factor	Number of Societies Involved (Dem. & Dict.)	% of Dem. Societies Having the Adj. Factor	% of Dict. Societies Having the Adj. Factor	Difference (in percentage points)	Probability of the Difference Being Due to Chance
A. Personnel					
Professional judges ..	5 & 4	40%	75%	−35	Above .20
Appointive judges ..	4 & 3	50	67	−17	Above .20
Jurors	5 & 3	40	33	+07	Above .20
Lawyers	5 & 3	40	67	−27	Above .20
B. Sources of Criteria					
Vigilantism	4 & 4	50	25	+25	Above .20
Supernaturalism	5 & 4	40	25	+15	Above .20
Little discretion	5 & 3	60	0	+60	Slightly above .20
Promulgation	5 & 4	60	75	−15	Above .20
C. Purposes					
Defense-oriented	4 & 4	75	0	+75	.05 to .20
Rehabilitation	4 & 3	50	33	+17	Above .20
D. Techniques					
Private emphasis	5 & 4	40	50	−10	Above .20
Only short delays ...	5 & 4	40	50	−10	Above .20
Discrimination	4 & 4	25	75	−50	Above .20
Frequent bribery	5 & 3	20	67	−47	Above .20
Adversary system ...	5 & 3	20	0	+20	Above .20
Rehearings	5 & 4	40	75	−35	Above .20

ated with defense orientation and judicial discretion are strong enough
to have chance probabilities almost below .20, in spite of the small
samples. The specific societies that illustrate these relations are shown
in Table 7–5. The democratic system emphasizes the importance of the
people sometimes at the expense of the state or the government. This
factor possibly explains why democratic societies tend to place numerous
obstacles in the way of finding an accused person guilty of violating
the social norms. In such societies, the prevailing philosophy is that
it is frequently better that no sanctions be enforced at all for a violation
of the norms of the collectivity than that innocent people be swept
up in the sanctions.

TABLE 7–5

THE SOCIETIES WHICH ILLUSTRATE THE MORE STATISTICALLY SIGNIFICANT FINDINGS
WITH REGARD TO DEMOCRACY AS A DETERMINANT OF ADJUDICATION SYSTEMS

	Dictatorial	Democratic		Dictatorial	Democratic
Defense-oriented		American Cheyenne French	Little judicial discretion to individualize		American Eskimo French
Prosecution-oriented	Chinese Egyptian Soviet Trobriand	Ifugao	Much judicial discretion to individualize	Chinese Egyptian Soviet	Cheyenne Ifugao

Table 7–4 also tends to show that societies with a democratic political
organization are more likely than societies with a dictatorial political
organization to have adjudication systems in which there is relatively
little judicial discretion. Just as the economic specialization involved in
industrialization carries over to a society's adjudication system, the popular restraints on political chieftains involved in democracy probably
also carry over to a society's adjudication system. One of the major
ways to prevent undue discretion on the part of adjudicators is to require
through tradition or law that present adjudicators apply the rules of
past adjudicators without attempting to individualize decisions to the
parties.

IV. COLLECTIVISTIC AND INDIVIDUALISTIC COMPARISONS

Table 7–6 shows how the adjudication systems of societies that emphasize collective ownership of property differ from those of societies that emphasize individual ownership. Three of the relationships are below or nearly at the .20 level of chance probability. Table 7–7 shows the

TABLE 7–6

How the Adjudication Systems of Collectivistic Societies Differ from Those of Individualistic Societies

Adjudication Factor	Number of Societies Involved (Coll. & Ind.)	% of Coll. Societies Having the Adj. Factor	% of Ind. Societies Having the Adj. Factor	Difference (in percentage points)	Probability of the Difference Being due to Chance
A. Personnel					
Professional judges ..	3 & 6	33%	67%	−34	Above .20
Appointive judges ..	3 & 4	33	75	−42	Above .20
Jurors	3 & 5	33	40	−07	Above .20
Lawyers	3 & 5	33	60	−27	Above .20
B. Sources of Criteria					
Vigilantism	3 & 5	33	40	−07	Above .20
Supernaturalism	3 & 6	67	17	+50	Above .20
Little discretion	3 & 5	33	40	−07	Above .20
Promulgation	3 & 6	67	67	0	No difference
C. Purposes					
Defense-oriented	2 & 6	50	33	+17	Above .20
Rehabilitation	3 & 4	100	0	+100	.05 to .20
D. Techniques					
Private emphasis	3 & 6	33	50	−17	Above .20
Only short delays ...	3 & 6	67	33	+34	Above .20
Discrimination	3 & 5	0	80	−80	.05 to .20
Frequent bribery	3 & 5	0	60	−60	Slightly above .20
Adversary system ...	3 & 5	0	20	−20	Above .20
Rehearings	3 & 6	33	67	−34	Above .20

specific societies that illustrate these relationships. All the societies that have collectivistic property systems emphasize rehabilitation over revenge or deterrence in their criminal proceedings, whereas none of the societies with individualistic property systems do so. This finding is possibly attributable to the fact that in a collectivistically organized society each member tends to feel a greater responsibility for each other member. Thus, when one member becomes a social deviant there is a greater tendency to blame the environment than to blame the individual. Furthermore, in a collectivistically organized society there is a greater feeling of unity and a lesser feeling of competitiveness. When a member of such a society becomes a social deviant, this feeling of unity discourages his being labeled an outlaw and encourages an attempt to bring him back into the fold through rehabilitation.

As shown in Table 7–6, collectivistic societies are less likely than in-

TABLE 7–7

THE SOCIETIES WHICH ILLUSTRATE THE MORE STATISTICALLY SIGNIFICANT FINDINGS WITH REGARD TO COLLECTIVISM AS A DETERMINANT OF ADJUDICATION SYSTEMS

	Individualistic	Collectivistic		Individualistic	Collectivistic
Rehabilitation emphasis		Cheyenne Eskimo Soviet	Frequent income or ethnic discrimination	American Chinese Egyptian Trobriand	
Deterrence or revenge emphasis	Chinese Egyptian French Ifugao		Rare factors in determining winners	Ifugao	Cheyenne Eskimo Soviet

	Individualistic	Collectivistic
Relatively frequent bribery	American Chinese Egyptian	
Relatively rare bribery	French Ifugao	Cheyenne Eskimo Soviet

dividualistic societies to have in their adjudication systems discrimination whereby members of higher classes or ethnic groups have a better chance of winning an adjudication than do others. This finding can possibly be explained by the fact that a collectivistic society is less likely to have sharp property differentials on which economic classes can be based. In addition, the greater feeling of unity and cooperation that tends to exist within collectivistic societies helps to discourage categorizing of people for purposes of unequal treatment.

A third finding Table 7–6 tends to reveal is the greater presence of bribery of adjudicators in societies with individualistic rather than collectivistic property systems. The explanation possibly lies in the fact that there is greater competition for material acquisition in an individualistic society than in a collectivistic society. Such material acquisitiveness provides an incentive to adjudicators to solicit or at least accept bribes, which incentive is relatively lacking in most collectivistically organized societies.

These hypotheses, findings, and theories relating to collectivistic and individualistic societies, like those relating to manufacturing and non-manufacturing societies or democratic and dictatorial societies, are not based on sufficient data to merit acceptance as proven propositions. This exploratory study, however, is readily capable of being expanded into a research design, using more societies, more information sources, and more variables. It has been a success to the extent that it throws light on the relationships involved and to the extent that it provokes more expansive studies of the cross-cultural context of adjudicative and other legal processes.

B. The Contestants

CHAPTER 8

The Litigants: Disparities in
Safeguards and Sentencing

Studies have previously been made of disparities in the sentencing of defendants who have different background characteristics in a given city or state.[1] It is the purpose of this chapter to analyze some data relevant to disparities at all stages in the administration of criminal procedure, not just the sentencing stage, and to do so with a nationwide sample of both state and federal cases. This chapter also considers the causes of and remedies for the substantial disparities found.

The writer gratefully thanks Lee Silverstein of the American Bar Foundation and Ronald Beattie of the Administrative Office of the United States Courts for their generous cooperation in allowing him to have access to their data on state and federal criminal cases, respectively. The data can now be obtained on magnetic tape or punched cards from the Inter-University Consortium for Political Research at Ann Arbor, Michigan. The writer also thanks Robert Byars and Lois Chatlain (political science students at the University of Illinois and University of Arizona respectively) for their participation in early phases of this study. Thanks are also owed to John Gilbert (the statistical consultant at the Center for Advanced Study in the Behavioral Sciences) for his help in processing some of the data and to the participants in the 1965 judicial process seminar at the East-West Center for their helpful comments.
[1] Green, Judicial Attitudes in Sentencing; A Study of the Factors Underlying the Sentencing Practice of the Criminal Court of Philadelphia (1961); Bullock, *Significance of the Racial Factor in the Length of Prison Sentences*, 52 J. Crim. L., C. & P.S. 411 (1961); Wolfgang, Kelly & Nolde, *Comparison of the Executed and the Commuted among Admissions to Death Row*, 53 J. Crim. L., C. & P.S. 301 (1962). For a listing of earlier related work, see the six-page annotated bibliography Institute of Judicial Administration, Disparity in Sentencing of Convicted Defendants (1954), although many of the items listed there emphasize differences among types of judges rather than types of defendants. For a judge-focused study of disparities, see Nagel, *Judicial Backgrounds and Criminal Cases*, 53 J. Crim. L., C. & P.S. 333 (1962) (Chap. 18 *infra*).

I. BASIC MATTERS

A. The Raw Data

The raw data for the state cases were obtained by the American Bar Foundation from a detailed study of trial court dockets for the year 1962 in a sample of 194 counties located in all 50 states. The data was gathered under the direction of Lee Silverstein as part of a study of the procedures available for providing attorneys to indigent defendants in criminal cases.[2] Fortunately, the American Bar Foundation had the foresight to include many interesting variables that are only distantly relevant to the immediate needs of the defense attorney project. The total sample consisted of 11,258 cases.

The 194 counties were chosen in accordance with a procedure especially developed for the project by the National Opinion Research Center. The procedure was designed to relate the likelihood of each county's being included in the sample to the quantity of criminal cases that each county has. Within each sampled county, individual felony cases were selected by random numbers in such a way as to make the ratio of sampled county cases divided by the total sample roughly equal to the ratio of total county cases divided by the universe of 1962 American state felony cases.

In processing the total sample of 11,258 criminal cases as part of the defense attorney project, Lee Silverstein weighted each case by the ratio between the number of total state cases divided by the number of sampled county cases. Assignment of weights to the sampled cases is not used in the tables of this study of disparities in criminal procedure because only larceny and assault cases (not the full 11,258 cases) have been used here in order to hold the crime constant, and also because this study is not designed to compare specific states with each other. Furthermore, preliminary cross-tabulation runs, with the cases receiving differential weights, did not produce findings significantly different from the unweighted runs in spite of the greater complexity involved in handling the weighting procedure.

The raw data for the federal cases were obtained by the Administrative Office of the United States under the direction of Ronald Beattie, Will Shafroth, and Warren Olney as part of their expanding program of gathering data on federal court cases.[3] The federal cases

---

[2] Silverstein, Defense of the Poor in Criminal Cases in American State Courts (1965).

[3] Director of the Administrative Office of the United States Courts, Annual Report—1963 (1964); Administrative Office of the U.S. Courts, Federal Offenders in the United States District Courts—1963 (1964).

do not represent a sample but, rather, the complete universe of the 36,265 federal criminal cases decided in 1963. In this study, however, only the assault and interstate larceny cases are used, and cases from the District of Columbia and from American territories are excluded.

There are 846 felonious assault cases and 1,103 grand larceny cases among the state cases, and there are 196 assault cases and 785 interstate larceny cases among the federal cases. Just two crimes are analyzed in this study because it has been found that the type of crime with which one is charged has a substantial influence on the criminal process, particularly at the sentencing[4] and bail stages.[5] Working with two crimes also makes the data more manageable for processing on a small budget. Assault and larceny are used as the two crimes because they represent the most frequently occurring crimes against persons and property, respectively.[6] They are also the types of crimes committed by a variety of people in all parts of the country, and at both the state and federal level. All the cases are felony cases with the exception of 51 of the federal assault cases, which involved nonaggravated assault. All cases in which the defendant was simultaneously charged with more than one crime are excluded from the analysis.

B. The Criminal Procedure Stages

The purpose of this subsection is to define briefly what is meant by each stage in the administration of criminal procedure, how information on each stage is recorded, and to indicate the importance of the stages to the overall process. The distribution of the cases on the procedural variables is also indicated.

The first stage on which data are available is the preliminary hearing. The main purpose of a preliminary hearing is for the judge, justice of the peace, or police magistrate to determine whether there is probable cause to maintain a criminal proceeding against the accused suspect, thereby possibly saving some innocent persons from humiliation, expense, delay, and inconvenience. It is preliminary to the prosecutor's formal accusation or to a grand jury indictment. Besides helping to sift out the innocent, the preliminary hearing also frequently (1) deters the

---

[4] Green, *op. cit., supra* note 1, at 29–41, 97–103; Bullock, *supra* note 1.

[5] Ares, Rankin & Sturz, *The Manhattan Bail Project—An Interim Report on the Use of Pre-Trial Parole*, 38 N.Y.U. L. Rev. 67 (1963).

[6] Federal assault cases refer to assaulting federal officials. 62 Stat. 758 (1949), 18 U.S.C. §§ 111, 113, 1153 (1950); and 68A Stat. 855 (1954), 26 U.S.C. § 7212 (1963). For the elements of state assault, see Miller, Criminal Law 302–12 (1934). Federal interstate larceny refers to thefts of goods involved in interstate commerce. 62 Stat. 729 (1949), 18 U.S.C. §659 (1950). In both sets of data, larceny means appropriating another's property by means other than burglary, auto theft, embezzlement, fraud, forgery, or robbery. Miller, *op. cit. supra* at 340–74 (1934).

use of third degree interrogation, (2) allows for the appearance of counsel and the granting or revising of bail, and (3) reveals that the accused is in the custody of the police so that he may resort to habeas corpus, right to a copy of the complaint, and other legal guarantees.[7]

In Tables 8–1, 8–2, and 8–3 "percent who received no preliminary hearing" refers only to those who are eligible for a preliminary hearing. It thus excludes from the base of the percentage all cases arising in counties whose laws do not provide preliminary hearings in the specific cases involved, as well as cases on which information is not available. Thus, as shown in column 1 of Tables 8–1 and 8–2, of the 1,168 usable state cases (i.e., 492 assault plus 676 larceny), the accused suspect received no preliminary hearing in 434 (i.e., 134 plus 300) or over one third of them. In 357 of the 434 cases, the accused was listed as having waived his statutory right to a preliminary hearing, possibly without realizing the importance of the right he had waived. The rest of the 434 cases were recorded as "no preliminary hearing, reason unknown."

The main purpose of releasing an accused suspect on bail is to minimize his hardship, especially if he is subsequently found to be innocent. It also improves the ability of the accused to investigate and prepare his case.[8] Of the 1,552 state cases on which information was available 689, or 44 percent, involved suspects who were not released on bail. Of these 689, 562 were subsequently found guilty, 71 were not found to be guilty (by reason of acquittal or dismissal), and guilty information was not available for 56. By the time the 71 nonconvicted suspects had been released, 20 had stayed in jail for 2 months or less, 13 had stayed in jail for over 3 months, and length of delay was not available for 38. Five of the nonconvicted suspects who were not released on bail were recorded as having, in effect, served jail terms of over six months before disposal of their cases.

The next procedural stage relates to the matter of defense counsel. For the state cases, the variable refers to having no lawyer whatsoever. All the state cases are felonies involving the possibility of more than a year in prison; yet, the defendants in 183 of the 1,561 cases had no lawyer to represent them, and only 13 of these 183 defendants were recorded as having waived counsel. For the federal cases, the variable refers to not having one's own lawyer, since all the federal defendants seem to have been provided with a lawyer of some kind unless there was an explicit waiver to the contrary. However, information on waivers is not present in the 1963 federal data. Because waiver information is not given, a few defendants who are recorded as not having had an assigned lawyer may have had no lawyer rather than their own

---

[7] Orfield, Criminal Procedure from Arrest to Appeal 49–100 (1947).

[8] Wald & Rankin, *Pretrial Detention and Ultimate Freedom—A Statistical Study*, 39 N.Y.U. L. Rev. 631 (1964).

lawyer. At least 390 of the 1,151 federal defendants did not have their own lawyer. A lawyer is essential to a felony defense in order to have a proper handling of such matters as investigation of the facts, negotiation with the prosecutor (especially where a guilty plea is involved), the direct and cross-examination of witnesses, and presentation of legal and factual arguments to the judge and jury. Although a court-assigned lawyer is surely better than no lawyer, his work may suffer from lack of experience, finances, and enthusiasm, and from lateness in being appointed.[9] There are no professional public defenders at the federal level outside the District of Columbia.

Like the preliminary hearing and the actual trial, the grand jury process, although time-consuming, is theoretically designed to aid in filtering out innocent suspects. The alternative to a grand jury indictment is to let the prosecutor alone make the judgment of whether the suspect should be held over for trial. Of the 915 federal cases that involved either indictment by the grand jury or by the prosecutor alone, 344 involved just the prosecutor. Of these 344 cases only half are recorded as involving a waiver of the grand jury by the defendant. The method of indictment or formal accusation was not included by the American Bar Foundation in the state data.

On the matter of delay, in 162 of the 405 cases in which the accused suspect was not released on bail, there was a delay of more than 2 months from his arrest to his release or trial, whichever came first. In many of these delayed cases, the defendant's attorney may have asked for at least one postponement of the trial, but information on postponements is not included in the raw data. Two months was used as a cutoff because approximately half the cases lasted more than two months and half lasted less than two months. The American Law Institute Code of Criminal Procedure provides that if a defendant is held for more than three months without trial due to no fault of his own, he is to be set free without being subject to rearrest for the same crime unless extremely extenuating circumstances are present.[10] A long delay, especially in jail, can penalize an innocent defendant or overpunish a guilty one as well as decrease the reliability and possibly the availability of valuable witnesses. Since the federal data did not indicate who was released on bail, the delay variable for the federal cases unfortunately does not distinguish between those awaiting trial in jail and those awaiting trial out of jail. In almost half the federal cases, however, there was more than a two months' delay from arrest to disposition.

In the state data, 63 percent of the cases that actually went to trial had no jury present, whereas only 48 percent of the related federal

---

[9] Carlin & Howard, *Legal Representation and Class Justice*, 12 U.C.L.A. L. Rev. 381, 418–21 (1965).

[10] ALI, Code of Crim. Proc. § 292 (1931).

cases were tried without a jury. The state cases that went to trial, however, include some in which a guilty plea was made during the course of the trial (generally a bench trial), whereas (because of the undifferentiated way the federal data was recorded) the federal percentage excludes all cases involving guilty pleas made at any time. The main advantage to the defendant of a jury trial over a bench trial is that conviction by a jury requires unanimous agreement by 12 persons, thereby decreasing the likelihood that an innocent person will be convicted.[11] The collective attitude of a jury may also be more balanced than that of some judges, and the attitudes of juries may be more like those of the defendant. In a sample of 1,500 criminal cases tried by jury, the University of Chicago Jury Project found that the judge and jury agreed on the verdict 81 percent of the time, but in the 19 percent of the cases when the judge and jury disagreed, "the judges were considerably more prone to convict."[12]

On the other hand, seeking a jury trial may mean a substantially greater delay as indicated by the high correlation between jury trial and long delay in Tables 8–3 and 8–6, even though the type of crime is, in effect, held constant by the low correlation between crime (larceny versus assault) and jury trial.[13] Seeking a jury trial may also mean that if the defendant is found guilty he is more likely to be denied probation than if he had a bench trial, as indicated in Tables 8–3 and 8–6. The relation between jury trial and probation denial may represent a penalty for having sought an expensive jury trial, or it may reflect the possibility that more severe larceny and assault cases are tried by juries.

The remaining criminal procedure variables do not involve procedural safeguards for the innocent but, rather, the results of the process. Thus, both the state and federal data indicate whether or not the defendants were found guilty. It is apparent that a high proportion of the defendants are found guilty, but it is also apparent that a substantial minority

---

[11] FELLMAN, THE DEFENDANT'S RIGHTS 85–89 (1958).

[12] Broeder, *The University of Chicago Jury Project*, 38 NEB. L. REV. 744, 749 (1959). The greater likelihood of conviction by a judge rather than a jury is partially indicated by the positive correlation between having a bench trial and being found guilty in Tables 8–3 and 8–6. At the state level, 82 percent of the bench trials in which there was a not-guilty plea resulted in a guilty finding, whereas only 64 percent of the jury trials resulted in a guilty finding. Some of this correlation, however, may be due to the possibility that guilty defendants are less likely to ask for jury trials.

[13] For the benefit of those who may not be statistically oriented, a correlation coefficient can range from −1.00 (perfect inverse correlation between the variables being correlated) to 0 (no correlation) to +1.00 (perfect direct correlation). Any correlation coefficient in Tables 8–3 or 8–6 can be read in four differently worded but logically equivalent ways. For example, the −.24 correlation between *not* having a lawyer and long delay can also be read as a +.24 correlation between having a lawyer and *long* delay, as a −.24 correlation between having a lawyer and *short* delay, or a +.24 correlation between *not* having a lawyer and short delay.

are not so found after having been subjected to criminal proceedings. To be more exact, approximately one out of five of the state and federal defendants are not considered to be guilty. Of those who are considered guilty, 83 percent plead guilty; and of those who plead guilty, the state data indicate 25 percent plead guilty to a lesser offense than the original charge (possibly after negotiating with the prosecutor).[14] Some of the background characteristics in the federal data cannot be correlated with the guilty variable because the Administrative Office of the United States Courts records race, sex, age, and prior record information only for those who have pleaded or been found guilty.

The data also indicate whether the guilty defendants were given a prison sentence by the judge, as contrasted with a suspended sentence or probation. Along related lines, the federal data indicate whether guilty defendants were recommended for prison or probation by the federal probation officer. This probation officer variable correlates highly with the related judicial decision variable; Table 8–7 shows a +.76 correlation coefficient between the two variables. When there is disagreement, the judge is more likely to grant probation than is the probation officer. It may be interesting to note that almost half of the defendants found guilty are given suspended sentences or probation.

The final variable relates to whether those who were imprisoned received sentences of more than one year as opposed to one year or less. Those defendants who were not imprisoned or who received indeterminate sentences were excluded from consideration on this variable. The one-year mark was used to separate relatively long from relatively short sentences, since it is the cutoff that frequently distinguishes local jail sentences from state penitentiary sentences and misdemeanors from felonies.

II. DISPARITIES RELATING TO THE CHARACTERISTICS OF THE DEFENDANTS

A. ECONOMIC CLASS

The first set of disparities to be discussed are those that relate to economic class. This variable is not only of interest in itself but is also relevant to explaining some of the disparities found in the other

---

[14] Whether a defendant pleads guilty rather than not guilty at the arraignment is not used as a variable largely because it correlates highly with the more important variable of being considered guilty rather than not guilty (+.47 in the federal data). It was, however, processed for the federal data where it correlated substantially with being over age 22 (+.19), being charged with larceny rather than assault (+.25), not receiving a grand jury indictment (+.31), receiving less than two months delay (+.24), and receiving a sentence of one year or less (+.28). All the other variables had a +.10 or less correlation with pleading guilty.

background variables, particularly race and, to a lesser extent, education. Class is defined in the state data in a legalistic rather than a sociological way, although the differences are probably not significant for the purposes of this study. The definition of class used by the Bar Foundation survey involved categorizing people as being indigent or not indigent. In this context, being indigent generally means being not financially competent to hire one's own lawyer. Because it tends to have that meaning, one can look in the federal data to the type of attorney the defendant had in order to obtain a roughly comparable measure of class. This explains the perfect correlation in Table 8–6 between being indigent and having assigned counsel.

1. Presentencing. Table 8–1 indicates that 34 percent of the indigent defendants failed to receive a preliminary hearing in the state felonious assault cases, whereas only 21 percent of the nonindigent defendants lacked such a hearing.[15] The percentages in the grand larceny cases of Table 8–2 go in the same direction, although to a lesser extent. The bail variable, however, produces the greatest disparity in the economic class column, since the ability to be released on bail is more closely related to one's economic status than any of the other procedural variables. With regard to the percent who were not released on bail in the assault cases, 52 percentage points separate the indigent from the nonindigent, and there is a 42 percentage point spread in the larceny cases.

Before going further, it should perhaps be pointed out that even though a difference between two percentages in Tables 8–1, 8–2, 8–4, and 8–5 is only a little larger than 10 percentage points, it might still be

---

[15] Tests of chance probability or statistical significance are not mentioned in this paper because the sample sizes are generally large enough that the differences emphasized are not readily attributable to chance. Exceptions are mentioned as they arise. The exceptions particularly relate to sex in the federal data and education in the state data.

To estimate the base of any percentage in the tables simply (1) determine the percent of cases in the category for which one wants to know the base (e.g., in the first table, 60 percent, or 374, of the 622 state assault cases on which applicable class information was available fell into the category of having nonindigent defendants) and (2) multiply it by either (a) the denominator of the fraction at the far left of the row (e.g., 492 cases had preliminary hearing information) or by (b) the sum of the two categories at the bottom of the column (e.g., 622 cases for class), whichever is smaller between (a) and (b). Thus where Table 8–1 says 21 percent of the nonindigent received no preliminary hearing, this means 21 percent of approximately 295 cases (i.e., 295 = 60 percent multiplied by 492). Such an estimation method is based on the fact that the set of cases inapplicable on the variable with *more* inapplicables usually contains a high proportion of the set of cases inapplicable on the variable with less inapplicables. To avoid overestimation the estimated base can be reduced by about 20 percent. This would reduce the 295 to 236, which is quite close to the exact base of 238 cases. The exact base for each percentage is not shown in order to avoid cluttering the tables with unneeded numbers.

an interesting difference if (1) it involves an important constitutional right or a jail sentence, (2) it is consistent with other related differences in the tables, and (3) it is consistent with known disparities between the groups in related matters other than criminal procedure. One may also bear in mind that there are many variables besides class, sex, race, age, education, urbanism, and region of the defendant that determine what will happen to him at a given procedural stage. These other variables may be lowering the correlation, although sometimes they may make it appear higher. Likewise, a near-zero difference may be important if conventional thought would have expected a much larger difference.

On the matter of having a lawyer, an interesting negative correlation appears in Tables 8–1 and 8–2. It seems that in many states an accused must be legally indigent before he can receive a court-appointed lawyer. Thus, there is possibly a curvilinear relation between economic class and having a lawyer; the poor are likely to obtain a free, court-appointed lawyer, the rich are likely to obtain their own hired lawyer, and the lower middle group may be the group most likely to lack legal representation, although the relation is clouded by the legal rather than sociological definition of indigency that is used. The relation between class and legal representation cannot be meaningfully determined in the federal cases, since indigents there, by definition, are those defendants who did not have their own lawyer.

On the matter of delay, the indigent defendant is more likely to be in the category of those who experienced over two months' delay while in jail from arrest to disposition or trial commencement. This is probably mainly due to the strong definitional relation in the state data between the variable relating to long delay while in jail and the variable relating to not being released on bail, which, in turn, is closely associated with being indigent. Thus, in the federal data when delay is measured irrespective of whether the defendant is in or out of jail, there is a negative correlation between being indigent and long delay, meaning the indigent tend to receive shorter delays than do the non-indigent. This is possibly because, by definition, all the indigent in the federal data have court-appointed lawyers, and court-appointed lawyers probably devote less time to their cases, or at least ask for fewer continuances, than hired lawyers do. A more important reason for faster action when indigent defendants are involved may be the incentive to get the indigent defendant out of jail, where he must stay if he is unable to pay the bail bond.

Tables 8–4 and 8–5 show the indigent federal defendant is much less likely to have a grand jury indictment than is the nonindigent defendant in either assault or larceny cases. Perhaps the indigent defendant can be more easily persuaded to waive a grand jury indictment than can a nonindigent defendant. Likewise, the indigent seems more likely than the nonindigent to receive a bench trial rather than a jury trial, particularly at the federal level. This may be due to the desire of his court-appointed counsel to accelerate the proceedings and to indigent defendant's lack of knowledge of the decreased likelihood of being found guilty by a unanimous 12-man jury. The jury disparity against indigent defendants is much less at the state level, possibly because middle class defendants may be reluctant to place their cases in the hands of state juries, which they perceive to disproportionately represent lower class values in contrast to the possibly higher status of federal juries.[16] Also, state court congestion may encourage more nonjury trials at that level.

With respect to being found guilty, 85 to 95 percent of the indigents were so found in contrast to consistently lower percentages for the nonindigent in the four types of cases. This disparity may be simply because indigent defendants are, in reality, more often guilty and are so found. The +.13 correlation between being indigent and having a prior record possibly lends support to the notion of greater criminality among the indigent. It is interesting to note, however, that the economic class disparity with regard to being found guilty is greater at the federal level where indigency and inability to hire one's own lawyer are synonymous. Thus, some of the disparity may be due to inferior legal representation and to the possibly greater passivity of indigent defendants with regard to fighting for an acquittal.

2. Sentencing.   Of those defendants who are found quilty, the indigent are much less likely to be recommended for probation by the probation officer or to be granted probation or a suspended sentence by the judge. Since the crime is held constant in Tables 8–1, 8–2, 8–4 and 8–5, these big differences cannot be attributed to differences in the crimes committed by indigents, unless one wants to argue that when indigents commit assault or larceny they do so more severely than nonindigents do. It seems more reasonable, at least with regard to larceny, to say that the *non*indigent defendants tend to steal larger sums, which partially explains why they are nonindigent. The tendency of nonindigent larceny defendants to steal larger amounts is probably the explanation for why, among those larceny defendants who are imprisoned, nonindigent defendants receive longer sentences. The negative relation between being indigent and receiving a long prison sentence shows up in both the state and federal larceny cases, in spite of the positive relation in the assault cases and (with the understandable exceptions

[16] The characteristics of federal juries have been studied. Mills, *A Statistical Study of Occupations of Jurors in a United States District Court,* 22 Md. L. Rev. 205 (1962); Robinson, *Bias, Probability, and Trial by Jury,* 15 Am. Soc. Rev. 73 (1950). Perhaps the future publications of the University of Chicago Jury Project will contain related data on state juries.

of the variable relating to being provided with a lawyer and the one relating to short delay) the positive relation on every one of the other variables.

It should also be pointed out that the disparities relating to the failure to grant probation or a suspended sentence to indigents cannot be completely attributed to the fact that they are more likely to have a prior record, since the disparities are larger than the correlation between being indigent and having a prior record. More important, however, are the findings revealed in Table 8–7, where prior record is held constant by using only larceny cases in which all the defendants had a prior record, and then by using only larceny cases in which the defendants had no prior record. A similar table is not shown for the assault cases on which prior record information is available because there are too few for this additional breakdown and because of a desire to limit the quantity of tables presented. A prior record breakdown is also less relevant to procedural variables other than the sentencing decision, and, as will be seen, is less theoretically relevant and less statistically applicable to background characteristics other than class and race. There is no information on prior record in the state data, but if disparities still exist at the federal level when prior record is equalized, then they probably also still exist at the state level.

Table 8–7 shows that the positive disparity between being indigent and not being recommended for or being granted probation or a suspended sentence is still large even when the presence of prior record is held constant. It might be argued, however, that the indigent may have more severe prior records than the nonindigent do. If a more severe prior record is interpreted to mean the number of previous crimes, this may be true, although the information is not included in the federal data. If, however, more severe prior records for larceny cases means the amount of money previously stolen, then the indigent are not likely to be ahead of the nonindigent. It should also be pointed out that there are no degrees of severity with regard to having no prior record, and the positive disparities are still present on the right side of Table 8–7, which uses only federal larceny cases. In those cases, a search was made by the federal authorities, and none of the defendants were found to have a prior record.

At first glance, these findings seem to conflict with those in the study of Edward Green,[17] who found a lack of sentencing disparities when crime and prior record were held constant. However, he worked with background variables other than economic class. His was also a one-city study of Philadelphia rather than a nationwide study. He also did not clearly separate the decision of whether to imprison or grant probation

---

[17] GREEN, *op. cit. supra* note 1.

from the decision of how many years to imprison after probation had been denied. In addition, he holds constant the severity of each crime as measured by its statutory penalty instead of holding constant the crime itself.

The reasons for the economic class sentencing disparities, holding crime and prior record constant, are due possibly to the quality of legal representation that the indigent receive and probably to the appearance that an indigent defendant presents before a middle class judge or probation officer. In other words, some class-biased attitudes may be present among judicial personnel, irrespective of the quality of legal representation provided to the indigent.

B. Sex

With regard to disparities relating to sex, the situation is much less clear than with regard to disparities relating to economic class. Many of the relationships shown in Tables 8–1, 8–2, 8–4, and 8–5 involve either disparities or sample sizes of females that are too small to be significant. Where there is a large disparity based on sufficient sample sizes, the disparity tends to favor the female, particularly at the sentencing stage. This type of favoritism cannot be attributed to economic class, since there is only a +.02 and a +.03 correlation between being a male and being indigent in the state and federal data, respectively. The difference seems to be attributable to American chivalry toward women, stemming from medieval traditions and possibly biological functions. Offsetting this, however, may be the possibly greater docility of women with regard to waiving their procedural rights and a possibly greater emphasis on procedural informality in processing female defendants.

With regard to pretrial procedure, male defendants in assault and larceny cases are much less likely than female defendants to be released on bail they can afford. Women, however, seem less likely to receive jury trials, although the findings are not consistent from assault to larceny cases. There were virtually no differences with regard to having a preliminary hearing, a lawyer, or a jury trial in the state data. The federal findings generally tend to show that female defendants receive more favorable treatment than male defendants, but the number of females in the federal cases is so small that the federal findings with regard to sex can be almost completely ignored. Likewise, a sample of trivial size seems to explain the finding in the state data on delay that of those defendants who are confined to jail pending trial, females are more likely to stay there longer. There were 56 females in the state assault cases and 77 in the larceny cases, which is generally large enough to reveal meaningful relations in Tables 8–1 and 8–2. The state delay variable, however, is worded in such a way that the only cases that can be positioned on it are those in which the defendant was not released on bail and in which hard-to-get delay information was available. Thus only 6 of the assault cases usable on the delay variable involve female defendants, and only 10 of the larceny cases do.

With regard to the results of the state criminal process, the sample sizes are large enough to say with reasonable confidence that the female defendant is more likely than the male to be found innocent, and if found guilty is more likely to receive a suspended sentence or probation. Like the economic class findings, these sex findings with regard to guilt and probation deviate from Edward Green's findings, probably for similar methodological reasons. The findings with regard to length of prison sentence shown at the bottom of Tables 8–1 and 8–2 are unreliable, since they are based on the very few cases in which women were given prison sentences.

C. RACE

Unlike the sexual disparities, the racial ones can be partly accounted for by the relation between being a Negro and being indigent. This relation has a +.16 correlation in the state data and a +.23 correlation in the federal data. It seems, however, that indigent defendants suffer more discrimination than Negro defendants in the administration of criminal justice.

For instance, the Negro disparities with regard to receiving a preliminary hearing are substantially less than the class disparities. The Negro is not so likely as the white defendant to be released on bail but is much more likely to be released than is the indigent defendant. That many Negro defendants are also indigent defendants probably explains why the Negro is slightly more likely to have a lawyer than is a white defendant, given the indigency prerequisite for receiving a court-appointed lawyer. When the Negro has a lawyer, his lawyer is much more likely to be court-appointed than are the lawyers of white defendants, as is shown in the federal data, particularly the larceny cases in which 52 percent of the Negroes did not have their own retained lawyers as contrasted with 25 percent of the Whites.

Like the indigent defendant, the Negro awaiting trial with his court-appointed lawyer tends to be subjected to *less* delay than the white defendant, particularly when delay is measured irrespective of whether the defendant has been released on bail. In fact, being subjected to delay seems to be a sign of high status rather than an indication of discrimination. Thus, in the state data there is a high +.24 correlation between having a lawyer and having a long delay, and in the federal data there is an even higher +.33 correlation between long delay and having one's own lawyer rather than a court-appointed lawyer. Apparently, there is a relation between delay and the shortage of trial attorneys in criminal cases similar to the relation that has been found in personal injury civil cases.[18] Delay can also benefit the guilty defendant by prolonging his freedom and by weakening the memories of witnesses.

The Negro is much less likely than the white defendant to have a grand jury indictment in either federal assault or larceny cases. If he goes to trial, he is even more unlikely to have a jury trial in comparison with white defendants. Indeed, 86 percent of the Negroes in federal assault cases failed to receive a jury trial in contrast to a 26 percent figure for white defendants. It appears that the constitutional rights of a grand jury indictment and of trial by jury are, in effect, mainly the white man's constitutional rights. This may be due to the possibility that Negroes and their lawyers perceive white juries as being more discriminatory than white judges. Some of the disparity, however, may be due to the possibility that Negroes tend to commit the less severe larcenies and assaults, which are less associated with grand jury indictment and trial by jury.

On the matter of receiving or being recommended for a prison sentence rather than a suspended sentence or probation, the Negro seems to be particularly discriminated against, especially in larceny cases. Thus, 74 percent of the guilty Negroes received prison sentences, whereas only 49 percent of the guilty Whites were imprisoned in the state larceny cases. Likewise, in the federal larceny cases 63 percent of the guilty Negroes were recommended for prison rather than probation, whereas only 44 percent of the guilty Whites were. These disparities still hold up in the cases of Table 8–7, where prior criminal record is held constant.

In the assault cases, the probation disparities were in the same direction but to a substantially lesser extent. This difference between the larceny and assault cases can possibly be explained by the fact that the victim is more likely to be a White when a Negro commits larceny than when the Negro commits assault.[19] It is financially less rewarding to commit larceny against a fellow Negro, although one more often commits assault against those groups with whom he has frequent contact.

It is interesting to note that the Negro–White disparity in federal cases is greater at the probation officer level than at the judicial level. There is a 15 percentage point spread between Negroes and Whites with regard to probation officer recommendations in assault cases, but only a 6 percentage point spread with regard to whether the judge granted probation. Perhaps probation officers base their decisions more on the characteristics of the defendants, whereas judges base their deci-

---

[18] Kalven, *The Bar, the Court and the Delay,* 325 Annals 37 (1960).

[19] Wolfgang, Crime and Race—Conceptions and Misconceptions (1964); Bullock, *supra* note 1.

sions more on the nature of the crime. Federal probation officers are also less well educated and may be less objective than judges. This same pattern (of greater disparities being associated with probation officers than with judges) shows up with regard to disparities relating to most of the other background characteristics as well.

The last line of the tables tends to show that of those imprisoned, the Negro defendant is more likely to receive a lighter sentence, particularly in larceny cases. Like the indigent defendant, the Negro defendant in larceny cases possibly steals smaller sums than white defendants. Someone skeptical of this explanation may argue that the shorter imprisonments received by Negroes are an indication of pro-Negro discrimination rather than a reflection of the relatively low severity of Negro larceny and assault. However, such an alternative explanation would be contrary to the strong anti-Negro disparities shown with regard to granting or denying probation. It would also be contrary to anti-Negro discrimination patterns in other activities such as employment and housing. The shorter imprisonments for Negroes also show up in the southern state larceny cases, where one would not expect to find pro-Negro discrimination. Furthermore, if Negro defendants tended to steal more than or as much as white defendants, one might expect to find a lower or negative correlation between being a Negro defendant and being indigent. Nevertheless, some specific instances probably exist in which a sympathetic or paternalistic white judge bends over backward to give a defendant a break partly because the defendant is Negro.

In a set of tables not presented, the state racial data were broken down into northern cases and southern cases.[20] The discrimination against the Negro was, in general, only slightly greater in the southern cases than in the northern cases, although where racial differences were present the discrimination was usually greater in the South for cultural reasons. Thus, the spread between Negroes and Whites with regard to being released on bail was somewhat greater in the southern cases than in the northern cases, as was the spread with regard to having a lawyer, being found guilty, and more so with regard to being sentenced to prison and being sentenced for a long term. For instance, when assault and larceny cases are combined, 13 percentage points separate the Negroes from the Whites with regard to being imprisoned on being found guilty in the North, whereas 22 percentage points separate them in the South. Racial discrimination is also slightly greater at the state level than at the federal level, particularly at the sentencing stages, possibly because federal judges are more self-conscious of racial discrimination than are state judges.

---

[20] See notes 21 and 22 *infra*, and the accompanying text with regard to how the North and South were defined.

D. AGE

In the state data, age was divided at under 21 versus 21 and over, because many states maintain such a division in processing criminal cases and because that is a breaking point in the American Bar Foundation's system of recording age. In the federal data, age was divided at under 22 versus 22 and over because the Federal Youth Corrections Act applies through age 21.

Nearly all the background characteristics involve some disparities that favor and some that disfavor the background characteristic. This is particularly true of the age variable; young defendants are less likely to receive the procedural safeguards received by older defendants, but are more likely to receive lighter sentences at the sentencing stage.

Thus, 66 percent of the defendants aged 21 or less did not have their own lawyer in the federal assault cases, whereas this was true for only 36 percent of the older defendants. There is a spread in the same direction, although not so large, in the federal larceny cases and in the state assault and larceny cases. Likewise, the younger defendants are much less likely to have a grand jury indictment. The age disparity is even greater with regard to a younger defendant's low likelihood of receiving a jury trial at the federal level. There seems to be no consistent substantial difference, however, with regard to receiving a preliminary hearing or being released on bail. Some of the disparity between younger defendants and older ones in the absence of a personal lawyer, a grand jury indictment, and a jury trial may be attributable to the discouragement of formalities in processing youthful offenders on the theory that informality decreases criminal stigma and increases rehabilitation emphasis. At the state level, younger defendants are subjected to greater delays than are older defendants, although they are subjected to lesser delays than are older defendants at the federal level, where the data tends to indicate a more paternalistic attitude toward the young.

On the other side of the criminal process, the young defendant is more likely to be recommended for probation by the probation officer, and he is more likely to be given probation or a suspended sentence by the judge, particularly in federal cases and particularly in larceny cases. Some of this is because young defendants are less likely to have a prior record as indicated by the −.12 correlation in Table 8–6, but some of it is also probably due to the rehabilitation emphasis and to the protective attitude that courts tend to have toward youngsters and women. Those relatively few young defendants who are sent to prison generally receive shorter sentences, at least at the state level. The exception represented by the federal larceny cases may be due to the smallness of the usable sample at the final stage of the procedure, or it may be due to the possibility that those few youthful defendants who cannot obtain federal probation are more likely to be hardened criminals than are the older defendants.

E. EDUCATION

Information about the educational level of criminal defendants is available only in the state data, and then for only a relatively small number of the 1,949 cases. Nevertheless, the relations are worth presenting because they tend to be internally consistent and not necessarily duplicative of the economic class relation. The education variable was divided into those who had completed no more than eight grades of elementary school and those who had completed one or more years of high school.

The less educated defendants have the greatest disparity of any of the background groups (including the indigent and the Negroes) with regard to being denied a preliminary hearing in either assault or larceny cases. This can be at least partly attributed to the apparent ignorance of the less educated with regard to their procedural rights and to their docility in being denied such rights. The less educated are also more likely to be confined to jail pending trial rather than be released on bail. A part of that disparity can be attributed to the relation between having only an elementary education and being indigent, although the correlation is only +.06. The less educated person is also more likely to have no lawyer to assist him in spite of the slight correlation between being indigent and being less educated. These disparities may not only indicate that the less educated are ignorant of the procedures involved in obtaining a preliminary hearing, bail, or a lawyer, but may also indicate that those responsible for providing these aspects of criminal procedure sometimes take advantage of the less educated, at least at the state trial court level.[21]

The findings with regard to delay while in jail and length of prison term are clouded by the especially small samples. The findings with regard to having a jury trial or being found guilty involve small or counterbalanced differences. The disparities among the guilty with regard to being imprisoned or granted a suspended sentence or probation are, however, substantial and consistent. Thus, 67 percent of the less educated went to prison in grand larceny cases, whereas only 48 percent of the more educated did. Perhaps some of this disparity can be explained by the possibility that the less educated make poorer rehabilitation risks

---

[21] Trebach indicates that poor education handicaps defendants at many points in the criminal process, particularly in dealing with the prosecutor. TREBACH, THE RATIONING OF JUSTICE: CONSTITUTIONAL RIGHTS AND THE CRIMINAL PROCESS 81 (1964).

or are thought to make poorer rehabilitation risks by the more educated probation officers and judges who make these decisions.

III. DISPARITIES RELATING TO THE CHARACTER- ISTICS OF THE COURTS

A. URBANISM AND REGION

There is no indication in the state or federal data about whether the defendant comes from an urban or rural background or a northern or southern background. Nonetheless, the data are capable of throwing light on the more interesting questions of how urban courts differ from rural courts and how northern courts differ from southern courts with regard to various aspects of criminal procedure, irrespective of the characteristics of the defendant. The answer is frequently contrary to the civil libertarian image of northern urbanism and the anticivil libertarian-ism image of southern ruralism.

In the state data, counties were the legal units determining the jurisdiction of the courts. A state court was defined as relatively urban if its county had 100,000 or more population and relatively rural if its county had less than 100,000 population. In the federal data, federal judicial districts were the legal units, and a more sophisticated measure of urbanism was used. It involved determining the counties within each federal district by consulting the United States Code, and then determining whether or not a majority of the people in each district lived in a standard metropolitan area by consulting the United States Census Reports. If the majority of the people in a district did live in a standard metropolitan area, then the district was considered relatively urban. Otherwise, it was considered relatively rural or nonurban. In both the state data and the federal data, most of the cases, particularly larceny cases, are tried in urban courts as above defined.

For both the state and federal data, the South was defined as those 11 states that were members of the Confederate States of America.[22] The six border states that had legalized slavery in 1860 but did not join the Confederacy were considered neither South nor North.[23] The remaining 33 states constituted the North. The urbanism and region variables are discussed together in this section because of the substantial correlation between being urban and being northern, at least in the federal data (+.37), and, more important, because both variables tended to reveal quite similar types of disparities, particularly in the federal

---

[22] Alabama, Arkansas, Florida, Georgia, Louisiana, Mississippi, North Carolina, South Carolina, Tennessee, Texas, and Virginia.
[23] Delaware, Kentucky, Maryland, Missouri, Oklahoma, and West Virginia.

data, where a more meaningful measure of urbanism was used. The regional differences are, however, generally greater than the urban–rural differences.

1. Pre-Sentencing. On the matter of providing a preliminary hearing, the rural–urban differences shown are small and counterbalanced between the assault and larceny cases, but they are substantial and consistent in the North versus South comparison. Thus, 38 percent of the northern assault cases contained no preliminary hearing in spite of laws providing for such hearings, whereas only 10 percent of the southern assault cases lacked a preliminary hearing. Perhaps the traditionalism of the South has been responsible for retaining this common law procedure.

Being released on bail also shows a small counterbalanced difference on the rural–urban split but a large consistent difference on the northern–southern split. This difference can probably be largely attributed to the high correlation between being indigent and not released on bail (+.46) and between being classified as indigent and being northern (+.19).

Not having any lawyer at all is quite disproportionately associated with being rural or southern in both assault and larceny cases. This finding is consistent with the finding of the National Legal Aid and Defender Association in 1959 that of the 15 states in the United States that did not have laws providing for the assignment of compensated counsel, 8 are in the South and 2 are border states.[24] This also means that 8 of the 11 southern states did not assign compensated counsel, possibly because of the conservatism and smaller financial resources associated with southern state governments. In the federal data where assigned counsel is available and where the lawyer variable relates to whether the defendant had his own lawyer or an appointed lawyer, the rural or southern defendants who had a lawyer were more likely to have their own lawyer (rather than an appointed lawyer) than the urban or northern defendants. This relation might be explainable by the greater percentage of defendants who were labeled indigent in the urban–northern courts and by the greater expensiveness of urban–northern lawyers.

On the matter of court delay, the urban and northern courts seem to be particularly congested, as they are in civil cases. Thus, in the state assault cases, 56 percent of the urban defendants remained in jail for over 2 months before disposition or trial in contrast to 31 percent of the rural defendants. There is also a 25 percentage point difference

---

[24] SPECIAL COMM. TO STUDY DEFENDER SYSTEMS, ASS'N OF THE BAR OF THE CITY OF NEW YORK & THE NAT'L LEGAL AID AND DEFENDER ASS'N, EQUAL JUSTICE FOR THE ACCUSED at inside front cover (1959).

between northern and southern defendants in federal larceny cases. Differences in the same direction, although not so large, appear in all four comparisons of urban versus rural cases and (with only one minor exception in the state larceny table) in all four comparisons of northern versus southern cases. Much has been written about congestion and delay in urban personal injury cases, but the problem of congestion and delay in urban criminal cases also appears to need attention. Congestion and delay are probably disproportionately associated with urban courts because their districts contain larger populations and more of the economic and social-psychological factors that breed criminality without a proportionate increase in criminal court judges and attorneys.

Jury trials and grand jury indictments in *assault* cases are more likely to be dispensed with in northern courts than in southern courts. On the other hand, jury trials and grand jury indictments in *larceny* cases are more likely to be retained in northern courts than in southern courts, whether state or federal. The findings are similar with urban and rural courts, although not so consistent. Perhaps a southern defendant accused of assault will seek a jury trial and a grand jury hearing more often than will a southern defendant accused of larceny. Maybe the southern defendant (or rather his lawyer) perceives southern juries as condoning assault more than larceny, particularly in comparison with northern juries.

2. Sentencing.   On the matter of finding guilt, the urban–rural and northern–southern differences tend to be negligible at both levels of government in both types of crimes. There are, however, some sharp differences with regard to sentencing. The urban and northern courts, whether state or federal, are clearly *more* likely than the rural and southern courts to imprison a defendant convicted of *assault* rather than to grant him probation or a suspended sentence. On the other hand, the urban and northern courts are clearly *less* likely than the rural and southern ones to imprison a defendant convicted of *larceny*. It thus seems that a greater stigma is attached to assault than to larceny in urban and northern areas than in rural and southern ones. The assault differences may be based on notions of self-defense associated with more agricultural societies, as opposed to the defense by professional police associated with more industrialized societies. The larceny differences may be due to the emphasis in agricultural societies on property that belongs to individual persons, as contrasted with the emphasis in industrialized societies on property that belongs to businesses and corporations.

On the other hand, when a defendant is imprisoned by a rural or southern court he seems more likely to receive a harsher sentence, at least at the state level. Thus, in the state larceny cases 66 percent of the southern defendants who were imprisoned received sentences of over 1 year, whereas only 34 percent of the northern defendants did. Likewise, there were 28 percentage points separating the southern and northern defendants on length of term in the state assault cases. The rural–urban differences found were similar in direction, though smaller in size. The federal larceny cases were the only substantial exception, and longer northern sentences there might be due to larger amounts of money stolen. Southern sentencing severity is also indicated by the fact that in capital cases the southern states make the most frequent use of capital punishment.[25] This relative emphasis on severe retribution may be partly attributable to the religious fundamentalism and rural individualism associated with the South.

B. State versus Federal Courts

Because the procedural variables in the state data are frequently measured differently than in the federal data, comparisons between the two levels of government cannot always be so systematic as one would like. Nevertheless, one can hypothesize certain similarities and differences that might be testable in a later study or partially testable in the present study.

Largely because of constitutional wording and judicial interpretation, the grand jury process and the right to counsel are more prevalent at the federal level than at the state level, at least during the years 1962 and 1963 when the data were compiled. The data do not indicate at which level preliminary hearings and release on bail are more prevalent. A preliminary hearing, however, is less a necessity if grand jury indictments are present. Likewise, release on bail is not so necessary if delays are short, and when one examines the time from arrest to disposition, irrespective of whether the defendant was released on bail, delays are much shorter at the federal level. The shorter delay is probably due in large part to the smaller caseload per federal judge and to the stricter federal interpretation of the constitutional requirement of a speedy trial. If one ignores all the federal and state guilty-plea cases, one also finds that a slightly higher percentage of the federal cases going to trial involve jury trials than do the state cases.

With regard to case outcomes, as contrasted to preverdict procedure, both the federal and state criminal process results in guilty pleas or findings in approximately 80 percent of the cases. Both render a guilty decision in a smaller percentage of assault than larceny cases, possibly because assault is a more subjective matter than larceny, or possibly because suspects are charged with assault on weaker evidence, since

---

[25] Mattick, The Unexamined Death—An Analysis of Capital Punishment 26–27 (1963).

it is generally a less serious crime. Use of probation and suspended sentences seems to be substantially more prevalent at the federal level. This may be an indication of a greater emphasis on rehabilitation in federal criminal procedure. Of those sentenced to prison in assault cases, however, the federal defendants are more likely to receive longer sentences, possibly because federal assault (at least in these cases) involves more serious elements than state assault does.[26] Length of sentence in larceny cases is more equal between the two levels of government.

Differences between the two levels of government with regard to their relative tendencies to discriminate against various groups were discussed as they arose. It was pointed out, for instance, that disparities between Negroes and Whites tend to be slightly greater at the state level than at the federal level. In addition, juveniles and youthful offenders are more likely to be deprived of procedural safeguards but given lighter sentences at the federal level than at the state level. In general, however, where the background characteristics were measured in the same way at both levels, similar types of disparities tended to show up in the analysis.

IV. INTEGRATING AND REDUCING THE DISPARITIES

A. Integrating the Disparities

At the risk of oversimplification, Table 8–8 attempts to integrate and summarize the major findings of this chapter. The neutral word "disparities" is used to tie the findings together, rather than a word like "discrimination" or "inequities." "Discrimination" implies a deliberate attempt on the part of judicial process decision makers to favor one group over the other. In reality, some of the differences reflect the nondiscriminatory application of legal rules that inherently divide people along class lines, such as the institution of bail or regional differentiation that is not imposed by a discriminatory national authority. Likewise, the word "inequities," or even "inequalities," implies unfairness when, in reality, some of the differences, such as those based on age groupings, may be socially justifiable.

Table 8–8 combines the background groups into three categories: the disadvantaged (i.e., indigents, Negroes, and the less educated), the paternalized (i.e., juveniles and females), and the industrialized (i.e., northern and urban defendants). Each of these concepts attempts to

---

[26] The maximum statutory penalty for simple and felonious assault is greater in the federal statutes (i.e., assault against federal officials) than it was in seven randomly sampled state statutes. For differences between federal and state assault and larceny, see note 6 *supra.*

isolate the key characteristic that explains the causes of the favorable or unfavorable treatment the included groups receive in criminal proceedings. Being disadvantaged refers to one's chances for a successful occupational career. Being paternalized refers to being treated by various social institutions in a somewhat fatherly way. Being industrialized refers to being part of a society in which only a small percentage of the people lead a farmer's way of life and most work for corporate manufacturing or distributing firms. Being a northern or urban defendant in this context refers to the court where one is tried rather than to where one is from.

The criminal procedure stages have also been combined into three categories because various stages showed similar types of disparities. The preverdict stages are referred to as safeguards for the innocent in order to emphasize their major purpose. Sentencing is divided into assault and larceny because different types of sentencing disparities occurred, depending on the type of crime involved. The safeguards are not so divided because the safeguard disparities were less influenced by the type of crime. Likewise, there is no state versus federal split on the vertical axis of the table because such a split was also not generally relevant to the type of disparities present.

By analogy, one can probably substitute various forms of murder and battery for assault and various forms of stealing for larceny. By analogy, one may also hypothesize that the types of disparities likely to be found at the decision to arrest and the decision to grant parole are similar to those present at the decision to grant probation. Similarly, in view of the economics of taking an appeal, the disparities present with regard to whether one receives an appellate hearing are probably closest to those relating to whether one is released on bail.

Each of the nine cells indicates whether the groups at the top of the table received generally favorable or unfavorable treatment in the criminal procedure stages to the left of the table. The words "favorable" and "unfavorable" can be read as if they were always preceded by the word "relatively" and followed by the word "treatment." "Relatively" in this context means relative to the groups opposite to those at the top (i.e., relative to the advantaged, the nonpaternalized, and the less industrialized). Strong examples and exceptions to the favorable and unfavorable labels are shown in each cell.

Summaries of the specific findings and explanations could also be shown in a matrix like that of Table 8–8, but that kind of information would require a large matrix of about 96 cells, covering 8 background groups (including the federal versus state group), multiplied by 12 procedural variables (including the 2 lawyer variables and 2 delay variables). Such a matrix would bring out more clearly the more subtle relations between each background group and its relative treatment.

It would also show more clearly that similar explanations cannot necessarily be offered for similar disparities involving (1) a given background group at different procedural stages or (2) a given procedural stage vis-à-vis different background groups. As indicated, however, the general explanations can be roughly summarized by referring to the characteristics associated with the basic concepts of being disadvantaged, paternalized, or industrialized.

B. REDUCING THE DISPARITIES

The data analyzed indicate there are significant disparities at various stages in the administration of criminal justice with regard to class, sex, race, age, education, urbanism, and region.[27] Some of these disparities are perhaps socially justifiable. For instance, the nature of the crime and the prison record of the defendant are legally relevant to sentencing, but not relevant to providing procedural due process. Also, it may be more appropriate to place a youthful rather than an older offender on probation on the theory that the older offender is expected to be a more responsible person. Perhaps penalties should vary somewhat from one regional culture to another. Thus, it is understandable that in the frontier days of the early West, horse thieves were severely treated but those who committed assault were not. Nevertheless, most of the disparities shown in Tables 8–1 through 8–6 probably cannot be logically justified in terms of societal interest, especially when crime and prison record are held constant.

What can be done to reduce these disparities? Remedies vary with the particular disparity involved. As a basic and general matter, however, it should be pointed out that there would probably be no criminal procedure disparities between the groups compared if the opposed groups did not exist or if the groups were not given differential treatment in society in general. Thus, there would be no indigent to be discriminated against in criminal procedure if the war on poverty were a complete success. Likewise, there would be no Negro–White discrimination in criminal procedure if there were no racial discrimination in other activities. Therefore, the problem of criminal procedure disparities is inherently tied to attempts to remove distinctions that are considered undesirable between the city and the country and the North and the South, and

---

[27] The characteristics of defendants, along with other variables, could conceivably be used by attorneys to predict outcomes at specific stages of the criminal process, particularly the trial stage. See Nagel, *Predicting Court Cases Quantitatively*, 63 MICH. L. REV. 1411 (1965). The purpose of the present chapter, however, is not to aid judicial predictability. On the contrary, one underlying purpose is to decrease the extent to which some characteristics of defendants do influence outcomes.

to attempts to further emancipate women, as well as to decrease the indigent and the uneducated and to eliminate general racial discrimination.

As regards a more piecemeal attack on specific disparities, such as the disparities relating to release on bail, one may mention the work of the Vera Foundation in New York City[28] and the National Bail Conference.[29] Partly as a result of the studies of organizations like these, the federal courts have been enlarging the proportion of defendants considered trustworthy enough to be released pending trial without any bail bond, and the state of Illinois will now release most defendants pending trial if they can afford the 10 percent down payment on the bail bond that commercial bondsmen generally charge as a premium or interest.[30] A large-scale campaign to provide competent counsel for the indigent has been initiated by the National Legal Aid and Defender Association[31] and the American Bar Association.[32] The problem of delay would probably benefit from studies and proposals like those made for the civil courts.[33] In the realm of sentencing disparities, the Administrative Office of the United States Courts is currently conducting an educational program to encourage more rational sentencing practices[34] and a statistical program designed to indicate more clearly what the current sentencing practices are.[35]

This chapter has been designed mainly to indicate the degree to which disparities involving different types of groups are present at various stages of criminal proceedings. It is, of course, unrealistic to expect that increased awareness of a problem will necessarily result in its amelioration. A study like the one described, however, could conceivably help to reduce certain disparities to the extent that those responsible for the disparities consider it desirable to make changes in light of the differences shown. Perhaps a similar study 5 or 10 years from now will reveal greater equality in the administration of criminal justice than is presently so.

---

[28] Ares, Rankin & Sturz, *supra* note 5; Sturz, *An Alternative to the Bail System*, 26 FED. PROB. 49 (1962).

[29] Goldfarb, *The Great Bail Scandal*, THE NEW REPUBLIC, June 6, 1964, pp. 14–17; *One Year's Progress in Bail Reform: May, 1964–April, 1965*, 49 J. AM. JUD. SOC'Y 65 (1965).

[30] ILL. REV. STAT. ch. 38, § 110 (1963).

[31] See the multilithed, *Defender Newsletter*, which the association publishes.

[32] Silverstein, *op. cit. supra* note 2. See also Marden, *Equal Access to Justice—The Challenge and the Opportunity*, 19 WASH. & LEE L. REV. 153 (1962).

[33] ZEISEL, KALVEN & BUCHHOLZ, DELAY IN THE COURT—AN ANALYSIS OF THE REMEDIES FOR DELAYED JUSTICE (1959).

[34] U.S. BUREAU OF PRISONS & ADMINISTRATIVE OFFICE OF THE U.S. COURTS, DESKBOOK OF SENTENCING—PRELIMINARY DRAFT (1961).

[35] ADMINISTRATIVE OFFICE OF THE U.S. COURTS, FEDERAL OFFENDERS IN THE UNITED STATES DISTRICT COURTS—1964 (1965).

TABLE 8-1

DISPARITIES IN STATE FELONIOUS ASSAULT CASES

Fraction in Sample	Criminal Procedure Treatment	Class		Sex		Race		Age		Education		Urbanism		Region	
		Indigent	Non	Male	Female	Negro	White	Under 21	21 & over	Elem.	High	Urban	Rural	North	South
134/492	% who received no preliminary hearing	34 (+) 21		27 + 26		24 + 23		32 + 28		40 (+) 22		28 + 24		38 (+) 10	
274/678	% who were not released on bail	73 (+) 21		42 (+) 23		49 (+) 36		38 – 48		47 + 37		41 + 36		45 (+) 30	
74/682	% who had no lawyer	2 – 12		11 – 12		13 + 9		15 + 7		8 + 5		7 (–) 24		6 (–) 21	
82/160	% who had over two months delay from arrest to disposition or trial while in jail	57 (+) 43		51 (–) 83		60 (+) 49		62 (+) 50		36 (–) 59		56 (+) 31		51 + 42	
134/236	% who had no jury trial of those tried	59 + 55		55 (–) 81		71 (+) 54		55 – 63		60 – 64		60 (+) 39		55 + 49	
541/714	% who pleaded or were found guilty	85 + 76		77 (+) 64		80 + 74		87 + 79		94 + 84		75 – 79		78 + 72	
288/454	% who received a prison sentence rather than a suspended sentence or probation	73 (+) 58		64 + 56		67 + 62		71 + 62		77 + 68		64 + 62		67 + 58	
75/185	% who received over one year prison terms of those imprisoned	42 + 35		43 (+) 11		50 (+) 29		27 (–) 38		0 (–) 13		37 (–) 50		23 (–) 51	
846	Number in sample	248	374	749	56	232	227	67	346	38	63	669	177	408	301

+ = the group on the left has a percent greater than the group on the right.
– = the group on the left has a percent less than the group on the right.
The sign is circled where the difference is greater than 10 percentage points.

TABLE 8-2

DISPARITIES IN STATE GRAND LARCENY CASES

Fraction in Sample	Criminal Procedure Treatment	Class		Sex		Race		Age		Education		Urbanism		Region	
		Indigent	Non	Male	Female	Negro	White	Under 21	21 & over	Elem.	High	Urban	Rural	North	South
300/676	% who received *no* preliminary hearing	48 + 40		45 + 43		35 − 43		42 + 41		57 (+) 43		42 − 50		55 (+) 35	
415/874	% who were *not* released on bail	73 (+) 31		50 (+) 24		58 (+) 45		55 (+) 47		62 + 50		46 − 53		49 + 46	
109/879	% who had *no* lawyer	2 (−) 14		13 + 10		10 − 17		16 + 12		24 (+) 9		8 (−) 25		12 − 17	
80/245	% who had over two months delay from arrest to disposition or trial while in jail	37 (+) 29		33 − 40		22 (−) 35		46 (+) 29		50 + 48		31 − 36		38 (+) 24	
167/243	% who had *no* jury trial of those tried	73 + 66		69 (+) 53		68 − 70		60 − 70		57 − 67		72 (+) 58		53 (−) 78	
820/958	% who pleaded or were found guilty	91 + 87		87 (+) 76		91 + 88		91 91		93 −100		87 + 82		90 + 83	
414/735	% who received a prison sentence rather than a suspended sentence or probation	65 (+) 45		57 (+) 36		74 (+) 49		49 (−) 60		67 (+) 48		56 56		51 − 60	
148/266	% who received over one year prison terms of those imprisoned	45 (−) 58		55 (−) 67		46 − 53		46 − 49		38 (+) 19		54 − 61		34 (−) 66	
1103	Number in sample	337	465	967	77	197	397	159	379	42	120	810	293	490	463

TABLE 8–3

CORRELATION COEFFICIENTS AMONG THE STATE VARIABLES

(1,949 cases)

	Indigent	Male	Negro	Under 21	Elem. Ed.	Urban	North	Larceny not Assault	No Prelim.	No Bail	No Lawyer	Long Delay	No Jury	Guilty	Prison	Long Term
Indigent	—	02	16	-02	06	07	19	02	11	46	-20	13	07	09	19	-03
Male		—	-05	03	-09	-02	-01	-01	01	12	01	-07	-03	08	08	04
Negro			—	-08	12	11	-06	-17	-07	12	-03	00	06	03	18	05
Under 21				—	-09	-15	-12	16	04	01	08	08	-08	05	-06	-06
Elem. ed.					—	-02	05	-12	11	08	13	-08	-07	-01	15	01
Urban						—	16	-07	-03	-03	-23	06	13	01	01	-09
North							—	-06	20	06	-13	15	-14	08	-02	-33
Larceny not assault								—	18	07	02	-19	12	12	-07	14
No preliminary									—	17	09	-16	-05	05	03	01
No bail										—	08	X	07	15	36	12
No lawyer											—	-24	08	01	04	16
Long delay												—	-37	-08	10	-06
No jury													—	30	-12	-05
Guilty														—	X	X
Prison															—	X
Long term																—

Coefficients greater than 10 are underlined.
X = related by definition or unknown.
Decimal points are eliminated.

TABLE 8-4

DISPARITIES IN FEDERAL ASSAULT CASES

Fraction in Sample	Criminal Procedure Treatment	Class		Sex		Race		Age		Urbanism		Region	
		Indigent	Non	Male	Female	Negro	White	Under 22	22 & over	Urban	Rural	North	South
73/194	% who did *not* have own lawyer	X	X	42 − 44		41 + 40		66 ⊕ 33		37 − 38		42 ⊕ 29	
67/171	% who did *not* have grand jury indictment	50 ⊕ 34		42 ⊖ 67		52 ⊕ 34		72 ⊕ 36		36 − 43		50 ⊕ 21	
87/195	% who had over two months delay from filing to disposition	25 ⊖ 56		39 ⊕ 0		41 − 46		16 ⊖ 46		52 ⊕ 38		48 + 43	
40/80	% who had *no* jury trial of those tried	59 ⊕ 45		52 ⊖ 100		86 ⊕ 26		75 ⊕ 36		49 − 51		54 + 52	
154/195	% who pleaded or were found guilty	89 ⊕ 74		X	X	X	X	X	X	81 + 77		80 + 75	
41/76	% who were *not* recommended for probation by probation officer	60 + 50		53 ⊖ 100		70 ⊕ 55		43 ⊖ 58		61 ⊕ 44		57 + 53	
81/154	% who received a prison sentence rather than a suspended sentence or probation	60 ⊕ 47		52 − 56		62 + 56		48 − 54		57 + 47		55 ⊕ 41	
54/81	% who received over one-year prison terms of those imprisoned	72 + 62		68 ⊕ 40		55 ⊖ 73		67 − 68		70 + 63		63 − 71	
196	Number in sample	73	121	145	9	32	81	44	109	100	96	111	68

TABLE 8-5

DISPARITIES IN FEDERAL INTERSTATE LARCENY CASES

Fraction in Sample	Criminal Procedure Treatment	Class		Sex		Race		Age		Urbanism		Region	
		Indigent	Non	Male	Female	Negro	White	Under 22	22 & over	Urban	Rural	North	South
$\frac{242}{771}$	% who did *not* have own lawyer	X	X	35 (+) 10		52 (+) 25		44 (+) 33		33 (+) 26		32 (+) 25	
$\frac{277}{744}$	% who did *not* have grand jury indictment	52 (+) 31		43 (+) 30		54 (+) 37		67 (+) 41		35 (−) 48		32 (−) 42	
$\frac{347}{772}$	% who had over two months delay from filing to disposition	20 (−) 56		38 (−) 60		22 (−) 48		23 (−) 41		49 (+) 29		54 (+) 29	
$\frac{60}{129}$	% who had *no* jury trial of those tried	62 (+) 41		49 (+) 0		65 (+) 39		100 (+) 36		42 (−) 70		43 (−) 58	
$\frac{647}{771}$	% who pleaded or were found guilty	92 (+) 80		X X		X X		X X		83 − 86		83 − 87	
$\frac{184}{365}$	% who were *not* recommended for probation by probation officer	66 (+) 42		51 (+) 33		63 (+) 44		47 − 51		51 + 49		49 − 49	
$\frac{303}{647}$	% who received a prison sentence rather than a suspended sentence or probation	58 (+) 41		47 (+) 30		54 (+) 40		38 − 48		46 − 52		43 (−) 54	
$\frac{150}{303}$	% who received over one year prison terms of those imprisoned	43 (−) 55		50 (+) 33		42 (−) 58		74 (+) 47		48 − 54		54 (+) 34	
785	Number in sample	242	529	637	10	190	412	71	575	644	141	536	164

TABLE 8–6

CORRELATION COEFFICIENTS AMONG THE FEDERAL VARIABLES
(981 cases)

	Indigent	Male	Negro	Under 22	Urban	North	Larceny not Assault	Prior Record	No Own Lawyer	No Grand Jury	Long Delay	No Trial Jury	Guilty	No Proba. Recom.	Prison	Long Term
Indigent	—	03	23	14	02	06	05	13	100	19	-33	17	16	21	16	-07
Male	—	—	-09	-01	05	08	11	08	03	-01	02	08	X	00	02	05
Negro	—	—	—	01	-06	-17	03	07	23	16	-22	30	X	17	12	-17
Under 22	—	—	—	—	-29	-06	-20	-12	14	18	-16	45	X	-05	-05	13
Urban	—	—	—	—	—	37	29	00	02	-09	14	-12	00	04	-03	-05
North	—	—	—	—	—	—	13	00	06	-01	18	-07	-01	00	-05	12
Larceny not assault	—	—	—	—	—	—	—	02	-05	-02	00	-03	05	-03	-05	-14
Prior record ...	—	—	—	—	—	—	—	—	13	04	-04	-23	X	32	35	03
No own lawyer ..	—	—	—	—	—	—	—	—	—	19	-33	17	16	21	16	-07
No grand jury ...	—	—	—	—	—	—	—	—	—	—	-42	19	23	03	00	-32
Long delay	—	—	—	—	—	—	—	—	—	—	—	-31	-28	-04	01	15
No trial jury	—	—	—	—	—	—	—	—	—	—	—	—	07	-45	-48	-08
Guilty	—	—	—	—	—	—	—	—	—	—	—	—	—	X	X	X
No probation recommendation	—	—	—	—	—	—	—	—	—	—	—	—	—	—	76	X
Prison	—	—	—	—	—	—	—	—	—	—	—	—	—	—	—	07
Long term	—	—	—	—	—	—	—	—	—	—	—	—	—	—	—	—

TABLE 8-7

CLASS AND RACIAL DISPARITIES IN SENTENCING WHILE EQUALIZING PRIOR RECORD IN FEDERAL INTERSTATE LARCENY CASES

Criminal Procedure Treatment	Some Prior Record					No Prior Record				
	Fraction in Sample	Class		Race		Fraction in Sample	Class		Race	
		Indigent	Non	Negro	White		Indigent	Non	Negro	White
% who were *not* recommended for probation by probation officer	$\frac{164}{270}$	74 ⊕ 52		72 ⊕ 54		$\frac{17}{90}$	27 ⊕ 16		22 + 18	
% who received a prison sentence rather than a suspended sentence or probation	$\frac{212}{380}$	62 + 52		66 ⊕ 50		$\frac{33}{195}$	23 + 15		20 + 14	
Number in sample	380	148	232	138	232	195	44	151	46	143

TABLE 8-8

SUMMARIZING THE DISPARITIES IN CRIMINAL PROCEDURE TREATMENT

	Disadvantaged Groups (Indigents, Negroes, or Less Educated)	Paternalized Groups (Juveniles or Females)	Industrialized Groups (Northern or Urban Defendants)
Safeguards for the innocent	Unfavorable, especially on bail, but favorable on being provided with a lawyer.	Unfavorable for juveniles, especially on jury trial, but unclear for females.	Unfavorable on preliminary hearing and delay, but favorable on providing lawyers. Mixed on jury trial, depending on the crime.
Assault sentencing	Unfavorable, especially on the probation officer decision.	Favorable, especially at the federal level.	Unfavorable on whether to grant probation, but favorable on length of imprisonment.
Larceny sentencing	Unfavorable (more so than assault) on whether to imprison, but favorable on length of imprisonment.	Ditto above.	Relatively favorable treatment.

Based on 1,949 state cases and 981 federal cases from all 50 states for the years 1962–63 in which the defendant was charged with a single charge of assault or of larceny.

CHAPTER 9

The Attorneys: Disparities
in Victory

A number of sociologists and legal scholars have studied the background characteristics of different types of lawyers.[1] No researcher, however, seems to have yet analyzed the possible relationships between these general characteristics and courtroom results. It is the purpose of this chapter to offer some findings relevant to those relationships. The basic theoretical position of this chapter is that in substantial samples of cases the characteristics of the opposing attorneys are, in general, relatively trivial predictive or explanatory variables, especially in comparison with the predictive power of the correlations between the outcomes of cases and the factual elements within those cases. The characteristics discussed are those for which there is data in the *Martindale-Hubbell Law Directory*, and which, one would suspect, might correlate with legal ability and thereby make a difference in courtroom results.

I. THE RESEARCH DESIGN

The data shown in Table 9–1 were compiled by working backward from the 1962 to the 1959 volume of *American Law Reports Annotated, Second Series*, until 100 cases were found in which just one attorney was listed for each side and both attorneys were listed in the *Martindale-*

---

[1] See, e.g., CARLIN, LAWYERS ON THEIR OWN (1962); Ladinsky, *The Impact of Social Backgrounds of Lawyers on Law Practice and the Law*, 16 J. LEGAL ED. 127 (1963); Lortie, *Laymen to Lawmen: Law School, Careers, and Professional Socialization*, 29 HARV. EDUCATION REV. 352 (1959); Comment, *The Jewish Law Student and New York Jobs—Discriminatory Effects in Law Firm Hiring Practices*, 73 YALE L. J. 625 (1964); Carlin, Current Research in the Sociology of the Legal Profession, 1962 (a paper presented at the annual meeting of the American Sociological Association).

Hubbell Law Directory for the year in which each case was decided.[2] By using the *American Law Reports,* important cases could be readily obtained from throughout the nation on a wide variety of subjects. Also, the cases annotated in A.L.R. are those that presumably could have gone either way on the law. This quality of relative neutrality helps to minimize a variable that is otherwise very difficult to control and, thus, in that respect makes A.L.R. cases more sensitive indicators of the ability to win. Given 100 cases, there are thus 200 lawyers in the full sample.[3] Each hypothesis in Table 9–1, however, is tested only on cases in which there is a group 1 lawyer opposing a group 2 lawyer. Thus, the number of usable cases varies with each hypothesis. This research design necessitates dividing each background characteristic at some point. For instance, age is split into two categories at average age 47. The difference column in Table 9–1 is equivalent to the correlation coefficient between being in group 1 rather than group 2 and being a winner rather than a loser. These correlation coefficients can range from +1.00 (perfect direct correlation) down to 0 (no correlation) down to −1.00 (perfect inverse correlation).[4] The last column indicates the probability that the difference found is attributable to chance, given the size of the difference and the number of lawyers involved. Differences having chance probabilities greater than 0.05 are readily attributable to chance.[5]

An alternative research design might involve determining what percent of their 1963 cases a selected group of 200 lawyers won. However, differences in the victory records of lawyers in such a research design could be readily attributed to the cases they handle rather than to their background characteristics. For example, divorce lawyers tend to win more cases than do criminal defense lawyers, regardless of background. The research design used in this chapter, in effect, makes comparisons only

---

[2] 85 A.L.R.2d (1962) through 67 A.L.R.2d (1959). A copy of the appendix to this paper, showing the cases, the lawyers, and their characteristics, can be obtained from the senior writer.

[3] The 200 attorneys seem to comprise a representative national sample of the diverse types who practice in cases important enough to be included in the *American Law Reports.* By making comparisons between types of cases and types of courts within this sample, one can roughly extrapolate to some other types of cases and some other types of courts. See the text material in the paragraph subsequent to note 13 *infra.*

[4] The difference column equals the phi correlation coefficient, since both the independent variable and the dependent variable are divided at the median. This means that exactly half the lawyers used were in each background group and were winners. For further detail on correlation, see GUILFORD, FUNDAMENTAL STATISTICS IN PSYCHOLOGY AND EDUCATION 135–38, 311–15 (1956). Table 9–2 also contains phi correlation coefficients.

[5] Technically speaking, the chance probabilities in Table 9–1 are one-tailed chi-squares as are (for ease in comparison) the chance probabilities referred to later with regard to Table 9–2. See *id.* at 228–37; EDWARDS, STATISTICAL METHODS FOR THE BEHAVIORAL SCIENCES 258–61 (1954).

TABLE 9-1

How Lawyers of Differing Backgrounds Fare when They Oppose Each Other

Group 1 (Hypothesized to be more likely to win)	Group 2 (Hypothesized to be less likely to win)	Number of Paired Lawyers (½ in each group)	% of Group 1 Lawyers Who Won	% of Group 2 Lawyers Who Won	Difference (= correlation coefficient)	Probability of Positive Diff. Being Due to Chance
Age						
1. Over 47	47 and under	82	56%	44%	+.12	.10 to .15
2. 36 through 54	Under 36 or over 34	120	60	40	+.20	.01 to .02½
Experience						
3. Over 20 years	20 and under	84	55	45	+.09	.20 to .25
4. 11 through 34	Under 11 or over 34	94	57	43	+.14	.05 to .10
Age & Experience						
5. Older (both within 5 yrs. on exper.)	Younger	54	48	52	−.04	.35 to .40
6. More Exper. (both within 5 yrs. on age)	Less Exper.	34	53	47	+.06	.35 to .40
Education						
7. More than 1 degree	1 degree or none mentioned	84	55	45	+.10	.15 to .20
8. More than 1 degree	No degrees mentioned	32	62	38	+.24	.05 to .10
9. Pre-1920 AALS approval	Other law schools	58	45	55	−.10	.20 to .25
Associations						
10. Member of ABA	Nonmember of ABA	88	45	55	−.10	.15 to .20
11. Member of a firm	Nonmember of a firm	106	53	47	+.06	.25 to .35
12. Public office holder	Nonoffice holder	30	53	47	+.06	.35 to .40
Evaluations						
13. High rating	Fair or no rating	90	53	47	+.06	.25 to .35
14. Very high recommendation	No recommendation	94	55	45	+.10	.15 to .20
15. Worth $10,000 or more	Under $10,000 or no listing	22	64	36	+.28	.10 to .15
Nationality						
16. British surname	Non-British surname	100	50	50	00	no difference

between lawyers who directly opposed each other. The emphasis is thus on the outcomes of individual cases, not on the victory records of individual lawyers over time. It may also be noted that by using only cases where one lawyer opposes one other lawyer, the effect of their respective backgrounds is brought out more clearly than if the backgrounds of both sides were diluted by injecting the additional variables that would necessarily accompany the introduction of one or more extra individuals.

II. THE BASIC FINDINGS

A. Age and Experience

The average age of the 200 lawyers in the sample was 47. Table 9–1 indicates that if a lawyer above age 47 opposes a lawyer 47 years old or younger, the older lawyer is more likely to win. However, if the lawyers are divided into three categories—namely, those who might be considered quite young (35 and under) to be practicing at the appellate court level (which is the court level for nearly all cases reported in the *American Law Reports*), those who might be considered middle aged (36 through 54), and those who might be considered approaching retirement (55 and over)—then the correlation with being a winner becomes stronger and is revealed to be curvilinear. Thus, the middle aged lawyer seems to fare the best in that, in the sample studied, he was generally capable of defeating both the younger, less experienced lawyer and the older, possibly slower lawyer.

As one might suspect, the relation between experience and victory is similar to the relation between age and victory. Thus, the lawyer with more than the average number of years since being admitted to the bar (over 20 years) generally won over the lawyer with less than the average. Likewise, when experience is divided into three categories (10 years or under, 11 through 34 years, and 35 years or over), a strengthened curvilinear relation is revealed. The greater importance of experience over mere age is shown by the figures on lines 5 and 6. Line 5 shows that an older lawyer has little advantage over a younger lawyer (irrespective of the age level or the age gap) and may possibly be at a slight disadvantage, if experience is held constant by comparing only lawyers who are within five years of each other on experience. On the other hand, a more experienced lawyer seems to have some advantage over a less experienced lawyer when age is similarly held constant. The correlations on lines 5 and 6 are as small as they are because one of the two variables was controlled within narrow limits on each line. This technique admittedly leaves something to be desired, but it is justified on the ground that no better technique is available. That is, it is difficult to assemble a significant sample of 60-year-old lawyers with only 5 years of experience or of 25-year old lawyers with 10 years of experience.

B. Education

The average lawyer in the sample had one college degree, which was usually a law degree. Of the lawyers who had two degrees or more (of any kind), 55 percent were victorious when faced by opponents who had one degree or who did not mention having a degree. Since this relationship is linear rather than curvilinear (unlike age and experience), the wider the educational gap, the greater the likelihood that the more educated lawyer will win. Thus, line 8 shows that when lawyers with two degrees or more (of any kind) are compared with lawyers who did not mention having a degree (thus eliminating the middle group of lawyers who have one degree), the correlation with victory rises from +.10 to +.24.

On the other hand, the attempt to correlate education *quality* with victory by determing when each law school was approved by the American Association of Law Schools revealed the correlation to be negative. This negative correlation, however, is small enough and based on few enough cases to be readily attributable to chance, unless further analysis reveals the operation of some meaningful explanatory variables. It should also be pointed out that year of AALS approval is not a perfect measure of law school quality.[6] Another explanation might be that graduates from the less prestigious law schools who are engaged in appellate advocacy tend to rank higher in their classes than do their opponents from the more prestigious law schools. This would set in motion a selective process that would produce the unexpected result revealed above.

C. Associations

American Bar Association membership, held by 63 percent of the lawyers in the sample, is another characteristic whose correlation with victory did not turn out as hypothesized. If the correlation were positive, however, one would not attribute it to a causal relation, since merely joining the ABA clearly does not make one a better lawyer. Furthermore, as Table 9–2 reveals, the ABA members in this sample of appellate court lawyers were disproportionately the younger, less experienced lawyers.

---

[6] For a list of the member schools of the AALS and when they were admitted, see American Association of Law Schools, Proceedings 271–73 (1961). This booklet also contains a provocative debate on the meaning of AALS approval. Year of ABA approval is even less meaningful as a measure of quality among approved law schools, since so many of the approved law schools were approved simultaneously in the 1920's. More meaningful results in categorizing the quality of the law schools might be obtained by using the average Law School Admissions Test scores for the entering classes of each law school. This data, however, is made available only for studies sponsored by the Educational Testing Service.

TABLE 9–2
How the Attorney Characteristics Correlate with Each Other

	Over 47 Yrs. Old	Over 20 Yrs. Exper.	Two Ed. Degrees	Pre-1920 AALS	ABA Member	Firm Member	Public Office	Very High Recom.	Anglo-Saxon
Over 47 yrs. old	—	+.79	−.27	+.01	−.08	−.12	−.01	+.20	+.05
Over 20 yrs. exper.		—	−.30	+.07	−.18	−.09	−.04	+.13	+.07
Two ed. degrees			—	+.30	+.10	+.11	+.02	+.03	−.06
Pre-1920 AALS				—	−.03	−.13	−.01	+.03	−.06
ABA member					—	+.28	+.02	+.30	−.07
Firm member						—	−.16	+.33	−.04
Public office							—	−.02	−.13
Very high recom.								—	+.04
Anglo-Saxon									—

Unlike ABA membership, being in a law firm (as an associate or a partner) does have a positive correlation with victory, although the linear correlation would probably be higher if lawyers from large firms had been compared with both solo practitioners and lawyers from very small firms. Information on firm size was not available, but Jerome Carlin's research supports the large versus small firm hypothesis, since he finds that the characteristics of small firm lawyers are more like those of solo practitioners than those of large firm lawyers.[7]

Lawyers who were currently holding public office (which usually meant being an attorney for a governmental unit) had a slight tendency to win over their opposition. The higher the governmental unit, the greater this tendency would probably have been. Such a hypothesis would conform to Eloise Snyder's finding that litigants possessing greater governmental and political power tend to win over litigants possessing lesser power.[8] She attributes this finding to the respect such litigants can evoke and to the able legal talent they can hire.

D. Evaluations

In the *Martindale-Hubbell Law Directory*, which was the source for the above characteristics, certain evaluation scores are also given. One such score refers to "estimate of legal ability."[9] It is based on "age, practical experience, nature and length of practice, and other relevant qualifications." It can range from *a* (very high), *b* (high), *c* (fair), to no rating at all (the publishers indicate the "absence of rating characters must not be construed as derogatory"). More than half of the lawyers in the sample of 200 had *a* (24 percent) or *b* (29 percent) ratings, and the rest had *c* ratings (7 percent) or were unrated (40 percent). The *a* and *b* lawyers did have a better victory record than the other lawyers, but not sufficiently better to place much weight on these ratings.

Martindale-Hubbell also indicates whether recommendations received for the listed lawyers have been "very high," but no distinction is made between derogatory recommendations and no recommendations. Of the 200 lawyers, 58 percent received "very high" recommendations and did show some tendency to win (+.10 phi correlation) when opposed by lawyers who did not receive such recognition.

The most potent predictor from *Martindale-Hubbell*, however, was net worth. Although only 20 percent of the lawyers were given net worth

---

[7] Carlin, Current Research in the Sociology of the Legal Profession, 1962, at 8–16 (a paper presented at the annual meeting of the American Sociological Association).

[8] Snyder, *Political Power and the Ability to Win Supreme Court Decisions,* 39 Soc. Forces 36 (1960).

[9] Quotations in this paragraph come from the inside front cover of Martindale-Hubbell Law Directory (1960).

evaluations, when those who were scored $10,000 and over were compared with the under $10,000 and unrated lawyers, a correlation of +.28 with being a winner rather than a loser resulted. The difficulty of assigning the proper significance to cause and effect, respectively, at this point and the possibility that reciprocal causation between wealth and victory is at work here complicates the evaluation of this correlation.

E. NATIONALITY

The last line in Table 9–1 deals with ancestral nationality. To make the comparisons involved, each lawyer's surname and its parts were taken to the *Dictionary of American Family Names*[10] in order to estimate whether a lawyer had a British (i.e., English, Scotch, Welsh) or non-British background. Of the surnames, 60 percent were determined to be British, 15 percent German, 14 percent Irish, 3 percent Scandinavian, 2 percent southern European (Italy, Greece, Spain), 2 percent eastern European (Polish, Balkan, Russian), 1 percent French, 1 percent Dutch, 2 percent unidentified non-British, and 2 percent unknown. Lawyers with British surnames defeated lawyers with non-British surnames in exactly half of the cases so paired. A sample selected in this way may contain individual instances in which a lawyer's surname obscures mixed ancestral nationality or does not reflect his ancestral nationality at all, but this possibility probably cannot account for the zero correlation. This result may be contrary to what one would expect, given the relatively disadvantaged backgrounds of non-Anglo-Saxon lawyers reflected in the findings of Jack Ladinsky.[11] The significance of ethnic differences is apparently lessened substantially when other variables, such as type of law practice and level of court practiced before, are held constant.

Related to the ancestral nationality variable are the religious and racial variables. The religious variable is closely correlated with ancestral nationality, since Catholics and Jews are disproportionately non-British. There is no data in *Martindale-Hubbell* on racial characteristics, but even if there were, race would not be a very good predictive variable, since a high proportion of all lawyers are white. In those few cases, however, where a Negro lawyer does oppose a white lawyer, one might suspect that the Negro lawyer would be at a slight disadvantage by virtue of a

---

[10] SMITH, DICTIONARY OF AMERICAN FAMILY NAMES (1956) gives the nationality origin and meaning of over 10,000 family names. When more than one ancestral nationality was given, the first one was used. SMITH, THE STORY OF OUR NAMES (1950) also gives, among other things, the national origin of various family name prefixes, roots, and suffixes, which can be used to estimate nationalities of names not given in Smith's Dictionary.

[11] Ladinsky, *Careers of Lawyers, Law Practice, and Legal Institutions*, 28 AM. SOC. REV. 47 (1963).

possible educational handicap, the existence of conscious or unconscious prejudice, and the likelihood that he would be defending in a criminal case.[12]

F. OTHER ELEMENTS

Perhaps a comparison of attorneys having different personality characteristics such as extroversion–introversion and dominance–submissiveness might prove significant. It might also be revealing to compare lawyers who differ in preparation techniques, appearance, or oratorical style. But none of these characteristics are described in *Martindale-Hubbell*.[13] Even if they were, however, one might still hypothesize that *Martindale* ratings, experience, and amount of education are probably better *general* predictors of courtroom success, at least at the appellate court level, although these other variables may be important in specific anecdotal instances.

If a table with a format like Table 9–1 is prepared for just federal courts and another table for just state courts, the two tables do not differ significantly. Likewise, if a table like Table 9–1 is prepared for northern courts and another table for southern courts there is also no significant difference between the tables. Finally, if a table is prepared for criminal, tort, family, and labor cases, on the one hand, and another table is prepared for business, property, and tax cases, the two tables are still very much alike. Thus, the correlations measured by this study seem to remain fairly constant, regardless of appellate court level, region, or type of case. Because several new variables are introduced at the trial level (especially the increased subjectivity of jury decisions), one might expect to find significant differences between these tables and a table prepared for trial court cases. This hypothesis cannot be tested with the present sample, however, since it lacks trial court cases.

One might hypothesize that, in general, the attorney whose characteristics are most like those of the deciding judge might have a slight edge. One could test this hypothesis by determining for each characteristic in Table 9–1 whether the tendency of lawyers in group 1 to win over lawyers in group 2 correlates positively with the incidence of group 1 judges. No data, however, was compiled in this study on the characteristics of individual judges.

It might also be noted that the appellees (the winners at the trial court level) won 58 percent of the 100 cases, while the appellants won 42

---

[12] Hale, The Career Development of the Negro Lawyer in Chicago, 1949 (unpublished dissertation in University of Chicago Library).

[13] The writer is in the process of undertaking a systematic content analysis of the transcripts of the oral arguments and judicial reactions in a sample of cases before the United State Supreme Court.

percent. Being an appellee correlated to a significant extent only with amount of education (+.19), holding a public office (+.17), and being a firm member (+.15). One could control for the effect that being an appellee has on the result shown on line 11 of Table 9–1 by using a set of cases all of which pitted firm member against solo practitioner and in half of which the firm member was the appellee. Similar controls could be applied to the correlation with amount of education and with holding public office. Such statistical controls would even further reduce the differences shown in Table 9–1.

III.   INTERRELATIONS AMONG THE CHARACTERISTICS

Table 9–2 shows how the attorney characteristics correlate with each other. Each cell indicates the correlation coefficient between the variables involved. The number of lawyers involved in each correlation is 200, except where meaningful information was occasionally not available for some lawyers (e.g., as to ancestral nationality, three lawyers were un- classifiable). Given 200 lawyers and the formula for calculating chance probability, any correlation coefficient larger than +.11 or −.11 is not readily attributable to chance.[14] Table 9–2 might have been more useful for interpreting the findings of Table 9–1 had only those lawyers been included in a given correlation who had participated in a usable case involving both of the variables to be correlated. Such an attempt to relate Table 9–2 more closely to Table 9–1, however, results in unduly small sample sizes for the cells, although the absolute size of the correlation coefficients is almost always substantially larger.

Figure 9–1 summarizes the relationships in Table 9–2 that were both statistically significant below the 0.05 level of chance probability and greater than 0.11 in phi coefficient size. The only statistically significant relations from Table 9–2 that were excluded from Figure 9–1 are the relations between experience and degrees (spurious if age is statistically controlled), between age and rating (spurious if experience is statisti- cally controlled), and between public office and firm membership (a negative tautology in part). Education quality was excluded from Figure 9–1 because of its unexplained correlations. Figure 9–1 also integrates most of the findings from Table 9–1 on courtroom victory. The arrows in the figure indicate what seem to be the causal connections on the basis of analyzing the correlations coefficients,[15] the time sequences, and the literature available on the sociology of the legal profession.

---

[14] See notes 4 and 5 *supra* and accompanying text.

[15] The Blalock-Simon method of testing causal models by analyzing correlation coefficients was used, and a high degree of goodness of fit or internal consistency was achieved. See Blalock, *Correlation and Causality: The Multivariate Case,* 39 Soc. Forces 246 (1961).

FIGURE 9–1

THE MOST STATISTICALLY SIGNIFICANT RELATIONS AMONG ATTORNEY
CHARACTERISTICS AND COURTROOM RESULTS

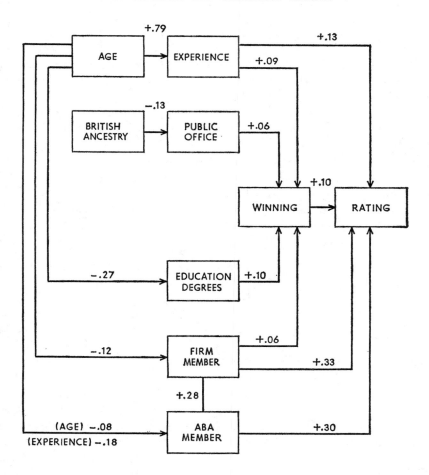

Reading from left to right and downward, one sees that there is a very high correlation between age and experience, as expected. There is also a less expected high negative correlation between age and quantity of education, which indicates that younger lawyers are obtaining more degrees than older lawyers have obtained. The younger lawyers are also more likely to be associated with a firm, whereas the older lawyers are more likely to be solo and general practitioners.

The only variable with which British ancestry correlated significantly was holding public office, and this was a negative correlation. Of the 77 non-Anglo-Saxon lawyers in the sample, 12 percent were attorneys for a governmental unit, whereas only 5 percent of the 120 Anglo-Saxon lawyers in the sample held such office. The difference might be explained by the fact that there is less discrimination in governmental hiring than in private hiring and sometimes even active recruitment of minority group representation for government positions.

Experience correlates positively with winning and also with having "very high" recommendations in *Martindale-Hubbell*. On the other hand, a smaller proportion of the older, more experienced lawyers in the sample were members of the American Bar Association (52 percent) than was true of the younger, less experienced lawyers (70 percent). If this relation holds in a larger sample of lawyers, it may help to explain why the American Bar Association has become somewhat more liberal in its pressure group activities during the 1950's than it was in the 1930's, although ABA leaders might argue that in both periods the ABA was merely defending the law and the judicial process.

Holding public office correlates positively with winning in court, as does quantity of education. Being a firm member correlates positively with winning, with having a very high *Martindale-Hubbell* evaluation, and with being an ABA member. Being an ABA member also correlates positively with the *Martindale-Hubbell* ratings, as does being on the winning side in the cases compiled. The three different *Martindale-Hubbell* evaluations all correlated highly with each other, but the recommendations evaluation was used in Figure 9–1 because it correlated more highly with the other attorney characteristics.

IV. CONCLUSIONS

As is shown in Table 9–1, there are definite and meaningful relationships between attorney characteristics and courtroom results. The relations in general, however, are smaller than might have been expected, particularly in comparison with the relationships among the characteristics themselves, which are shown in Table 9–2. Thus, one might conclude by saying that some characteristics of lawyers are reasonably potent for predicting other characteristics of the same lawyers (especially when statistical controls are used), but these same characteristics are, in general, not very potent for predicting courtroom results. Legal scholars, practicing lawyers, and social scientists interested in decisional outcomes can get much better predictability by analyzing the factual elements within the cases,[16] the characteristics of the judges or jurors,[17] and the characteristics of the litigants.[18]

---

[16] Kort, *Content Analysis of Judicial Opinions and Rules of Law,* in JUDICIAL DECISION-MAKING 133 (SCHUBERT ed. 1963).

[17] Rodell, *For Every Justice, Judicial Deference Is a Sometime Thing,* 50 GEO. L. J. 700 (1962).

[18] Bullock, *Significance of the Racial Factor in the Length of Prison Sentences,* 52 J. CRIM. L., C. & P.S. 411 (1961).

C. Evidentiary and Other Facts as Predictors

CHAPTER 10

Correlation Analysis Explained: Criminal Cases

Justice Holmes believed that a major object of legal analysis should be the prediction of what courts will do when faced with given situations. A major object of all social science analysis might also be the prediction of what individuals or groups being studied will do when faced with given situations. Past events are especially valuable in making such predictions. Sometimes, however, if they are handled merely in an impressionistic manner, past events are too complex to serve as a basis for accurate prediction. Then a quantitative technique supplemented by nonquantitative considerations may be in order.

I. THE PROBLEM

Most litigation situations revolve around legislative or judicial rules of law that specify that certain individual variables or combinations of variables will lead to certain judicial decisions. The predictive method presented here applies mainly to litigation situations involving rules of law that do *not* specify exactly which combinations of variables will lead to one result and which to the opposite result. For example, in deciding whether there is a violation of due process in obtaining a criminal confession, the United States Supreme Court has never specified the combinations of variables that would lead it to the decision that a confession was inadmissible.

Fred Kort's provocative work greatly helped to generate the ideas presented here, especially his articles *Predicting Supreme Court Decisions Mathematically: A Quantitative Analysis of the "Right to Counsel" Cases,* 55 AM. POL. SCI. REV. 1 (1957); and *The Quantitative Content Analysis of Judicial Opinions,* PROD at 11 (1960). Both methods described in Kort's articles, however, are far more complicated than the method described here. See Nagel, *Weighting Variables in Judicial Prediction,* 60 MODERN USES OF LOGIC IN L. 93 (1960).

125

It is possible to predict how the court will go in a future case, however, from a quantitative analysis of both the variables present in past cases and the decisions reached. This is possible *provided* the court is consistent with the underlying pattern it has established (or that has been established for it, if a lower court's decision is being predicted), and *provided* that the presence of the relevant fact-variables in the future case is not so subject to dispute that one cannot know what fact-variables will be found present by the court. These are some variables that the Supreme Court has found relevant in deciding some criminal confession cases in favor of the defense: that the defendant has been detained for more than 12 hours incommunicado during which time he confessed; that the defendant is a Negro in a southern jurisdiction; and that the defendant has been subjected to protracted questioning.

II.   THE METHOD OF SOLUTION

To illustrate the predictive method proposed here, five hypothetical past criminal confession cases (A, B, C, D, and E), involving four hypothetical variables (*p*, *q*, *r*, and *s*), will be used to predict one hypothetical future case, case X. In actual applications, more past cases and more variables are likely to be involved.

STEP 1

Compile a list of the cases in the jurisdiction involved, dealing with the issue involved. Use only cases in which one can determine what variables were present that the court considered relevant. This usually means confining oneself to cases with published opinions as sources for predictive material. For purposes of our example, we assume that five criminal confession cases are located—A, B, C, D, and E.

STEP 2

Compile a list of the separate variables present in the Step 1 cases which the court probably considered relevant to a decision in favor of the affirmative position. These prodefense variables, present in one or more cases, we shall call *p*, *q*, *r*, and *s*.

STEP 3

Prepare a chart, showing what variables were present (to the degree specified in defining the variables) in the cases and who won on the issue being predicted. In case X, the case to be predicted, variables, *q*, *r*, and *s* are present. None of the past cases alone indicates how case X will go. In case E, the defense won with *p*, *r*, and *s*, but is *q* in case X equivalent to *p?* In case D, the defense won with *p* and *r,* but are *q* and *s* in case X equivalent to *p?* These questions can be answered only by some method that quantitatively or subjectively gives weights to the variables.

TABLE 10–1

EXAMPLE OF STEP 3

Cases (in time sequence)	Who Won on the Issue	p	q	r	s
A	Prosecution		Present		
B	Defense	Present	Present	Present	Present
C	Prosecution	Present	Present		
D	Defense	Present		Present	
E	Defense	Present		Present	Present

STEP 4

Prepare as many four-cell tables as there are variables. Each four-cell table shows the correlation between the presence of the variable involved and the victory of the affirmative position.

TABLE 10–2

EXAMPLE OF STEP 4

	Prosecution Wins	Defense Wins
Variable *p* Present	Cell a 1	Cell b 3
Variable *p* Absent	Cell c 1	Cell d 0

	Prosecution Wins	Defense Wins
Variable *q* Present	a 2	b 1
Variable *q* Absent	c 0	d 2

	Prosecution Wins	Defense Wins
Variable *r* Present	a 0	b 3
Variable *r* Absent	c 2	d 0

	Prosecution Wins	Defense Wins
Variable *s* Present	a 0	b 2
Variable *s* Absent	c 2	d 1

Step 5

Calculate a two-place correlation coefficient for each four-cell table where the correlation coefficient =

$$\frac{bc - ad}{\sqrt{(a + b)(c + d)(a + c)(b + d)}}$$

A correlation coefficient indicates the direction and intensity of the correlation between the presence of the variable and a victory for the affirmative position. Square roots can be determined by consulting a square root table, and the arithmetic operations can easily be done with a desk calculator or by hand if necessary.

TABLE 10–3

Example of Step 5

Table	Correlation Coefficient	
p	$\dfrac{3 - 0}{\sqrt{4 \cdot 1 \cdot 2 \cdot 3}}$	$= +\ .61$
q	$\dfrac{0 - 4}{\sqrt{3 \cdot 2 \cdot 2 \cdot 3}}$	$= -\ .67$
r	$\dfrac{6 - 0}{\sqrt{3 \cdot 2 \cdot 2 \cdot 3}}$	$= + 1.00$
s	$\dfrac{4 - 0}{\sqrt{2 \cdot 3 \cdot 2 \cdot 3}}$	$= +\ .67$

For greater precision, the correlation coefficient for each variable can be calculated while the influence of the other variables is eliminated through the technique of partial correlation. See J. P. Guilford, Elementary Statistics in Psychology and Education, 316–18, 405–9 (Mc-Graw-Hill Co., Inc., New York, 3d ed. 1956). For still greater precision, winning and losing in multijudge decisions can be measured on a continuum in terms of the probability of obtaining the voting split of each case purely by chance. The lower the chance probability of the split, the greater is the victory, if it occurred, or the greater the loss, if a loss occurred. *Id.* at pp. 237–38. Precision is also gained by measuring the presence of the variables along a continuum, rather than as a dichotomy, whenever the variables are of such nature that it is possible to do so. This may necessitate a more complex correlation coefficient, however. *Id.* at pp. 297–305, 135–51.

STEP 6

Calculate a point value for each variable where the point value equals 100 + (100 times the correlation coefficient of the variable). This step is designed to eliminate decimal points and negative numbers.

TABLE 10–4

EXAMPLE OF STEP 6

Variable	Point Value
p	$100 + (100 \cdot \quad .61) = 161$
q	$100 + (100 \cdot \ -.67) = \quad 33$
r	$100 + (100 \cdot \ 1.00) = 200$
s	$100 + (100 \cdot \ -.67) = 167$

STEP 7

Calculate a composite value for each case where the composite value equals the sum of the point values of the component variables of each case.

TABLE 10–5

EXAMPLE OF STEP 7

Past Case	Composite Value
A	$33 \qquad\qquad\qquad = \quad 33$
B	$161 + 33 + 200 + 167 = 561$
C	$161 + 33 \qquad\qquad = 194$
D	$161 \qquad + 200 \qquad = 361$
E	$161 \qquad + 200 + 167 = 528$

STEP 8

Arrange the cases in order of their composite values and note the lowest composite value corresponding to a victory for the affirmative position and the highest composite value corresponding to a victory for the negative position.

A composite value of 361 or higher indicates the defense will win. A composite value of 194 or lower indicates the prosecution will win.

TABLE 10–6

EXAMPLE OF STEP 8

Past Case	Composite Value	Who Won on the Issue		
B	561	Defense		
E	528	Defense		
D	361	Defense	<	cutoff
C	194	Prosecution	<	points
A	33	Prosecution		

STEP 9

Apply the point allocations of step 6 to the variables present in the case being predicted.

TABLE 10–7

EXAMPLE OF STEP 9

Future Case	Variables Present	Composite Value	Predicted Winner on the Issue
X	q, r, & s	33 + 200 + 167 = 400	Defense

STEP 10

Each time a new case is decided, insert its contents and decision into steps 1 through 8 in order to arrive at point values for new variables, to arrive at new point values for old variables, and to determine new cutoff points. This new material, in turn, should be used for the prediction of future cases.

TABLE 10–8

EXAMPLE OF STEP 10

If Defense Wins Case X		If Prosecution Wins Case X	
Variable	New Point Value	Variable	New Point Value
p	125	p	171
q	50	q	29
r	200	r	171
s	171	s	133
No new variable		No new variable	
New cutoff points: 325 and 175		New cutoff points: 342 and 333	

III.   LIMITATIONS

There are five types of situations in which the quantitative method should not be used. *First,* if a prior case has the same variables as the case being predicted, and no other variables, one should generally predict the same decision that was given in the prior case, regardless of the quantitative analysis. *Second,* if certain variables in a prior case led to an affirmative decision and the case being predicted has the same variables and more, the new case should also have an affirmative decision. *Third,* if a negative decision was given in a prior case with certain variables and the present case lacks any of these variables and has no others, the present case should also have a negative decision. *Fourth,* if a prior case explicitly says that the presence of a certain variable or a certain combination of variables will result in a decision for the defendant, such a rule should generally be followed in making predictions, regardless of the point values of the variables. *Finally,* if the composite value of the case being predicted falls between the cutoff points, or if no cutoff points have been established because all the cases have gone one way or because there have been no cases, or if the case being predicted contains a new variable not encountered by prior cases, then one must resort to at least partially subjective weighting in making a prediction, provided none of the other four situations apply.

IV.   USE OF COMPUTERS

The simple arithmetical and verbal rules presented can easily be programmed into a small electronic computer for many types of cases. The computer can bring up-to-date the point values of the variables on being told, by punched cards, the decisions and the variables present in new cases. Likewise, it can do the predicting and punch out the result on being told, by a punched card, the variables present in the case to be predicted. The American Bar Association has already established a Committee on Electronic Data Retrieval that has as one of its interests the investigation of such predictive systems.

V.   CONCLUSION

The method presented here is in no way meant to replace the traditional methods used to analyze judicial precedents. The method presupposes that legal scholars and social scientists will continue to point out the cases and the variables that are relevant to deciding particular issues in particular jurisdictions. If, however, the prediction problem involves allocating weights to the variables, and the court or the legislature has not done so, then a quantitative method of analysis such as the one presented here may prove more accurate (and much faster if electronic equipment is used) than a purely subjective method of weighting factual variables in precedents.

CHAPTER 11

Correlation Analysis Applied:
Reapportionment Cases

I. THE CASES AND THE VARIABLES

A few years ago, an article appeared in *The American Behavioral Scientist* and in *The Practical Lawyer,* titled "Using Simple Calculations to Predict Judicial Decisions."[1] Since then, the article has been reprinted[2] and commented on[3] in various places, but no detailed application has yet been reported of the methodology presented.[4] It is the purpose of this chapter to present such an application in the hope that others might thereby be stimulated to apply it further. The application involves reapportionment cases, although almost any field of law could have been used for illustrative purposes. Technical aspects of the methodology have been placed in the footnotes so as not to disrupt the continuity of the application to the nontechnical-oriented reader.

From *Colegrove* v. *Green*[5] through *Baker* v. *Carr,*[6] nine major reapportionment cases have been decided in the federal and state courts.[7] Table 11–1 shows the name, citation, year, and state of each case as

---

[1] Nagel, *Using Simple Calculations to Predict Judicial Decisions,* 4 AM. BEHAV. SCI. 24 (1960), PRAC. LAW. (March 1961) at 68 (chap. 10 *supra*).

[2] LAW IN SOCIETY (Schwartz & Skolnick eds. forthcoming); 18 Mo. B.J. 362 (1962).

[3] Fagan, *Some Contributions of Mathematical Reasoning to the Study of Politics,* 55 AM. POL. SCI. REV. 888, 889 (1961); Lawlor, *What Computers Can Do: Analysis and Prediction of Judicial Decisions,* 49 A.B.A.J. 337, 341 (1963); Schubert, *A Psychometric Model of the Supreme Court,* 5 AM. BEHAV. SCI. 14 (1961).

[4] In a recent article, however, Ulmer reports without providing the data that "application of Nagel's correlation analysis to . . . 20 facts in . . . 19 cases gave a perfect separation of pro and con cases." Ulmer, *Quantitative Analysis of Judicial Processes: Some Practical and Theoretical Applications,* 28 LAW & CONTEMP. PROB. 164, 173 (1963).

[5] 328 U.S. 549 (1946).

[6] 369 U.S. 186 (1962).

[7] LARSON, REAPPORTIONMENT AND THE COURTS (1963).

of the time *Baker* v. *Carr* was decided. The application could easily be extended to cover more reapportionment cases, but doing so would make it more difficult for the reader to perceive the methodology involved.

An analysis of the nine cases indicates that one who attacks an apportionment must meet certain prerequisites in order to win, regardless of the other variables in his case. These prerequisites require the attacking party (1) to cite the equal protection clause, the Fifteenth Amendment, or the state equivalents rather than the republican form of government clause; (2) to exhaust satisfactorily his available lower judicial and nonjudicial remedies; and (3) to seek such remedies as a declaratory judgment or a temporary at-large election rather than an affirmative redistricting order or a nullification of legislation passed by a malapportioned legislature. The cases also indicate there is one element that will bring victory for the attacker, regardless of the other variables present—namely, the legislature's taking affirmative statutory action to make the districts more unequal. The cases further indicate that certain variables, although not prerequisites to victory, will weigh in favor of the attacker if they are present, and will weigh against him if they

TABLE 11–1

THE REAPPORTIONMENT CASES AND THEIR CRUCIAL FACTS
(from *Colegrove* v. *Green* through *Baker* v. *Carr*)

The Cases		Variables Present			
(arranged chronologically)	Who Won	One	Two	Three	Four
Colegrove v. *Green,* 328 U.S. 549 (1946) (Ill.)	Defender	No	Congress	No	Federal
Dyer v. *Abe,* 138 F. Supp. 220 (1956) (Hawaii)	Attacker	Yes	Territory	Yes	Federal
Magraw v. *Donovan,* 163 F. Supp. 184 (1958) (Minn.)	Attacker	Yes	State	Yes	Federal
Asbury Park Press, Inc. v. *Woolley,* 33 N.J. 1, 161 A.2d 705 (1960)	Attacker	Yes	State	Yes	State
Scholle v. *Secretary of State,* 360 Mich. 1, 104 N.W.2d 63 (1960)	Defender	No	State	Yes	State
W.M.C.A., Inc. v. *Simon,* 196 F. Supp. 758 (1961) (N.Y.)	Defender	No	State	No	Federal
Maryland Committee v. *Tawes,* Circ. Ct. Arundel County (1961) (Md.)[8]	Defender	No	State	Yes	State
Grills v. *Anderson,* 29 U.S.L. WEEK 2443 (1961) (Ind.)	Attacker	Yes	State	No	State
Baker v. *Carr,* 369 U.S. 186 (1962) (Tenn.)	Attacker	Yes	State	Yes	Federal

Variable 1: Did the relevant constitution or organic act expressly require districts of equal population per representative?
Variable 2: Was a territorial, state, or congressional apportionment attacked?
Variable 3: Could less than 35 percent of the population choose more than 50 percent of the legislative membership involved?
Variable 4: Did a federal court or a state court decide the case?

---

[8] *Aff'd* 229 Md. 406, 184 A.2d 715 (1962).

are absent. These variables are indicated at the bottom of Table 11–1.[9]

It is important to note that the presence or absence of each of these kinds of variables can be determined reasonably well before each case is decided. Highly subjective variables are not useful for prediction purposes. It is also worth noting that a lengthy list of variables is not a prerequisite to prediction. Nor is it necessary that all the relevant cases be decided by the same court or by multijudge courts.[10] Note also that some of the variables can relate to legal requirements (variable 1), to evidentiary facts (variables 2 and 3), to place and personnel (variable 4), to time and overrulings (see note 9), and to other relevant matters.[11]

The most difficult aspect of applying correlation analysis to case prediction is in formulating the hypotheses as to what the relevant variables are. This process can be partially mechanized by converting the full text of the relevant cases into punched tape either by a typist or an optical scanner.[12] Which side won in each case, as well as the full text, should be punched on the tape. The punched tape can then be processed by a programmed computer to read out each word (including its grammatical variations and synonyms) that has a +.20 correlation or more (at a given level of probability) with victory for a given side (e.g., the apportionment attacker). If too few or too many predictive words are read out, the specified correlation or probability levels can be raised or lowered accordingly. The resulting list of predictive words should generate insights about what some of the relevant predictive variables are.

---

[9] To get at the influence of the "climb on the bandwagon effect" after *Baker*, all the reapportionment cases starting from *Colegrove* might be positioned on the new variable of: "Was the case decided before or after *Baker* v. *Carr?*" In predicting cases subsequent to *Wesberry* v. *Sanders*, 376 U.S. 1 (1964), one should probably drop variable 2 unless a differential judicial behavior toward congressional and state legislative redistricting continues to be maintained in spite of the *Wesberry* predecent.

Likewise, in spite of the pronouncements of *Reynolds* v. *Sims*, 84 Sup. Ct. 1362 (1964), a somewhat more lenient judicial attitude may continue to exist toward malapportionment in state upper houses as compared to state lower houses. Thus, variable 1 may continue to have some predictive power, although less than previously. As time goes on, the 35 percent figure of variable 3 will probably have to be raised to give better predictability.

[10] One defect in some of the methodological techniques of Fred Kort is that they are restricted to the United States Supreme Court or at least to multijudge courts with equal numbers of judges. See Kort, *Simultaneous Equations and Boolean Algebra in the Analysis of Judicial Decisions*, 28 LAW & CONTEMP. PROB. 143 (1963); Kort, *Predicting Supreme Court Decisions Mathematically: A Quantitative Analysis of the Right to Counsel Cases*, 51 AM. POL. SCI. REV. 1 (1957).

[11] The points made in this paragraph, as well as in other parts of this article, are particularly relevant to the criticism made by Wiener, *Decision Prediction by Computers: Nonsense Cubed—and Worse*, 48 A.B.A.J. 1023 (1962).

[12] The relevant cases can be found by traditional search techniques or by electronic search techniques. See Eldridge & Dennis, *The Computer as a Tool for Legal Research*, 28 LAW & CONTEMP. PROB. 78 (1963).

II. THE WEIGHT OF EACH VARIABLE AND EACH CASE

Table 11–1 shows how each case was positioned on each variable as well as who won. A simple correlation coefficient can be calculated to show the degree of relation between victory for the attacker and the presence of each variable.[13] The correlation coefficients can range from −1.00 (completely inverse relationship) to 0.00 (indicating no relationship) to +1.00 (completely direct relationship).[14] A quick way of approximating a correlation coefficient is simply to subtract (1) the percentage of cases *lacking* X variable that the affirmative side won from (2) the percentage of cases *having* X variable that the affirmative side won.[15] Thus, there is a correlation of +1.00 between victory and whether the state constitution or organic act expressly requires districts of equal population.[16] There is a +.50 correlation between victory and the level of government whose apportionment is being attacked.[17] There is a correlation of +.32 between victory and whether less than 35 percent

---

[13] Tests of chance-probability or statistical significance are inappropriate to apply to the correlation coefficients in this context because (as is brought out more clearly in Table 11–3) one is attempting only to weight the variables relative to each other as of the time the next case is being predicted. One is not attempting to generalize from a sample to an infinite population of apportionment cases or even to a population greater than N plus one.

[14] Unlike Boolean algebra, correlation coefficients do get at the degree of relation between the variables and case outcome. Boolean algebra uses "if . . ., then . . ." reasoning which specifies the presence of a relation in given circumstances but not the degree of the relation. See Lawlor, *Foundations of Logical Legal Decision Making,* 63 MODERN USES OF LOGIC IN L. 98 (1963), Kort, *Simultaneous Equations and Boolean Algebra in the Analysis of Judicial Decisions,* 28 LAW & CONTEMP. PROB. 143 (1963).

[15] See Nagel, *Testing Empirical Generalizations in Legal Research,* 15 J. LEGAL ED. 365 (1963) (chap. 2 *supra*). It can be shown algebraically that a phi correlation coefficient equals the difference (D) between the two percentages times $\dfrac{1+R}{1+C}\sqrt{\dfrac{C}{R}}$ where R equals the ratio between the larger row total and the smaller row total, and C equals the ratio between the larger column total and the smaller column total provided the fact-variable is on the columns and the outcome variable is on the rows. Thus, big differences between phi and D exist only where there are very big differences between R and C.

[16] A phi correlation coefficient is used here, since both variables are measured dichotomously and since the phi coefficient requires no assumptions about bell-shaped distributions. See GUILFORD, FUNDAMENTAL STATISTICS IN PSYCHOLOGY AND EDUCATION 311 (1956).

[17] The basic Pearsonian product-moment correlation coefficient is used here, since one of the two variables is measured in three ordinal categories. See GUILFORD, *op. cit. supra* note 16, at 138–39; WALKER & LEV, STATISTICAL INFERENCE 286 (1953). In such a situation, the point-biserial correlation coefficient would also be appropriate. See GUILFORD, *op. cit. supra* note 16, at 301–5. When a variable has multiple nominal categories, one can use the contingency coefficient divided by its maximum to give the coefficient a zero to 1.00 range. WALKER & LEV, *op. cit. supra,* at 287.

of the population can choose more than 50 percent of the legislative membership involved.[18] Finally, there is a +.10 correlation between victory and whether the case is being heard before a federal judge rather than a state judge.[19]

Variable 1 seems to be relevant because of the obligation of the courts to follow promulgated law where the law is explicit. Variable 2 is relevant probably because of the understandable reluctance of the courts to interfere with a legislature operating at a coordinate or higher level in the federal hierarchy. Variable 3 is relevant because it involves a method for measuring the severity of a malapportionment that is meaningful, simple, and frequently used by the courts. Variable 4 is possibly relevant because of the apparent conservatism and ruralism of the average state court relative to the average federal court, especially with regard to the allocation of local political power.

In order to make the correlation coefficients easier to manipulate, each one can be multiplied by 100 to eliminate the decimal point and added to 100 to eliminate any negative numbers that may have occurred.[19a] The resulting score indicates the numerical weight of each variable to which the original correlation pertained. Thus, 200 is the numerical weight of attacking an apportionment where the relevant constitution or organic act requires districts of equal population.[20] Table

---

[18] Data on the minimum percent of the population needed to elect more than 50 percent of the legislative membership involved was obtained by consulting NATIONAL MUNICIPAL LEAGUE, COMPENDIUM ON LEGISLATIVE APPORTIONMENT (1962) iii–iv (for the 1960 census); Dauer & Kelsay, *Unrepresentative States*, 44 NATIONAL MUNICIPAL REV. 571 (1956) (for the 1950 census); 52 CENSUS OF POPULATION 8 (1953) (for Hawaii); *Colegrove* v. *Green*, 328 U.S. 549, 562 (1946); 42 CENSUS OF POPULATION 500 (1943) (for Illinois). When both houses of a state legislature were involved, the sum of the minimum population percentages needed to control the lower house plus the upper house was divided by two in order to get one percentage figure.

[19] Although it did not occur in any of the nine cases, a phi coefficient or an estimated phi coefficient (see note 16 *supra*) can be calculated without trouble, even if both the attacker and the defender of an apportionment had won approximately half a victory in the same case. One simply adds 0.5 to the appropriate win cell and to the appropriate loss cell of the fourfold table from which the phi coefficient is to be calculated.

[19a] However, adding 100 to each correlation coefficient is unnecessary and sometimes undesirable because all the variables should have positive correlations with victory for the affirmative side if they are worthwhile variables, and because adding 100 may create a distorted point-spread between cases having certain variables and cases lacking those variables. The predictive power of the tables in the reapportionment application presented would be improved if this change were applied. A variable having an inverse correlation with outcome can be reworded to produce a positive correlation by reversing the order of its categories.

[20] Instead of expressing the weight of each variable in terms of the phi coefficient or the estimated phi coefficient, one could conceivably use phi squared or Fisher's z transformation of phi, but these measures overemphasize high correlation variables, and they are unduly complex. See GUILFORD, *op. cit. supra* note 16, at 182 & 378.

TABLE 11–2

THE REAPPORTIONMENT CASES AND THEIR POINT VALUES

	Points for Variables				Total Points	Who Won
Cases	One	Two	Three	Four		
Colegrove	0	0	0	110	110	Defender
Dyer	200	150	132	110	592	Attacker
Magraw	200	125	132	110	597	Attacker
Asbury Park	200	125	132	0	457	Attacker
Scholle	0	125	132	0	257	Defender
W.M.C.A.	0	125	0	110	235	Defender
Tawes	0	125	132	0	257	Defender
Grills	200	125	0	0	325	Attacker
Baker	200	125	132	110	567	Attacker

11–2 shows the numerical weights for the other variables present in the cases.[21] It also shows the total points for each case.[22]

III. PREDICTING OUTCOMES

A quick perusal of Table 11–2 reveals that if the attacker of an apportionment in the next case to arise after *Baker* v. *Carr* can muster 325 points he will probably win his case, assuming he meets the above-mentioned prerequisites.[23] Likewise, if the attacker cannot muster more than 257 points he will probably lose his case, assuming the defender does not have to justify any affirmative statutory action that has made the districts more unequal. It is interesting to note that the next appor-

---

[21] All of the +.50 correlation of variable number 2 was allocated to the most favorable position on the variable (attacking a territorial apportionment). Half of the +.50 correlation was allocated to the middle position on the variable (attacking a state apportionment). As with the dichotomous variables, no points were allocated to the unfavorable position (attacking a congressional apportionment).

[22] The method presented can also handle variables that have a curvilinear correlation with decision outcomes, such as where being very high or being very low correlates positively with victory for the affirmative position, but being in the middle on the variable correlates negatively. To obtain a simple curvilinear correlation coefficient, one can put the data into a table with three columns (categories on the fact-variable) and two rows (categories on the outcome variable). Then (with the percentages totaling down to 100 percent in each column) add the percentage appearing in the top cell of the first column to the percentage in the top cell of the third column, and subtract the percentage in the top cell of the second column from this sum. The result should be allocated to the weight of cases falling in either extreme where the correlation is upright U-shaped or in neither extreme where the correlation is inverted U-shaped.

[23] See the text accompanying notes 7–9.

tionment case decided after *Baker* v. *Carr* was *Sims* v. *Frank*.[24] The predictive scheme indicated that the attacker would muster 567 points in that case, since all four variables were present, and he would thus be a winner, provided judicial consistency prevailed. On April 14, 1962, the federal district court for Alabama did decide as predicted. As new cases are decided, the correlation coefficients and cutoff levels should be recalculated to keep the predictive scheme up-to-date. If the sample sizes are large enough to give statistical significance, however, then the weights and cutoff levels need to be recalculated only occasionally.

As a further test of the predictive scheme presented, one might try to predict the second case from the first case, the third case from the first two, and so on.[25] Table 11–3 shows the cutoff levels for each prediction, the total points for each case being predicted as of the time of the prediction, the predicted winner, whether the prediction was correct, and whether an accurate prediction could have been made merely on the basis of one of the prior cases, provided that the prior case used does not conflict with another prior case.[26] The table indicates that after the first two cases a quantitative prediction could be made for six of the eight remaining cases, including *Sims* v. *Frank*.[27] Of the six cases for which a prediction could be made, all six were correctly predicted by the quantitative method, and two of the six correct predictions could not have been known from any one nonconflicting prior

---

[24] 205 F. Supp. 245 (M.D. Ala. 1962).

[25] Table 11–3 should indicate the decision in each prior case as of the time of each prediction (not just as of the time of *Baker* v. *Carr*), since the decision sometimes changes as the case moves up the appellate hierarchy. It just so happens, however, that the decision in each case in Table 11–3 was the same at the time of the next prediction as it was at the time of *Baker* v. *Carr*.

[26] For the sake of simplicity, all the calculations for Table 11–3 were made with variable number 2 dichotomized rather than trichotomized. In other words, variable 2 was reworded to read, "Was a territorial or state apportionment rather than a congressional apportionment attacked?" In general, very little extra precision in predicting is gained by trichotomizing a variable rather than dichotomizing it at some meaningful point unless the correlation is curvilinear. See note 22 *supra*. A numerical variable can be tentatively dichotomized after one winning case and one losing case have been decided by splitting the variable at a point that represents the average between the size of the variable in the winning case and the size of the variable in the losing case. It is also mathematically desirable in using this weighting scheme to have the same number of categories on all variables. GUILFORD, *op. cit. supra* note 16, at 423.

[27] 205 F. Supp. 245 (M.D. Ala. 1962). The total points in cases 5 and 9 fell between the two cutoff levels. In such a situation, one could predict the outcome corresponding to the nearest cutoff level, but such a procedure is quite inaccurate. It is inaccurate because one has no way of knowing how much of the middle area belongs above the true upper cutoff level and how much of it belongs below the true lower cutoff level until cases with total points in the middle area are decided. Note that the influence of the presence or absence of variable 4 was not calculable until after the fourth case, since the first three cases all had variable 4 present.

TABLE 11–3

Predicting Each Case from Its Prior Cases

Case Being Predicted	Basis of Prediction (case numbers)	Cut-off Levels	Total Points in the Case Being Predicted	Predicted Winner	Was the Quantitative Prediction Correct?	Could Have Been Accurately Predicted by One Nonconflicting Prior Case
1. Colgrove	None	—	—	No prior case	—	No
2. Dyer	1	—	—	No cutoff levels	—	No
3. Magraw	1–2	0–600	600	Attacker	Yes	Yes (Dyer)
4. Asbury	1–3	0–600	600	Attacker	Yes	No
5. Scholle	1–4	67–600	400	Between the cutoff levels	—	No
6. W.M.C.A.	1–5	322–522	278	Defender	Yes	No
7. Tawes	1–6	316–516	316	Defender	Yes	Yes (Scholle)
8. Grills	1–7	290–490	335	Between the cutoff levels	—	No
9. Baker	1–8	264–338	564	Attacker	Yes	Yes (Magraw or Dyer)

case.[28] The odds are 63 to 1, or about 0.02, that six correct predictions could be made purely by chance out of 6 opportunities.[29]

Partly because of coincidence and partly because of human consistency, no decision involved in Table 11–3 was inconsistent with any prior decision. In other words, no case in which the attacker won had fewer points

[28] A case can be predicted on the basis of one prior case if the case being predicted has exactly the same variables as the prior case (an all-fours prediction), if the case being predicted has the same variables plus other variables and the prior case was decided for the affirmative party (an affirmative a fortiori prediction), or if the case being predicted has less variables and no different ones and the prior case was decided for the negative party (a negative a fortiori prediction). A case cannot be predicted on the basis of one prior case if the one prior case conflicts with another prior case unless one has some system for weighting the precedent value (as contrasted to the point value) of cases. On weighting precedent value, see Nagel, *Sociometric Relations among American Courts*, 43 Southwestern Social Science Q. 136–42 & n.9 (1962).

[29] For the conservative bettor or lawyer, the empirical probabilities of correct predictions can be improved by widening the cutoff levels, but doing so decreases the proportion of cases in which a prediction can be made.

than a prior case in which the attacker lost. Likewise, no case in which the attacker lost had more points than a prior case in which the attacker won. If some of the precedents being used as a basis of a prediction are inconsistent, and adding or eliminating variables will not help, then one should draw the cutoff lines in a way that minimizes the number of inconsistent cases. Where there are two or more ways to draw the cutoff lines with the same minimum number of inconsistencies, then one should draw the cutoff lines in a way that both the winning cases with the lowest total points for the affirmative position and the losing cases with the highest total points are called inconsistencies.[30]

One can easily extend the line of predictions shown in Table 11–3 on through the numerous reapportionment cases that have been decided subsequent to *Sims* v. *Frank.* The National Municipal League has published chronologically over 15 volumes of *Court Decisions on Legislative Apportionment,* which can be used to supply the raw data. If the correlation analysis is applied through the 23rd case, all the predictions are that the attacker will win, except in two cases where the total points fell within the cutoff level. All these predictions ultimately on appeal proved to be accurate.[31] As of 1968, the variable having dominant predictive importance is the equality measurement variable, with the others reduced to relative insignificance.[32]

---

[30] If the number of cases or the number of inconsistencies is large, then a more systematic way to draw the cutoff lines would involve calculating:

$$\frac{\text{avg. total points of winning cases} + \text{avg. total points of losing cases}}{2}$$

The total points for the case immediately above this figure represents the best upper cutoff line, and the total points for the case immediately below this figure represents the best lower cutoff line.

[31] For an application of correlation analysis and related techniques to a longer line of cases, see Chapters 12 and 13, below. The addition of new variables or the subtraction of old variables as the cases increase does not affect the basic methodology.

[32] For a discussion of more sophisticated ways of measuring equality (variable 3) and of the courts reactions to the alternatives, see DIXON, DEMOCRATIC REPRESENTATION: REAPPORTIONMENT IN LAW AND POLITICS 439–55 (1968). Variable 1 became unimportant when the Supreme Court declared that Article 1 of the Constitution impliedly requires equality in federal redistricting (*Wesberry* v. *Sanders,* 367 U.S. 1, 1964), and that the Fourteenth Amendment impliedly requires equality in state redistricting, regardless what the state constitutions say (*Reynolds* v. *Sims,* 377 U.S. 567, 1964). Variable 2 became unimportant when the Supreme Court extended reapportionment to the lowest levels in the hierarchy of legislative bodies (*Avery* v. *Midland County,* 390 U.S. 474, 1968). With regard to variable 4, a recent empirical study fails to reveal statistically significant differences between state and federal courts (Beiser, *A Comparative Analysis of State and Federal Judicial Behavior: The Reapportionment Cases,* 62 AM. POL. SCI. REV. 788 [1968]).

IV. PARTIAL CORRELATION AND DISCRIMINANT ANALYSIS

To make the predictive scheme more accurate although more complicated, one can weight each variable not in terms of its simple phi coefficient but, rather, in terms of its correlation with victory or defeat when the overlapping of the other variables is statistically held constant.[33] Thus, if one were predicting the 10th case from the first 9, he would calculate the correlation between variable 1 and outcome while variables 2, 3, and 4 are held constant; the correlation between variable 2 and outcome while variables 1, 3, and 4 are held constant; and variable 3 and outcome while variables 1, 2, and 4 are held constant; and likewise with variable 4.

To calculate these partial correlation coefficients by hand is quite laborious, but electronic computer programs for doing so are available at most university and other computing centers. One merely converts each case into an IBM card by assigning a certain IBM column to each variable and punching a 0 if the variable is absent and a 1 is the variable is present. The data cards, the correlation program, and a set of parameter cards (indicating which columns are to be intercorrelated and which are to be held constant) are then fed into the computer, and shortly thereafter the requested correlation coefficients are printed out.[34] Partial correlation, however, tends to give meaningless results if any variable has a perfect 1.00 correlation with outcome or with another variable. This is likely to happen when the number of cases is small. To achieve the goals of partial correlation without the extra math or computer work, one should try to use variables that are as logically independent of each other as possible.[35]

---

[33] WALKER & LEVI, *op. cit. supra* note 17, at 341–43.

[34] If a partial correlation program is not available, one can use a regression analysis program, since the square of the partial correlation coefficient of X correlated with Y when Z is held constant equals the regression weight of X correlated with Y when Z is held constant multiplied by the regression weight of Y correlated with X when Z is held constant. *Id.* at 343. If, however, one uses a regression program rather than a partial correlation program, then instead of weighting the variables in terms of their partial correlation coefficients one can weight the variables in terms of their unstandardized regression coefficients, thereby producing approximately the same prediction result. See BLALOCK, SOCIAL STATISTICS 343–46 (1960); GUILFORD, *op. cit. supra* note 16, at 390–95; Tanenhaus, *The Supreme Court Certiorari Jurisdiction: Cue Theory,* in JUDICIAL DECISION-MAKING 111–32 (SCHUBERT ed. 1963).

[35] Stepwise computer programs are available which reduce the variable to those that have a high correlation with case outcome and a low correlation with each other before calculating partial coefficients or regression weights. What constitutes a high or low correlation can be specified by the user. The variables can also be reduced by a complicated technique called factor analysis. See GUILFORD, PSYCHOMETRIC METHODS 470–538 (1954); Kort, *Content Analysis of Judicial Opinions and Rules of Law,* in JUDICIAL DECISION-MAKING 133–97 (SCHUBERT ed. 1963).

For an even more accurate weighting scheme, especially where case outcomes are dichotomous,[36] one can use a technique related to correlation analysis, called discriminant analysis.[37] To be practical, this type of weighting scheme also requires an electronic computer. Unfortunately because of the relative newness and infrequent use of the technique, not many computing centers have available discriminant analysis programs. The author, however, can make available a copy of the University of Illinois discriminant analysis program[38] to anyone who would like a copy.[39]

V. CONCLUSION

Improved predictability in reapportionment litigation should enable the parties to plan their strategies better in this growing field of litigation. The real potentiality of the basic method presented, however, lies in the fact that such a method can be easily applied to analyzing a wide variety of cases. For each field of law analyzed, the user needs to be supplied only with the point values for the variables and the cutoff levels, both of which can be periodically up-dated by a loose-leaf service.[40] Such an analysis conceivably could have some value to such people as theoreticians who seek to understand the judicial process, legislators who are concerned with judicial reactions, judges who are concerned with stare decisis, members of the public who seek to comply with the law, as well as practitioners who are interested in aids to case prediction.

---

[36] When degrees of case outcomes are involved, one can use regression analysis (see note 32 *supra*) or multiple discriminant analysis. COOLEY & LOHNES, MULTIVARIATE PROCEDURES FOR THE BEHAVIORAL SCIENCES (1962).

[37] TINTNER, ECONOMETRICS 95–102 (1952); GUILFORD, *op. cit. supra* note 16, at 432–33. This method of case prediction was first suggested by Fisher, *The Mathematical Analysis of Supreme Court Decisions: The Use and Abuse of Quantitative Methods*, 52 AM. POL. SCI. REV. 321, 336 (1958). Ulmer also mentions having used a variation of it in Ulmer, *supra* note 4.

[38] Correlation, discriminant, regression, and factoring programs are also available from the Health Sciences Computing Facility at U.C.L.A. See BIOMEDICAL COMPUTER PROGRAMS (1964).

[39] In order to facilitate prediction where the variables involve multiple-nominal categories instead of dichotomies, the author is experimenting with the Glueck prediction techniques. See GLUECK, PREDICTING DELINQUENCY AND CRIME 18–32 (1959). Any variable involving multiple nominal categories, however can be made into one yes–no dichotomy for each category on the variable by hand or by a recoding program.

[40] See, for example, the loose-leaf services of the Jury Verdict Research Corporation of Cleveland, Ohio, reviewed in Nagel, *Statistical Prediction of Verdicts and Awards*, 63 MODERN USES OF LOGIC IN L. 135 (1963). The big defect in their analysis, however, is that they mainly deal with the effect of only one variable at a time rather than the simultaneous effect on case outcomes of a combination of relevant variables.

CHAPTER 12

Correlation Analysis Compared: Civil Liberty Cases

This chapter illustrates and systematically compares three methods for quantitatively predicting case outcomes. The three methods are correlation,[1] regression,[2] and discriminant analysis,[3] all of which involve standard social science research techniques. Two prior chapters[4] have generated requests for a study dealing with the problems involved in handling a larger number of cases and predictive variables. The present chapter is also designed to provide such a study. It does not presuppose that the reader has read the earlier chapters, although such a reading might help to clarify further some of the points made here. The cases used to illustrate the methods consist of 149 civil liberties cases decided by the United States Supreme Court from 1956 through 1960. The list of cases was obtained from a series of articles by Sidney Ulmer and Glendon Schubert.[5] Technical aspects have been eliminated from the

The author is very grateful to Dorothy Anna Shipley for allowing him to use some of the data she compiled for her bachelor's thesis, Predictive Generalizations in Civil Liberties Cases, August 1963 (in the University of Illinois Library). Thanks are also owed to John Gilbert, statistical consultant at the Behavioral Sciences Center, for his helpful comments.

[1] For further details than this chapter provides on correlation analysis, see Nagel, *Applying Correlation Analysis to Case Predictions*, 42 TEXAS L. REV. 1006 (1964) (chap. 11 *supra*); and Nagel, *Using Simple Calculations To Predict Judicial Decisions*, PRAC. LAW. (March 1961) at 68 (chap. 10 *supra*).

[2] For further details on regression analysis, see BLALOCK, SOCIAL STATISTICS 273–358 (1960); GUILFORD, FUNDAMENTAL STATISTICS IN PSYCHOLOGY AND EDUCATION 365–72, 390–434 (1956).

[3] For further details on discriminant analysis, see COOLEY & LOHNES, MULTI-VARIATE PROCEDURES FOR THE BEHAVIORAL SCIENCES 116–33 (1962); TINTNER, ECONOMETRICS 95–102 (1952).

[4] See the articles cited in note 1 *supra*.

[5] Schubert, *The 1960 Term of the Supreme Court—A Psychological Analysis*, 56 AM. POL. SCI. REV. 90, 98 (1962); Ulmer, *A Note on Attitudinal Consistency in the United States Supreme Court*, 22 INDIAN J. POL. SCI. 195, 201 (1961); Ulmer,

body of this chapter, leaving a simple explanation that should be sufficient to enable the nontechnical reader to employ the methods in his legal research.

I. THE METHODS

A. THE BASIC PROCEDURE

All three methods rely on the relationship between case outcomes and various predictor variables. In this article, the outcome to be predicted is whether a given civil liberties case will be decided in the direction of narrowing civil liberties or in the direction of broadening civil liberties. The civil liberties cases deal with freedom of speech and religion, civil liberty aspects of criminal procedure, and equal protection under law. The predictor variables relate to the law, evidence, prior events, and other matters relevant to the cases, and are set out in Table 12–1.

Each of the three methods applies a variation of the following formula to the individual case in order to predict its outcome:

$$S = (W_1 \cdot X_1) + (W_2 \cdot X_2) + \ldots + (W_n \cdot X_n).$$

In the formula, X_1 represents the number of units of variable 1 that are present in the case being predicted; X_2 represents the number of units of variable 2 present; and so on to X_n, the last variable. If a variable provides for only two degrees of units (e.g., absent versus present), its X can have only a value of zero or one. The W_1 represents the numerical prediction weight or importance of variable 1; W_2 represents the weight of variable 2; and so on to W_n, the last weight. The S represents the score obtained by summing the WX products in the formula.[6] If two possible case outcomes are involved (e.g., narrowing civil liberties versus broadening), a summation score less than a certain amount (the cutoff level) indicates a narrowing decision is more likely to be reached; a score greater than a certain amount indicates a broadening decision is more likely to be reached.

Scaling Judicial Cases, 4 AM. BEHAV. SCI. 31, 32 (April 1961); Ulmer, *The Analysis of Behavior Patterns on the United States Supreme Court*, 22 J. POL. 629, 649 (1960); and Ulmer, *Supreme Court Behavior and Civil Rights*, 13 W. POL. Q. 288, 297–99 (1960).

[6] S is a general symbol. The S for correlation analysis is symbolized T, and the S for discriminant analysis is symbolized Z. The S for regression analysis plus the *a*-coefficient described later is symbolized Y.

TABLE 12–1

THE WEIGHTS FOR 8 VARIABLES IN 149 CIVIL LIBERTIES CASES

Variables of the Cases	Weights of the Variables		
	Correla-tion	Regres-sion	Discrimi-nant
1. Having been decided negatively in the lower court rather than positively	.07	.23	.61
2. Having originated in the South, West, or District of Columbia, rather than the East or Midwest	.35	.32	.85
3. Involving state, local, private, or military action rather than federal civilian action ..	.11	.20	.55
4. Mainly involving legislative, police, or administrative action rather than chief executive, regulatory agency, or judicial action	.20	.12	.31
5. Mainly involving 1st, 4th, 6th, or 8th Amendments rather than Article 1, or 5th or 14th Amendments	.19	.24	.64
6. Mainly involving free speech or equal protection rather than freedom of religion or criminal procedure matters	.13	.04	.11
7. Mainly involving murder, theft, fraud, assault, or no crime rather than contempt or other crimes	.21	.15	.39
8. Involving amicus curiae briefs by a combination of pressure groups or none rather than just one pressure group	.19	.31	.83
Minimum S score .... (equals 0 if minimum X always equals 0)	0	0	0
Maximum S score .... (equals sum of weights if maximum X always equals 1)	1.45	1.61	4.30
a-coefficient		−.49	
Cutoff score .... (equals average S Score of the cases for correlation and discriminant analysis; equals .5 for regression analysis if outcome is a 0 vs. 1 dichotomy)	.859	.500	2.734

B. THE RAW DATA

The three methods differ mainly in their manners of calculating the weights of the variables employed in the above formula. All three methods, however, require the same kinds of data in order to calculate the weights. The data consist of how each one of a set of past cases is positioned with regard to the outcome and with regard to each of the variables thought to be relevant for prediction.[7] The categories on the outcome variable and on each of the predictor variables should either be dichotomies or be capable of being arranged in a meaningful ascending or descending order. Region of the litigation-provoking incident (e.g., East, Midwest, West, South) is a variable that generally must be dichotomized (e.g., East and Midwest versus West and South).[8] Age of the defendant is a variable that can be arranged in equal 1-year or 10-year categories.

In correlation analysis, the values of the predictor and outcome variables should range only from zero (absent) to one (present), unless a variation called partial correlation analysis is used. In regression analysis, both the predictor and outcome variables can have any range, including millions, decimals, and negative numbers. In discriminant analysis, the predictor variables again can have any range, but the outcome variable is usually dichotomized (zero and one), although discriminant analysis can, if necessary, handle more than two groups.

C. Assigning Weights to the Variables

1. Correlation Analysis. For the weight of a given predictor variable, correlation analysis uses the correlation coefficient (symbolized r) between the variable and the outcome. When both the predictor variable and the outcome variable provide for only two categories or degrees apiece, the correlation coefficient is approximately equal to (1) the percentage of cases *positive* on the predictor variable that are also positive on the outcome variable minus (2) the percentage of cases *negative* on the predictor variable that are positive on the outcome variable.[9] Correlation analysis is simpler but somewhat less accurate than the other two methods. It is simple enough to be readily usable without a computer,

---

[7] Nothing practical is to be gained by reducing the variables to their underlying factors, since one can more efficiently predict with the variables themselves. Fruchter, Introduction to Factor Analysis (1954).

[8] *But see* notes 14 and 15 *infra* and the accompanying text.

[9] See Nagel, *Testing Empirical Generalizations in Legal Research*, 15 J. Legal Ed. 365, 372 (1963) (chap. 2 *supra*). One is led to erroneous results if one merely uses the percentage of cases *positive* on the predictor variable that are also positive on the outcome variable (without considering the percentage of cases *negative* on the predictor variable that are also positive on the outcome variable) as was done in Jury Verdict Research Corp., How To Predict Personal Injury Verdicts 26 (1963). Their prediction formula, in effect, is $S = (P_1/P) (P_2/P) \cdots (P_n/P) (P)$, where P equals the percentage of cases won by the affirmative position in the total sample and where $P_1, P_2, \ldots$ and P_n equal the percent of cases won by the affirmative position when variable 1, 2, . . . or n is present. S thus supposedly equals a percentage or empirical probability of victory. This approach is inconsistent with the Bayes probability theorem. See Mosteller, Rourke, & Thomas, Probability with Statistical Applications 143–50 (1961).

although a desk calculator would be helpful. But, if one has access to a computer, it would generally be wasteful to do a less accurate correlation analysis instead of a regression or discriminant analysis. The correlation analysis method was designed for the practicing lawyer or legal scholar who does not have easy access to a computer.

2. Regression Analysis. For a given weight, regression analysis uses what is called the unstandardized partial regression weight (symbolized *b*) between the predictor variable and the outcome. The user of this method need not know how to calculate a *b*-weight, because standard computer programs are available at most computing centers and can quickly and accurately calculate the *b*-weights for a set of variables in a set of cases. It is enough to know that, given the data, regression analysis will yield predictions that statistically minimize error in what statisticians call a "least squares sense." This roughly means that, if each case were plotted as a point on a multidimensional graph, with the outcome on one axis and the predictor variables on the other axes, then the regression weights would determine a line through these points such that the sum of the squares of the deviations from the points to the line would be minimized.

As a highly simplified example of how regression analysis assigns a weight to a variable, assume one is trying to use regression analysis to predict the height (the outcome variable) of a specific person (the case at bar) from his width (the predictor variable). Suppose further that the only basis for prediction is the height and the width of three prior persons (the precedents). What regression analysis, in effect, does by numerical formulas is draw a two-dimensional graph, with various units of height (starting with zero) marked on the left side of the graph and various units of width marked on the bottom. The height and width of each prior person is then shown as a dot drawn over from the appropriate marking on the left side and up from the appropriate marking at the bottom. Then, one slanted line (called a regression line) is drawn as close to all three dots as is possible, with overall proximity measured by the sum of the distances squared from each point to the line. If a right triangle is drawn anywhere along this regression line so that all or part of the line forms the diagonal side, the *b*-weight is the ratio between the length of the vertical side of the triangle and the horizontal side of the triangle. The closer this ratio is to 1.00, the closer is the relation between the two variables. The *a*-coefficient represents the number of units up from the O point on the graph (i.e., the intersection of the left side and the bottom) to the point where the regression line crosses the left side of the graph.

3. Discriminant Analysis. For a given weight, discriminant analysis uses a value (symbolized k) that maximizes the difference between (1) the S scores of the cases decided in a positive direction and (2) the S scores of the cases decided in a negative direction. Computer programs for discriminant analysis are now increasingly available at computing centers. The discriminant approach generally provides the most accurate predictions in the sense of quantity right divided by predictions made. However, when all the predictor variables and the outcome variable have been dichotomized, discriminant analysis produces practically the same predictions as does regression analysis or a variation of correlation analysis, called partial correlation analysis.[10]

Again, a highly simplified example will serve to illustrate the method of assigning a weight to a variable. Suppose one is trying to use discriminant analysis to predict the sex of a person from his or her width. As before, assume that the only bases of prediction are the sex and width of three prior persons. What discriminant analysis, in effect, does by numerical formulas is to find a number (called a discriminate weight) by which to multiply the width of each prior male. The average of these products is then determined. The width of each female is also multiplied by the number, and the average of those products is determined. The number or weight is ideal for discriminant analysis if there is no other number that will produce a wider divergence between the average of the male products and the average of the femal products.

To use a computer program for regression or discriminant analysis, one punched card per case is needed, unless the number of variables necessitates the use of more. Certain columns on each card should be set aside for each variable. Thus, if hole 1 is punched on column 12 of the card corresponding to case 23, this punch may indicate that a certain variable was present. If hole 3 is punched on column 19 of the same card, this punch may indicate that case 23 fell into interval 3 on the amount of medical expenses claimed by the plaintiff. Once the cards are punched by a typewriter-like keypunch, the personnel at the particular computing center being used can quickly inform the user how to combine his deck of data cards with a deck of standard program cards in order to obtain the kind of printed output shown in the columns of Table 12–1.

Both regression and discriminant analysis provide weights for each variable, while the other variables are statistically held constant or partialed out. Thus, in regression and discriminant analysis (but not ordinary correlation analysis) the weight of a given variable depends on what

---

[10] BLALOCK, *op. cit. supra* note 2, at 343–46; Rulon, *Distinctions Between Discriminant and Regression Analysis,* 21 HARV. EDUCATION REV. 80, 89 (1951).

other variables are included. If two similar variables are included, at least one will have a lower weight than it would have had if only that one had been included.

D. Determining the Cutoff Level

The three methods also differ with regard to how they determine what S score is likely to lead to a negative decision and what S score is likely to lead to a positive decision. Both correlation analysis and discriminant analysis use the average S of the cases as a cutoff score. Any future case having an S greater than this average is likely to be decided in a positive direction; similarly, if the S value is less than the determined average, the case is likely to be decided in a negative direction.[11]

In regression analysis, if the S plus an a-coefficient is greater than or equal to 0.5 (i.e., closer to 1 than to 0), then a positive decision is more likely; the converse is true if the S plus a is less than 0.5 (i.e., closer to 0 than to 1). Since any computer program that does regression analysis will also supply the appropriate a-coefficient, the object of regression analysis is to predict the outcome (Y) value, which can be 0 or 1 if the outcome has been dichotomized. If the outcome value were height, regression analysis would give an answer in inches or feet, depending on the unit of measurement used, whereas correlation and discriminant analysis would give an answer that would be a purely abstract number above or below the cutoff between being tall or short.

II.   THE ILLUSTRATION

A. Dichotomizing the Variables

Table 12–1 shows the predictor variables that were used, the correlation, regression, and discriminant weights for each variable, and the cutoff scores for each method.[12] For the sake of simplicity, each vari-

---

[11] In Nagel, *Applying Correlation Analysis to Case Prediction,* 42 Texas L. Rev. 1006, 1015 (1946) (chap. 11 *supra*), the cutoff score was calculated by adding the average S of the cases that were decided in a positive direction to the average S of the cases that were decided in a negative direction and by dividing this sum by two. Merely determining the average S of all the cases is simpler, and the difference in accuracy is very slight. Likewise, with a large sample of cases it is unnecessary to have an upper cutoff score (equal to the S score of the case immediately above the average S) and a lower cutoff score (equal to the S score of the case immediately below the average S).

[12] The discriminant weights and the discriminant cutoff score were originally in thousandths, but they were multiplied by 100 to eliminate the zeros to the right of the decimal point. The cutoff scores are carried to one decimal place more than the weights so as to prevent some summated S scores from exactly equaling the cutoff scores.

able was dichotomized by collapsing together into one category the categories in which a relatively high percentage of the cases were decided in a positive direction, and by collapsing together into a second category the categories in which a relatively high percentage of the cases were decided in a negative direction. Most computing centers have cross-tabulation programs that will quickly indicate the percentage of cases decided in a positive direction for each category on each variable, although these percentages can be calculated by hand. One should also attempt to create categories that are internally homogeneous and externally different from each other, regardless of their relation with outcome. The dichotomous categories are also more useful if they contain approximately equal quantities of cases.

If there are N categories on a predictor variable, the quantity of ways in which the variable can be dichotomized can be readily calculated by applying the formula for determining the number of combinations that can be made out of N things taken J at a time.[13] For example, if there are 6 categories on a variable, the 6 can be taken 5 at a time in 6 ways, 4 at a time in 15 ways, and 3 at a time in 20 ways (half of which produce duplicate dichotomies). Thus, a variable that has 6 categories can be dichotomized into 6 plus 15 plus 10, or 31 different ways. Only one dichotomy per variable can be fed into the correlation analysis. However, all the dichotomies can be fed into a regression or discriminant analysis if the computer program is capable of initially taking that many input variables and if the program is capable of throwing out the dichotomies it determines to be weak in relative predictive power. It is more efficient, however, to not feed the regression or discriminant analysis any dichotomies that are obviously relatively weak.

If desired, the dichotomizing process can be avoided by using only variables that are natural dichotomies (e.g., sex) or that have ascending or descending categories (e.g., social class) or by using the Glueck prediction method, which is, in effect, a method for weighting categories on predictor variables rather than a method for weighting the variables themselves.[14] One can also avoid the dichotomizing process with the correlation method by ranking the categories from the one having the highest percentage of victories for the affirmative outcome down to the one having the lowest percentage. The X value of a case with regard

---

[13] The formula is $N!/J!\ (N\text{-}J)!$ where $N!$ (i.e., N factorial) means 1 times 2 times 3 on up to N, and likewise with $J!$ ADAMS, INTERMEDIATE ALGEBRA 295, 336–38 (1960).

[14] The Glueck prediction method is discussed in GLUECK & GLUECK, PREDICTING DELINQUENCY AND CRIME 18–32 (1959) and in Nagel, *Judicial Prediction and Analysis from Empirical Probability Tables*, 41 IND. L. J. 403 (1966) (Chap. 13 *infra*) which compares and discusses in detail the nondichotomizing prediction methods briefly mentioned in this paragraph and elsewhere.

to such a variable then equals $(C\text{-}R) \div (C\text{-}1)$, where C equals the number of categories (e.g., region was previously mentioned with four categories) and R equals the rank of the category in which the case is located. For example, if the region variable with four categories has a correlation weight of 0.11 with outcome and if the categories are associated with outcome in the order of East, West, Midwest, and South, then a case from the East would receive an X in the basic summation formula equal to $(4\text{-}1) \div (4\text{-}1)$ or 1. A case from the West would receive an X of $(4\text{-}2) \div (4\text{-}1)$ or 0.67; a case from the Midwest would get a 0.33; and a case from the South would get a 0. The basic summation formula involves summing the product of the W and X for each variable in order to determine the total points of each case.[15] It should also be mentioned that the dichotomizing process can even be avoided while the regression or discriminant method is used by substituting for the value of X the percentage of cases falling into the affirmative outcome position for each category on each variable.

B. INAPPLICABLE AND MISSING INFORMATION

The weights and cutoff scores in Table 12–1 were calculated on the basis of 149 of the 175 civil liberties cases on which data were gathered.[16] The original group of 175 cases had to be reduced to 166, because 9 of the cases could not be objectively classified as having broadened or narrowed civil liberties. The 166 cases were then reduced to 149, because for 17 cases complete information was not available or the categories were inapplicable for some of the variables. As an alternative to eliminating all 17 cases, one or more variables could have been eliminated, or missing information for a case could have been replaced with the average category on the variable involved, or the category "unknown" could have been collapsed into a positive or negative category, depending

---

[15] An appropriate correlation coefficient in this context is a contingency coefficient. SIEGEL, NON-PARAMETRIC STATISTICS FOR THE BEHAVIORAL SCIENCES 196–202 (1956). To give this coefficient a 0 to 1.00 range, it should be divided by 0.71, because it can be shown algebraically that when the outcome variable has been dichotomized, 0.71 is the maximum contingency coefficient that can be obtained. Another appropriate coefficient in this context is Cramer's multinominal coefficient. CRAMER, MATHEMATICAL METHODS OF STATISTICS 282 (1946).

[16] The 175 cases do not contain all the civil liberties cases decided by the Supreme Court from 1956 through 1960, because the articles from which the list was obtained excluded unanimous cases (see note 5 *supra*), although a small, roughly random sample of unanimous civil liberties cases was found in the court reports and added to the original list bringing it to 175 cases. This incompleteness, however, does not affect the nature of the methods described in this article, and it probably does not substantially affect the weights shown in Table 12–1. Nevertheless, if additional unanimous cases had been used, the rate of correct predictions would probably have been substantially higher, since the outcome of unanimous cases is generally easier to predict than is the outcome of sharply divided cases.

on the percentage of positive decisions among the cases falling into
the unknown category on the variable. The technique chosen for each
variable should be the technique that will maximize the sample size,
will retain powerful variables and nonduplicative variables, and will
make no unreasonable assumptions.[17]

C. Why the Variables Seem To Be Relevant

Variable 1 seems to be relevant because of a tendency by the Supreme
Court to use its certiorari power more to reverse than to affirm lower
court decisions. Variable 2 may be relevant because civil liberties violations may be greater in the South and West and because the Supreme
Court may apply higher standards to the District of Columbia. Likewise,
civil liberties violations may be greater at the state, local, private, and
military levels than at the federal civilian level (explaining variable
3) and greater in the legislative, police, and other administrative spheres
than in the executive, regulatory agency, or judicial spheres (explaining
variable 4); or it may be that the Supreme Court has a more negative
bias toward the state (etc.) levels and legislative (etc.) spheres in comparison with the federal (etc.) levels and executive (etc.) spheres of
decision making.

Variables 5 and 6 are closely related, although Fourteenth Amendment
cases might cover all the categories in variable 6. Apparently, the Supreme
Court was more solicitous of violations of free speech and equal protection
than of violations of freedom of religion and criminal procedure during
the base period. When a crime was involved, it seems that the pro-
civil liberties position was more likely to win when the crime was more
serious and the defendant had more at stake. The last variable may
be relevant because the most important civil liberties cases in terms
of the interests at stake have the most amicus curiae briefs filed, and
nearly all are filed by pro-civil liberties groups. When only one pressure
group was involved, it was generally the American Civil Liberties Union,
attempting to influence a criminal procedure case.

D. Applying the Results of the Analysis

To illustrate how the data in Table 12–1 are applied, take the 1954
school desegregation case of *Brown* v. *Board of Education*[18] as an

---

[17] By "powerful variable" is meant a predictor variable that has a high correlation with the outcome variable. By "nonduplicative variable" is meant a variable that
has a low correlation with the other predictor variables. Good variables, in addition
to being powerful and non-duplicative, should be ones on which data can generally
be found previous to the making of the decision being predicted.

[18] 347 U.S. 483 (1954). Since *Brown* was decided prior to 1956, it was not one of
the cases used to calculate the weights.

example. Applying the formula previously described for correlation analysis, *Brown* had all the variables present except variable 5, giving it a summation score of (.07) (1) + (.35) (1) + (.11) (1) + (.20) (1) + (.19) (0) + (.13) (1) + (.21) (1) + (.19) (1), which equals 1.26 out of a maximum of 1.45 and a minimum of 0. Since this summation score exceeds the cutoff score of 0.859, one would predict that *Brown* would be decided in a broadening direction, as it unanimously was. Similarly, *Brown* gets a score of 1.37 using the regression weights, and this S plus the *a*-coefficient of −.49 exceeds the 0.500 cutoff score. Likewise, *Brown* gets a discriminant S of 3.66, which is greater than the 2.734 cutoff score.

III. THE UTILITY OF QUANTITATIVE CASE PREDICTION

Table 12–2 indicates that 95 percent of the cases like *Brown* having a discriminant S that falls into the interval 3.65 to 4.20 were decided in favor of the broadening position. Knowing the rough probability of victory in cases before the Supreme Court might be helpful in rationing scarce resources or revising the briefs of a law firm, a pressure group, or the solicitor general's office, although even if one has a case that falls into the extreme intervals in Table 12–2, it may still be worth participating in an appeal if the gain to be achieved in a victory is enough to offset the low probability of victory, or if some special characteristic is present that indicates the probability of victory is much higher than calculated (e.g., the other side had no standing to sue).

The seven intervals in Table 12–2 all contain as equal a quantity of cases as is possible, in spite of many tied scores and the fact that 149 is not evenly divisible by 7. A more detailed table could be created, using more than seven intervals, although the denominator of the percentages may become too small to give meaningful percentages. Theoretically, as many intervals or classes as there are combinations of characteristics among the cases could be provided.[19] A similar table and similar intervals could likewise be created for the regression scores or for the correlation scores. If the variables, the prediction method,

---

[19] For each combination, one could also indicate a predicted percentage of victory (as well as an actual percentage) by applying the regression formula with the *a*-coefficient. See Tanenhaus, Muraskin, Rosen, & Shick, *The Supreme Court Certiorari Jurisdiction—Cue Theory*, in JUDICIAL DECISION-MAKING 111, 129 (SCHUBERT ed. 1963). As a simpler alternative, one could create a single regression equation from the data contained in a table such as Table 12.2. GUILFORD, *op. cit. supra* note 2, at 365–72. The data shown there, for instance, yields the equation $P = -.36 + .33\ S$, where P is the probability of victory for the broadening position and S is the summation score of the case being predicted. Such an equation, however, is a summarizing device; thus, it may lose some of the detail provided by the percentages in Table 12–2, especially if the percentages ascend unevenly rather than in a smooth incline.

TABLE 12–2

PERCENTAGE OF VICTORY AT VARIOUS LEVELS OF DISCRIMINANT SCORES

Interval of Discriminant Scores	Number of Cases in Interval	Percentage of Cases Decided in Broadening Direction
.61 to 1.84	19	11%
1.86 to 2.20	22	23
2.38 to 2.69	21	48
2.70 to 2.83	23	48
2.85 to 3.24	22	68
3.26 to 3.56	23	78
3.65 to 4.20	19	95

and the clerical work were perfect, then all the intervals up to a score of 2.734 (the cutoff score) would have 0 percent of their cases decided in a broadening direction, and all the intervals beyond 2.734 would have 100 percent of their cases so decided.

"Predicting" cases from which the weights were calculated is, of course, really postdicting. It is, however, interesting to note that, given the variables and cases used, the correlation method correctly postdicted 104 cases, or 70 percent of the 149 cases; the regression analysis correctly postdicted 109, or 73 percent; and the discriminant analysis was correct on 111 cases, or 74 percent of the 149. If a method cannot postdict reasonably well, it is unlikely to predict reasonably well.

By chance alone, one could accurately predict only approximately 75 cases (or 50 percent). By always predicting the most frequent outcome (which was a broadening decision), one could accurately predict only 79 cases or 53 percent. Obtaining 111 correct postdictions and 38 incorrect ones, as the discriminant analysis did, could occur purely by chance only about once in a billion times.[20] A similar accuracy probability can be determined for the correlation and regression analysis postdictions.[21]

---

[20] Such a probability can be determined by calculating $(111-38)^2/149$ and then reading the probability corresponding to this quotient in the first row of a chi-square table. GUILFORD, *op. cit. supra* note 2, at 238, 540. If the above quotient goes beyond the maximum of the chi-square table, then determine the square root of this quotient and read the probability corresponding to this square root from a large normal-curve table. *Id.* at 534.

[21] If the discriminant analysis were used on the 149 cases and flipping a coin were used on the 26 eliminated cases, then approximately 124 cases (i.e., 111 plus 13) or 72 percent of the 175 would be postdicted correctly. One can, of course, improve on the coin-flipping technique by predicting a broadening outcome on the 26 eliminated cases or by replacing the missing information for 17 of the 26 cases with the average category or other reasonable estimate on the predictor variables involved.

The postdiction power, and thus the prediction power, might have been increased even further if the author had used additional or different variables, a narrower set of cases, a greater proportion of unanimous cases, or more precise categorization. Nevertheless, this demonstration allows the conclusion that the use of quantitative prediction of court cases *plus* traditional prediction techniques is probably better than the use of the traditional alone.

CHAPTER 13

Empirical Probability Tables:
International Dispute Cases

A previous chapter [1] described how some statistical techniques could be applied to synthesizing judicial precedents and to predicting the outcomes of future cases. For simplicity of presentation, the characteristics or variables in the precedent cases were made into either–or dichotomies. For example, the region of the country where the litigation-provoking incident occurred was dichotomized to read "originated in (1) the South, West, or District of Columbia, rather than (2) the East or Midwest." It is the purpose of this chapter to describe some related techniques that are particularly applicable to working with variables that consist of more than two nonnumerical categories. The present techniques represent an improvement not only in broadened applicability but also in predictive power, simplicity, and in utility for building a behavioral science of law. The article presupposes no prior reading, and technical matters have been relegated to the footnotes and to an appendix.

A second purpose of this chapter is to emphasize that the quantitative processing of cases can be useful to understanding why a set of cases was decided the way it was as well as to predicting future decisions. "Prediction" involves knowing how a case or entity will be positioned on a decision or dependent variable by knowing (1) how it is usually

---

The author is very grateful to Martin Goodman for allowing him to use some of the data he compiled for his bachelor's thesis, The United States as a Party in International Law Disputes, 1964 (in the University of Illinois Library). The author is also grateful to John Gilbert, the statistical consultant at the Center for Advanced Study in the Behavioral Sciences, for his many helpful comments made while the author was a fellow at the Center. Thanks for helpful comments are also owed to the members of the 1965 seminar on judicial prediction at the U.C.L.A. Law-Science Research Center.

[1] Nagel, *Predicting Court Cases Quantitatively*, 63 MICH. L. REV. 1411 (1965) (chap. 12 *supra*).

positioned, (2) what the trends over time are with regard to its position-ing, *or* (3) how it is positioned on an independent variable. "Analysis" or "understanding" involves knowing what facts or independent variables are relevant to making a prediction and how much they are relevant, especially when other intervening variables are equalized among the cases or entities. Too many quantitative case content studies in the past have perhaps overemphasized prediction at the expense of analysis.[2]

The set of cases used to illustrate the methodology consists of 137 disputes, involving international relations in which the United States was a party. These 137 cases represent all cases of the above type included in four leading international law casebooks.[3] The field of in-ternational law was used because of its potential social importance and because it is an important field of law that has had almost no quantitative analysis. The outcome to be predicted in these illustrative cases is whether the United States will lose or win. In the sample of 137 cases, the United States won 65 percent of the time.

I.   HOW TO USE EMPIRICAL PROBABILITY TABLES

Tables 13–1 and 13–2 are empirical probability tables in that they show for given sets of cases what percentage of the cases actually resulted in victory for the United States. For example, in the set of 53 cases mentioned at the top of Table 13–1 in which United States domestic law was the main body of law being applied, the United States won 85 percent of the time. If winning or losing a case were like flipping a coin, the a priori or the by-chance probability of victory as contrasted to the empirical probability would always be 50 percent. A priori prob-abilities, however, have little value in judicial prediction or analysis unless they are used to determine how much an empirical probability or other statistic deviates from chance.

In Table 13–1, each of the seven variables or characteristics on which the cases are positioned is designated by an arabic numeral. Each of the categories or positions on the variables is designated by a small letter. Only categories into which some of the 137 cases fell are included in Table 13–1. Thus, on variable 6 relating to the industrial power of the opponent of the United States one could provide a category for cases in which the opponent had greater industrial power than the

---

[2] This point is also made by Theodore Becker in *Judicial Structure and Its Func-tioning in Society: New Approaches to Teaching and Research in Public Law*, 30 J. POL. 302 at 317 (1967); and in *The Fall and Rise of Political Scientific Jurispru-dence: Its Relevance to Contemporary Legal Concerns*, 45 N. CAR. L. REV. 142 at 646 (1967); and by Lon Fuller in *An Afterword: Science and the Judicial Process*, 79 HARV. L. REV. 1551 (1966).

[3] BISHOP, INTERNATIONAL LAW (1952); HUDSON, INTERNATIONAL LAW (1951); KATZ & BREWSTER, INTERNATIONAL TRANSACTIONS & RELATIONS (1960); ORFIELD & RE, INTERNATIONAL LAW (1955).

United States had, but there were no such cases in the sample of 137, although a larger and more historically oriented sample might have had such cases. The categories are supposed to be mutually exclusive so that no case can fall into more than one category on the same variable. The variables in Table 13–1 are arranged in the order of the correlation weight (symbolized r) that was assigned to each variable by a method that will be described shortly. The categories on each variable are arranged in the order of their respective victory percentages.

A. For Prediction Purposes

Table 13–2 shows the percentage of cases decided in favor of the United States when the cases are grouped into seven approximately equal sets, depending on what summation score each case has received. To calculate an unweighted summation score for a given case, one merely determines into what category the case falls on each of the seven variables, and then sums the seven corresponding empirical probabilities or percentages.[4]

For example, in 1949 a creditor of the I. G. Farben Company brought suit in Switzerland to stop the confiscation of I. G. Farben's Swiss assets by the United States and the Allied Powers unless payment were made to I. G. Farben's legitimate creditors.[5] In terms of the seven variables in Table 13–1, the case involves the domestic law of another country ($P = .25$), the U.S. seeking reparation ($P = 0$),[6] a non-British foreign court ($P = .33$), the U.S. taking a position that neither favors the creditor nor the debtor ($P = .61$), no civil liberty interest ($P = .65$), a noncountry opponent of the U.S. ($P = .70$), and a resident of a foreign country as the plaintiff ($P = .73$). The sum of these percentages is 3.27. If Tables 13–1 and 13–2 were available prior to the I. G. Farben decision, one would say that the case had less than a .22 probability of being decided in favor of the United States, as is indicated in the top row of Table 13–2. The case, incidentally, was decided against the position of the United States.[7]

---

[4] To make Table 13–1 more usable, it should be supplemented by more detailed descriptions of the categories so as to make the positioning of future cases easier and more objective. Because of the methodological nature of this article, the full substantive details are not provided here, although some elaboration is made at various points in this article. One can find greater substantive detail in the bachelor's thesis mentioned above, which is available on loan from the University of Illinois Library.

[5] German Assets in Switzerland (I. G. Farben) Case, 45 Schweizerische Juristen-Zeitung 341 (1949).

[6] Where a category has a victory percentage of 0 or 100, one should check the relevant judicial opinions and legislation to determine whether the judges or legislators have indicated that cases in that category are always supposed to be decided in a certain direction, regardless how the cases are positioned on the other variables.

[7] The unweighted summation method is essentially the same as the prediction system used by Sheldon and Eleanor Glueck for predicting delinquency and other forms of criminal behavior. Glueck & Glueck, Predicting Delinquency and Crime 18–32 (1959).

TABLE 13-1

THE EMPIRICAL PROBABILITY OF VICTORY FOR THE UNITED STATES FOR
EACH CATEGORY ON EACH VARIABLE

Variables, Weights, and Categories (Arranged in rank order)	Quantity of Cases in Category	Percent of Cases Won by U.S. in Category
1. Main Source of Law ($r = .35, k = .24$)		
a) U.S. domestic law	53	85%
b) International law and custom	63	56
c) Treaty	17	47
d) Domestic law of other country	4	25
2. Main Subject Matter and U.S. Position ($r = .30, k = .27$)		
a) National territory and U.S. seeking change	3	100
b) National territory and U.S. seeking status quo	1	100
c) Jurisdiction and U.S. seeking it	26	85
d) Hostilities between countries and U.S. repelling interference	6	67
e) Diplomatic or consular intercourse and U.S. seeking redress	3	67
f) Individual in international law and U.S. seeking curtailment of his rights (e.g., deportation and alien rights)	26	65
g) Responsibility of other country asserted by U.S. generally for damages	17	65
h) Individual in international law and U.S. seeking to expand or maintain his rights (e.g., U.S. representing citizen in suit)	20	60
i) Treaty and U.S. seeking broad definition	10	60
j) Diplomatic and consular intercourse and redress sought from U.S.	2	50
k) Responsibility of U.S. asserted generally for damages	15	47
l) Treaty and U.S. seeking narrow definition	7	43
m) Hostilities between countries and U.S. seeking to interfere or obtain reparations	1	0
3. Decision-Making Tribunal ($r = .27, k = .17$)		
a) U.S. Supreme Court	41	76
b) Lower federal court	32	69
c) Ad hoc tribunals	56	61
d) British court	2	50
e) Non-British foreign court	3	33
f) Hague	3	0
4. Economic Interests and U.S. Position ($r = .24, k = .25$)		
a) U.S. liberal in antitrust cases	9	100
b) U.S. liberal in debtor–creditor cases	3	100
c) U.S. conservative in business v. labor cases	1	100
d) No economic interests involved or U.S. position neutral	119	61
e) U.S. conservative in debtor–creditor cases	5	60
5. Civil Liberty Interests and U.S. Position ($r = .23, k = .38$)		
a) U.S. liberal in noncriminal procedure matters	4	100
b) U.S. liberal in criminal procedure	6	83
c) U.S. conservative in noncriminal procedure matters	10	80
d) No civil liberty interest involved or U.S. position neutral	99	65
e) U.S. conservative in criminal procedure	16	44
6. Industrial Power of U.S. Opponent ($r = .21, k = .20$)		
a) Same	6	100
b) Not countries	70	70
c) Less	66	56

TABLE 13–1–*Cont.*

Variables, Weights, and Categories (Arranged in rank order)	Quantity of Cases in Category	Percent of Cases Won by U.S. in Category
7. Nature of Plaintiff ($r = .19, k = .34$)		
a) State in U.S.	1	100
b) Alien in U.S.	10	80
c) Resident of foreign country	11	73
d) U.S. itself	75	68
e) U.S. citizen	14	57
f) Business firm	18	50
f) Business firm	8	50
g) Other country	18	50

TABLE 13–2

THE EMPIRICAL PROBABILITY OF VICTORY FOR THE UNITED STATES FOR
EACH INTERVAL OF SUMMATION SCORES

Interval of Summation Scores	Number of Cases in Interval	Percentage of Cases Decided in Favor of the U.S.
I. Unweighted Scores		
3.27 to 4.17	18	22%
4.18 to 4.31	19	37
4.32 to 4.41	21	62
4.42 to 4.61	19	68
4.62 to 4.76	20	75
4.79 to 5.03	20	85
5.05 to 5.84	20	100
II. Weighted Scores		
.903 to 1.112	19	16%
1.127 to 1.156	19	42
1.158 to 1.177	20	60
1.179 to 1.222	21	62
1.223 to 1.263	20	85
1.266 to 1.347	20	90
1.348 to 1.580	18	100

For a more accurate prediction method, one can sum the products of each percentage times the discriminant weight (symbolized k) of each variable instead of merely summing the percentages. Using that alternative, the I. G. Farben case would receive a summation score of $(.24) \cdot (.25) + (.27) \cdot (0) + (.17) \cdot (.33)$ and so on summing to .903. According to Table 13–2, if an international dispute case like those in the sample of 137 has a weighted summation score of .903 the United States has less than a 16 percent chance of winning. If the score were 1.130, the United States would have between a .16 probability and a .42 probability of winning.

If all 137 cases are given weighted summation scores and are listed in rank order, then predicting a victory for the United States in all cases with a score greater than 1.157 (and a defeat in all cases with a lower score) would have resulted in 105 accurate predictions and 32 inaccurate ones. A cutoff score of 1.157 represents the best cutoff from the point of view of minimizing inaccurate predictions of victory or defeat. If the unweighted scores and a cutoff based on them had been used, 32 inaccurate predictions would have also resulted, although weighting the variables normally improves predictability, especially if there are only a few variables or only a few categories per variable.[8]

B. For Analytic Purposes

In addition to being potentially useful for prediction purposes, an empirical probability table like Table 13–1 can perhaps be even more useful for analyzing or understanding why the cases in a group were decided the way they were. A good predictive method is generally a good analytic method, although not necessarily. An example of a conflict between the two perspectives is a prediction method based on predicting the most frequently occurring outcome. If, for instance, the United States had won 90 percent of the cases and the future were like the past, one could predict accurately 9 times out of 10 by always predicting victory for the United States, but such a method provides no understanding of why some cases are won by the United States and why some cases are lost. It says nothing about what the predictor variables are or what their relative importance is.

How to weight the variables also depends partly on whether one is mainly interested in prediction or analysis. The k-weights or discriminant weights in Table 13–1, for instance, indicate the importance of each variable primarily for predictive rather than analytic purposes. By using such weights as multipliers in calculating summation scores, one can minimize prediction errors. The discriminant weights, however, have no meaning out of the context of the seven predictor variables used. This is so because each discriminant weight is lowered by the presence of other partially overlapping predictor variables. On the other hand, the r-weights or correlation coefficients do indicate the extent to which each variable correlates with victory for the United States, irrespective of what other variables are included.

---

[8] Guilford, Fundamental Statistics in Psychology & Education 422–25 (1956). Weighting the seven variables in this example was also less important in that the seven variables were chosen from a larger set of variables by a method called stepwise regression analysis that substantially decreases the presence of overlapping variables. See the text material following note 16 *infra*.

Correlation coefficients are especially helpful for indicating the direction (positive or inverse) as well as the intensity (high or low) of the relation between a predictor variable and case outcomes where the categories on the variable have some inherently meaningful ascending or descending order. Intervals of length or time as used by physicists have such a character, but the kinds of variables most relevant to analyzing court cases are not so measurable. Since the correlation coefficients in Table 13–1 do not indicate what categories are associated with victory and what categories are associated with defeat, one has to determine this by looking at the category percentages under each variable.

An examination of the percentages tends to reveal that two important underlying elements determine whether the United States will win or lose in this set of 137 international cases. One element has to do with playing on one's home grounds. Thus, the United States is much more likely to win where American domestic law is the main body of law being applied, rather than international custom, treaty, or foreign law. The United States also is more likely to win before the United States Supreme Court and lower federal courts than before international tribunals or foreign courts. In this sense, granting broader jurisdiction to international tribunals may be partly detrimental to the United States, but the net result may still be highly beneficial if some conflicts are thereby resolved that might otherwise lead to international hostilities.[9]

The other important underlying element has to do with the liberalism of the position taken by the United States, as is shown in variables 4 through 7. The United States thus fares better when it is taking the liberal position in cases involving economic interests (i.e., a pro-antitrust, prodebtor, or prolabor position), or the liberal position in cases involving civil liberties (i.e., prosafeguards for the innocent, pro-equal protection, or pro-freedom of speech or religion). Likewise the United States does better when it has in past history faced an opponent of approximately equal industrial power rather than lesser industrial power. Along related lines, the United States does slightly better when it is the plaintiff than when it is being sued.

Some of the effects of taking a more liberal position also show up on variable 2, although many of the percentages on that variable are unmeaningful because of the small number of cases on which they are based, which illustrates a disadvantage of providing too many categories on a variable. Nevertheless, if one concentrates on just those categories having 10 or more cases, it appears that the United States is more likely

---

[9] For a discussion of the desirability of granting broader jurisdiction to international and foreign tribunals, see A.B.A. Section of International & Comparative Law, Report on the Self-Judging Aspect of the United States Domestic Jurisdiction Reservation to its Adherence to the Statute of the International Court of Justice (1959).

to win (1) if it is seeking to establish rather than reject the jurisdiction of some tribunal, (2) if it is seeking to collect damages rather than seeking to avoid paying them, and (3) if it is seeking a broad interpretation rather than a narrow interpretation of a treaty. The United States fares about equally well when it is (1) curtailing an individual's rights in a deportation or alien proceeding before an American tribunal or (2) expanding an individual's rights by suing on his behalf before a claims commission or other tribunal. The equality in percentages between these two categories is possibly because one involves the home grounds element and the other involves the liberalism element.

Being on its home grounds favors the United States possibly because of relatively pro-American attitudes in American domestic law and among American judges. Taking a liberal position possibly helps the United States because of the liberalism of the United States Supreme Court since the 1930's and the possible liberalism of international tribunals. These explanations for the probability patterns observed may not be the best of all possible explanations. The important thing, however, is that the patterns of behavior revealed by an empirical probability table like Table 13–1 might not have been observed by merely briefing the cases in the traditional law school way.[10]

II.   HOW TO PRODUCE EMPIRICAL PROBABILITY TABLES

In order to produce tables like Tables 13–1 and 13–2 either by hand or with the aid of computers, one must first determine (1) what set of cases are to be used as precedents, (2) what variables and categories on the variables may be useful in predicting or explaining the alternative outcomes one is interested in, and (3) what category each case belongs in on each variable. For these three initial steps, one mainly needs a knowledge of traditional legal research techniques, a little creative imagination, and some careful clerical work. The clerical work will, of course, benefit from having a few people checking on the work of one another in order to obtain a consensus on the categorizing done.

On the matter of picking the cases and the variables, a predictive goal might conflict with an analytic goal. For example, if one wanted to pre-

---

[10] Instead of ordering the categories of a multiple-category variable in terms of the extent to which each category is associated with victory for the United States, Hubert Blalock advocates ordering the categories in terms of the extent to which each category is associated with the underlying explanatory elements. Blalock's type of ordering thus emphasizes analysis rather than prediction. Ordering the categories in terms of their association with the outcome variable, as is done in Table 13–1, however, does help to reveal what the underlying explanatory elements are. See Blalock, Nominal Scales, Generalizations to Populations and the Formulation of Scientific Laws (1965) (a paper presented at the annual meeting of the American Sociological Association).

dict the outcome of a case involving an international boundary dispute one would probably only use other boundary dispute cases as precedent cases and not a sample of 137 diverse international law cases. If, however, one wanted to analyze a variety of international law cases for the purpose of inferring some broad generalizations, then one would probably not confine himself to boundary disputes. Likewise, for predictive purposes exclusively legalistic variables might be the most appropriate ones; but for theoretical-analytic purposes one might want to see the relation to outcome of some sociological, psychological, or political variables.

A. By Hand

After each precedent case has been positioned on each variable, the data processing differs depending on whether or not one has access to a computer. If one does not have access to a computer, it is recommended that only the unweighted summation method be used, unless there are only a small number of variables and cases. One index card can be set aside for each case. On the card can be indicated how each case was positioned on each variable, using whatever symbols are convenient. For each variable, the cards can be sorted into as many piles as there are categories on the variable. Then, one can count the total number of cards in each pile and the subtotal of cards that were decided in an affirmative direction on the outcome variable. By dividing this subtotal by the total for each pile, one can determine the victory percentage for each category and thus the contents of a table like Table 13–1.

After a table like Table 13–1 is created, one can use it along with the classification symbols on each index card to determine the summation score for each case, which can also be written on the index card. The cards can then be rearranged in rank order from the case with the lowest summation score to the one with the highest. Next, the cards can be divided into approximately seven piles as equal in number as is possible, even though there are ties and the number of cases may not be evenly divisible by seven.[11] For each such pile of cards, one can count the total number of cards and the subtotal of cards decided in an affirmative direction. Dividing this subtotal by the total for each pile yields the victory percentage for each summation interval and thus the contents of a table like Table 13–2.

---

[11] Equal piles are used to avoid having some of the denominators become too small to yield statistically meaningful percentages and to avoid having others become too large for differentiating among the many cases within the group. With 137 cases, 7 piles seem appropriate, although one could use fewer piles with fewer cases or more piles with more cases.

B. With a Computer

If a computer is available, then one can use one IBM-type card per case instead of one index card. On each IBM card set aside one column for each variable and punch hole 1 on the column if the case falls into category 1, and hole 2 if it falls into category 2, and so on. If a variable has more than 10 categories (which is more than the maximum number of usable positions on an IBM-card column), then use 2 columns for that variable, and for a case in category 11 punch hole 1 on the first column and hole 1 in the second column, and likewise for category 12, and so on. The variables and categories can be in any order. Somewhere on each card a case identification number can also be punched. This process will result in as many data cards as there are cases, unless there are so many variables that one needs more than one data card per case.

To obtain the victory percentages for each category for making a table like Table 13–1, one merely puts the data cards along with some appropriate control cards in the input box at whatever computer center he has access to. In order to know how to prepare the control cards, one needs to consult whatever statistical users manual is available at the computing center. For example, at the Stanford University Computing Center where the widely used *BMD* manual is available,[12] one would place five control cards in front of the data cards and two control cards behind them. The first two cards are different forms of user identification cards. They mainly indicate the user's name and that he wants the computer to apply the BMD02S cross-tabulation program to his data cards. The next control card punched in accordance with the instructions in the manual mainly indicates to the computer how many data cards and how many variables it is to process. Then comes a control card that indicates how many categories are present on each variable, followed by a control card that indicates what columns have been set aside for each variable. Next come the data cards, followed by a card that indicates that each predictor variable is to be cross-tabulated or correlated with the outcome variable, not with each other. The final card simply has the word "finish" punched on it.

After one has obtained the percentages output and made a table like Table 13–1, then the same data cards can be resubmitted with a set of BMD09S transgeneration control cards designed to create a new data deck. The control cards for this run mainly indicate what victory percentages correspond to each category on each variable.[13] In the new

---

[12] BMD—Biomedical Computer Programs (1964). This manual and its computer programs are available at many university computing centers.

[13] For greater predictive accuracy, the percentages can be indicated to more than two decimal places.

deck, which the computer will create, each card still corresponds to one case. Every two columns correspond to a different variable. The big difference between the new data deck and the old one is that if case 12 falls into category 3 on variable 7, then a 3 is not punched on the new deck in the columns set aside for variable 7. Instead, the victory percentage for category 3 on variable 7 is punched.[14] This repunching, like the calculation of the percentages, can be handled by the IBM 7090 computer at Stanford in less than two minutes.

The final computer step involves submitting the new data deck along with a few simple control cards for a discriminant analysis run calling for a program like BMD04M. The program will not only give discriminant weights like those shown in Table 13–1, it will also calculate a weighted summation score for each case and then print out the cases arranged in the rank order of their summation scores, along with how each case was decided.[15] From this rank-order listing one can block off approximately seven sets of cases equal in number and then calculate the percentages needed for a table like Table 13–2. One can also look at this listing to determine what summation score represents the best cutoff level such that there is a minimum number of negatively decided cases above the level and affirmatively decided cases below the level.

As an alternative or supplement to the discriminant analysis step, one can run the new data deck through a regression program like BMD02R or a correlation program like BMD03D to obtain a different set of weights.[16] Prior to using the discriminant analysis program, one can have the data cards applied to a stepwise regression program like BMD02R, which is designed to aid in reducing the number of variables. The stepwise program will rank the variables in terms of their relative potency in accounting for the variation in outcome among the cases and will indicate how much additional variation each additional variable accounts for. Additional variables after approximately the first half-dozen generally tend to be redundant. Personnel at the computing center can be helpful in setting up the control cards for any of these runs.

---

[14] Where the outcome variable is a numerical score rather than a win–lose dichotomy, one can substitute the average outcome score of each category (rather than the percent of wins) for the category number.

[15] If the new data deck is run through a Pearsonian product moment correlation program, the resulting correlation coefficients are identical to those obtained by applying Cramer's V for multiple-category variables to the old data deck. For a description of Cramer's V, see BLALOCK, SOCIAL STATISTICS 230 (1960).

[16] For an alternative set of weights, the percentages on the new data deck can be transferred into logarithms or square roots by exercising certain transgeneration options in the BMD04M discriminant analysis program. This sometimes improves predictability, particularly if the distribution of percentage scores on a predictor variable is unbalanced away from one side of the average percentage. See WALKER & LEV, STATISTICAL INFERENCE 423–25 (1953).

For a more detailed description of discriminant, regression, and correlation weighting, see Nagel, *supra* note 1, and the references cited therein.

III. SOME BROADER IMPLICATIONS

Empirical probability tables in combination with the traditional non-quantitative techniques developed by lawyers can probably be helpful in predicting the outcome of court cases, especially if the tables are prepared and periodically updated in consultation with the lawyers who will be using them. Such tables are currently prepared on a subscription basis for personal injury lawyers by the Jury Verdict Research Service of Cleveland. Unfortunately, however, their tables do not provide any data on intervals of summation scores and the corresponding empirical probabilities. Their category percentages thus represent a mass of numbers that cannot be meaningfully integrated unless summation data are provided or unless the user is informed of the applicability of the Bayes prediction method.[17] Nevertheless, it is heartening to see this kind of commercial venture into the realm of case prediction. Perhaps in time this firm and other firms will expand into other fields of law, using a more sophisticated and more useful methodology.

The possibly more important implications of quantitative case analysis have to do with the development of a behavioral science of law. In developing such a science, it seems necessary at first to emphasize the development of scientific tools for the analysis of legal phenomena. The next stage logically seems to be the application of such tools to the testing of empirical generalizations. When a lot of such testing has been done, a body of empirical propositions will be developed. In the third stage, one can inductively build broader theories of law from these empirical propositions.

Although one can talk conceptually of three stages, in reality all three types of work can be going on simultaneously by different persons or by the same person in different studies or even in the same study. Methodology helps to test propositions, and propositions help to generate theory, but theory can also stimulate hypotheses that when tested become propositions. Likewise, the desire to test certain hypotheses may generate new methodologies. Nevertheless, in the early development or redevelopment of a behavioral or social science, methodology may be emphasized more than it is later.

Over the last 10 years, a number of articles and books have called for a more scientific analysis of the legal process, and additional ones will probably appear in the next few years.[18] This chapter has advocated the

---

[17] See the appendix to this chapter for a description of the Bayes method of prediction.

[18] SCHUBERT, QUANTITATIVE ANALYSIS OF JUDICIAL BEHAVIOR (1959); Cowan, *Decision Theory in Law, Science, and Technology,* 17 RUTGERS L. REV. 499 (1963); Nagel, *Testing Empirical Generalizations in Legal Research,* 15 J. LEGAL ED. 365 (1963).

use of empirical probability tables, correlation coefficients, and various summation methods for analyzing court cases. It should, however, be pointed out that the same techniques can be used to analyze such behavior as that of legislators, administrators, attorneys, and the general public. The techniques can also be applied to entities other than individuals such as countries and time periods. Nevertheless, it is hoped that the near future will see less emphasis on methodological discussions and more emphasis on the application of such techniques to the testing of empirical generalizations and to the building of inductive theories of the legal process.

APPENDIX

Alternative Predictive and Analytic Techniques Applicable to Multiple-Category Variables

The purpose of this appendix is to discuss some alternative techniques for predicting with multiple-category variables other than the summation methods presented in the chapter. This discussion is placed in an appendix because it is more technical than the rest of the chapter, and because the techniques discussed are generally inferior to the summation methods on both predictive power and ease of application.

The first alternative technique is the Bayes method.[19] It involves application of the following formula to the empirical probabilities of Table 13–1 in order to arrive at a composite probability of victory for the United States or

$$P(W \text{ given } S) = \frac{P(W) \cdot P(S \text{ given } W)}{[P(L) \cdot P(S \text{ given } L)] + [P(W) \cdot P(S \text{ given } W)]}$$

where P = probability, W = win for U.S., L = loss for U.S., S = any set of categories. For example, suppose all one knows about a case is that it involves a treaty and the United States is seeking the jurisdiction of some tribunal. With this information, the numerical value of the formula becomes:

$$.74 = \frac{\left(\frac{89}{137}\right)\left(\frac{(17)\,(.47)}{89} \cdot \frac{(26)\,(.85)}{89}\right)}{\left(\frac{48}{137}\right)\left(\frac{(17)\,(1-.47)}{48} \cdot \frac{(26)\,(1-.85)}{48}\right) + \left(\frac{89}{137}\right)\left(\frac{(17)\,(.47)}{89} \cdot \frac{(26)\,(.85)}{89}\right)}$$

The formula takes into consideration that there were 137 cases, 89 of which were decided in favor of the United States and 48 of which were

---

[19] Mosteller, Probability with Statistical Applications 143–50 (1961).

decided against the United States. The quantities 17 and 26 and the decimals .47 and .85 correspond to categories 1c and 2c. By analogy, one could apply the formula to a case where one knows how it is positioned on all seven variables rather than on just two variables.

A big defect in this method is that it assumes all variables are independent or nonoverlapping relative to each other. The weighted summation method, on the other hand, allocates a discriminant weight to each variable, which statistically eliminates or partials out the overlap between the variables used. Another defect is the laboriousness of the calculations, especially if many variables are used, although the calculations can be made easier and more accurate by using a desk calculator.[20]

Another alternative might be called the every-combination method. This method requires the preparation of an empirical probability table that shows the percentages of cases won by the United States in every possible combination of categories. For example, if one were working with just variables 1 and 2, an empirical probability would have to be shown for cases that were in category *a* on 1 and *a* on 2; *a* on 1 and *b* on 2; and so on. Since there are 4 categories on variable 1 and 13 categories on variable 2, there are 52 (i.e., 4 times 13) combinations to be provided for with just the first two variables. Given the number of categories on each of the seven variables, 163,800 combinations must be provided for if all seven variables are used. In effect, the method converts 7 variables with from 3 to 13 categories apiece into 1 variable with 163,800 categories.

An obvious defect in this approach is that with only 137 cases many combinations have not occurred; for those combinations that have occurred, the denominator of the percentages may be too small to give meaningful percentages. The percentages are also difficult to interpret for analytical purposes. In spite of these serious defects, a variation of this every-combination method has been proposed by James Coleman.[21]

John Sonquist and James Morgan of the University of Michigan have proposed a method related to the every-combination method.[22] Their

---

[20] Given the assumption of independence of the variables, the Bayes method can be deductively proved to be valid. *Ibid.* The Jury Verdict Research Corporation has proposed a method for handling multiple category variables which, at first glance, looks like a version of the Bayes method, but the JVR method can be shown algebraically to be inconsistent with the Bayes method. See JURY VERDICT RESEARCH CORP., HOW TO PREDICT PERSONAL INJURY VERDICTS 26 (1963); and Nagel, *supra* note 1, at 1414.

[21] COLEMAN, INTRODUCTION TO MATHEMATICAL SOCIOLOGY 219–24 (1964). His variation of the every-combination method also has the defect of laborious complexity, and it is able to handle only one multiple-category variable among the predictor variables.

[22] Sonquist & Morgan, The Detection of Interaction Effects—A Report on a Computer Program for the Selection of Optimal Combinations of Explanatory Variables (1964).

approach is, in effect, a selective combination method, since their computer program generates a maximum of 63 combinations. The particular combinations that the program presents in its output are the combinations most different from each other with regard to their positioning on the outcome variable, with each combination being required to meet a minimum level of predictive importance. The combinations are worded in such a way that every case falls into one of them and only one of them. The computer program splits multiple-category variables (e.g., variable 1) into one category and its opposite (e.g., treaty cases versus nontreaty cases).

The Sonquist-Morgan approach is probably the best alternative discussed in this appendix. It is, however, substantially more difficult to apply than the summation method discussed in the chapter. Indeed, it is almost impossible to apply if one does not have access to their computer program plus an IBM 7090 computer that operates like the one at the University of Michigan. The output of the program is also more difficult to interpret, particularly for analytic purposes. Moreover, the program's ratio of accurate predictions to predictions made may be less than the weighted summation method, possibly because of information lost in dichotomizing the variables. Their approach, though, is quite new and needs more use to be fully evaluated.

Several alternative methods might be useful for obtaining accurate predictions, but they have little value for understanding why some cases are decided one way and why some are decided another way. Predicting the most frequently occurring outcome was previously mentioned as being such a method. Trend analysis is closely related, since it involves, in effect, predicting the most frequently occurring recent outcome. Thus, if in the series of 137 cases the United States won the first 89 but lost the last 48, then one might logically predict the United States will lose the next case. Predicting the most frequent outcome is an especially poor predictive technique if the most frequent outcome of two possible outcomes occurs only a little more than 50 percent of the time. Likewise, projecting trends is an especially poor predictive technique if the trend line is flat—that is, the United States or other affirmative position has been consistently winning or losing approximately the same proportion of cases over time.[23]

---

[23] Bruce Jacobs of the Massachusetts Institute of Technology has devised a form of trend analysis that involves plotting over time the number of judges on the Supreme Court who agreed with a given argument in a given type of case. He then combines the trend lines for a number of arguments in order to predict the voting split on the Supreme Court for a case at a future point in time. His method, in effect, involves plotting decisions on issues rather than decisions on cases, but it reveals nothing with regard to what variables correlate with the alternative decisions on the issues plotted. Bruce Jacobs, A Quantitative Analysis of Supreme Court Decision-Making in Congressional Reapportionment Cases (unpublished manuscript).

Another predictive method that has little analytical or causal value is the judgmental method. It involves making a small or large survey of lawyers or other experts in the field of law involved in order to determine how they think a case or set of cases will be decided. Such a prediction method may be quite powerful, depending on the expertise of those asked and the sophistication of the handling of the data,[24] but unless systematic probing questions are asked with regard to why the cases will be decided as predicted, this method is not likely to reveal anything with regard to the variables correlated with or responsible for the decisions reached.

Finally, it should also be mentioned that several approaches to case prediction are applicable only if the multiple-category variables are numerical (like age) or if they are converted into either–or dichotomies. This is true of such techniques as factor analysis,[25] simultaneous equations,[26] or Boolean algebra.[27] The information lost in dichotomizing may be of value to improved predictive power and especially to a theoretical interpretation of the elements responsible for the decisions. These three methods are also unduly complex. Boolean algebra, in addition, seems to be particularly incapable of yielding empirical probabilities. Thus, it can say only that a future case will be won or lost, and cannot give a probability of victory like those associated with the summation intervals in Table 13–2, or with the Bayes method, or the selective combinations method of Sonquist and Morgan.[28]

---

[24] One way to handle the data might involve presenting the experts with a description of the set of cases to be predicted and asking them to classify each case into five outcome categories. If the cases are international disputes in which the United States is a party, the outcome categories might be (1) U.S. is very likely to win, (2) U.S. is more likely to win than lose, (3) U.S. has an even chance, (4) U.S. is more likely to lose than win, and (5) U.S. is very likely to lose. Each case can be given an average category score (which is equal to the sum of the category numbers in which it was placed divided by the number of experts involved) or a more sophisticated scale score can be given to each case in accordance with the principles of psychometric measurement. GUILFORD PSYCHOMETRIC METHODS 223–44 (1954).

[25] KORT, *Content Analysis of Judicial Opinions and Rules of Law*, JUDICIAL DECISION-MAKING 133–97 (1963).

[26] Kort, *Simultaneous Equations and Boolean Algebra in the Analysis of Judicial Decisions*, 28 LAW & CONTEMP. PROB. 143–63 (1963).

[27] Lawlor, *Foundations of Logical Legal Decision Making*, 63 MODERN USES OF LOGIC IN L. 98 (1963).

[28] Reed Lawlor is currently developing a technique that combines the summation approach with Boolean algebra so as to enable his Boolean algebra approach to yield empirical probabilities of victory.

Part Three

THE POLICYMAKERS AND
THE POLICY APPLIERS

Part Three deals with the legal decision makers who represent the organism in stimulus–response theory or the conversion structure in input–output theory. The decision makers convert the normative and factual stimuli into legal policies and adjudications, which, in turn, become stimuli to lower level administrators and policy recipients who then convert them into the ultimate policy effects. This section discusses (1) research methodologies for studying the role of decision makers, (2) methods of recruitment, (3) background and attitude characteristics, (4) accounting for decisional variation, and (5) interaction between legislators and judges.

The big problem in designing research on the role of decision makers is in devising a way to determine the extent to which various differences among the decision makers result in differences in their decisions. The difficulty arises mainly because no substantial set of judges will be hearing the same cases, and their decisions will thus lack comparability. To resolve this problem, one can try presentation of the same hypothetical cases to many judges, but such a procedure means a small sample of cases, a low response, and a lack of reality. As an alternative, one can try to find judges from different courts who have heard cases that are similar in subject matter and in ease of deciding in a liberal or conservative direction, but that procedure involves subjective considerations on the part of the researcher, which may greatly muddy the findings. The most meaningful alternative seems to be that of making comparisons among different judges from the same multijudge court where they are simultaneously hearing identical cases. This is basically the approach recommended in Chapter 14. The chapter also discusses some of the problems involved in sampling and positioning the judges on their characteristics and decisions, as well as the problems involved in analyzing the data and explaining the findings.

Chapter 15 raises the basic policy problem of whether judges should be elected or appointed. The chapter is particularly concerned with whether elected judges are more likely to vote in accordance with their political party position than are appointed judges. It also deals with the influence of nonpartisan elections and of length of tenure. On-going research not presented further shows that when one compares elected judges on the same court with interim-appointed judges, using the within-court methodology of Chapter 14, the findings are mixed, but elected judges do tend to come out somewhat more liberal in their decisions and more representative of the general public in their backgrounds.

Chapters 16 and 17 describe some of the attitudes and backgrounds of legal policymakers. Chapter 16 compares the liberalism–conservatism of judges, legislators, and administrators, and attempts to explain the causes and effects of these attitudinal differences, as well as what can be done to decrease the influence of personal prejudices on judicial and other forms of decision making. The chapter also discusses some methodological aspects of attitude measurement. Chapter 17 deals with political party affiliation as the most important judicial background characteristic. The chapter emphasizes (1) the extent to which party representation on the courts is not proportionate to party representation among the general public, (2) the need for bipartisanship as an important check on judicial bias, and (3) devices for obtaining greater bipartisanship.

Chapters 18 and 19 apply the methodology of Chapter 14 to accounting for within-court decisional variation. Chapter 18 deals with differences among judges with regard to their propensity to decide for the defense in criminal cases. The key variables that account for the biggest variations include political party affiliation, pressure group membership, former occupation, religion, and liberalism attitudes. Chapter 19 deals with differences among commissioners on the federal independent regulatory agencies with regard to their propensity to decide for the liberal position and their propensity to dissent. The key variables here are party, region, appointer, ideology, the majority position on the agency, and various combinations of these variables.

The last two chapters in this section deal with the interaction that exists between legislative and judicial decision makers. Chapter 20 discusses the role of politics in the Supreme Court's exercise of judicial review over acts of Congress. The frequency and direction of judicial review is shown to be influenced by (1) the degree of party differences between Congress and the Court, (2) which party is in power, and (3) the party affiliation of individual judges, although not by the degree of interparty friction in Congress, as some have hypothesized. Chapter 21 deals with the other side of the coin—namely, the role of politics and other variables in Congress' exercise of its power to pass or at least consider bills to curb the powers of the Court. The frequency and success of Court-curbing bills is shown to be influenced by the quantity and subject matter of the judicial provocation, by catalytic factors, particularly of a political nature, within Congress, and by the judicial counter-action.

Future studies of judicial and other decision makers will possibly make more use of interviewing techniques, particularly with regard to how judges view their roles.[1] There will also be more concern for trial court judges,[2] and for judges in a cross-cultural context.[3] Such studies should help to increase the ability to generalize about the role of judges in the legal process.

---

[1] Becker, *Surveys and Judiciaries, or Who's Afraid of the Purple Curtain*, 1 LAW & SOC. REV. 133 (1966); Vines, *The Judicial Role in American States* in J. TANENHAUS & J. GROSSMAN, FRONTIERS IN JUDICIAL RESEARCH (1969).

[2] K. DOLBEARE, TRIAL COURTS IN URBAN POLITICS (1967).

[3] G. SCHUBERT & D. DANELSKI, COMPARATIVE JUDICIAL BEHAVIOR—CROSS-CULTURAL STUDIES IN POLITICAL DECISION-MAKING IN THE EAST AND WEST (1969).

SECTION I
Research Methods

CHAPTER 14

Testing Relations between
Characteristics and Decision Making

I. GOALS AND TRADITIONAL SOLUTIONS

One useful contribution that a behavioral approach can possibly make to the public law field of political science is in the testing of relations that may exist between judicial characteristics on the one hand and judicial decision-making propensities on the other.

An analysis of these relations is useful for at least four purposes. It is useful primarily to provide a better theoretical understanding of the nature of the judicial process.[1] Furthermore, if one finds that some judges have a higher correlation between their background characteristics and their decisional propensities than do other judges, then one can make statements about methods of decreasing these correlations by analyzing how the low-correlation judges or their courts differ from the high-correlation judges. In addition, if one finds that certain background characteristics, like party affiliation, religion, and regionalism, have a significant relation to certain judicial propensities, then one can better demonstrate the need for making judges more representative of the people over whom they judge with regard to these characteristics. Finally, an analysis of these relations can provide some data that can be helpful to voters in the selection of judges and to lawyers in the selection of jurors.[2]

---

[1] The importance of the judiciary in government policy formation is shown in V. ROSENBLUM, LAW AS A POLITICAL INSTRUMENT (1955); J. PELTASON, FEDERAL COURTS IN THE POLITICAL PROCESS (1955); and Dahl, *Decision-Making in a Democracy: The Role of the Supreme Court as a National Policy Maker,* 6 J. PUB. L. 286–94 (1957).

[2] When a governor appoints a judge or when a lawyer tries to get a case heard before a particular judge, he generally has knowledge of the prior judicial or non-judicial records of the judges involved and need not resort to prediction from background characteristics. Such decisional data, however, is generally not possessed by voters when they elect judges or by lawyers when they empanel a jury.

Various scholars within the public law field of political science (such as John Schmidhauser, Cortez Ewing, and Rodney Mott) have already compiled data on differences in the backgrounds of American judges, but they have not yet shown that these background characteristics correlate with differences in the decisions of the judiciary.[3] Various other scholars within the public law field of political science (such as Glendon Schubert, C. Herman Pritchett and S. Sidney Ulmer) have compiled data on the different decisional tendencies of American judges, but they likewise have not shown that these decisional propensities correlate with differences in the backgrounds of the judiciary.[4] Before a bridge can be built between these two fields of public law research, a method must be devised for empirically testing relations between judicial characteristics and judicial decision making.[5]

Can the traditional approach to public law provide such a testing method? That approach has emphasized the analysis of the doctrines presented in judicial opinions. However, seldom, if ever, will a judge mention in an opinion that his background or personal values were influential in the decision he reached, even if they actually were influential. He may, on the other hand, explicitly state that his background or personal values were not influential, as Justice Frankfurter did in the *Barnette* flag salute case.[6] In view of this understandable desire of judges to avoid indicating in their opinions any relation between their personal characteristics and their decisions, the reading of judicial opinions alone cannot provide a method of testing whether and in what form these relations exist. The traditional approach in public law has also involved the writing of judicial biographies, particularly of judges on the United States Supreme Court. A judicial biography may reveal relations between personal characteristics of an individual judge and some of his decisions,

---

[3] Schmidhauser, *The Justices of the Supreme Court: A Collective Portrait,* 3 MID-WEST J. POL. SCI. 1–57 (1958); C. EWING, THE JUDGES OF THE SUPREME COURT, 1789–1937 (1938); and Mott, *Judicial Personnel,* 167 ANNALS 143–55 (1933). But see Schmidhauser, *Judicial Behavior and the Sectional Crisis of 1837–1860,* 23 J. POL. 615–40 (1961).

[4] G. SCHUBERT, QUANTITATIVE ANALYSIS OF JUDICIAL BEHAVIOR (1959); C. HERMAN PRITCHETT, THE ROOSEVELT COURT: A STUDY IN JUDICIAL POLITICS AND VALUES, 1937–1947 (1948); and Ulmer, *The Analysis of Behavior Patterns on the United States Supreme Court,* 22 J. POL. 629–53 (1960). See also Gaudet, *Individual Differences in Sentencing Tendencies of Judges,* 32 ARCHIVES OF PSYCH. 1–58 (1938).

[5] See speculations by Haines, *General Observations on the Effects of Personal, Political, and Economic Influences on the Decisions of Judges,* 17 ILL. L. REV. 96–116 (1922); R. CARR, THE SUPREME COURT AND JUDICIAL REVIEW 231–57 (1942); and Hall, *Determination of Methods for Ascertaining the Factors That Influence Judicial Decisions in Cases Involving Due Process of Law,* 20 AM. POL. SCI. REV. 127–34 (1926). See also J. FRANK, COURTS ON TRIAL: MYTH AND REALITY IN AMERICAN JUSTICE 146–56, 165–85 (1950).

[6] *West Virginia State Board of Education* v. *Barnette,* 319 U.S. 624 (1943).

but an individual biography alone cannot provide a method of testing generalizations about these relations.

II.   BEHAVIORAL SOLUTIONS

On the other hand, can the behavioral approach provide a method for testing these relations? The behavioral approach to public law has emphasized the quantitative analysis of judicial phenomena, but how may a quantitative analysis be applied to interrelating judicial characteristics and judicial decisions?

A. FORMULATING THE HYPOTHESES

First some hypotheses have to be formulated in which one of the variables in each hypothesis is a judicial characteristic (like party affiliation, American Bar Association membership, age, or religion) and in which one of the other variables in each hypothesis relates to a decisional propensity in a certain type of case (like criminal cases, business regulation cases, or free speech cases). For illustrative purposes, the hypothesis can be used that Democratic judges have a greater tendency to decide for the defense in criminal cases than do Republican judges.

B. SAMPLING THE JUDGES

After formulating a hypothesis, the testing problem then involves determining what judges should be studied in order to test the hypothesis. State or federal supreme court judges make a more desirable sample to study than intermediate appellate or trial court judges do for three reasons. First, as a practical matter, there are fewer of them, and data on them are easier to find. Second, if characteristics in the backgrounds of state and federal supreme court judges are found to influence their decisions, then one can conclude that characteristics in the backgrounds of lower court judges probably influence their decisions even more. Such a conclusion is reasonable because of the relative absence of formal opinions jointly arrived at to justify decisions reached in lower court proceedings, and because lower court proceedings involved more subjective factual issues about who did what as contrasted to legal issues about what can be legally done.[7] Third, only on supreme courts can one find so many judges hearing exactly the same cases simultaneously. If one judge votes more frequently for the defense than do his fellow judges on the same supreme court hearing the same cases, then one cannot attribute this decisional difference to a difference in the cases heard, since all the

---

[7] FRANK, *op. cit. supra* note 5.

judges heard the same cases. On the other hand, if the judges had been trial court judges, the difference in their decisional records could possibly be attributed to a difference in the cases each judge heard or to a difference in the law under which each judge operated if the judges were from different jurisdictions, rather than to a difference in the backgrounds or attitudes of the judges themselves.

What state or federal supreme court judges should one sample? If one samples all the judges who ever sat on the U.S. Supreme Court, he will have a maximum sample as of January 1, 1962, of only 92 judges, some of whom would be unusable because they did not serve long enough for comparison with their contemporaries. Using a historical sample also brings in the complicating factor of the changing meaning of political party labels or the changing meaning of whatever the judicial characteristic is. If, however, one uses for his sample all those judges who sat on the state and federal supreme courts during any recent year, he will then have a fair-sized sample of over 300 contemporary judges and at least 49 different courts to work with. In the beginning of 1955, for instance, 313 judges were serving on the 49 state and federal supreme courts.[8]

To test the party affiliation hypothesis, one should eliminate from the sample all those courts that did not have at least one Democratic and one Republican judge, because if there are all Democrats or all Republicans on a court, then comparisons within the court between judges from the two parties cannot be made. Likewise if Catholic judges, for instance, are being compared with Protestant judges or if younger judges are being compared with older ones, only those courts should be used on which members of both groups being compared are represented.[9] In 1955, for example, 152 judges were serving on the 24 state and federal supreme courts in which both Democratic and Republican judges were represented. One should also exclude from the sample those judges who did not sit out the full year or other time period with which one is working. Otherwise, the number of cases that can be used will be greatly reduced, since no case should be used unless it was heard by all the judges on the court who are included in the sample. For example, 6 of the 152 judges on the 24 bipartisan courts of 1955, who were listed as being present at

---

[8] A list of state and federal supreme court judges in 1955 can be found in DIRECTORY OF AMERICAN JUDGES (LIEBMAN ed. 1955). For other years since 1935, the BOOK OF STATES (1935 to date), provides such lists.

[9] The judicial characteristics involved should generally be split into two categories so there will be many courts to work with that have at least one judge in each category. If more than two categories are used, one is not likely to find so many courts having at least one judge in each category. The dividing line between the two categories may divide the judges into two nominal labels (e.g., Democrats and Republicans), or it may divide the judges at the mean or median of the total sample (e.g., above and below age 63.2) or into the upper and lower third of the total sample (e.g., above age 65 and below age 60).

the beginning of the year, did not sit out the year, and thus they should be eliminated from the sample.

C. Positioning the Judges

Once the sample of judges has been drawn, the problem then becomes one of determining where to place each judge on each variable. To determine a background characteristic of a judge, such as his party affiliation, one may consult such biographical sources as *Who's Who in America*, the *Directory of American Judges*, the *Martindale-Hubbell Law Directory*, or the governmental directories published by many states. For attitudinal characteristics, one may conduct personal interviews of the judges or send them mailed questionnaires.[10]

For their decisions in criminal cases, for instance, each judge should be given a decision score, which will indicate his propensity to decide for the defense or the prosecution relative to his fellow judges on his own court.[11] Such a decision score can be based on the ratio between the number of times that each judge voted for the defense rather than for the prosecution and the number of times that each judge voted in criminal cases. Likewise, similar decision scores can be calculated for each judge in other types of cases in which the researcher is interested. For example, in 1955 the 7 judges of the Pennsylvania Supreme Court heard 21 criminal cases in which all 7 judges voted.[12] Justice Bell voted for the defense

---

[10] For suggestive attitudinal items, see the tests mentioned in the various editions of O. Buros (ed.), Mental Measurements Yearbook (1938–59). For ideas on maximizing the utility of mailed questionnaires or personal interviews see William Goode and Paul Hatt, Methods in Social Research, 132–208 (1952).

[11] Criminal cases can be defined as cases in which one party (the defense side) has been charged with committing an act subject to fine, imprisonment, or other penalty owed to the collectivity (the prosecution side) rather than to the individuals who may have been particularly harmed. These cases may involve questions of guilt, punishment, or procedure. Tax cases and business regulation cases, however, were excluded from the tables presented here because they were analyzed separately in the larger study of which this chapter is a part. Regardless of what type of case one is working with, he should clearly indicate what the type refers to and what the general positions are that the judges can vote for. Types of cases need not be mutually exclusive. Thus, a labor union versus management case may produce an explicit controversy between the judges over the free speech aspects of picketing and thereby also be a free speech case.

[12] The 21 Pennsylvania full-court criminal cases of 1955 were: *Commonwealth v. Burdell*, 380 Pa. 43 (1955); *Commonwealth v. Edwards*, 380 Pa. 52 (1955); *Commonwealth v. Mackley*, 380 Pa. 70 (1955); *Commonwealth v. Grays*, 380 Pa. 77 (1955); *Commonwealth ex rel. Dunn v. Ruch*, 380 Pa. 152 (1955); *Commonwealth ex rel. Lane v. Baldi*, 380 Pa. 201 (1955); *Commonwealth v. Chaitt*, 380 Pa. 352 (1955); *Commonwealth v. LaRue*, 381 Pa. 113 (1955); *Commonwealth v. Lane*, 381 Pa. 293 (1955); *Commonwealth v. Thompson*, 381 Pa. 299 (1955); *Commonwealth v. Mason*, 381 Pa. 309 (1955); *Commonwealth v. Cisneros*, 381 Pa. 447 (1955); *Commonwealth v. Bolish*, 381 Pa. 500 (1955); *Commonwealth ex rel. Matthews v. Day*, 381 Pa. 617 (1955); *Commonwealth v. Farrow*, 382 Pa. 61 (1955);

in 4 of these cases, giving him a decision score in the criminal cases of that year of 4/21 (when the decision score is expressed as a fraction) or .19 (when the decision score is expressed as a decimal).

Cases for any given court should be used only if all the judges on the court voted who were included in the sample. Otherwise, if a court decided a criminal case *against* the defense when one of the listed judges was absent due to illness, then that judge might thereby receive a higher decision score *for* the defense than would his co-judges. His relatively high decision score for the defense might be unwarranted, since if he had been present for the case he also might have decided against the defense.[13]

Sometimes, a judge casts his vote in a case contrary to the way some of his fellow judges voted, but neither wholeheartedly for the plaintiff nor wholeheartedly for the defendant but, rather, toward a middle position. He can do this in five different ways: (1) by explicitly voting for only some of the parties on each side where multiple parties are involved; (2) by explicitly voting for only one of the claims or charges on each side where multiple claims or charges are involved; (3) by voting for both sides where cross appeals or counterclaims are involved; (4) by voting for or against a third party where third parties are involved; or (5) by concurring with a majority or dissenting opinion while expressing strong doubts or reservations in favor of the other side.[14] In one of the 21 Pennsylvania criminal cases of 1955, for example, Justice Musmanno concurred with the majority decision for the prosecution while expressing strong doubts and reservations favoring the defense.[15] As a result of this

---

Commonwealth v. *Capps*, 382 Pa. 72 (1955); *Commonwealth* v. *Wable*, 382 Pa. 80 (1955); *Commonwealth* ex rel. *Taylor* v. *Superintendent of the County Prison*, 382 Pa. 181 (1955); *Commonwealth* ex rel. *Bishop v. Maroney*, 382 Pa. 324 (1955); *Commonwealth* v. *Thomas*, 382 Pa. 639 (1955); *Commonwealth* v. *Moon*, 383 Pa. 18 (1955).

[13] If in a rehearing of a case a judge changed his decision, his later position is the one that probably should be recorded, even if the rehearing occurred beyond the time period with which one is working. The decisions analyzed can include memorandum decisions that merely state the result of the case, giving little, if any, of the facts or law involved provided that one examines the lower court opinion to determine the nature of the parties involved (assuming the decision score is phrased in terms of the nature of the parties). Multiple cases decided under one opinion need not be counted as more than one case unless there was a different distribution of votes in the separate cases.

[14] A jurisdictional dissent to a case decided on its merits could conceivably be counted as an in-between vote, as an instance of nonparticipation, or as a vote for the party who would benefit from a denial of jurisdiction. If one defines the decision score in terms of the parties benefited rather than in terms of the reasons offered, then the rare phenomenon of a jurisdictional dissent should be counted as a vote for the party who would benefit from a denial of jurisdiction.

[15] *Commonwealth* v. *Edwards*, 380 Pa. 52 (1955). If cases involving in-between voting by some of the judges are eliminated from the analysis, then data useful in differentiating the judges may be lost. Likewise, if such cases are eliminated for the judges so voting, then distortions of the relative decisional propensities of the judges may result.

halfway decision, Musmanno's decision score in the 21 cases was 11.5/21 (or .55) instead of 11/21 or 12/21.

Although one can talk about a middle position between a vote for the plaintiff and a vote for the defendant, there is no objective way of weighting cases in order to say, for example, that a clear vote for the defense in case A is worth twice as much as a clear vote for the defense in case B. Classifying cases as "more important" and "less important" is an extremely subjective and awkward process, especially on the state supreme court level where the cases receive less commentary by treatise and periodical writers than do cases of the United States Supreme Court. Likewise, the frequency with which a case is cited in *Shepard's Citations* is not necessarily a measure of its impact on society, but is only a measure of the extent to which similar facts tend to recur in contexts sufficiently different to merit rehearing.

Table 14–1 shows the decision score in criminal cases for each of the judges serving on the Pennsylvania and New Jersey Supreme Courts in 1955.[16] It also shows the party affiliation of each judge as given in various biographical directories published in the 1950's. Judges giving no party affiliation in any of these directories probably do not closely identify themselves with either political party. Had Justice Brennan been appointed to the United States Supreme Court in the middle of 1955 instead of in the middle of 1956, then he would have been completely excluded from the analysis as if he had never been on the court so that cases could be used on which he did not sit.

D. ANALYZING THE DATA

Suppose that the supreme courts of Pennsylvania and New Jersey were the only bipartisan courts hearing criminal cases in 1955. How might one use the data of Table 14–1 to test the hypothesis that Democratic judges have a greater tendency to decide for the defense in criminal cases than do Republican judges?

---

[16] The 28 New Jersey full-court criminal cases of 1955 were: *Lenkowski,* 17 N.J. 191 (1955); *State v. Schmelz,* 17 N.J. 227 (1955); *State v. Newton,* 17 N.J. 271 (1955); *State v. Wobertz,* 17 N.J. 569 (1955); *State v. Rios,* 17 N.J. 572 (1955); *State v. Borrell,* 18 N.J. 16 (1955); *State v. Kaufman,* 18 N.J. 75 (1955); *State v. Low,* 18 N.J. 179 (1955); *State v. Cianci,* 18 N.J. 191 (1955); *State v. Arartro,* 18 N.J. 201 (1955); *Johnstown v. State,* 18 N.J. 422 (1955); *State v. Riccardi,* 18 N.J. 441 (1955); *State v. Huber,* 18 N.J. 447 (1955); *White,* 18 N.J. 449 (1955); *State v. Haines,* 18 N.J. 550 (1955); *State v. Dantonio,* 18 N.J. 570 (1955); *State v. Wise,* 19 N.J. 59 (1955); *State v. Rogers,* 19 N.J. 218 (1955); *State v. Browning,* 19 N.J. 424 (1955); *State v. Fary,* 19 N.J. 431 (1955); *State v. Pontery,* 19 N.J. 457 (1955); *Application of Berlin and Diamond,* 19 N.J. 522 (1955); *State v. Dunphy,* 19 N.J. 531 (1955); *State v. D'lppolita,* 19 N.J. 540 (1955); *State v. DeMeo,* 20 N.J. 1 (1955); *State v. Landeros,* 20 N.J. 69 (1955); *State v. Kociolek,* 20 N.J. 92 (1955); and *State v. Benny,* 20 N.J. 238 (1955).

TABLE 14–1

DATA ON PARTY AFFILIATIONS AND CRIMINAL CASE DECISION SCORES FOR THE
1955 PENNSYLVANIA AND NEW JERSEY SUPREME COURT JUDGES
(using all the 1955 full-court criminal cases)

Judges	*Party*	*Decision Score*[*]	*Above or below the Average of One's Court*
Pennsylvania			Average of court .221
Arnold	Republican	3/21 or .14	Below
Bell	Republican	4/21 or .19	Below
Chidsey	Republican	4/21 or .19	Below
Jones	Democratic	4/21 or .19	Below
Musmanno	Democratic	11.5/21 or .55	Above
Stearne	Republican	3/21 or .14	Below
Stern	Republican	3/21 or .14	Below
New Jersey			Average of court .253
Brennan	Democratic	8/28 or .29	Above
Burling	None given	5/28 or .18	Below
Heher	Democratic	11.5/28 or .41	Above
Jacobs	None given	6/28 or .21	Below
Oliphant	Republican	6/28 or .21	Below
Vanderbilt	Republican	6/28 or .21	Below
Wachenfeld	Democratic	7/28 or .25	Below

[*] Decision score = proportion of times voting for the defense in criminal cases.

By simple addition and division, one could find that the average decision score of the five Democratic judges in Table 14–1 is 34 percent for the defense. Likewise, one could find that the average decision score of the seven Republican judges in Table 14–1 is only 17 percent for the defense. It would, however, be fallacious to conclude from the difference between these two averages that the Democratic judges involved have a greater tendency to decide for the defense in criminal cases than do the Republican judges. It would be fallacious to draw such a conclusion because it is quite possible that if the Pennsylvania Republican judges had been sitting on the New Jersey Supreme Court, hearing the facts in the New Jersey cases and operating under the New Jersey law, then the Pennsylvania Republicans might have received as high or even higher decisions scores for the defense than did the New Jersey Democrats.

Failure to control or account for differences in the cases they hear when comparing judges can easily lead to spurious results. For example, Glendon Schubert compares northern trial judges with southern trial judges in union–management cases later heard by the U.S. Supreme Court, and he finds the southern trial judges decided in favor of the union about the same percentage of times as the northern judges.[17]

---

[17] G. SCHUBERT, JUDICIAL BEHAVIOR: A READER IN THEORY AND RESEARCH 458 (1964).

Southern union–management cases, however, may be much easier to decide in favor of the union given the facts involved. Likewise, the findings of some other studies are somewhat muddied by not accounting for differences in the cases among groups of judges.[18] Richard Schwartz, on the other hand, has clearly indicated awareness of this comparability problem.[19]

In order to remedy this noncomparability of judges on different courts, one should compare the Democratic with the Republican judges of the Pennsylvania Supreme Court and the Democratic with the Republican judges of the New Jersey Supreme Court. This can be done by separately calculating the average decision score for each court and then seeing which judges are above and which are below the average of their respective courts. The average decision score for the Pennsylvania Supreme Court was 22 percent for the defense.[20] Only Justice Musmanno was above this average.[21] The average decision score for the New Jersey

---

[18] Schmidhauser, *Stare Decisis, Dissent, and the Background of the Justices of the Supreme Court of the United States*, 14 TORONTO L. J. 194 (1962); Goldman, Politics, Judges and the Administration of Justice, unpublished Ph.D. dissertation, Harvard University 1965; and Bowen, The Explanation of Judicial Voting Behavior from Sociological Characteristics of Judges, unpublished Ph.D. dissertation, Yale University, 1965.

[19] Schwartz, *Judicial Objectivity and Quantitative Analysis,* 1963 M.U.L.L. 139 (1963).

[20] The average decision score of a court is calculated by adding together the decision scores of the individual judges and dividing by the number of judges. As an alternative, one could calculate the median decision score, which represents the middle decision score when the individual scores are arranged numerically and there is an odd number of scores, or which represents the average of the two middle decision scores when there is an even number of scores. This alternative, however, has disadvantages: (1) it results in too many judges being at the splitting point, especially where there are only a few occasional dissenters; (2) its reliability varies too much from sample to sample; and (3) it particularly results in grouping judges together as above or below the median who are more different in their decisional propensities than is the situation when judges are grouped together as above or below the average.

[21] A test of the reliability or consistency of positioning a judge as being above or below can be made by determining the degree of correlation between (1) being above or below the average of one's court on the decision score using only the odd-numbered nonunanimous cases (numbered in chronological order), and (2) being above or below the average of one's court on the decision score using only the even-numbered nonunanimous cases. See J. P. GUILFORD, FUNDAMENTAL STATISTICS IN PSYCHOLOGY AND EDUCATION 435–60 (1956). Judges positioned on the basis of only one case, however, cannot be used in such a test. Only the nonunanimous cases are relevant because these are the only cases that affect a judge's position relative to his co-judges. An alternative test for consistency is to see if the voting patterns on court after court tend to form a scale using the Guttman scaling technique. See G. SCHUBERT, QUANTITATIVE ANALYSIS OF JUDICIAL BEHAVIOR (1959). Using a small number of cases to position the judges is not a serious handicap if the case type involved has reasonably high unidimensionality. If, for example, voting for the defense rather than the prosecution tends to mean roughly the same thing from one case to the next, then adding more criminal cases beyond the first few is largely redundant, especially where business regulation and tax cases have been excluded from the category of criminal cases. More important than the reliability or internal consistency of the decision variable is the

Supreme Court, on the other hand, was 25 percent for the defense.[22] Justices Brennan and Heher were both above this average.[23] There is no mathematical reason to prevent any Democrat or Republican from being above, below, or at the average decision score of his court. It should also be pointed out that if all the full-court cases for a time period are used, as was done in Table 14–1, or if only the nonunanimous full-court cases for a time period are used, as was done in Table 14–2, then the same judges will be above, below, or at the average decision score of their respective courts. The positioning is identical because the unanimous cases of a court have no bearing on who is above, below, or at the average of the court. Considerably less work, however, is involved if one needs only to consult the cases that are nonunanimous on the issue being decided in order to position the judges on a court as being above, below, or at the average decision score of their court.[24]

From the data in Table 14–1 or in Table 14–2, a four-cell table, like that of Table 14–3, can easily be constructed to show the relation between being a Democrat and being above the average of one's court on the decision score, "proportion of times voting for the defense in criminal

---

validity or meaningfulness of the correlations between the decision variables and various judicial characteristics in light of correlations involving (1) the characteristics of other judges and their decisions; (2) the same judges and other decisions; or (3) the characteristics of legislators, voters, jurors, or related decision makers and their decisions.

[22] The average decision score in criminal cases for the New Jersey Supreme Court included the decision scores of those judges who gave no party affiliation. If such judges were excluded from the calculation, then a different average criminal decision score for each court would have to be calculated every time the effect of a different judicial characteristic was studied. This would unduly complicate a study involving many judicial characteristics and many types of cases. Where there are many judges who fall into neither of the two categories used, then they should be excluded from the calculation of the averages of their respective courts to prevent distortions.

[23] Instead of classifying each judge as being merely above or below the average decision score of his respective court, one could utilize percentage points. Then, instead of determining the percent of (1) Democratic or (2) Republican judges who were above the average decision score of their respective courts, one would determine (1) the average number of percentage points that the Democratic or (2) the Republican judges were above or below the average decision score of their respective courts. This alternative method, however, results in an unduly complex research design and in unduly complex tabular presentations. A more important reason for rejecting it is that while one can feel confident in saying on the basis of a limited number of cases that a judge is above or below the average decision score of his court, one cannot feel nearly so confident in trying to pinpoint his percentage points above or below the average decision score of his court.

[24] When the formal opinion is unanimous, the judges may have initially disagreed in the conference room before unity was established. There is no reason why the background-behavior relations should be significantly different in conference room disagreement from what they are in formal opinion disagreement. Formal disagreement, however, only arises in approximately 10 percent of the state supreme court cases, with wide variations among different types of cases.

TABLE 14–2

DATA ON PARTY AFFILIATIONS AND CRIMINAL CASE DECISION SCORES FOR THE
1955 PENNSYLVANIA AND NEW JERSEY SUPREME COURT JUDGES
(using all the 1955 full-court *non-unanimous* criminal cases)

Judges	Party	Decision Score[*]	Above or below the Average of One's Court
Pennsylvania			Average of court .183
Arnold	Republican	0/9 or .00	Below
Bell	Republican	1/9 or .11	Below
Chidsey	Republican	1/9 or .11	Below
Jones	Democratic	1/9 or .11	Below
Musmanno	Democratic	8.5/9 or .94	Above
Stearne	Republican	0/9 or .00	Below
Stern	Republican	0/9 or .00	Below
New Jersey			Average of court .313
Brennan	Democratic	5/13 or .38	Above
Burling	None given	2/13 or .15	Below
Heher	Democratic	8.5/13 or .65	Above
Jacobs	None given	3/13 or .23	Below
Oliphant	Republican	3/13 or .23	Below
Vanderbilt	Republican	3/13 or .23	Below
Wachenfeld	Democratic	4/13 or .31	Below

[*] Decision score = proportion of times voting for the defense in criminal cases.

cases."[25] Table 14–3 shows that 60 percent of the 5 Democratic judges involved were above the average decision score of their respective courts, whereas 0 percent of the 7 Republican judges involved were above the average of their respective courts.[26]

[25] Those judges who were *at* the average decision score of their respective courts were placed with those judges who were *below* the average decision score of their respective courts in light of conventional practice especially where small samples are involved. S. SIEGEL, NON-PARAMETRIC STATISTICS FOR THE BEHAVIORAL SCIENCES 112–15 (1956). To the extent that judges in non-unanimous decisions tend to be slightly skewed toward the conservative or prosecution direction, judges at the average tend to be closer to those below the average than they are to those above the average.

[26] The alternative method is to determine, first, on how many courts the Democrats had higher average decision scores than the Republicans and, second, on how many courts the Republicans had higher average decision scores than the Democrats. With regard to the data in Table 14–1, there are two courts of the first type and zero courts of the second type. The probability of obtaining purely by chance X number of courts of the first type and only Y number of courts of the second type can be determined by a two-cell chi-square test or a two-cell t-test. See SIEGEL, *op. cit.* 42–47. This courts approach (as contrasted to the judges approach that Table 14–3 applies to the data of Table 14–1) involves a greatly decreased sample size, since there are many more judges than there are courts, and it involves giving undue weight to smaller courts since all courts figure equally in the courts approach, regardless of their size. Most important, it loses information partially preserved in the

TABLE 14–3

THE RELATION BETWEEN PARTY AFFILIATION AND CRIMINAL CASE DECISION SCORES
USING THE 1955 PENNSYLVANIA AND NEW JERSEY SUPREME COURT JUDGES

	Republican Judges	Democratic Judges
Above the average of one's court on the decision score*	0 (0 percent of 7)	3 (60 percent of 5)
At or below the average of one's court on the decision score	7 (100 percent of 7)	2 (40 percent of 5)
Totals	7	5

* Decision score = proportion of times voting for the defense in criminal cases.

As a matter of curiosity, one might ask what is the relation between party affiliation and criminal case decision scores using all the 1955 bipartisan supreme courts, not just those of Pennsylvania and New Jersey? Table 14–4 provides the answer.[27] It tends to indicate that Democratic judges have a greater tendency to decide for the defense in criminal cases than do Republican judges in that 55 percent of the 40 democratic judges, involved were above the average decision score of their respective courts, whereas only 31 percent of the 45 Republican

---

judges approach on the *degree* of difference between the Democrats and Republicans on a court. The ideal method is probably one that gives the figures for both the judges approach (e.g., 60 percent of the 5 Democrats and 0 percent of the 7 Republican judges were above the average of their respective courts) and the courts approach (e.g., on two of the courts the Democratic judges had a higher average decision score than did the Republicans, whereas on none of the courts did the Republican judges have a higher average decision score than did the Democratic judges).

[27] An alternative to both the judges and the courts approach is a cases approach, usable only in the special situation where one is willing to weight all the cases in the sample equally, as when one is interested in discussing the background-decisional relations on a single court over time. For example, of the 55 cases from 1789 through 1960 in which the United States Supreme Court nullified provisions in congressional acts authorizing governmental regulation or taxation, 22 cases (or 40 percent) involved a positive correlation between being a Democratic judge and voting against nullification; 18 (or 33 percent) involved a zero correlation; and only 15 (or 27 percent) involved a negative correlation. The probability of such a breakdown purely by chance can be determined by using a two-cell chi-square test (if zero-correlated cases are eliminated) or a three-cell chi-square test (if zero-correlated cases are retained). See J. P. GUILFORD, *op. cit.* 236–39. By a positive correlation in any single case is meant a *greater* proportion of the participating Democratic judges voted against nullification than did the participating Republican judges. Likewise, a negative correlation means a *lesser* proportion of the Democratic judges in the case so voted, and a zero correlation means both groups had equal proportions of antinullification voters. See *ibid.* 305–15.

judges involved were above the average of their respective courts.[28] This distribution is statistically significant in that the difference shown is not readily attributable to chance, given the size of the difference and the size of the groups involved.[29] The 85 judges involved in Table 14–4 include all the usable judges on the 15 bipartisan state supreme courts that heard nonunanimous criminal cases in 1955.[30] On 10 of these 15 courts, the Democratic judges had a higher average decision score for the defense than did the Republican judges.[31] On the remaining five courts, the pattern was reversed, but the average difference was considerably smaller.[32]

---

[28] This type of relationship can also be expressed in terms of a correlation coefficient which can range from +1.00 (perfect positive correlation) to −1.00 (perfect negative correlation). The phi correlation coefficient is appropriate to use for the data because it takes into consideration (1) the dichotomous phrasing of the variables and (2) that the judicial characteristic with which one is working may not be measurable in degrees or may not be distributed in a bell-shaped distribution, although the decision variable may be. See H. WALKER and J. LEV, STATISTICAL INFERENCE 271–75 (1953). The phi correlation for Table 14–4 is a +.24 correlation between being a Democratic judge and being above the average decision score of one's court where the decision score represents the proportion of times voting for the defense in criminal cases.

[29] The t-test is the appropriate test of statistical significance to use on this type of data to determine the probability of attributing the differences found to chance because (1) it takes into consideration the smallness of the samples involved and because (2) the judges distribute themselves approximately in a bell-shaped manner on the decision variables being measured. Some judges in the total sample are very much above the average of their respective courts on a decision score, while some are very much below, but most judges are approximately at the average. Individual courts may be skewed in various directions, but the overall distribution of the total sample of judges on the dependent variable tends toward a bell shape. See H. YUKER, A GUIDE TO STATISTICAL CALCULATIONS 64–66 (1958) for the formula for making such a t-test. The probabilities so found should be halved if the hypothesis specifies the direction of the difference, not merely that there will be a difference. See SIEGEL, *op. cit.* 13–14. So long as there is no expected-by-chance frequency less than 10 in any of the cells, the chi-square test may also be applied, giving exactly the same results as the t-test. See J. P. GUILFORD, *op. cit.* 231–35. The probability is between 1 and 2.5 out of 100 of obtaining purely by chance the difference of 24 percentage points, which is shown in Table 14–4 with Republican and Democratic group sizes of 45 and 40 judges, respectively. Such a computation is useful in that it enables one to give less weight to high correlations found with a small set of judges and to give more weight to low correlations found with a large set of judges.

[30] By usable judges in this context is meant judges listed in the DIRECTORY OF AMERICAN JUDGES at the beginning of 1955 who served to the end of the year and who listed themselves as either Democrats or Republicans in the directories consulted.

[31] These 10 courts that went in accordance with the hypothesis were the supreme courts of California, Colorado, Idaho, Maryland, Michigan, Montana, New Jersey, Pennsylvania, Rhode Island, and North Dakota. The average difference on these courts was 45 percentage points between the average decision score of their Democrats and the average decision score of their Republicans.

[32] These five courts that went contrary to the hypothesis were the supreme courts of Illinois, New York, Ohio, Utah, and the United States Supreme Court. The average difference was only 24 percentage points between the average decision score of their Republicans and the average decision score of their Democrats.

Another important way of interpreting Table 14–4 is to point out that knowing a judge is a Republican or a Democrat enables one to predict accurately whether a judge will be above or below the average decision score of his court approximately 53 out of 95 times, or approximately 56 percent. This is so since 31 plus 22 of the 45 plus 40 judges behaved in

TABLE 14–4

THE RELATION BETWEEN PARTY AFFILIATION AND CRIMINAL CASE DECISION SCORES
USING ALL THE 1955 BIPARTISAN SUPREME COURTS

	Republican Judges	Democratic Judges
Above the average of one's court on the decision score*	14 (31 percent of 45)	22 (55 percent of 40)
At or below the average of one's court on the decision score	31 (69 percent of 45)	18 (45 percent of 40)
Totals	45	40

* Decision score = proportion of times voting for the defense in criminal cases. Unanimous cases were excluded, since they have no bearing on the direction of the position of judges relative to their co-judges sitting on the same court.

accordance with the hypothesis that Republican judges tend to be below and Democratic judges tend to be above the decision scores of their courts.[33]

E. EXPLAINING THE FINDINGS

No test of the relation between a judicial characteristic and a form of judicial decision making should be considered complete unless some meaningful explanation is offered to account for the findings. Two factors, for example, might account for the difference found between the decisions in criminal cases of Democratic judges and those of Republican judges. First, to some extent a criminal case represents a conflict of social groups in that the defendant generally tends to be a member of the lower middle or working class (particularly if tax and business regulation cases

---

[33] An alternative interpretation is to square the difference between the 55 percent and the 31 percent of Table 14–4, giving .24 squared or 6 percent. To say that political party as a variable accounts for only 6 percent of the variance in the cases may have some technical statistical meaning, but it has no commonsense meaning.

are analyzed separately),[34] and the prosecutor tends to be a member of the upper middle or upper class, enforcing laws promulgated by upper middle and upper class legislators and judges.[35] Second, various studies have shown that Democratic voters and legislators tend to be more working-class oriented in their values than are Republican voters and legislators.[36] Given the average nature of criminal cases and the average nature of Democrats and Republicans who are not judges, it is understandable that the Democratic judges generally tended to have a higher decision score for the defense in criminal cases than did their fellow Republican judges on the same court. In other words, being a Democratic judge does not cause one to become relatively defense-minded, but, rather, having a certain set of values possibly causes one to be both a Democrat and a relatively defense-minded judge.[37]

On the other hand, various offsetting factors prevent the correlation from being perfect. For one, party choice is frequently determined by considerations other than the similarity between the values of the individual and those of the party he has chosen. Even if an individual has chosen his party on the basis of value considerations, he may deviate from others within his party on a narrow but relevant issue, such as leniency toward criminal defendants. In addition, two judges may have the same value systems and thus possibly be of the same party, but one of the two judges may hold his values with a greater intensity and may frequently dissent without being joined by his less vigorous associate of the same party. Lack of homogeneity in the cases and the presence of clerical errors may also disrupt the correlation.

III. OTHER INTERRELATIONAL HYPOTHESES

Other tables like Table 14–4 were compiled in a project carried on at Northwestern University in 1960, using different judicial characteristics and different types of cases. The other judicial characteristics include pressure group affiliations, prejudicial occupations, education, age, urbanism, regionalism, and ethnic group affiliations. The other types of cases include those dealing with administrative regulation, civil liberties, taxation, family relations, business relations, and personal injury matters. Many of these other tables also showed statistically significant correla-

---

[34] D. TAFT, CRIMINOLOGY 131–33 (1950).

[35] D. MATTHEWS, THE SOCIAL BACKGROUND OF POLITICAL DECISION-MAKERS 23–30 (1954).

[36] A. CAMPBELL, G. GURIN, & W. MILLER, THE VOTER DECIDES 118–19 (1954); J. TURNER, PARTY AND CONSTITUENCY: PRESSURES ON CONGRESS 60 (1951).

[37] Values cause party affiliation more than party affiliation causes values, but party affiliation and its accompanying activities can reinforce prior values as is recognized in Adamany, *The Party Variable in Judges' Voting: Conceptual Notes and a Case Study*, 63 AM. POLI. SCI. REV.—(1969) and Nagel, *Political Party Affiliation and Judges' Decisions*, 55 AM POLI. SCI. REV. 843 (1961) at p. 847.

tions between the judicial characteristics and the decisional propensities involved.[38]

Various projects are now being carried on at the University of Illinois to test hypotheses concerning correlations between certain variables that do not involve judicial characteristics and certain decisional processes and outcomes. Some of the relations being tested include the relation between the type of property system different societies have and the degree of judicial bribery present within these societies; the relation between voting for party and nationality factors, and whether a judicial election or a general election is involved; the relation between the per capita income of different states and the citation influence of their state supreme courts; and the relation between the socioeconomic status of different defendants in criminal cases and the severity of the penalties they receive.

Indeed, quantitative behavioral methods can possibly make their greatest contribution to public law by way of this concept of *testing generalizations concerning interrelations* between certain judicial characteristics or other variables on the one hand and certain decisional processes or outcomes on the other hand. The findings of such studies should definitely bring the field of public law closer to one of its goals of providing a better understanding of the nature of the judicial process.

---

[38] Nagel, *Political Party Affiliation and Judges' Decisions*, 55 Am. Pol. Sci. Rev. 843–50 (1961) (partly in chap. 15 *infra*). This article deals with the relations between political party affiliation of judges on the one hand and their decisions scores in 15 different types of cases on the other. Nagel, *Judicial Backgrounds and Criminal Cases*, J. Crim. L., C., & P. S. (1962) (chap. 18 *infra*). This article deals with the relations between 14 different background and attitudinal variables of judges on the one hand and their criminal case decision scores on the other.

SECTION II
Methods of Recruitment

CHAPTER 15

Election versus Appointment

Judicial appointment, a nonpartisan ballot, and long terms of office have been proposed or defended as devices for decreasing the role of partisan influences on judicial decisions. Judges selected or holding office where these devices are operative possibly have a greater tendency to vote contrary to their party pattern than other judges. To test these hypotheses, a measure of "voting contrary to one's party pattern" is needed.

I have attempted such a test, using three types of cases—namely, administrative regulation of business, unemployment compensation, and employee injury cases. These were selected because in the decisions on them one can most confidently say that political party patterns emerged.[1] Some of the judges did not hear all three types of cases. For purposes of this study, however, a judge was considered to have voted contrary to the pattern of his party if he was a Republican who was above (or a Democrat who was below) the average of his court on the decision score on all three or two out of three or, if he did not vote on all three, then on both of the two or on the one of the types of cases he heard. A judge was considered to have voted in accordance with the pattern of his party, conversely, if he was a Republican who was below (or a Democrat who was above) the average of his court on the decision score in all three, two out of three, two out of two, or the one of these types of cases he voted on. Judges who fell between these limits—i.e., whose decision scores departed from their court averages in one of two of the case types—were not counted either way. Using these definitions, 65 judges serving through 1955 on

---

[1] See Nagel, *Political Party Affiliation and Judge's Decisions,* 55 AM. POL. SCI. REV. 843–48 (1961).

bipartisan state and federal supreme courts were counted as having voted either contrary to or in accordance with the pattern set by their respective parties.

Table 15–1 shows the relationships between being a judge who operated under each of the various arrangements listed and being a judge who voted contrary to his party pattern. It includes all those judges who could be assigned a voting position contrary to or in accordance with their party pattern. According to row one of Table 15–2, 7 of the 18 appointed judges voted contrary to their party patterns, whereas only 7 of the 47 elected judges did so.[2] This was the most striking of the

TABLE 15–1

JUDICIAL TENURE, METHODS OF SELECTION, AND CONFORMITY
TO PARTY VOTING PATTERNS, 1955

Group 1	Group 2	Number of judges in each group (1)	(2)	% in Group 1 who voted contrary to their party pattern	% in Group 2 who voted contrary to their party pattern	Probability of the positive difference being due to chance
Appointed judges	Elected judges	18	47	39	15	.02½ to .05
Judges elected by a nonpartisan ballot	Judges elected by a partisan ballot	29	18	14	17	*
Judges with terms longer than 8 years	Judges with terms of 8 or less years	37	28	27	14	.15 to .20
Elected judges with terms longer than 8 years	Elected judges with terms of 8 or less years	20	27	15.0	14.8	*
Appointed judges with terms longer than 8 years	Elected judges with terms longer than 8 years	17	20	41	15	.02½ to .05

* Negative or negligible difference.

several differences that emerged, and it was statistically significant slightly below the 0.05 level of chance probability.[3] The nonpartisan versus partisan ballot comparison showed an insignificant negative relation between being a judge elected by a nonpartisan ballot and being a judge

[2] Elected and appointed judges were sorted out from the entries and the designation table in the DIRECTORY OF AMERICAN JUDGES (1955).

[3] These probabilities were calculated by using a chi-square formula with a Yates correction in view of the skew toward voting in accordance with party patterns. See J. P. GUILFORD, FUNDAMENTAL STATISTICS IN PSYCHOLOGY AND EDUCATION 207–8, 228–39 (1956).

who voted contrary to his party pattern.[4] As for length of term, eight years was the median term in 1955 for supreme court judges[5] A greater proportion of the judges with terms longer than this median voted contrary to their party pattern than did the judges with shorter terms. This difference, however, disappears when long-term judges are compared with short-term judges, while the method of selection is held constant as is shown on the fourth row of Table 15–2. On the other hand, if length of term is held constant, as in the fifth row, the difference between appointed and elected judges still remains strong. Thus, the method of selection can account for the difference between the long- and short-term groups, but the length of term cannot account for the difference between the appointed and elected groups.

What is there about appointed judges, in contrast to elected judges, that might account for the significantly higher percentage of them who voted contrary to their party patterns? Appointed judges probably reflect their personal values in their decisions just as much as do elected judges.[6] The difference may lie in the possibility that the values of appointed judges are less clearly correlated with their party affiliation than are the values of elected judges. In other words, appointed judges who are Democrats possibly tend to be nontypical Democrats in their values, and appointed judges who are Republicans likewise possibly nontypical Republicans, at least more so than elected judges. In terms of liberalism and conservatism, appointed judges serving on bipartisan courts are possibly more likely to be conservative Democrats or liberal Republicans. Two considerations support this hypothesis.

First, appointive systems for choosing state supreme court judges generally provide for a nonpartisan or bipartisan body to nominate or approve the executive appointments to the court. In Missouri and California, for example, there is a special nominating commission composed of distinguished members of the bar, the judiciary, and the lay public. Such a nominating commission is less likely to consider party consistency in picking judges than are the nominators for an elected court at a party caucus, convention or primary. It is somewhat more debatable

---

[4] Judges elected on a nonpartisan ballot were identified by first determining, through the DIRECTORY entries, in what year the most recent term (prior to 1955) of each judge began and then checking the judicial election law for his state in that year in the BOOK OF STATES (1938–1955).

[5] The terms of office were traced through the same sources as the methods of selection.

[6] This hypothesis was partially tested by using the attitudinal data obtained from a mailed questionnaire to see if any correlation existed between (1) being an appointed rather than an elected judge and (2) voting contrary to rather than in accordance with one's value position in criminal cases. The correlation, as hypothesized, was practically zero with a sample of 65 judges.

whether a prospective judge on the federal or the New Jersey Supreme Court is helped toward a bipartisan senate confirmation if he is not too closely identified with a political party; but evidently that might handicap him in a partisan election system.

Second, appointive systems for choosing supreme court justices may provide by tradition or law that the executive should occasionally appoint judges not of his own party to the court. The appointed courts covered in Table 15–2 were the supreme courts of California, Missouri, New Jersey, and the United States. From 1910 to 1960, 9 of the 33 judges appointed to the United States Supreme Court were not of the President's party.[7] In a survey of state supreme courts, conducted by the Council of State Governments, the question was asked as to what attempts, if any, were made by each state to obtain supreme courts of a bipartisan composition.[8] The responses and subsequent checking indicated that the appointive course systems of California, Missouri, New Jersey, Delaware, and New Hampshire made such attempts by tradition or law, whereas no elective court system did so. If a Democratic governor or President appoints a Republican, he is likely to appoint a Republican with values closer to the relatively liberal wing than to the relatively conservative wing of that party. Likewise, a Republican governor or President who appoints a Democrat will probably choose one with values closer to the relatively conservative wing than to the relatively liberal wing of the Democratic Party. Electorates, on the other hand, are never required to choose judges of the party opposite to their own.[9]

The reason for the near-zero correlation with regard to the nonpartisan ballot hypothesis is probably the near-meaninglessness of nonpartisan ballots where there are organized and competing political parties running the elections behind the scenes. Three states—Michigan, Tennessee, and Arizona—have nonpartisan ballots for supreme court elections, but openly recognize the role of political parties by providing partisan primaries or party conventions to pick the judges who run on the nonpartisan ballot.[10] Even nonpartisan elections preceded by nonpartisan primaries may have partisan influences behind the formalities of the election and nomination procedure. If party affiliation does make a difference in judicial behavior, as the data from Table 15–1 tend to show, then non-

---

[7] SCHUBERT, CONSTITUTIONAL POLITICS: THE POLITICAL BEHAVIOR OF SUPREME COURT JUSTICES AND THE CONSTITUTIONAL POLICIES THAT THEY MAKE 37, 711–12 (1960).

[8] COURTS OF LAST RESORT OF THE FORTY-EIGHT STATES Table 4 (1955).

[9] The mailed questionnaire survey mentioned in note 6 showed no positive correlation between (1) being an appointed judge rather than an elected judge on a bipartisan court and (2) being a conservative Democrat or a liberal Republican rather than a liberal Democrat or a conservative Republican. The slightly negative correlation, however, was only a −.04 phi coefficient and was only based on 25 judges.

[10] COURTS OF LAST RESORT OF THE FORTY-EIGHT STATES, *op. cit., supra* note 8.

partisan ballots only deprive the voter of information useful to him in intelligently voting for judges, assuming he does not learn their party affiliation by some other means.

The reason for the zero correlation with regard to the length-of-term hypothesis is probably that a long term does not cause a judge's value system and his party affiliation to become inconsistent if they were formerly consistent. A long term of office may well make a judge more independent of a party boss. Judges on state supreme courts, however, as previously stated, probably vote in accordance with their party pattern because their value system determines both their voting behavior in certain cases and their party affiliation, not because some party boss asked them to do so.

Regardless of judicial tenure and modes of selection, there probably will always be a residue of party-correlated judicial subjectivity as long as political parties are at least partly value-oriented and as long as court cases involve value-oriented controversies. Ultimately, the problem becomes not how to remove this irreducible residue of judicial subjectivity but, rather, what direction it should take. If judges should have value positions that are representative of the public at large, then it seems arguable that judges (at least on the higher court levels) should be elected, since presumably a judge elected at large will tend to have more representative values than a judge chosen in any other manner.

SECTION III

Background and Attitude Characteristics

CHAPTER 16

Judicial Attitudes and Those of Legislators and Administrators

Since 1960, at least two articles and one book have been published with titles indicating that they deal with the attitudes of some segment of the American judiciary.[1] Closer examination, however, reveals that those materials are concerned only with the on-the-bench attitudes of judges (as manifested in judicial decisions). As yet no published survey seems to have been made to ascertain, on the basis of a questionnaire, the degree of liberalism or other broad set of attitudinal characteristics present among members of the American judiciary, especially in comparison with legislators and administrators.[2] It is the purpose of this chapter to describe some findings based on such a study, to discuss the causes and effects of the differences found, and to test some proposals for decreasing the role of personal attitudes in judicial decision making.[3]

---

[1] Spaeth, *An Approach to the Study of Attitudinal Differences as an Aspect of Judicial Behavior*, 5 MIDWEST J. POL. SCI. 165–80 (1961); Tanenhaus, *Supreme Court Attitudes toward Federal Administrative Agencies*, 22 J. POL. 502–24 (1960); and PAUL, CONSERVATIVE CRISIS AND THE RULE OF LAW: ATTITUDES OF BAR AND BENCH, 1887–1895 (1960).

[2] "We know courts are, at least in this country a generally conservative social force, and more like a brake than a motor in the social mechanism, but we have no scientific factual comparison of judicial, legislative, and executive organs of government." Quoted from Cohen, *Transcendental Nonsense and the Functional Approach*, 35 COLUM. L. REV. 845 (1935), reprinted in his READINGS IN LEGAL PHILOSOPHY AND JURISPRUDENCE 481 (1951).

[3] For further details concerning methodological and various other matters involved in this chapter, see an earlier version, *Off-the-Bench Judicial Attitudes*, which appears in JUDICIAL DECISION-MAKING 481 (G. SCHUBERT ed. 1963). The earlier version, however, does not contain the judicial-legislative-executive comparisons presented here.

I. THE QUESTIONNAIRE

In comparison with a questionnaire approach, the traditional analysis of court cases will not, for a variety of reasons, so clearly reveal the nature of off-the-bench judicial attitudes. For one thing, judges differ among themselves in the extent to which they suppress their personal attitudes in their decisions. Judges in general probably suppress their personal attitudes more so than do legislators and administrators when reaching similar decisions. In addition, just because many courts, particularly the United States Supreme Court, have in the past frequently declared liberal economic legislation unconstitutional does not necessarily indicate that judges are more conservative than legislators and governors. The legislation declared unconstitutional may have reflected unusually liberal viewpoints, not the average viewpoints of legislators across the country as a whole.[4] Along similar lines, if the Supreme Court nullifies some conservative free speech legislation, this may not tell us much about the relative sympathy of judges and legislators for freedom of speech if the legislation was a nontypical legislative product. The judiciary almost never nullifies conservative economic legislation or liberal free speech legislation because it is almost never presented with such cases. Of course, any analysis based solely on the Supreme Court lacks broadness if one wants to talk about a wider sample of judges. A questionnaire approach has the further advantage of holding the stimulus constant for more meaningful comparisons among the respondents. A questionnaire approach also avoids the circularity of saying "conservative judges reach conservative decisions" where both the conservatism of the judges and the conservatism of their decisions have been determined by reading their decisions.

Figure 16–1 shows both sides of the questionnaire that was mailed along with an explanatory letter to the 313 state and federal supreme court judges who were incumbent in 1955 according to the *Directory of American Judges.* Each questionnaire had a different identification number typed on its last line so that the responses of the judges who replied could be correlated with their judicial decisions and their background characteristics.

The questionnaire is designed to determine operationally the degree of liberalism of one who answers it. "Liberalism" is used conceptually in this chapter to refer to a viewpoint associated with the interests of

---

[4] Charles Warren makes the further argument that the conservative economic decisions of the Supreme Court between 1890 and 1935 have been distortedly overpublicized relative to their social impact, relative to the work of Congress, and relative to the liberal economic decisions of the Court. C. WARREN, CONGRESS, THE CONSTITUTION, AND THE SUPREME COURT 222–45 (1935).

the lower or less privileged economic or social groups in a society and, to a lesser extent, with acceptance of long-run social change. The term "conservative," on the other hand, is used primarily to refer to a viewpoint associated with the interests of the upper or dominant groups in a society, and with resistance to long-run social change.[5] Since liberalism is a continuum concept, one cannot be considered a liberal or a conservative in an absolute sense, but only more, less, or equally liberal in comparison with someone else. The liberalism–conservatism attitude was chosen over other attitudinal or personality characteristics because it seemed to represent the frame of mind most likely to account for why some political decision makers tend to decide in one direction on controversial issues and other political decision makers tend to decide in an opposite direction. Various studies have shown that liberalism is composed of or correlated with a number of subattitudes.[6] These subattitudes include: (1) working class and socialistic sympathy, (2) internationalism and pacifism, (3) criminal rehabilitationism and tolerance of deviant behavior, (4) naturalism as contrasted to supernaturalism, (5) ethnic equalitarianism, (6) approval of marital and family planning, (7) democraticness (i.e., advocacy of majority rule and tolerance of deviant beliefs), and (8) sex equalitarianism.

The 24 items in the questionnaire were taken with slight changes from the 40 items in a liberalism questionnaire devised by Hans Eysenck.[7] The Eysenck liberalism questionnaire was chosen because: (1) it clearly distinguished British Socialists and Communists on the one hand from British Conservatives and Fascists on the other hand as a test of its validity; (2) it has items relating to all eight of the subattitudes of liberalism; (3) it has been subjected to an analysis that determined that all the items were measuring the same underlying factor; (4) it provides for the agree–disagree method of scoring, which is easy for respondents and test interpreters to handle; (5) its items are worded relatively concisely, unambiguously, and maturely; (6) it is relatively free from being timebound or culturebound in its concepts; (7) it has enough items to produce a meaningful scale; and (8) it has some items worded in a liberal direction and some in a conservative direction. None of the other proposed liberalism questionnaires have all these advantages.[8]

[5] R. MacIver, THE WEB OF GOVERNMENT 215–17 (1951).
[6] H. Eysenck, Psychology of Politics (1954); Kerr, *Correlates of Political-Economic Liberalism-Conservatism,* 20 Social Psychology 61–77 (1944); and Vetter, *What Makes Attitudes and Opinions Liberal or Conservative,* 47 J. of Abnormal & Social Psych. 125–30 (1947).
[7] Eysenck, *op. cit.,* 122–24. Portions of the questionnaire are reproduced here with the permission of Routledge and Kegan Paul, London, England.
[8] For many of the alternative liberalism questionnaires, see Mental Measurements Yearbook (O. Buros ed. 1938–59).

FIGURE 16–1

THE QUESTIONNAIRE

Below are 24 statements that represent widely held opinions on various social questions selected from speeches, books, newspapers, and other sources. They were chosen in such a way that most people are likely to agree with some and disagree with others. After each statement please record your completely confidential personal opinion regarding the statement, using the following system of marking:

++ if you strongly agree with the statement.
+ if you agree on the whole but not strongly.
0   if you cannot decide for or against or if you think the question is worded in such a way that you cannot give an answer.
— if you disagree on the whole but not strongly.
—— if you strongly disagree.

	Your Frank Opinion
Opinion Statements	
1. Colored people are innately inferior to white people.	————
2. Present laws favor the rich as against the poor.	————
3. War is inherent in human nature.	————
4. Our treatment of criminals is too harsh: we should try to cure, not to punish them.	————
5. In the interests of peace, we must give up part of our national sovereignty.	————
6. Sunday observance is old-fashioned, and should cease to govern our behavior.	————
7. It is right that men should be permitted greater sexual freedom than women by society.	————
8. Unrestricted freedom of discussion on every topic is desirable in the press, in literature, and on the stage.	————
9. More collectivism, like the TVA, should be introduced into our society.	————
10. Conscientious objectors are traitors to their country, and should be treated accordingly.	————
11. Only by going back to religion can civilization hope to survive.	————
12. Marriages between white and colored people should be greatly discouraged.	————
13. There should be far more controversial and political discussion over the radio and television.	————
14. Divorce laws should be altered to make divorce easier.	————
15. Nationalization in any industry is likely to lead to inefficiency.	————
16. It is right and proper that non-sectarian religious education in schools should be compulsory.	————

FIGURE 16–1—*cont.*

17. Men and women have the right to find out whether they are sexually suited before marriage.   _____

18. The principle "Spare the rod and spoil the child" has much truth in it, and should govern our methods of bringing up children.   _____

19. Women are not the equals of men in intelligence and organizing ability.   _____

20. The Jews have too much power and influence in this country.   _____

21. Differences in pay between men and women doing the same work should be abolished.   _____

22. Birth control, except when medically indicated, should be made illegal.   _____

23. The death penalty is barbaric, and should be abolished.   _____

24. Only people with a definite minimum of intelligence and education should be allowed to vote.   _____

Your father's main occupation (a possibly relevant background item not published in the directories)_____

Correlation number (for IBM computer purposes) _____

The 40 items were reduced to 24 in order to have a less bulky questionnaire and thereby presumably a higher response. The particular 24 items selected were chosen in such a way that there would be three items for describing each of the eight subattitudes, anticipating that correlations would be made with each subattitude in addition to the overall attitude of liberalism. The particular three items chosen to represent each subattitude were those three items that had the highest correlation with the factor of liberalism. Slight changes were made in the wording of some items that which were a little ambiguous, out of date, or out of place geographically. Changes were generally avoided in order to keep the items in the derived questionnaire like the corresponding items in the original questionnaire so that Eysenck's extensive research with the original questionnaire could be related to the results obtained with the derived questionnaire.[9] According to the Eysenck method of scoring, a liberal by definition expresses agreement with items 2, 4, 5, 6, 8, 9, 13, 14, 17, 21, and 23, and disagreement with items 1, 3, 7, 10, 11, 12, 15, 16, 18, 19, 20, 22, and 24; a conservative would be expected to respond in the opposite way.

_____

[9] The most significant changes related to toning down the items favorable to socialism so as to get a more diverse response from an American sample. Thus, item 9 originally read, "Ultimately, private property should be abolished and complete socialism introduced"; item 15 originally read, "The nationalization of the great industries is likely to lead to inefficiency, bureaucracy, and stagnation." Item 16, which expressed a sentiment favorable toward church and state coordination, also was toned down, since it originally read, "It is right and proper that religious education in schools should be compulsory."

II.   THE RESPONSES

Of these 313 state and federal supreme court justices, 118 sent back answered questionnaires. Of the 195 remaining judges, 38 are known to have died between 1955 when the *Directory* was published and 1960 when the questionnaires were sent out (known through information received from relatives, the Post Office, and the court reports), 21 wrote back but failed to answer the questions, and 136 failed to reply.[10]

To make the average responses of the judges more meaningful, one should try to say whether the average judge on various items was more or less liberal than some person or group whose degree of liberalism is reasonably well known. The groups chosen for a standard in Table 16–1 consist of a 1948 sample of 250 members of the British Conservative Party, 250 Liberal Party members, and 250 Laborites, all of whom were of the middle class. These groups were chosen because most political scientists have a roughly similar image of how liberal these three relatively homogeneous groups are, and also because they are the only substantial groups for whom Eysenck has published detailed data.

For ease in reading, Table 16–1 groups the items into the subattitudes previously mentioned. The subattitudes are arranged in order of their relevance to the factor of liberalism as measured by the correlation coefficients each component item had with the factor of liberalism in Eysenck's study. An (L) or (C) after each item indicates whether the item is worded in a liberal or a conservative direction. Entries in the difference columns of Table 16–1 are derived by determining the number of percentage points by which the percent of judges agreeing with the item differs from the percent of the nonjudge group agreeing with the item. An "L" in the difference columns indicates the nonjudges were more liberal on the item involved, whereas a "C" indicates the nonjudges were more conservative. One can determine the approximate percent of judges disagreeing with an item by subtracting from 91 percent the percent of judges agreeing. We use 91 percent rather than 100 percent because an average of 9 percent of the participating judges gave a neutral response or nonresponse to each item.

As Table 16–1 indicates, the judges were more conservative on 18 of the 24 items in comparison with the Laborites. The judges were more conservative on 16 of the 24 items in comparison with the Liberals. They were likewise more conservative than the British Conservatives on 10 items, and the British Conservatives were more conservative on 13 items, and both groups were alike on one item. Thus, the average

---

[10] A few judges, legislators, and administrators sent back completed questionnaires too late to be included in the analysis.

TABLE 16–1

The Responses of the Judges and Those of Other Political Groups

Questionnaire Item (C) = worded in conserv. direction (L) = worded in liberal direction (See Figure 16–1 for exact wording.)	% of Judges Agreeing	*Percentage Points Different from:				
		British			American	
		Labor-ites	Liber-als	Tories	Admin-istrators	Legis-lators
Socialistic Sympathy						
2. Laws favor rich (L)	9	L 56	L 28	L 18	L 13	L 17
9. Have more TVA's (L)**	12	L 44	L 3	C 9	L 5	L 9
15. Nationalization means stagnation (C)**	86	L 70	L 28	0	L 12	L 9
Internationalism and Pacifism						
3. War is inherent (C)	33	C 1	C 24	C 34	C 6	C 13
5. Abandon some sovereignty (L)	40	L 36	L 20	C 8	C 15	C 15
10. Conscientious objectors are traitors (C)	10	L 1	C 6	C 18	C 3	C 7
Criminal Rehabilitationism						
4. Criminal treatment is too harsh (L)	20	L 52	L 38	L 19	L 18	C 1
18. Spare rod, spoil child (C) ...	69	L 31	L 20	L 13	C 3	0
23. Abolish death penalty (L) ...	34	L 30	L 8	C 4	L 1	C 5
Religiosity						
6. Sunday observance is old-fashioned (L)	11	L 57	L 33	L 25	L 2	L 7
11. Go back to religion (C)	66	L 30	L 10	L 1	L 2	L 2
16. Have religion in schools (C)**	31	C 1	C 24	C 35	C 2	L 4
Ethnic Equalitarianism						
1. Colored are inferior (C)	37	L 18	L 10	C 5	L 4	C 5
12. Discourage miscegenation (C)	88	L 39	L 22	L 11	L 13	L 16
20. Jews are too powerful (C) ..	9	C 30	C 43	C 59	C 9	C 14
Marital and Family Planning						
14. Make divorce laws easier (L)	14	L 47	L 28	L 19	L 1	C 2
17. Premarital sex is permissible (L)	15	L 47	L 25	L 20	L 10	L 10
22. Make birth control illegal (C)	12	L 4	C 10	C 10	L 1	C 5
Faith in Free Speech and Democracy						
8. Have unrestricted discussion (L)	49	L 30	L 30	L 26	L 2	L 1
13. Have more controversy on radio and TV (L)	64	L 20	L 7	L 3	L 12	L 13
24. Have education test for voting (C)	37	C 2	C 10	C 18	C 6	C 15
Sex Equalitarianism						
7. Give men more sex freedom (C)	13	C 7	C 16	C 21	C 3	0
19. Women are inferior to men (C)	17	C 11	C 13	C 23	L 5	L 3
21. Have equal pay for both sexes (L)	69	L 14	L 8	C 1	L 4	C 11

* An "L" in the difference columns indicates the non-judges were more liberal on the item involved. A "C" indicates the non-judges were more conservative. The number indicates how many percentage points separated the two groups.
** The American questionnaire was slightly different from the British questionnaire on items 9 and 15 making the judges look less conservative than they otherwise would be in comparison with the British sample. The reverse was true on item 16.

American supreme court judge of 1955 seems to be about as liberal as the average middle class member of the British Conservative Party of 1948 to the extent that the data presented is representative of the two groups.

In order to obtain a better understanding of political decision makers, it is interesting to compare the responses of the supreme court judges with the responses obtained from a sample of legislators and cabinet-level administrators on the state and federal levels. To make these comparisons, the same questionnaire without identification numbers was sent to a random sample of 304 state legislators drawn from the *Book of the States* and 9 federal legislators drawn from the *Congressional Directory* for the 1955 term. Of these, 139 legislators sent back completed questionnaires. The questionnaires were also sent to a random sample of 304 state governors, lieutenant-governors, secretaries of state, attorney generals, treasurers, auditors, and superintendents of education drawn from the *Book of the States* for 1955, and a similar sample of 9 federal officials drawn from the *United States Government Organization Manual.* These executive officials sent back 120 completed questionnaires. The 304-to-9 ratio of state and federal representation was used to preserve the same ratio as was present in the sample of judges.

Table 16–1 shows how the responses of the judges compared with those of the legislators and the executive officials. As the table indicates, the judges seem to be substantially more conservative than both the administrators and the legislators on the economic issues and the free speech issues. On the other hand, the judges seem to be substantially less provincial on matters of internationalism than are either the administrators or the legislators, and they are less in favor of restricting the electorate. They are more conservative toward criminal treatment than are administrators but less conservative than are legislators. Likewise, they are more conservative on family planning than are administrators, but are less conservative than legislators. There are no substantial differences between the groups on religiosity, although the judges tended to be slightly more conservative. There are also no consistent differences between the groups on ethnic equalitarianism, although the judges tended to be more prejudiced toward Negroes and less prejudiced toward Jews. All three groups seem to think approximately alike with regard to sexual equality. In general, if one emphasizes the economic and First Amendment issues, which are so important in constitutional law, the administrators seem to be the most liberal; the legislators, next; and the judges, the most conservative of the three sets of political decision makers.

A further picture of the judicial-legislative-executive comparisons can be obtained by examining the unsolicited comments given by some of the respondents. The items dealing with the TVA and nationalization provoked such typical comments among the judges as "incompatible with democracy," "costing us billions annually," "managerial inefficiency," and "God forbid that this government shall ever become socialistic." On the other hand, the legislators who commented on these items said such things as "does not lead to inefficiency," "depends on what [is nationalized]," and "Public utilities [should] accept government regulation." The few administrators who commented on these items all objected to referring to the TVA as collectivistic. In the realm of freedom of speech, one judge offered a quite conservative free speech standard in saying, "I would not permit discussion in literature, press, or on the stage topics that I would not want discussed in my home." By way of contrast, a legislator who agreed strongly that unrestricted freedom of discussion on every topic is desirable commented that the only restriction he would provide for is that the "source of information be available." The administrators offered some less creative comments touching on matters of obscenity, falsehood, and the nature of the speaker. Examples of unsolicited comments to other sets of items might also be given, but in general they merely tend to reinforce the findings based on the more systematic structured responses.

An interesting finding that comes from analyzing the strength of the responses instead of the direction of the responses reveals that of the three groups the judges were the least likely to agree or disagree strongly rather than mildly with the questionnaire items. The legislators, on the other hand, expressed the most frequent tendency to agree or disagree strongly with the items.

An examination of Table 16–1 might lead one to hypothesize that American political leaders, at least on the state level, are possibly more conservative on the average than is the general American population, particularly on economic matters. Since the questionnaire was not submitted to a cross section of the general public, this hypothesis cannot be directly tested with the data of this chapter. In 1958, however, Herbert McCloskey administered a related liberalism questionnaire to approximately 3,000 delegates of the previous Democratic and Republican national conventions and to a nationwide sample of 1,500 citizens. The data he provided in his subsequent *APSR* article tends to show that on the average the party delegates were significantly less liberal than the general public in the realm of tax policy, welfare and equalitarian legislation, public ownership, and foreign policy.[11] Since party delegates are somewhat analogous to administrators, legislators, and judges, such office holders would possibly also be less liberal than the general public.

Comparisons within individual courts revealed that the more conservative judges tended to be Republicans, members of conservative pressure

---

[11] McCloskey *et al., Issue Conflict and Consensus among Party Leaders and Followers,* 54 AM. POL. SCI. REV. 411–15 (1960).

groups, alumni of relatively high tuition law schools, older judges, and members of nationally dominant ethnic groups. Comparisons between courts matched for political party composition revealed that the more conservative judges tended to be Southerners, appointed judges, judges elected by districts rather than at-large, and state judges rather than federal judges.[12]

III.   CAUSES OF THE DIFFERENCES

How might one account for the relative conservatism of the judicial attitudes described in this chapter? One might point out that maybe the sample of respondents was an unrepresentative sample of those to whom questionnaires were sent. The sample-distorting influences that might be present, however, would generally affect the judges, legislators, and administrators all in the same manner. Certain sample-distorting influences did particularly affect the judges, but these distortions tend to make the judges more liberal relative to the legislators and administrators rather than more conservative. For one thing, a substantially higher percentage of nonrespondents among the judges than among the legislators and administrators were deceased nonrespondents because the judges of 1955 were substantially older than the legislators and administrators of 1955. These deceased nonresponding judges would have added to the conservatism of the judges, since these judges tended to be the older judges, and the older judges tended to be more conservative than the younger judges in both their decisions and their attitudes. For another thing, a higher percentage of nonrespondents among the judges than among the legislators and administrators were southern nonrespondents, possibly because the judges were sent their questionnaires from the northern state of Illinois and the legislators and administrators were sent their questionnaires from the southwestern state of Arizona. These southern nonrespondents would have added to the conservatism of the judges, since the southern judges who did respond were generally more conservative than the northern judges. In addition, since judges are reputed to be conservative[13] some of the judges might consciously or subconsciously upgrade the liberalism of their responses so as to reduce the correlation between their responses and their judicial decisions, which the letter accompanying the questionnaires told them were going to be made. No such correlations were mentioned to the legislators or administrators. Finally, given the sample

---

[12] Data on the characteristics of the judges were obtained by consulting THE DI-RECTORY OF AMERICAN JUDGES (LIEBMAN ed. 1955); WHO'S WHO IN AMERICA (W. SAMMONS ed. 1954–58); MARTINDALE-HUBBELL LAW DIRECTORY (1955); E. C. SMITH, DICTIONARY OF FAMILY NAMES (1956), and COURTS OF LAST RESORTS (1950).

[13] R. CARR, THE SUPREME COURT AND JUDICIAL REVIEW 33–36 (1942).

sizes involved, the chance probability is less than 5 out of 100 that the average response to any item could deviate from the true average by more than 10 percent.[14] This paragraph is particularly relevant to answering the critique of Theodore Becker, who emphasizes that only 118 judges responded. He fails to recognize, however, that if one can determine the direction of the nonresponse, as can be done here, then one can say meaningful things about how the results would have been affected if the response had been greater.[15]

Assuming that the samples are reasonably representative, why might supreme court judges be more conservative relative to the general population and relative to legislative and administrative officials? There may be several factors operating. Among the occupational and economic factors, it might be pointed out that all supreme court judges are lawyers; whereas legislators, administrators, and people in general are not so restricted in what occupational strata they come from.[16] Being a lawyer when party is held constant may correlate with conservatism because lawyers tend to come from financially well-to-do families[17] and also tend to be well-to-do themselves.[18] Over 80 percent of the responding judges said their fathers had been professional men, businessmen, or farm owners. As lawyers, the judges themselves tended to be disproportionately prosecuting attorneys and corporation lawyers. Of the few judges who indicated a legal specialty in the *Directory*, 24 said their specialty was corporation law, whereas only one said his specialty was labor law. Likewise, 121 mentioned having been prosecutors, but none mentioned having done criminal defense work. As judges, the 313 supreme court judges averaged a salary of $16,000 per year in 1955.[19] The constant

---

[14] M. J. Hagood & D. O. Price, Statistics for Sociologists 279–94 (1952), and M. Parten, Surveys, Polls, and Samples: Practical Procedures 290–330 (1950).

[15] T. Becker, Political Behaviorism and Modern Jurisprudence 23 (1964); and Becker, *Surveys and Judiciaries, or Who's Afraid of the Purple Curtain,* 1 L. & Soc'y Rev. 133 (1966).

[16] Only 28 percent of the legislators in a sample of 13 states during 1925–35 were lawyers. Hyneman, *Who Makes Our Laws,* 55 Pol. Sci. Q. 556–81 (1940). Although tabulated statistics on some of the background characteristics of governors are available, such statistics are not so available for lieutenant governors, secretaries of state, attorneys general, treasurers, auditors, and state school superintendents. It is also much easier to find data on federal legislators than on state legislators. See W. Bell et al., Public Leadership (1961), and D. Matthews, The Social Background of Political Decision-Makers (1955).

[17] Miller, *American Lawyers in Business and Politics: Their Social Backgrounds and Early Training,* 60 Yale L. J. 66–76 (1951).

[18] In 1954, the average gross income of nonsalaried lawyers was $16,719 with a net (after overhead) of $10,258. Liebenberg, *Income of Lawyers in the Post-War Period,* 36 Survey Current Bus. 29 (1956). The average income of salaried lawyers was slightly higher. *Ibid.*

[19] The Book of States 438 (1956). The relation between wealth and conservatism is discussed in R. Center, Psychology of Social Classes (1949).

looking back to precedents that is characteristic of lawyers in a common law system may also account for some of their conservatism, as may the vested interest that lawyers and judges have in preserving the law that they laboriously learned.[20]

In addition to occupational and economic factors, it might be noted that the 313 judges had a high average age of 63, and to the extent that advanced age brings increased conservatism, this too may explain some of the conservatism of the bench.[21] Furthermore, their ethnic characteristics (race, religion, and ancestral nationality) were heavily weighted in the direction of those ethnic characteristics associated with high socioeconomic status and with attitudinal conservatism.[22] The pressure group affiliations of the judges also appeared to be much more conservative on the average than might be expected of the legislators and administrators, but these affiliations come as a result of being conservative and do not generally operate as value-shaping factors except in a reinforcing sense. With regard to pressure groups, not even one judge indicated that he was a member of a liberal organization like the Americans for Democratic Action, the American Civil Liberties Union, the American Veterans Committee, or the National Lawyers Guild. On the other hand, many judges indicated they were members of conservative organizations like the Sons of the American Revolution, the American Bar Association, the American Legion, and various business groups. Relatively long tenure and frequent appointment may also make the judge less sensitive to popular demands and thereby more conservative.[23]

In addition to accounting for the relative conservatism of the judges, one should also attempt to account for why the gap between the judges, on the one hand, and the legislators and administrators, on the other, is not wider than it is. For one thing, the background characteristics of the judges, which tend to predispose one toward conservatism, are not so drastically different from those of legislators and administrators. All three groups tend to have had high social status occupations, to come from fathers with high social status occupations, to have substantial incomes, to be beyond middle age, and to have high social status ethnic affiliations. Furthermore, the judges have some counteracting characteristics, which tend to predispose them toward a liberal direction. They

---

[20] J. FRANK, COURTS ON TRIAL: MYTH AND REALITY IN AMERICAN JUSTICE 262–89 (1949). H. LASKI, A GRAMMAR OF POLITICS 572 (1925).

[21] The median age for both legislative houses of all 48 states was 48.4 in 1935. H. WALKER, THE LEGISLATIVE PROCESS: LAWMAKING IN THE UNITED STATES 149 (1948). Fifty-two years was the most frequent age of the federal executives serving on a level high enough to be worthy of inclusion in J. ROSOW, AMERICAN MEN IN GOVERNMENT xvii (1949).

[22] Nagel, *Ethnic Affiliations and Judicial Propensities*, 24 J. POL. 92–110 (1962).

[23] R. JACKSON, THE STRUGGLE FOR JUDICIAL SUPREMACY: A STUDY OF A CRISIS IN AMERICAN POWER POLITICS 313–15 (1949).

are better educated than either legislators or administrators, and they are chosen from larger constituencies more likely to encompass an urban area than are the legislators. These horizon-broadening factors possibly account for the relative liberalism of the judges in the realm of international relations.

Table 16–2 shows more graphically how the relevant background

TABLE 16–2

SOME CHARACTERISTICS WHICH TEND TO CORRELATE WITH CONSERVATISM

Characteristic	Supreme Court Judges	Compared with		
		General Public	Adminis-trators	Legisla-tors
Occupation (percent lawyers)	100% (Generally prosecuting or corporation)	Lower than judges	Lower	Lower
Father's occupation (percent professional, proprietor, official, or farmer)	82%	Lower	Lower	Lower
Salary (per year average)	$16,000	Lower	Lower	Lower
Ethnic affiliation (% white-Protestant)	86%	Lower	Lower	Lower
Age (average)	63	Lower	Lower	Lower
Conservative pressure group affiliations	Many conservative, almost none liberal	Lower	Lower	Lower
Long tenure (median period between elections)	8 years	Inapplicable	Lower	Lower
Recruitment (percent not chosen by direct popular vote)	25%	Inapplicable	19%	Lower
Lack of education (percent never attended college)	Almost zero %	Higher	Higher	Higher
Narrowness of constituency (percent chosen by district)	18%	Inapplicable	Lower	Higher

characteristics of the judges compare with the general public, the administrators, and the legislators. The characteristics are presented in the somewhat random order in which they were discussed. Most of the entries in the table pertaining to administrators, legislators, and the general public are based on common sense, on data concerning analogous officials, and on data dealing with only a segment of the group involved. Therefore, precise figures are given only for the judges.

Legislators and administrators were possibly more in favor of educational restrictions for voters because they are more dependent on the whims of the electorate for holding office than the judges are. In the realm of criminal rehabilitation and marital planning, the negative attitudes of the legislators possibly reflected a sensitivity to public opinion, which presumably demands harsh treatment of criminals and pays lip service to Victorian morals. The more positive attitude the judges manifested toward Jews as contrasted to Negroes may reflect the fact that members of the legal profession have closer relations with Jews than do members of many other occupations. The greater moderation the judges manifested by refusing to agree or disagree strongly rather than mildly with most of the items may be attributable to the norm of neutrality judges are supposed to follow, to the fact that judges represent more diverse constituencies than legislators, and to the fact that the responding judges were more identifiable than the administrators and legislators were.[24]

IV.   EFFECTS OF THE DIFFERENCES

A high degree of conservatism on the part of the American judiciary would have no particular significance if the values of judges had no bearing on the decisions they reach. In order to determine whether there is a relationship between judicial attitudes and judicial decision making, each judge was given a liberalism score that corresponded to the total of the liberalism scores he received for each item after the items were weighted in terms of the correlation each item had with the factor of liberalism in Eysenck's study. The median liberalism score was 109 on a scale that could range from 41 to 195. Of the 1955 supreme courts, 22 had at least one judge who scored above 109 and at least one judge who scored below 109. On these courts, as is shown in Table 16–3, the low-scoring (under 109) judges in their nonunanimous decisions of 1955 tended to vote for the *prosecution* in criminal cases, for the *business concern* in business regulation cases, for the party being sued (generally an *insurance company*) in motor vehicle accident cases, and for the *employer* in workmen's compensation cases more so than did the high-scoring (over 109) judges.[25] Too few diversely responding judges were involved in cases of other types for meaningful comparisons.

Correlations were also made between responses to a few of the specific items and various decisional propensities. For example, there was a

---

[24] Many of the responding legislators and administrators, however, could also be identified by the source of the postmark since most of the questionnaires were sent to home addresses. Some legislators and administrators voluntarily signed their names to the questionnaires or otherwise indicated their identity.

[25] The attitude–behavior correlations, however, were generally not based on enough judges nor were the correlations large enough to be statistically significant below the .05 level of chance of probability.

TABLE 16–3

How the Decisions of (1) Judges with Liberalism Scores above 109 Differ from Those of (2) Judges with Liberalism Scores at or below 109
(using the nonunanimous cases of the state and federal supreme courts of 1955 on which both groups are represented)

Decision Score (*percent of judgments for whom in what types of cases*)	*Number of Judges Involved in Each Group* (1) (2)	*Group 1 Judges Who Were above Their Court Avg.*	*Group 2 Judges Who Were above Their Court Avg.*	*Direction of the Difference*
For the *prosecution* in criminal cases	23 & 22	43%	73%	Positive
For the *business* firm in business regulation cases	16 & 16	25	62	Positive
For the party being *sued* in motor vehicle accident cases	20 & 16	40	56	Positive
For the *employer* in employee injury cases	20 & 20	50	55	Positive

high and statistically significant correlation between *disagreeing* with item 4 ("Our treatment of criminals is too harsh; we should try to cure, not to punish them.") and being above the average of one's court with regard to the proportion of times one voted for the *prosecution* in criminal cases.[26] Off-the-bench judicial attitudes thus do seem to correlate in a meaningful way with on-the-bench judicial decisions. If judges are disproportionately conservative relative to legislators, administrators, and people in general, it can be expected that their conservatism will be reflected in their decision making.

The personal attitudes of administrators and legislators also undoubtedly influence their decisions, but how much in comparison with that of judges? No attitude–decision study seems to have been made with administrators, but Warren Miller and Donald Stokes have made such a study with congressmen.[27] They found that there was a +.57 correlation between the diverse attitudes of congressmen and their roll-call voting behavior in social welfare controversies. This correlation is substantially higher than the correlations found between the attitudes of judges and their decisional voting behavior. The difference probably results from the greater restraints law and tradition place on the personalized voting

---

[26] See Nagel, *Judicial Backgrounds and Criminal Cases*, 52 J. Crim. L., C. & P. S. (1962) (chap. 18 *infra*). Likewise there were meaningful correlations between the response of the judges to each of the three economic liberalism items and their decisions in workmen's compensation and business regulation cases.

[27] Miller and Stokes, Policy Preferences of Congressional Candidates and Constituents at 8, a paper presented at the 1961 American Political Science Association meeting.

of judges as contrasted to legislators,[28] although legislators are restrained by party and constituency pressures, which sometimes conflict with their personal attitudes.

Attitudinal differences between judges, on the one hand, and legislators and administrators, on the other, may also affect the tranquility of judicial relations with the other two branches of government. When the differences suddenly become greater, sharp conflict may result. Thus, the political party representation in Congress had suddenly become substantially different from that on the Supreme Court in all three periods in American history when the Supreme Court had its most sudden upsurges of judicial review and when Congress had its strongest court-curbing debates. These conflicts reflect attitudinal differences to the extent that there is a correlation between political party affiliation and social attitudes. The three periods involved are the period of *Marbury* v. *Madison* and the Chase impeachment, the period of the Civil War cases and Lincoln's conflict with the court, and the period of the New Deal cases and Roosevelt's court-packing proposal. In general, it seems that when judicial conservatism increases relative to the legislature, then judicial review of economic regulatory legislation will also increase, and judicial review of legislation that narrows civil liberties will decrease. Likewise, when judicial liberalism increases relative to the legislature, then judicial review of economic regulatory legislation will decrease, and judicial review of legislation that narrows civil liberties will increase.

V. DECREASING THE ROLE OF PERSONAL ATTITUDES

How might one go about decreasing the role of political decision makers' personal attitudes in their decisions? This is more a problem with judges than with legislators and administrators because prevailing norms demand greater objectivity on the part of judges. However, there has been considerable discussion relevant to how legislators can be made more responsive to their political party[29] or to their constituents.[30] There has also been some discussion with regard to making administrators more responsive to legal rules and informal norms.[31] To make legislators more responsive to their political parties, changes are needed in party composition and organization, in legislative committees and scheduling, and in gubernatorial strength. To make legislators more responsive to

---

[28] K. Llewellyn, The Common Law Tradition: Deciding Appeals 19–61 (1960).

[29] APSA Committee on Political Parties, Toward a Responsible Party System (1950); and M. Jewell, State Legislatures: Politics and Practice (1962).

[30] V. O. Key, Public Opinion and American Democracy 480–99 (1961), and Eulau, *The Role of the Representative: Some Empirical Observations on the Theory of Edmund Burke*, 53 Am. Pol. Sci. Rev. 742–56 (1959).

[31] H. Simon et al., Public Administration 513–61 (1950).

their constituents, they need more homogeneous and politically competitive districts, plus better information facilities between constituency and legislator concerning the legislator's work and the constituency's desires. Administrators can be made more responsive to legal rules and informal norms if hierarchial, legislative, and judicial controls are increased and if professionalism and *esprit de corps* are promoted.

It is the primary purpose of this section of the chapter, however, to attempt to test empirically three proposals designed to decrease the role of judicial attitudes in judicial decision making. The three proposals are requiring judicial experience as a prerequisite to being either a state or federal supreme court judge, abandoning the wearing of robes by the judiciary, and requiring evidence of legal scholarship as a prerequisite to being a judge. Do judges operating under these devices tend to vote contrary to their off-the-bench attitudinal positions any more so than judges who do not operate under them? As the previous section of the chapter indicated, there was a statistically significant correlation between *disagreeing* with the opinion expressed in item 4 ("Our treatment of criminals is too harsh; we should try to cure not to punish them.") and being *above* the average of one's court with regard to the proportion of times one voted for the prosecution in criminal cases. Thus, a judge who *disagreed* with the statement (when other judges on his court agreed[32]) and yet was *below* the average of his court in his proportion of times voting for the prosecution seemed to be voting contrary to his value position with regard to criminal cases, as was a judge who *agreed* (when other judges on his court *disagreed*) but was *above* his court average in the prosecution direction. Likewise, a judge who *disagreed* and was *above* or who *agreed* and was *below* seemed to be voting in accordance with his value position in criminal cases. With these concepts of contrariety and accordance in mind, the logical question is raised about what those judges who voted contrary to their value position have in common, if anything.

Congress has occasionally been faced with proposed legislation to make a certain number of years of judicial experience a prerequisite to appointment to the United States Supreme Court.[33] The rationale offered for the legislation is that judges with such judicial experience will be less likely to be influenced by their personal values and will

---

[32] The previous version of this chapter referred to in note 3 failed to eliminate from the analysis those judges who sat on courts where the respondents were unanimous in their responses to item 4 of the questionnaire. Since such judges were neither liberal nor conservative relative to their fellow judges on the questionnaire item, they would not be expected to be relatively liberal or conservative in their criminal case decisions and should have been eliminated from the analysis. Eliminating them slightly changed the findings of this section.

[33] See, e.g., W. MURPHY & C. H. PRITCHETT, COURTS JUDGES AND POLITICS: AN INTRODUCTION TO THE JUDICIAL PROCESS 111 (1961).

be more technically competent. A possible effect of the legislation is to obtain a more conservative judiciary to the extent that the more years a judge has been on the bench, the older he is likely to be; and the older a judge is, the more conservative he is likely to be. This effect may be the real motivation of the proponents, but it does not refute their rationale. No attempt has been made in this chapter to measure the technical competence of judges, but something can possibly be said about the correlation or lack of correlation between judicial experience and judicial objectivity. The judicial experience of the 1955 state and federal supreme court judges as of the beginning of 1955 ranged from none at all for those whose terms begin in January, 1955, on up to Justice Lummus of the Massachusetts Supreme Judicial Court who had been serving as a judge on various courts for 48 years. The average judge in the group of 313 had 17 years of judicial experience. The first row of Table 16–4 shows the relationship between being a

TABLE 16–4

RELATIONSHIP BETWEEN BEING A JUDGE WITH CERTAIN QUALIFICATIONS AND BEING
A JUDGE WHO VOTED CONTRARY TO HIS VALUE POSITION

Group 1 (Hypothesized to Be More Subjective)	Group 2 (Hypothesized to Be More Objective)	Number of Judges Involved (1) (2)	% in Group 1 Who Voted Contrary to Their Value Position	% in Group 2 Who Voted Contrary to Their Value Position	Direction of the Difference
Judges with 17 years or less judicial experience	Judges with more than 17 years judicial experience	16 and 18	31%	38%	Positive
Judges who wear robes	Judges who do not wear robes	31 and 6	32	17	Negative
Judges who have not held scholarly positions	Judges who have held scholarly positions	23 and 11	26	36	Positive

judge with more than 17 years judicial experience and being a judge who voted contrary to his value position in criminal cases. The relationship is slightly positive in that a slightly greater percent of judges with high judicial experience voted contrary to their value position than did judges with low judicial experience.

Some legal scholars, such as the late Jerome Frank, have theorized that the wearing of robes encourages the public to think of judges as being different from ordinary humans in their ability to suppress their personal attitudes.[34] Such a public image of the judiciary supposedly enables judges to inject their personal attitudes into decisions with less fear of being detected. On 8 state supreme courts (Arizona, Arkansas, Kentucky, Missouri, North Dakota, Oklahoma, South Dakota, and Texas), the judges do not wear robes; on 40 state supreme courts and the federal Supreme Court the judges do wear robes.[35] Row 2 of Table 16–4 shows the relationship between being a judge who does not wear robes and being a judge who voted contrary to his value position in criminal cases. The table tends to indicate that there is a negative correlation between not wearing robes and suppressing one's personal attitudes. The negative correlation, however, is not large enough to be considered statistically significant given the sample sizes involved; nor does a negative correlation seem to have any logical substantiation.[36]

Attempts to raise the scholarly competence of members of the bench may result in judges who can move the docket along faster, who can spot legal issues easier, and who can more readily muster precedents and legal arguments to support their decisions. A nonlawyer serving as a judge or a justice of the peace would probably be more likely to resort to personal preferences, as contrasted to legal rules, than would a lawyer in deciding a case. Since all the supreme court judges are lawyers, however, there is probably no very substantial correlation between their scholarliness and their objectivity. Some indications of scholarliness include having been an honor student, a teacher, an author, or a member of a scholarly legal organization, like the American Law Institute. About one third of the state and federal supreme court judges of 1955 indicated they had held such positions. The last row of Table 16–4 shows the slightly positive relationship that exists between being a judge who held such a scholarly position and being a judge who voted contrary to his personal values in criminal cases.

Some reforms proposed to promote judicial objectivity cannot be tested with the research design of this chapter because no American jurisdiction has adopted them. These proposals include psychoanalysis of judges,[37] self-analysis by judges,[38] special interrogatories by lawyers to judges concerning their decisions,[39] and special qualifying examinations and

---

[34] Frank, *The Cult of the Robe,* 28 Sat. Rev. Lit. 41 (1945).

[35] Courts of Last Resort of the Forty-Eight States Table 3 (1950).

[36] None of the correlations in Table 16–4 are large enough or based on enough judges to be considered statistically significant below the 0.05 level of chance probability. By logical substantiation in this context is meant consistency with what is known about the behavior of nonjudges or people in general.

[37] Schroeder, *The Psychological Study of Judicial Opinions,* Cal. L. Rev. 89–113 (1918).

[38] Lasswell, *Self-Analysis and Judicial Thinking,* 40 Int. J. Ethics 342–62 (1930).

[39] Frank, *op. cit. supra* note 18 at 423, 141–43.

training.[40] A civil code system or a more stare decisis–oriented system, by decreasing judicial discretion, might also decrease judicial subjectivity, but the rigidities introduced by the cure might be worse than the subjectivities of the disease. Some reforms to promote judicial objectivity also cannot be tested with the research design of this study because they have been proposed for trial courts and lower appellate courts. These proposals include making appeals easier, making it easier to get a change of venue or a change in the judge, having multiple-judge trial courts so the diverse judges can counteract one another, and requiring the writing of opinions to justify the decisions reached. Some proposals for decreasing judicial subjectivity are particularly relevant to decreasing political partisan influences on judicial decisions. These include gubernatorial appointment, nonpartisan ballots, and long tenure. Their effect on decreasing background-decisional correlations was discussed in a recent article in the *American Political Science Review*.[41]

VI.   GENERAL CONCLUSIONS

In summary, the off-the-bench attitudes of state and federal supreme court judges seem to be more conservative relative to the general public, cabinet-level officials, and legislators. Since there were relatively few representatives from the federal government in the sample, this conclusion is more relevant to the state level of government.

The conservatism found can probably be largely attributed to factors of class, family background, pre-judicial occupations, training, age, and ethnic affiliations. The conservatism found seems to be reflected in decisions reached, because judges who gave more conservative responses to the questionnaire also had greater tendencies to decide for the prosecution in criminal cases, for the business firm in business regulation cases, for the party sued in auto accident cases, and for the employer in workmen's compensation cases.

Judges who have many years of judicial experience or who have received scholarly honors seem to inject their personal values into their decisions slightly less than other judges. Contrary to Jerome Frank, however, judges who do not wear robes seem to inject their values into their decisions just as much as judges who do wear robes. Nevertheless, as Jerome Frank emphasized 30 years ago, all judges are human.[42] Like legislators and administrators, they thus have values shaped by their differing backgrounds and manifested in their decisions.

---

[40] *Id.*, 247–53.

[41] Nagel, *Political Party Affiliation and Judges' Decisions*, 55 Am. Pol. Sci. Rev. 843–50 (1961) (partly in chap. 15 *supra*).

[42] Frank, *Are Judges Human?* 80 Pa. L. Rev. 17 (1931).

CHAPTER 17

Political Party Representation
on the Courts

The new federal judgeships have again raised the issue of equal party representation among the judiciary. Both the *Journal of the American Judicature Society* and the American Bar Association's House of Delegates have recommended that the Democratic Party and the Republican Party should have approximately equal representation on the federal judiciary.[1] This issue has not been raised regarding party representation among the justices of the supreme courts of the respective states, which together are at least as important as the federal courts. Various analyses have shown that such equality has not prevailed on the federal judiciary in the past.[2] It is the purpose of this chapter to describe, account for, and evaluate the party distribution among the justices of the state supreme courts.

For example, the *Directory of American Judges* shows that for 1955 (the only year for which this useful directory has been published), before Alaska and Hawaii became states, 304 judges were sitting on the 48 supreme courts.[3] The *Directory* gives a party affiliation for 236 of the 304 judges. *Who's Who in America* gives a party affiliation for 25 of the remaining 68 judges.[4] Various miscellaneous sources, particularly state governmental manuals, give a party affiliation for 10 of the remaining 43 judges.[5] The supreme court judges who give no party affiliation in any of

---

[1] *A Bi-Partisan Judiciary*, 43, J. Am. Jud. Soc'y 75 (1959); 84 ABA Rep. 173 (1959).

[2] PELTASON, FEDERAL COURTS IN THE POLITICAL PROCESS 31–2 (1955) and Miller, *Federal Judicial Appointments: The Continuing Struggle for Good Judges*, 41 ABA J. 125 (1955).

[3] *Directory of American Judges* (LIEBMAN ed. 1955).

[4] 28, 29, 30 WHO'S WHO IN AMERICA (SAMMONS ed. 1954, 1956, 1958).

[5] ALABAMA OFFICIAL AND STATISTICAL REGISTER 223 (Bannon ed. 1955); DIRECTORY OF THE STATE OF OKLAHOMA 8 (WINTERS ed. 1959); ITALIAN-AMERICAN WHO'S WHO 64 (1954); OHIO ELECTION STATISTICS 21 (1956); PENNSYLVANIA

the sources consulted probably do not closely identify themselves with any political party. Any reference to the party affiliation of one of the judges in a source not dated in the 1950's was not used because of the possibility that the judge may have changed or dropped his party affiliation. Table 17–1 shows that 50 percent of the 304 supreme court judges

TABLE 17–1

PARTY AFFILIATION OF THE 1955 STATE SUPREME COURT
JUDGES

Party	Number	Percent of 304 Total	Percent of 271 Dems. and Reps.
Democratic	153	50%	56%
Republican	118	39	44
No party given in the sources consulted	33	11	
Totals	304	100%	100%

were Democrats, 39 percent were Republicans, and 11 percent gave no party affiliation. Minor parties were not mentioned by any of the judges. Of the 271 judges who gave a party affiliation, 56 percent were Democrats and 44 percent were Republicans.

Table 17–1 thus shows an approximate equality of Democratic and Republican state supreme court judges in the nation as a whole. Table 17–2, however, shows that this equality is based on relatively high Democratic percentages on the southern supreme courts and relatively low Democratic percentages on the northern supreme courts. If the South is defined as including all the slaveholding states of 1860 plus the Oklahoma Territory, then the average southern state supreme court was 92 percent Democratic, with 14 of the 17 southern state supreme courts being 100 percent Democratic. If the North is defined as covering the other 31 states, then the average northern state supreme court was only 33 percent Democratic, with 9 of the 31 northern state supreme courts being 0 percent Democratic.

I.   STATE VERSUS FEDERAL COMPARISONS

It is more difficult to expect equal party representation on state supreme courts than on the federal judiciary for two reasons. First, the federal judiciary is appointed by the President, whereas in 1955 only 7 of

MANUAL 556 (1956); NORTH CAROLINA MANUAL 462 (1954); SCHUBERT, THE QUANTITATIVE ANALYSIS OF JUDICIAL BEHAVIOR 133 (1959); N. Y. *Times,* September 30, 1954, 32.

the 48 state supreme courts were appointed by their governors (California, Delaware, Maine, Massachusetts, Missouri, New Hampshire, and New Jersey).[6] This is relevant because it is easier for a single President or governor in making appointments to cross party lines than it is for a mass of legislators or voters to do so. In fact, judicial elections with partisan ballots are frequently characterized by party-label voting more so than other elections because the voters know so little about the candidates as individuals.[7] Of the six states which by law or tradition provide for a bipartisan supreme court (Alabama, California, Delaware, Missouri, New Hampshire, and New Jersey), five of them are among the seven states that have governor-appointed supreme courts.[8] The sixth, Alabama, has a provision in its constitution requiring bipartisan representation on the Alabama Supreme Court, but the provision is apparently ignored, since all seven Alabama supreme court judges are Democrats.

The second reason it is easier to have the parties equally represented on the federal judiciary than on given state supreme courts is because the nation as a whole from which the federal judiciary collectively draws its personnel is nearly equally divided between Democrats and Republicans. Individual states, on the other hand, may have populations overwhelmingly Democratic, like the deep southern states, or overwhelmingly Republican, like some of the New England states or some of the northern states between the Rocky Mountains and the Mississippi River. Thus, one cannot readily expect the Democrats of Georgia to give the relatively negligible number of Georgia Republicans equal representation on the Georgia Supreme Court, and likewise one cannot readily expect the North Dakota Republicans to give equal representation to the relatively negligible number of North Dakota Democrats.

II. JUDICIAL VERSUS CONGRESSIONAL COMPARISONS

One thus may be unrealistic in expecting the two parties to be equally represented on each of the state supreme courts. It does not seem unrealistic, however, to expect the two parties to be represented on each state supreme court in rough proportion to their party strength in each state. To what extent are the inequalities of party representation on the state supreme courts disproportionate to the distribution of Democrats and Republicans in the states? The congressional vote of 1954 can be used to determine the approximate proportion of Democrats and Republicans in each state population in the absence of more accurate state-by-state data on party affiliation.[9] Table 17–3 shows the Democratic and Republican

---

[6] DIRECTORY OF AMERICAN JUDGES, Designation Table (Liebman ed. 1955).

[7] Roper, STUDY OF VOTER AWARENESS OF JUDICIAL CANDIDATES IN ELECTIONS (1959).

[8] *Courts of Last Resort in the 48 States,* Table 4 (1950).

[9] JOINT COMMITTEE ON PRINTING, CONGRESSIONAL DIRECTORY 289–96 (1955).

TABLE 17-2

DEMOCRATIC AND REPUBLICAN STATE SUPREME COURT
REPRESENTATION IN 1955 BY STATES
(judges not giving a party affiliation in any of the
sources consulted are excluded)

State	Demo- crats	Repub- licans	Dems.° Dems. + Reps.
		South	
Alabama	7	0	100%
Arkansas	5	0	100
Delaware	1	2	33
Florida	7	0	100
Georgia	7	0	100
Kentucky	6	0	100
Louisiana	6	0	100
Maryland	3	2	60
Mississippi	8	0	100
Missouri	4	2	67
North Carolina	7	0	100
Oklahoma	9	0	100
South Carolina	5	0	100
Tennessee	5	0	100
Texas	9	0	100
Virginia	6	0	100
West Virginia	5	0	100
	Average = 92% Democratic		
		North	
Arizona	5	0	100%
California	2	2	50
Colorado	3	4	43
Connecticut	3	2	60
Idaho	1	3	25
Illinois	2	5	29
Indiana	0	4	0
Iowa	0	9	0
Kansas	0	7	0
Maine	1	5	17
Massachusetts	2	5	29
Michigan	2	6	25
Minnesota	1	4	20
Montana	2	1	67
Nebraska	2	5	29
Nevada	0	1	0
New Hampshire	2	3	40
New Jersey	3	2	60
New Mexico	4	0	100
New York	5	2	71
North Dakota	1	3	25
Ohio	3	4	43
Oregon	2	5	29
Pennsylvania	2	5	29
Rhode Island	3	2	60

° This column represents the percentage the Democratic judges constitute among the judges giving a party affiliation on the court involved.

TABLE 17-2—*cont.*

State	Demo-crats	Repub-licans	Dems.[*]
			Dems. + Reps.
South Dakota	0	4	0
Utah	3	1	75
Vermont	0	5	0
Washington	0	4	0
Wisconsin	0	5	0
Wyoming	0	2	0
	Average = 33% Democratic		

[*] This column represents the percentage the Democratic judges constitute among the judges giving a party affiliation on the court involved.

distributions in the general population by states as indicated by the 1954 congressional vote.

The Democrats are better represented on the southern supreme courts (92 percent average) than they are in the congressional vote of the southern states (76 percent average). This may be attributable to the fact that many conservative southerners vote for Republicans in national elections but only for Democrats in state and local elections,[10] and also to the possibility that there may be gerrymandering of representation by the dominant Democrats in the state governments to favor their own party.

The Democrats, on the other hand, are underrepresented among supreme courts in the north (33 percent average) relative to their northern state congressional vote (47 percent average). This Democratic underrepresentation on the northern supreme courts is even greater when one considers that the congressional vote was only from 1954, when Democratic popularity was lower than in previous years, whereas most of the supreme court judges were elected prior to 1952, when Democratic popularity was higher. Like the southerner who votes for Republicans in national elections only, many rural northerners are more prone to vote for Democrats in national elections than in local elections. Also like the southern situation in reverse, the disparity between Democratic representation on northern supreme courts as compared with Democratic representation in the northern congressional vote may be attributable to distortions in judicial allocations by rural dominated state governments or archaic state constitutions so as to favor Republican rather than Democratic areas. In Illinois, for instance, the seventh supreme court district elects only one seventh of the seven-man Illinois Supreme Court, but it has over half of the Illinois population, since it includes all of Chicago's Cook County plus four neighboring counties.[11] Other northern states

[10] CAMPBELL, GURIN AND MILLER, THE VOTER DECIDES 22–26 (1954).
[11] McNAMARA, ILLINOIS VOTER'S HANDBOOK 199, 190–92 (1954).

TABLE 17–3

DEMOCRATIC AND REPUBLICAN DISTRIBUTION IN THE GENERAL
POPULATION BY STATES AS INDICATED BY THE
1954 CONGRESSIONAL VOTE
(in thousands)

State	Demo-crats	Repub-licans	Dems.* / Dems. + Reps.
South			
Alabama	268	11	96%
Arkansas	285	0	100
Delaware	79	65	55
Florida	255	71	78
Georgia	315	30	91
Kentucky	432	236	65
Louisiana	208	8	96
Maryland	343	295	54
Mississippi	99	0	100
Missouri	665	519	56
North Carolina	390	213	65
Oklahoma	354	191	65
South Carolina	210	2	99
Tennessee	234	112	68
Texas	1095	155	88
Virginia	204	128	61
West Virginia	341	251	58
Average = 76% Democratic			
North			
Arizona	128	121	51%
California	1793	1872	49
Colorado	240	240	50
Connecticut	913	947	49
Idaho	103	123	46
Illinois	1635	1622	50
Indiana	747	832	47
Iowa	329	477	41
Kansas	267	347	43
Maine	109	133	45
Massachusetts	845	835	50
Michigan	1100	1033	52
Minnesota	600	532	53
Montana	118	107	52
Nebraska	157	249	39
Nevada	32	42	45
New Hampshire	87	105	45
New Jersey	862	903	49
New Mexico	222	154	59
New York	2399	2508	49
North Dakota	113	231	33
Ohio	1114	1341	45
Oregon	257	308	45
Pennsylvania	1873	1827	51

* This column represents the percentage the Democratic congressional
voters constitute among the voters either Democratic or Republican in
the state involved.

TABLE 17–3—*cont.*

State	Demo-crats	Repub-licans	Dems.* Dems. + Reps.
Rhode Island	196	131	60
South Dakota	94	137	41
Utah	117	146	44
Vermont	44	70	38
Washington	818	804	50
Wisconsin	540	600	47
Wyoming	48	61	44
Average = 47% Democratic			

° This column represents the percentage the Democratic congressional voters constitute among the voters either Democratic or Republican in the state involved.

possibly have similar distortions in their supreme court allocations. While reapportionment of congressional and state legislative districts is frequently discussed in apportionment literature, the problem of reapportionment of state judicial allocations is discussed comparatively seldom.

III.   EQUAL VERSUS PROPORTIONATE REPRESENTATION

One of the best checks on political partisanship in judicial decision making is to have multijudge benches composed of members of both parties who check and balance each other. Near-equality of party representation on every state supreme court is an unrealistic goal. Proportionate party representation, however, would bring the state supreme courts closer to near-equality of party representation than they presently are. Such proportionate representation can be achieved through redistricting of judicial districts, through various proportional representation voting devices,[12] and through bipartisan appointments. Promoting party balance on the state courts, particularly the state supreme courts, should be as high on the judicial reform agenda as promoting party balance on the federal courts.

[12] Bone, American Politics and the Party System 671–79 (1949).

SECTION IV

Accounting for
Decisional Variation

CHAPTER 18

Judicial Backgrounds and
Criminal Cases

I. THE RESEARCH FINDINGS

A. POLITICAL PARTY AFFILIATION

The first row of Table 18–1 tends to indicate that on the bipartisan supreme courts Democratic and Republican judges do differ from one another in deciding criminal cases. In 1955, 15 bipartisan state and federal supreme courts decided at least one nonunanimous criminal case on which all their judges sat. These courts were comprised of 85 judges who gave a party affiliation in the sources consulted. Of the 40 Democrats, 55 percent were above the average of their respective courts on the decision score, whereas only 31 percent of the 45 Republicans were above the average of their respective courts on the decision score.

The California Supreme Court illustrates this statistically significant difference. Two of the California judges, Justices Carter and Traynor, declared themselves as Democrats in the *Directory*, and two, Justices Shenk and Spence, declared themselves as Republicans. Justices Edmonds, Gibson, and Schauer did not indicate party affiliation. It is unusual for so many judges on a supreme court not to give party affiliation. The California Supreme Court, however, is not an elected court. Partly to eliminate partisan influence, the judges are appointed initially by the governor with the approval of a Commission on Qualifications, and they appear on the ballot for voter approval every 12 years thereafter. In 1955, only Missouri had a similar system of judicial election. In spite of this attempt to eliminate partisan divisions, Democrats Carter

227

and Traynor were on opposite sides of Republicans Shenk and Spence in a large number of cases of different types. All 7 judges of the court heard 14 criminal cases together in which nonunanimous decisions were reached.[1] The 2 Democrats had an average decision score in these cases of 85 percent for the defense, whereas the 2 Republicans had an average decision score in the same cases of only 18 percent for the defense. In the famous *Chessman* case of 1955, for example, the only two dissenters in favor of the defense were Democrats Carter and Traynor.

Other supreme courts in which the Democrats had a higher average decision score for the defense than did the Republicans include the supreme courts of Colorado, Idaho, Maryland, Michigan, Montana, New Jersey, Rhode Island, North Dakota, and Pennsylvania. Of the 15 courts with qualifying criminal cases, only the Illinois, New York, Ohio, Utah, and federal supreme courts followed an opposite pattern, although not to so great extent as the 10 courts that followed the general pattern.

B. PRESSURE GROUP AFFILIATIONS

Many of the judges were members of pressure groups that endorse various kinds of legislation. The types of pressure groups most frequently mentioned were professional groups (e.g., the American Bar Association), veterans' groups (e.g., the American Legion), business groups (e.g., chambers of commerce), and nativist groups (e.g., the Sons of the American Revolution). Decision scores of the judges who were members of these groups did not differ to a statistically significant extent from the decision scores of the nonmember judges, with the exception of the scores pertaining to membership in the American Bar Association. Table 18–1 shows that 52 percent of the judges who indicated (in the *Directory*, *Who's Who*, or *Martindale-Hubbell*) that they were not members of the ABA had decision scores above the average for their respective courts, whereas only 37 percent of the judges who indicated that they were members of the ABA had such scores.

On the United States Supreme Court, for instance, Justices Black, Douglas, Frankfurter, and Minton did not indicate ABA membership, while Mr. Chief Justice Warren and Justices Burton, Clark, Harlan, and

---

[1] *Lyons* v. *Superior Court*, 43 Cal. 2d 755, 278 P.2d 681 (1955); In re *Chessman*, 44 Cal. 2d 1, 279 P.2d 24 (1955); *People* v. *Sykes*, 44 Cal. 2d 166, 280 P.2d 769 (1955); *Bompensiero* v. *Superior Court*, 44 Cal. 2d 178, 281 P.2d 250 (1955); In re *Bartges*, 44 Cal. 2d 241, 282 P.2d 47 (1955); *People* v. *Cavanaugh*, 44 Cal. 2d 252, 282 P.2d 53 (1955); *People* v. *Terry*, 44 Cal. 2d 371, 282 P.2d 19 (1955); *People* v. *Cahan*, 44 Cal. 2d 434, 282 P.2d 905 (1955); *People* v. *Berger*, 44 Cal. 2d 459, 282 P.2d 509 (1955); *People* v. *Jackson*, 44 Cal. 2d 511, 282 P.2d 898 (1955); In re *Hess*, 45 Cal. 2d 171, 288 P.2d 5 (1955); *People* v. *Acosta*, 45 Cal. 2d 538, 290 P.2d 1 (1955); *People* v. *Tarantino*, 45 Cal. 2d 590, 290 P.2d 505 (1955); *Calhoun* v. *Superior Court*, 46 Cal. 2d 18, 291 P.2d 474 (1955).

Reed, did indicate such membership. In the 9 full-court nonunanimous criminal cases of 1955, the 4 non-ABA members had an average decision score of 70 percent for the defense, whereas the 5 ABA members had only an average decision source of 51 percent.[2] Subsequent to 1955, the Chief Justice withdrew from the ABA on ideological grounds. If Warren were considered a non-ABA member in 1955, then the average decision score of the non-ABA group would move up to 71 percent for the defense, and the average decision score of the ABA group would move down to 45 percent for the defense.

C. PRE-JUDICIAL OCCUPATIONS

Many of the judges indicated that they had formerly held occupations other than the private practice of law. The types of occupations most frequently mentioned were prosecuting attorney, legislator, corporation counsel, businessman, teacher, public administrator, attorney general, and regulatory agency attorney. The pre-judicial occupations thought to have the most relevance to decisional differences among judges in criminal cases were those of businessman and prosecuting attorney. Although judges who were former businessmen tended to have a lower decision score for the defense in criminal cases than did judges who were not, the difference was not quite statistically significant. However, 50 percent of the judges who did not indicate being former prosecutors had decision scores above the average for their respective courts, whereas only 36 percent of the judges who did indicate being former prosecutors had such scores.

The Pennsylvania Supreme Court exemplifies the general pattern found on supreme courts having some judges who were former prosecutors. On this court, three of the judges (Justices Arnold, Bell, and Chidsey) indicated they had been prosecutors before becoming judges. In the 9 nonunanimous criminal cases which the full court heard in 1955, the other 4 judges in the court (Justices Jones, Musmanno, Stearne, and Stern) had an average decision score of 26 percent for the defense, whereas the 3 judges who were former prosecutors had an average decision score for the defense of only 7 percent.[3] Mr. Justice Musmanno,

---

[2] *Bell* v. *United States,* 349 U.S. 81 (1955); In the Matter of *Murchison,* 349 U.S. 133 (1955); *Quinn* v. *United States,* 349 U.S. 155 (1955); *Emspak* v. *United States,* 349 U.S. 190 (1955); *Bart* v. *United States,* 349 U.S. 219 (1955); *Williams* v. *Georgia,* 349 U.S. 375 (1955); *Donaducy* v. *Pennsylvania,* 349 U.S. 913 (1955); *United States* ex rel. *Toth* v. *Quarles,* 350 U.S. 11 (1955); *Michel* v. *Louisiana,* 350 U.S. 91 (1955).

[3] *Commonwealth* v. *Edwards,* 380 Pa. 52, 110 A.2d 216 (1955); *Commonwealth* ex rel. *Dunn* v. *Ruch,* 380 Pa. 152, 110 A.2d 240 (1955); *Commonwealth* ex rel. *Lane* v. *Baldi,* 380 Pa. 201, 110 A.2d 409 (1955); *Commonwealth* v. *Chaitt,* 380 Pa. 532, 112 A.2d 379 (1955); *Commonwealth* v. *LaRue,* 381 Pa. 113, 112 A.2d 362

TABLE 18-1

How Judges of Differing Backgrounds and Attitudes Differ in Their Criminal Case Decisions

(based on the nonunanimous cases of the state and federal supreme courts of 1955 on which both groups being compared are present)

Group 1 (Hypothesized to Be Less Defense Minded)	Group 2 (Hypothesized to Be More Defense Minded)	Number of Judges Involved in Each Group (1)	(2)	% of Group 1 Above Their Court Average on the Decision Score*	% of Group 2 Above Their Court Average on the Decision Score*	Difference	Probability of the Positive Difference Being Due to Chance
Party							
Republicans	Democrats	45	40	31%	55%	+24	Less than .05
Pressure groups							
Members of a business group	Did not indicate such membership	15	71	47	52	+5	.20 to .50
Members of ABA	Did not indicate such membership	105	88	37	52	+15	Less than .05
Members of a nativist group	Did not indicate such membership	11	33	36	48	+12	.20 to .50
Occupations							
Former businessmen	Did not indicate such occupation	22	71	32	40	+8	.05 to .20
Former prosecutors	Did not indicate such occupation	81	105	36	50	+14	Less than .05

Education Attended high-tuition law school	Attended low-tuition law school	24	22	54	59	+5	.20 to .50
Age Over age 65	Under age 60	67	66	43	42	−1	Negligible diff.
Geography Practiced initially in small town	Practiced initially in large city	31	37	35	35	0	Negligible diff.
Religion and ancestral nationality Protestants	Catholics	39	18	31	56	+25	Less than .05
High income Prot. denomination	Low income Prot. denomination	54	54	41	50	+9	.05 to .20
Only British Ancestry	Part non-British ancestry	96	97	38	47	+9	.05 to .20
Attitudes Low general liberalism score	High general liberalism score	22	23	27	57	+30	Less than .05
Low criminal liberalism score	High criminal liberalism score	26	17	27	59	+32	Less than .05

* Decision Score = proportion of times voting for the defense in criminal cases.

the famous defense lawyer in the *Sacco-Vanzetti* case and other criminal cases, alone had a decision score of 94 percent for the defense in these cases.

D. Education, Age, and Geography

Approximately one third of the 313 supreme court judges serving in 1955 went to law schools whose annual tuition was under $120 in 1927 (the earliest year for which school-by-school tuition figures are available), and approximately one third went to law schools whose annual tuition was over $240.[4] A higher percentage of judges who went to low-tuition law schools (under $120) had decision scores above the average for their respective courts than did judges who went to high-tuition law schools (over $240). This difference, however, was not statistically significant. Likewise, there was no statistically significant difference between judges in the bottom third age group (under 60) and judges in the top third age group (over 65).

There was also no statistically significant difference between judges who practiced law initially in small towns with populations under 5,000 (the bottom third among the judges) and judges who practiced initially in large cities with populations over 100,000 (the top third among the judges).[5]

Because in this study comparisons are made only within courts, comparisons are not made between judges of different regions. If southern supreme courts were compared with northern supreme courts, however, one might hypothesize that the southern courts would have a higher percent of judgments granted to the defense than would the northern courts because (1) violence is possibly more condoned in the South than in the North, except violence by a Negro against a White, (2) less efficient southern police are possibly more likely to bring innocent persons to trial than are northern police, and (3) southern lower courts are possibly more likely to commit reversible error than are northern lower courts.

(1955); *Commonwealth* v. *Mason,* 381 Pa. 309, 112 A.2d 174 (1955); *Commonwealth* v. *Cisneros,* 381 Pa. 447, 113 A.2d 293 (1955); *Commonwealth* ex rel. *Taylor* v. *Superintendent of the County Prison,* 382 Pa. 181, 114 A.2d 343 (1955); *Commonwealth* v. *Thomas,* 382 Pa. 639, 117 A.2d 204 (1955).

[4] Tuition figures for the last law school each judge attended were taken from Reed, Review of Legal Education in the United States and Canada for the Year 1928 (1929).

[5] Population figures for the place of initial law practice of each judge were taken from 1 U.S. Bureau of the Census, Department of Commerce, Census of Population 178–320 (1920). The year 1920 was the census year nearest to the year when the average judge among the 313 judges began practicing law.

E. RELIGION AND ANCESTRAL NATIONALITY

Most of the judges with entries in the *Directory of American Judges* listed their religion in response to the *Directory* questionnaire. There were too few Jewish supreme court judges to make comparisons between Jewish and non-Jewish judges. However, 11 supreme courts had some Catholic and some Protestant judges, and heard some nonunanimous criminal cases with all judges present. These 11 supreme courts had 57 judges who indicated they were either Catholics or Protestants. Of the 18 Catholic judges, 56 percent had decision scores above the average for their respective courts, whereas only 31 percent of the 39 Protestants had such scores.

This statistically significant difference is illustrated by the New Jersey Supreme Court. Justices Brennan and Heher indicated they were Catholics; Justices Oliphant, Vanderbilt, and Wachenfeld indicated they were Protestants; and Justices Burling and Jacobs gave no religious affiliation. In the 12 nonunanimous criminal cases the full New Jersey Supreme Court heard in 1955, the 2 Catholics had an average decision score for the defense of 52 percent, whereas the 3 Protestants had an average decision score for the defense of only 28 percent.[6]

The members of certain Protestant denominations are traditionally thought to have a higher average income than that of members of other Protestant denominations. The relatively high income denominations are the Congregationalist, Episcopalian, Presbyterian, and Unitarian; and the relatively low income denominations are the Baptist, Lutheran, and Methodist.[7] When judges from each of the two groups sitting on the same supreme court criminal cases were compared, the judges from the relatively low-income denominations tended to have a higher decision score for the defense than did the judges from the relatively high-income denominations. The difference, however, was not quite statistically significant.

The ancestral nationality of each judge can be roughly determined by taking each judge's paternal and maternal family names or their component parts to Elsdon C. Smith's *Dictionary of Family Names* (1956),

---

[6] *State* v. *Schmelz*, 17 N.J. 227, 111 A.2d 50 (1955); *State* v. *Newton*, 17 N.J. 271, 111 A.2d 272 (1955); *State* v. *Low*, 18 N.J. 179, 113 A.2d 169 (1955); *State* v. *Cianoi*, 18 N.J. 191, 13 A.2d 176 (1955); *Johnson* v. *State*, 18 N.J. 422, 114 A.2d 1 (1955); In the Matter of *White*, 18 N.J. 449, 114 A.2d 261 (1955); *State* v. *Haines*, 18 N.J. 550, 115 A.2d 24 (1955); *State* v. *Wise*, 19 N.J. 59, 115 A.2d 62 (1955); *State* v. *Fary*, 19 N.J. 431, 117 A.2d 499 (1955); *State* v. *D'Ippolita*, 19 N.J. 540, 117 A.2d 592 (1955); *State* v. *DeMeo*, 20 N.J. 1, 118 A.2d 1 (1955); *State* v. *Kociolek*, 20 N.J. 92, 118 A.2d 812 (1955).

[7] Allinsmith, *Religious Affiliation and Politico-Economic Attitudes*, 12 PUBLIC OPINION Q. 377 (1948).

which in dictionary form gives the nationality origin of over 10,000 family names. If one compares judges whose ancestral nationality is exclusively British (which includes English, Scotch, or Welsh) with judges on the same court whose ancestral nationality is at least partly non-British (to the extent determinable in the Smith book), one finds that the judges of partially non-British derivation tend to have higher decision scores for the defense than do the judges of wholly British derivation on the same courts. This difference, however, is not quite statistically significant.

F. OFF-THE-BENCH ATTITUDES

In the spring of 1960, a mailed questionnaire was sent to each of the 313 state and federal supreme court judges of 1955 in order to determine their attitudes on various issues. Of these judges, 119 returned answered questionnaires. The questionnaire represented a condensed and revised version of a liberalism–conservatism questionnaire written by H. J. Eysenck.[8] The judges were asked to indicate whether on the whole they agreed a lot, agreed a little, neither agreed nor disagreed, disagreed a little, or disagreed a lot with a list of statements. The questionnaire was primarily designed to measure the degree of sympathy a respondent has for less privileged groups and the degree of acceptance he has toward long-run social change. These two components make up what is generally referred to as liberalism.[9] The questionnaire was scored in such a way that a respondent could receive a liberalism score ranging from 41 to 195. The median liberalism score actually received was 109. Seventeen supreme courts that heard full-court nonunanimous criminal cases had at least one judge with a score over 109 and at least one judge with a score at or below 109. Of the judges scoring above 109, 57 percent were above the average of the respondents of their respective courts on the decision score, whereas only 27 percent of the judges scoring at or below 109 were above the average of the respondents of their respective courts on the decision score. This difference is statistically significant, but a specific example cannot be given because the judges were promised anonymity if they responded to the questionnaire.

There was one particularly relevant statement the judges were asked to respond to by indicating whether and how much they agreed or disagreed. This statement read: "Our treatment of criminals is too harsh; we should try to cure not to punish them." Of the 119 responding judges, 24 indicated they strongly disagreed on the whole with the statement, 48 disagreed but not strongly, 22 neither disagreed nor agreed,

---

[8] EYSENCK, PSYCHOLOGY OF POLITICS 122–24 (1954).
[9] MACIVER, THE WEB OF GOVERNMENT 215–17 (1951).

20 agreed on the whole but not strongly, and 5 agreed strongly. The average responding judge was thus in between disagreeing mildly and being neutral. Of those who were neutral or who agreed with the statement, 59 percent were above the average of the respondents of their respective courts on the decision score, whereas only 27 percent of those who disagreed with the statement were above the average of the respondents of their respective courts on the decision score. This difference is statistically significant.

II. REASONS AND REMEDIES

How might one account for the relationships between judicial characteristics and judicial decision making that have been described? Some of the relationships found are easily attributable to chance. Others, however, are not. The nonattributable ones are those where the odds are more than 95 to 5, or 19 to 1, of obtaining the differences purely by chance given the size of the differences and the size of the groups. They include the differences between Democratic and Republican judges, non-ABA members and ABA members, non-former prosecutors and former prosecutors, Catholic judges and Protestant judges, and relatively liberal judges and relatively conservative judges as measured by their off-the-bench attitudes.

To some extent a criminal case represents a conflict of social groups, in that the defendant generally tends to be a member of the lower middle or working class (particularly if tax and business regulation cases are analyzed separately);[10] and the prosecutor tends to be a member of the upper middle or upper class, enforcing laws promulgated by upper middle and upper class legislators and judges.[11] Mass data show that persons holding certain positions (e.g., being a Democrat or a Catholic) with respect to background characteristics (e.g., party or religion) tend to have greater sympathy for lower economic and social groups than do persons holding obverse positions.[12] Given the nature of the average criminal case, judges holding such positions with respect to background characteristics are therefore likely to have a higher decision score for the defense than do judges holding obverse background positions. The correlation between a judge's position on background characteristics and his relative degree of sympathy for lower economic and social groups may account for the differences found concerning party, pressure groups, religion, and liberal–conservative attitudes.

---

[10] TAFT, CRIMINOLOGY 131–33 (1950).

[11] MATTHEWS, THE SOCIAL BACKGROUND OF POLITICAL DECISION-MAKERS 23–30 (1954).

[12] CAMPBELL, GURIN, & MILLER, THE VOTER DECIDES (1954); TURNER, PARTY AND CONSTITUENCY: PRESSURES ON CONGRESS (1951).

However, it probably does not account for the differences found between former prosecutors and their opposite number; judges who are former prosecutors are probably on the average not substantially more or less ideologically liberal than judges who have not been prosecutors. Their lower decision scores for the defense are possibly more attributable to a relatively pro-prosecution frame of reference, which caused them to become prosecutors or which they acquired or had reinforced when they served as prosecutors.

Many devices are available for minimizing the influence of judicial backgrounds, including the availability to defendants of easy appeals, the requirement that judges write opinions to justify their decisions, the use of multijudge courts with judges of diversified backgrounds, and the drafting of clearer and more detailed substantive statutes, thereby limiting the area of judicial discretion.

Because criminal cases frequently involve value-oriented controversies, however, and because different background and attitudinal positions tend to correspond to different value orientations, there will probably always be some correlation between judicial characteristics and judicial decision making in criminal cases.

CHAPTER 19

Regulatory Commissioners and
Party Politics

In 1936, Pendleton Herring asked "Does party allegiance mean anything in the functioning of our commissions?" On the basis of his extensive knowledge of individual commissioners, he answered: "Nominal party allegiance conveys nothing in itself."[1] In 1955, Marver Bernstein stated, "there is little evidence that commissioners decide on major policy issues according to their party affiliations."[2] No systematic quantitative study, however, seems to have been made of the presence, direction, or degree of correlation between party affiliation and decision making on the seven major regulatory agencies. It is the purpose of this chapter to offer some data relevant to that matter.

I. THE RESEARCH DESIGN[3]

The sample of commissioners involved in this study consists of all the commissioners who served in the CAB, FCC, FPC, FTC, ICC, NLRB, and SEC for the years 1936, 1946, and 1956, thereby providing 20 groups of commissioners (there was no CAB in 1936) and 100 separate commissioners.[4] Commissioners serving during more than one time period were used only for the first time period unless they sat on no non-unanimous adjudications in their first time period. Commissioners who served on only a small portion of the year's cases were excluded from

---

[1] HERRING, FEDERAL COMMISSIONERS: A STUDY OF THEIR CAREERS AND QUALIFICATIONS 10–11 (1936).

[2] BERNSTEIN, REGULATING BUSINESS BY REGULATORY COMMISSIONS 104 (1955).

[3] The research design used here is similar to the research design described in more detail in Nagel, *Testing Relations between Judicial Characteristics and Judicial Decision-Making*, 15 W. POL. Q. 425 (1962) (ch. 14 *supra*).

[4] A copy of the appendix showing the commissioners, their characteristics, and their decision scores can be obtained on request from the author.

the analysis. The seven agencies were chosen because of the high importance and large quantity of cases they adjudicate.[5] The three time periods were chosen in order to have a substantial sample of commissioners, while minimizing overlap between time periods and maximizing the likelihood of diversity of appointers within each time period.

Information on the party affiliation, state from which appointed, appointer, and other characteristics of the commissioners was obtained from *Who's Who in America,* the *Government Organization Manuals,* and from correspondence with the agencies. Information on their decisional propensities was obtained from the hearing reports of the agencies for the years 1936, 1946, and 1956. Each commissioner was given a score, indicating whether he was above or below the average of his agency for the year involved with regard to the proportion of times he decided nonunanimous decisions in what might be considered a liberal direction.

Only nonunanimous decisions were used because (1) these are the most controversial decisions and thus generally the most important decisions in terms of the conflicting interests involved, (2) because only nonunanimous decisions provide differences to be accounted for, and (3) because unanimous decisions do not affect whether a commissioner is above or below the average of his agency. Only about 5 percent of the total agency decisions, however, were nonunanimous, although this figure varied substantially, depending on the agency, the year, and the type of cases involved. By liberal direction is meant a decision in favor of the consumer, shipper, or investor (rather than the seller, producer, transporter, or broker), in favor of labor (rather than management), in favor of a small business or increased competition (rather than a larger firm or decreased competition). Borderline decisions that could not be readily positioned as liberal or conservative were excluded from the analysis, as were decisions decided by less than the full agency for the year involved.

II.   PARTY, REGION, APPOINTER, AND LIBERALISM

Table 19–1 shows the findings with regard to the relations between the party, region, appointer, and the decisions of the commissioners. The types within each group are arranged from the type of commissioners hypothesized to be most liberal down to the type of commissioner hypothesized to be least liberal. Lines 1 and 2 indicate that 54 of the 100 commissioners were Democrats and 40 were Republicans. The remaining six were independents. When the sum of the commissioners in a group of types does not total 100 in Tables 19–1 or 19–2, the

---

[5] ADMINISTRATIVE CONFERENCE OF THE U.S., STATISTICAL DATA RELATING TO ADMINISTRATVE PROCEEDINGS (1962).

remainder equals unknowns and inapplicables. Of the 54 Democratic Commissioners, 37 could be given liberalism scores (proportion of times deciding in a liberal direction), and 57 percent of these 37 were above their agency's average liberalism score. On the other hand, only 39 percent of the 31 scorable Republicans were above their agency's average liberalism score. This difference of 18 percentage points between 57 percent and 39 percent is larger than the corresponding differences in Table 19–1 between Northerners and Southerners and between Democratic-appointed and Republican-appointed commissioners, indicating that party is a better predictive or explanatory variable is than region

TABLE 19–1

RELATIONS BETWEEN PARTY, REGION, APPOINTER, AND THE DIRECTION OF COMMISSIONERS' DECISIONS

Type of Commissioners	Number with Background Info.	Number with Background & Liberalism Information	Percent of Type above Their Agency's Average Liberalism Score
Party			
1 Democrats	54	37	57%
2 Republicans	40	31	39
Region			
3 Northerners	64	50	54
4 Southerners	28	21	43
Party and region			
5 Dems. from the North	27	20	65
6 Dems. from the South	23	16	44
7 Reps. from the North	34	26	38
8 Reps. from the South	4	4	25
Appointer			
9 Appointed by Democrats	60	43	56
10 Appointed by Republicans	40	30	47
Party and appointer			
11 Dems. appointed by Democrats	39	26	54
12 Dems. appointed by Republicans	15	11	64
13 Reps. appointed by Democrats	16	13	46
14 Reps. appointed by Republicans	24	18	33
Party, region, and appointer			
15 Dems. from North apptd. within	19	13	69
16 Dems. from North apptd. across	6	5	80
17 Dems. from South apptd. within	15	11	46
18 Dems. from South apptd. across	8	5	40
19 Reps. from North apptd. across	15	12	42
20 Reps. from North apptd. within	18	13	31
21 Reps. from South apptd. across	0	0	—
22 Reps. from South apptd. within	4	4	25

or appointer. The Democratic–Republican difference is understandable in view of the history, urbanism, working-class orientation, and ethnic-group orientation of the Democratic Party relative to the Republican Party.

Lines 3 and 4 indicate that commissioners appointed from northern states are more likely to be found on the liberal side of split decisions than are commissioners appointed from southern states.[6] Similar decisional differences can be shown, although slightly less so if one uses region where born rather than region where appointed from for those few commissioners whose birthplace and appointment place differ. Much of the relative conservatism of the southern commissioners can probably be attributed to the effects of their relative ruralism, which places a greater emphasis on consumer and worker self-sufficiency and on face-to-face relations between consumers and sellers and between workers and employers.[7]

Lines 5 through 8 combine party and region. They reveal a difference of 40 percentage points between the percent of Democrats from the North who were above their agency's average liberalism score and the corresponding percentage for Republicans from the South. Democrats from the South and Republicans from the North had approximately equal propensities to be on the liberal side of split decisions with a slight edge to the southern Democrats. This near equality between southern Democrats and northern Republicans is probably due to the offsetting effects of combining liberal party affiliation with conservative regionalism and liberal regionalism with conservative party affiliation. As mentioned, however, party seems to be stronger than region in shaping commissioners' attitudes on these economic issues.

Lines 9 and 10 show that commissioners receiving their initial appointment from a Democratic president are more likely to be above their agency's average liberalism score than are commissioners receiving their initial appointment from a Republican president. A similar although less strong difference can also be shown if one uses the party of the most recent appointer for each commissioner rather than the party of his initial appointer. Possibly the difference is less strong because reappointments may be based more on inertia and less on ideological considerations than are initial appointments. The decisional differences

---

[6] The southern states consisted of Ala., Ark., Del., Fla., Ga., Ky., La., Md., Miss., Mo., N.C., Okla., S.C., Tenn., Texas, W. Va., and Va. The northern states consisted of the other 33. Two commissioners appointed from Washington, D.C., were excluded from the regional analysis.

[7] Commissioners who were appointed from cities larger than 100,000 were disproportionately more likely to be above their agency's liberalism score, to be Democrats, and to be Northerners than were commissioners from cities smaller than or equal to 100,000 in population.

attributable to the party of the appointers are accountable in terms of the same factors mentioned in accounting for the differences attributable to the party of the commissioners themselves. The appointer difference, however, is less than the party or regional difference, probably because Republican presidents so frequently appoint Democratic commissioners (15 out of 39 appointments as shown on lines 12 and 14) and because Democratic presidents so frequently appoint Republican commissioners (16 out of 55 appointments). The authorizing statutes of all seven agencies except the NLRB require some bipartisan appointments.

Lines 11 through 14 reveal a substantial difference of 21 percentage points (with regard to being above one's agency liberalism score) between Democratic commissioners appointed by Democratic presidents and Republican commissioners appointed by Republican presidents. Democratic commissioners appointed across party lines (generally by Eisenhower) seemed to be even more liberal than Democratic commissioners appointed within party lines. This strange difference may be partly due to post-1930 Republican presidential attempts to influence northern urban Democratic voters through regulatory appointments analogous to Eisenhower's appointment of Brennan and Hoover's appointment of Cardozo to the Supreme Court in contrast to Truman's appointments of Vinson, Clark, and Minton. Marver Bernstein states that "Franklin Roosevelt often appointed Republicans who were closer to the policy of his administration than many Democrats were."[8] The relatively small difference between the 64 percent on line 12 and the 54 percent on line 11 may also be due to chance, since relatively few scorable Democrats were appointed by Republicans in the sample of 100.

Lines 15 through 22 combine party, region, and appointer simultaneously. Forty-four percentage points separate the liberalism percentage for northern Democrats appointed within party lines from the southern Republicans appointed within party lines. The five northern Democrats appointed across party lines were again the only group deviating from the expected pattern. Southern Democrats and northern Republicans tend to occupy a middling to right-wing position on the economic decisional spectrum, as do their counterparts in the congressional arena.

It is interesting to note that some background characteristics other than party, region, appointer, and urbanism had correlations with being above the average liberalism score of one's agency. Thus, commissioners who were nonlawyers were somewhat more likely to be found on the liberal side of split decisions, as were commissioners who had held other federal positions before becoming commissioners. Alumni of the

---

[8] BERNSTEIN, *op. cit. supra* note 2, at 104.

higher tuition, more northeastern undergraduate schools were also more liberal. Whether or not a commissioner had been a former professor or had done corporate or business work did not make a difference.[9] The role of the religious variable could not be determined, since 41 commissioners were listed as Protestants, only 4 as Catholics, and none as Jews in *Who's Who in America.*

III. PARTY, IDEOLOGY, AGENCY DOMINATION, AND THE PROPENSITY TO DISSENT

As indicated above, each one of the 100 commissioners was given a liberalism score equal to the proportion of times he voted in favor of the liberal position in the full-agency nonunanimous decisions he participated in. Likewise, each commissioner was given a dissenting score equal to the proportion of times he dissented in those same decisions. The dissenting scores for the members of each agency in each time period can be totaled and divided by the number of agency members to determine the agency's average dissenting score. Table 19–2 indicates the percent of commissioners of various types who were above their agency's average dissenting score.

The patterns revealed in Table 19–2 on dissenting are less clear than those in Table 19–1 on liberalism. Two variables, however, do seem to account for most of the dissenting variation among the commissioner types. If a commissioner is in the ideological minority on his agency, it is understandable that he would dissent more than his fellow commissioners who are in the ideological majority. A commissioner who is liberal (pro-consumer, pro-union) also tends to be more likely to dissent than is a commissioner who is conservative (pro-seller, pro-management) regardless of what ideology or party dominates the agency, possibly because liberals may be more innovative and nonconformist.

The types within each group in Table 19–2 are arranged from the type of commissioners hypothesized to be most likely to dissent down to the type of commissioners hypothesized to be least likely to dissent. Lines 1 and 2 indicate there is a substantial relationship between being a Democrat and being a dissenter, since 57 percent of the 37 positionable Democrats were above their agency's average dissenting score, whereas only 35 percent of the 31 positionable Republicans were. This difference

---

[9] For some interesting impressionistic material on the impact of various occupations represented on the commissions, see the following articles by Lincoln Smith, *Businessmen as Regulatory Commissioners*, 31 J. Bus. U. Chi. 132 (1958); *Lawyers as Regulatory Commissioners*, 23 Geo. Wash. L. Rev. 375 (1955); *Accountants as Regulatory Commissioners*, 59 Pub. Util. Fort. 93 (1957); *Engineers as Regulatory Commissioners*, 60 Pub. Util. Fort. 718 (1957). These articles, however, are primarily concerned with the competence and expertise of these occupational groups of commissioners rather than their relative liberalism.

TABLE 19–2

RELATIONS BETWEEN PARTY, IDEOLOGY, AGENCY DOMINATION, AND THE
PROPENSITY TO DISSENT

Type of Commissioners	Number with Back- ground Info.	Number with Back- ground & Dissent Informa- tion	Percent of Type above Their Agency's Average Dissent Score
Party			
1 Democrats	54	37	57%
2 Republicans	40	31	35
Ideology			
3 Liberals	38	38	53
4 Conservatives	35	35	37
Ideology and party			
5 Liberal Democrats	21	21	67
6 Liberal Republicans	12	12	42
7 Conservative Democrats	16	16	44
8 Conservative Republicans	19	19	32
Party and agency domination			
9 Democrats on Rep. Agency	13	11	73
10 Democrats on Dem. Agency	39	26	50
11 Republicans on Dem. Agency	19	16	27
12 Republicans on Rep. Agency	19	16	44
Ideology and agency domination			
13 Liberals on Cons. Agency	13	13	92
14 Conservatives on Lib. Agency	12	12	50
15 Liberals on Liberal Agency	23	23	35
16 Conservatives on Cons. Agency	21	21	24

is possibly due to the relative liberalism of the Democrats in general and to the fact that the dissenting Democrats represented an especially liberal minority, even among the agencies numerically dominated by the nominal Democrats.

Lines 3 and 4 show a significant difference in dissenting rates between relative conservatives (i.e., those below their agency's average liberalism score) and relative liberals (i.e., those above their agency's average liberalism score), although not so large as expected. Lines 5 through 8 show how the differences in dissenting can be sharpened by combining party and liberalism, since 35 percentage points separate the liberal Democrats from the conservative Republicans. The liberal Republicans did not dissent more than the conservative Democrats, partly because most of the liberal Republicans happened to be coincidentally on agencies numerically dominated by liberals.

Lines 9 through 12 indicate the effect of being in the minority party on being a dissenter. The Democrats on Republican agencies (i.e., agencies having more Republicans than Democrats) dissented more than Democrats on Democratic agencies, although Republicans on Democratic agencies did not dissent so much as Republicans on Republican agencies. The influence of liberalism is also shown on lines 9 through 12 by the fact that dissenting by the minority is stronger when the Democrats are the minority than when the Republicans are the minority, and, likewise, Democrats on Democratic agencies dissented more than Republican agencies.

Lines 13 through 16 reveal the clearest pattern in Table 19–2. Of the liberals on conservative agencies (i.e., agencies having more commissioners below the average liberalism score of their agency than above), 92 percent were above the average dissenting score of their agency. Likewise, 50 percent of the conservatives on liberal agencies were above the average dissenting score of their agency. On the other hand, only 35 percent of the liberals on liberal agencies were above on dissenting, and only 24 percent of the conservatives on conservative agencies were above.

IV. CONCLUSIONS

Many important decisions of the regulatory agencies inherently involve value judgments correlated with party, region, and appointer. To offset the potentially biasing influence of these background factors, it does seem desirable that the authorizing statutes of nearly all the agencies currently require approximately equal party representation, with the odd seat going to the party occupying the Presidency.[10] It also seems desirable to know that informal pressures and senatorial courtesy promote a roughly proportional representation among the major geographical regions. In addition, the present five- to seven-year terms for commissioners also seem desirable, since they are short enough to allow for a diversity of appointers without hampering the ability of the commissioners to obtain and apply valuable experience over time.[11]

---

[10] At least one authority has argued to the contrary that "the bipartisan provision is obsolete and unnecessary." MANSFIELD, THE LAKE CARGO COAL CONTROVERSY 145 (1932).

[11] The Landis Report, however, advocates increasing commissioners' terms to at least 10 years. LANDIS, REPORT ON REGULATORY AGENCIES TO THE PRESIDENT-ELECT 68 (1960).

SECTION V

Interaction between
Legislators and Judges

CHAPTER 20

Curbing the Congress:
The Politics of Judicial Review

The literature of political science is reasonably fulsome with regard to the role of the American party system in the decision-making behavior of Congress[1] and (to a lesser extent) of the President.[2] However, until Wallace Mendelson and John Roche recently raised an interesting hypothesis concerning the subject,[3] little has been written about the general role of the American party system in the decision-making behavior of the Supreme Court, either by authorities studying the Supreme Court[4] or by authorities studying political parties.[5] It is the purpose of this

---

[1] See, e.g., TURNER, PARTY AND CONSTITUENCY—PRESSURES ON CONGRESS (1951) [hereinafter cited as TURNER]; Lowell, *The Influence of Party upon Legislation in England and America,* 1 AM. HIST. ASSOC. REP. 319 (1901) [hereinafter cited as Lowell].

[2] See, e.g., Odegard, *Presidential Leadership and Party Responsibility,* ANNALS, Sept. 1956, p. 66; Seligman, *The Presidential Office and the President as Party Leader,* 21 LAW & CONTEMP. PROB. 724 (1956).

[3] Mendelson, *Judicial Review and Party Politics,* 12 VAND. L. REV. 447 (1959). Address by Mendelson, *The Politics of Judicial Supremacy,* the American Political Science Association Annual Meeting, 1961. ROCHE, COURTS AND RIGHTS—THE AMERICAN JUDICIARY IN ACTION 22–24, 46 (1961) [hereinafter cited as ROCHE].

[4] See, however, John Schmidhauser's recent study of the relation between party affiliation and judicial decisions in the sectional controversies of the Taney period. *Judicial Behavior and the Sectional Crisis of 1837–1860,* 23 J. POL. 615 (1961). The need for investigating the role of political parties on the Supreme Court has been pointed out by S. Sidney Ulmer and Glendon Schubert. See Ulmer, *An Empirical Analysis of Selected Aspects of Lawmaking of the United States Supreme Court,* 8 J. PUB. L. 414, 436 (1959); SCHUBERT, QUANTITATIVE ANALYSIS OF JUDICIAL BEHAVIOR 142 (1959).

[5] Part five of KEY, POLITICS, PARTIES AND PRESSURE GROUPS (1952), is entitled *Party and Government,* but it deals only with legislation and administration. Chapter eight of LEISERSON, PARTIES AND POLITICS—AN INSTITUTIONAL AND BEHAVIORAL AP-

chapter to indicate what some of the relations might be between American political parties on the one hand and the history of judicial review on the other.[6]

I. THE ROLE OF INTERPARTY DISSIMILARITY

Writing for the *Vanderbilt Law Review* in 1959, Wallace Mendelson said: "This at least seems clear: court intrusion upon national policy has thrived in the United States only in periods of unusual weakness in our party system."[7] John Roche has also proclaimed "the major reason that judges have been able to exercise this enormous jurisdiction over public policy is the absence of a disciplined, internally cohesive national two-party system."[8]

Both Mendelson and Roche indicate that judicial intrusion is measurable by the occurrence of judicial review. By *the occurrence of judicial review* in this context is meant separate court opinions in which provisions of a congressional statute have been declared unconstitutional.[9] Using such a measure, Mendelson finds that the period from 1789 through 1864 was a period of low judicial review (only 2 instances), whereas the period from 1865 through 1936 was a period of high judicial review (74 instances). From 1937 to the present, there have been relatively few instances of judicial review (only 10 instances).[10]

During these three periods, what has been the average degree of interparty dissimilarity on the national level? According to Mendelson,

---

PROACH (1958) is similarly entitled "Parties and the Control of Government," but it also leaves out the judicial branch of government.

[6] For a discussion of the effect of judicial review on political parties as contrasted to the effect of political parties on judicial review, see HORN, GROUPS AND THE CONSTITUTION 93–121 (1956). For a discussion of the role of political parties in judicial recruitment as contrasted to judicial decision making, see Evans, *Political Influences in the Selection of Federal Judges*, 1948 WIS. L. REV. 330, and McCoy, *Judicial Selection and Judicial Conduct*, 24 SO. CAL. L. REV. 1 (1950). For a discussion of political parties and judicial decision making in a contemporary context as contrasted to a historical context, see Nagel, *Political Party Affiliation and Judges' Decisions*, 55 AM. POL. SCI. REV. 843 (1961) (partly in chap. 15 *supra*).

[7] Mendelson, *Judicial Review and Party Politics*, 12 VAND. L. REV. 447 (1959).

[8] ROCHE, *op. cit. supra* note 3, at 46.

[9] In this chapter, *occurrences* (*or instances*) *of judicial review, cases of judicial review*, and *opinions involving judicial review* are used interchangeably to refer to separate court opinions in which provisions of a congressional statute have been declared unconstitutional. A case in which the Supreme Court merely contemplates whether or not it should exercise judicial review is not in this sense an instance of judicial review. Sometimes, the term *judicial nullification* is used to refer to the exercise of judicial review, but the Supreme Court can, in effect, nullify provisions through interpretation without declaring them unconstitutional.

[10] Seventy-six instances of judicial review prior to 1937 are listed in GILBERT, PROVISIONS OF FEDERAL LAW HELD UNCONSTITUTIONAL BY THE SUPREME COURT OF THE UNITED STATES 148 (1936). Ten instances of judicial review since 1937 are listed in FREUND, SUTHERLAND, HOWE & BROWN, CONSTITUTIONAL LAW 21 (1961).

20. *Curbing the Congress: The Politics of Judicial Review*   247

the first and third periods have had relatively high degrees of interparty dissimilarity, whereas interparty dissimilarity was relatively low in the middle period. Hugh Bone, however, has stated that: "Perhaps the best way to judge party cleavages and loyalties is through a study of congressional roll calls on controversial policies. Real differences between the parties, if they exist, should be apparent in matters of legislation."[11] Julius Turner building on the work of A. Lawrence Lowell has devised such a roll-call measure of interparty dissimilarity. It involves determining what percentage of the nonunanimous roll-call votes were party-oriented votes. By *party-oriented votes,* Turner means a roll-call vote in which 90 percent or more of the members of one party vote in one direction and 90 percent or more of the members of the other party vote in exactly the opposite direction.

Lowell calculated the percentage of party-oriented roll-call votes for two terms of Congress prior to 1865.[12] The average percentage of party-oriented roll-call votes in those two terms was 20 percent. For seven terms of Congress between 1865 and 1937, which were analyzed by Lowell and Turner, the average percentage of party-oriented roll-call votes increased to 29 percent.[13] Indeed, the period of greatest dissimilarity between the Democratic party and the Republican party in American history as measured by this device occurred during the McKinley administration. Subsequent to 1937, as measured by four terms of Congress, the average percentage of party-oriented roll-call votes decreased to a low 13 percent.[14]

In other words, the Lowell and Turner data, summarized in Table 20–1, tend to show that the two long periods of low judicial review in American history corresponded to periods of low party dissimilarity, and the period of high judicial review in American history was a period when the parties differed most. These findings, therefore, seem to go contrary to Professor Mendelson's hypothesis, but they do not necessarily show an inverse relationship. A latitudinal analysis of the party systems[15]

---

[11] BONE, AMERICAN POLITICS AND THE PARTY SYSTEM 363 (1949).

[12] In 1845–47, 11 percent of the votes in the House of Representatives were party-oriented votes. Lowell, *supra* note 1, at 538. In 1863–65, 30 percent of the votes in the House were party-oriented votes. *Ibid.*

[13] In 1887–89, the percentage of party-oriented roll-call votes was 14 percent. In 1897–99, it was 51 percent; in 1899–1901, 49 percent. Lowell, *supra* note 1, at 539–41. In 1921, it was 29 percent; in 1928, 7 percent; in 1930–31, 31 percent; and in 1933, it was 23 percent. TURNER, *op cit., supra* note 1, at 28.

[14] In 1937, the percentage of party-oriented roll-call votes was 12 percent. In 1944, it was 11 percent. In the 1945–47 term of Congress, it was 14.5 percent (averaging the 18 percent of 1945 and the 11 percent of 1946). In the 1947–49 term of Congress, it was 15.5 percent (averaging the 15 percent of 1947 and the 16 percent of 1948). TURNER, *op. cit. supra* note 1, at 28.

[15] MODERN POLITICAL PARTIES (NEUMANN ed. 1956).

TABLE 20–1

INTERPARTY DISSIMILARITY AND JUDICIAL REVIEW[*]

Period	Percentage of Party-Oriented Votes in Congress	Occurrence of Judicial Review
1789–1864	20% average (based on 2 terms)	2 instances (.05 per term)
1865–1936	29% average (based on 7 terms)	75 instances (2.05 per term) 2.05 per term
1937–1960	13% average (based on 4 terms)	10 instances (.83 per term)

[*] Figures are calculated on a per-congressional-term basis.

and the judicial systems of various countries[16] reveals no particular relationship between interparty dissimilarity and the occurrence of judicial review. Likewise, a longitudinal analysis by Lowell[17] and Turner[18] of the British party system over time reveals that the two major British political parties tended to vote very much alike in the British Parliament during the 1800's and very much unalike during the 1900's, but the British judiciary never hinted at exercising any judicial review in either period. Thus, there is probably no substantial relationship between interparty dissimilarity and the occurrence of judicial review.[19] Neither a direct nor an inverse relationship seems to have any empirical or theoretical substantiation.

II. PARTY DIFFERENCES BETWEEN CONGRESS AND THE COURT

In spite of the lack of importance of interparty dissimilarity in explaining judicial review, further analysis reveals that there are some definite and meaningful relations between the American party system and judicial review. For one thing, many upsurges of judicial review have occurred when one of the two parties tended to dominate Congress and the other party was in strong control of the Supreme Court. For instance, when *Marbury* v. *Madison*[20] occurred, the Jeffersonians overwhelmingly

---

[16] McWHINNEY, JUDICIAL REVIEW IN THE ENGLISH-SPEAKING WORLD (1956); WHEARE, MODERN CONSTITUTIONS (1951).

[17] Lowell, *supra* note 1, at 538.

[18] TURNER, *op. cit. supra* note 1, at 24.

[19] In isolated instances, a causal relationship might be found. Thus, the fact that neither the Democratic party nor the Republican party in Congress was willing to do anything about segregation may have been a partially motivating factor in the Supreme Court desegregation decision in *Brown* v. *Board of Education*, 347 U.S. 483 (1954), and particularly in *Bolling* v. *Sharpe*, 347 U.S. 497 (1954), where a congressional act was nullified.

[20] 5 U.S. (1 Cranch) 137 (1803).

controlled both the House and the Senate,[21] but 100 percent of the Supreme Court Justices were Federalists.[22] Likewise, during the period of *Dred Scott*[23] and the Civil War instances of judicial review the Republicans were rising to the ascendancy in Congress, but the Democrats still controlled the Supreme Court. In the early 1930's, when the Democrats overwhelmed Congress, it was a Republican-controlled Supreme Court that scored a record 15 instances of judicial review.[24] This relationship is more clearly shown in Table 20–2.[25]

TABLE 20–2

CONGRESS-COURT PARTY DIFFERENCES AND JUDICIAL REVIEW

Periods of Upsurge in Judicial Review (Big Increase over Immediately Prior Years)	Party Controlling Congress	Party Controlling the Court
Marbury v. *Madison*	Democrats	Federalists
1865–1870	Republicans	Democrats
1932–1936	Democrats	Republicans

The logical explanation behind this relationship lies in the ideological and the partisan differences that exist between Democrats and Republicans.[26] During periods of relatively sudden political opinion change in American history, congressional membership has changed relatively fast in accordance with the changing times, but the Supreme Court has been significantly slower to change. The result in such periods has been diversity of party affiliation between Congress and the Supreme

---

[21] Data on the political party affiliation of members of Congress (including the breakdown of minor parties) is available in Legislative Reference Service of the Library of Congress, Political Classification of the Congress of the United States, 1798 to 1956 (1957). The *Congressional Directory* gives such data from 1899 to the present.

[22] Data on the political party affiliation of Supreme Court judges is available in SCHUBERT, CONSTITUTIONAL POLITICS—THE POLITICAL BEHAVIOR OF SUPREME COURT JUSTICES AND THE CONSTITUTIONAL POLICIES THAT THEY MAKE 707–12 (1960). According to 12 DICTIONARY OF AMERICAN BIOGRAPHY 127–28 (1933), McLean switched from being a Democrat to a Republican in approximately 1856. Davis switched in the opposite direction from being a Republican to a Democrat in approximately 1866. See 5 DICTIONARY OF AMERICAN BIOGRAPHY 110, 111 (1930).

[23] 60 U.S. (19 How.) 393 (1856).

[24] By *a record 15 instances* is meant that if judicial review frequencies were graphed on a year-by-year basis the period 1932 to 1936 would constitute the most peaked bulge in the curve.

[25] A fourth period of upsurge in judicial review was the period from 1920 through 1925 when 14 instances of judicial review occurred. At that time, both the Congress and the Court were dominated by Republicans, but 10 of the 14 instances involved statutes passed during the Democratic-dominated Congresses of the Wilson administration.

[26] See notes 32–38, 48, 49, 51, and 52 *infra* and the accompanying text.

Court. This diversity, in turn, has resulted in a clash of behavior between these two institutions, manifesting itself in an upsurge of judicial review.

III. THE PARTY IN POWER

In this context of party politics and judicial review, it is also meaningful to note that during the pre-1865 period of low judicial review, the Democrats averaged 61 percent control of both houses of Congress,[27] 66 percent control of the Presidency,[28] and 60 percent control of the Supreme Court.[29] In the period of high judicial review from 1865 through 1936, the Democrats averaged only 46 percent control of Congress, 31 percent of the Presidency,[30] and a lowly 34 percent control of the Court. Then again in the post-1936 period of low judicial review, the Democratic average rose to 58 percent in Congress, 67 percent in the Presidency, and 78 percent in the Supreme Court. There thus seems to be a high correlation between Democratic party control of the national government and the relative absence of judicial review as is shown in Table 20–3.

TABLE 20–3

THE PARTY IN POWER AND JUDICIAL REVIEW[*]

Period	(1) Average Percentage of Democrats in Congress	(2) Average Percentage of Democrats on Court	(3) Average Percentage of Democrats as President	(4) Average Number of Occurrences of Judicial Review
1789–1864	61%	60%	66%	.05
1865–1936	46	34	31	2.05
1937–1960	58	78	67	.83

* Figures are calculated on a per-congressional-term basis.

[27] The percentage of Democrats in Congress is calculated by adding the percentage of Democrats in the House of Representatives to the percentage of Democrats in the Senate and dividing by 2.

[28] Data on the political party affiliation of American presidents is available in ROSSITER, THE AMERICAN PRESIDENCY 162 (MENTOR ed. 1956).

[29] For all three branches of the national government, the Democratic percentage referred to here is the ratio between Democrats and Republicans, not to the ratio between Democrats and all other parties. *Democrats* includes the pre-1865 forerunners of the Democratic party who later flowed into the party—namely, the opposition party in the Congress of 1789, the Democratic-Republicans, and the Jacksonians. *Republicans* includes the pre-1865 forerunners of the Republican party who later flowed into the party—namely, the administration party of 1789 and 1825, the Federalists, the Anti-Masonics, the Whigs, and the Free-Soilers. On these matters of party history, see BINKLEY, AMERICAN POLITICAL PARTIES—THEIR NATURAL HISTORY (1959) [hereinafter cited as BINKLEY].

[30] Andrew Johnson is excluded from the analysis because some authorities classify him as a Republican, e.g., MAGRUDER, AMERICAN GOVERNMENT 423 (1951); others as a Democrat, e.g., ROSSITER, THE AMERICAN PRESIDENCY 162 (MENTOR ed. 1956); and still others as a Unionist, e.g., HICKS, THE AMERICAN NATION 24 (1955).

The explanation behind this relationship seems to lie in the meaning of being a Democrat or a Republican and in the nature of the average statute over which the Supreme Court has exercised judicial review.[31] A content analysis of the Democratic and Republican platforms since platforms originated reveals few references to the role of the Supreme Court.[32] Where these references do occur, however, the Republican party platform has shown a more favorable attitude toward positive Supreme Court action than has the Democratic party platform. For instance, in 1936 the Republican party platform proclaimed: "We pledge ourselves . . . to resist all attempts to impair the authority of the Supreme Court of the United States, the final protector of the rights of our citizens against the arbitrary encroachments of the legislative and executive branches of government."[33] Similar praise of judicial authority is found in the Republican platforms of 1912[34] and 1908.[35] Democratic party platforms, on the other hand, have either ignored the issue of judicial power or else they have called for constitutional amendments to get around Supreme Court decisions as in 1936,[36] 1924[37] and 1908.[38] In addition, the Jeffersonian-inspired Chase impeachment in 1804 and the Roosevelt court-packing plan of 1937 are well-known examples of Democratic attempts to stifle or lessen the general exercise of judicial review.[39]

In an article subsequent to his two previous papers (see note 3 *supra*), Wallace Mendelson takes the position that "The peculiarity of the middle period as revealed in Nagel's figures [referring to Table 20–3] was that the dominant party while heavily prevalent in the Court and the Presidency, had little more than bare control of Congress . . . which is central to my position."[40] This position, although it refers to data from Table 20–3 (which deals with the party in power as a cause of judicial review) is really more like the position of Section II of this chapter (which deals with differences between Congress and the Court as a cause). John Roche still persists in his original position that interparty similarity and lack of intraparty discipline is the major

---

[31] See notes 48 and 49 *infra* and the accompanying text. See also text accompanying notes 45 and 46 *infra*.

[32] See PORTER & JOHNSON, NATIONAL PARTY PLATFORMS, 1840–1956 (1956).

[33] *Id.* at 366.

[34] *Id.* at 184.

[35] *Id.* at 160.

[36] *Id.* at 362.

[37] *Id.* at 254.

[38] *Id.* at 147.

[39] The Civil War decade involved a Republican attempt to lessen judicial review, although only in the limited fields of military trials and greenback money. Both the southern Democrats and the conservative Republicans combined forces to attack the Supreme Court during the 1950's in the fields of segregation and subversion. See further, McCLOSKEY, THE AMERICAN SUPREME COURT (1960).

[40] Mendelson, *Politics and Judicial Review*, 12 J. PUB. L. 364 (1963).

reason for judicial review, as indicated in the second 1966 edition of his book (see note 3 *supra*).

IV. A JUDGE'S PARTY AFFILIATION AND JUDICIAL REVIEW

If there is a difference between being a Democrat or Republican and having a negative or positive attitude toward judicial review, the difference should be discernible in the voting behavior of Supreme Court justices. If one wishes to determine the direction of the correlation between being a Democratic judge on the Supreme Court and exercising judicial restraint in any individual case on which both political parties are represented, one can do so by determining in the case whether the percentage of Democratic judges voting against the exercise of judicial review was higher than, equal to, or lower than the percentage of Republican judges voting against the exercise of judicial review. For instance, in the famous 1922 child labor tax case *Bailey* v. *Drexel Furniture Co.*,[41] 33 percent of the 3 Democratic judges on the Court voted against exercising judicial review, whereas 0 percent of the 6 Republican judges on the Court did so. This case, therefore, involves a *positive* correlation between being a Democratic judge and exercising judicial restraint. On the other hand, in the 1960 court-martial case *McElroy* v. *United States ex rel. Guagliardo*,[42] 0 percent of the 4 Democratic judges voted against exercising judicial review, whereas 25 percent of the 4 Republican judges did so. This case, therefore, involves a *negative* correlation between being a Democratic judge and exercising judicial restraint. In every unanimous case there is a 0 correlation, although a 0 correlation can also occur in a nonunanimous case if the percentage of Democrats favoring judicial review is the same as the percentage of Republicans favoring judicial review.[43]

Voting in the majority (in any of the 86 instances of judicial review from 1789 through 1960) generally means the same as voting for the exercise of judicial review. There have, however, been a few instances in which judges voted in the majority in order to indicate they favored

---

[41] 259 U.S. 20 (1922).

[42] 361 U.S. 281 (1960). Frankfurter was classified as an independent because he is so classified by SCHUBERT, CONSTITUTIONAL POLITICS—THE POLITICAL BEHAVIOR OF SUPREME COURT JUSTICES AND THE CONSTITUTIONAL POLICIES THAT THEY MAKE 107 (1960), and MENDELSON, THE CONSTITUTION AND THE SUPREME COURT 515 (1959). Further, Frankfurter gives no party affiliation in any recent biographical directory.

[43] It is interesting to note that instead of testing the relation between judicial party affiliation and judicial review, the same methodology presented here could be used to test the relation between judicial age, ethnic affiliation, region, paternal background, education, prior occupation or any other judicial characteristic, on the one hand, and judicial review or any other type of judicial decision making, on the other. That, however, is another subject matter on which the writer is working.

the winning party, while expressly or impliedly stating they favored at least partially withholding the exercise of judicial review.[44] Likewise, there have been a few instances in which judges dissented in order to indicate they favored the losing party, while expressly or impliedly stating they had no objection to the majority's use of judicial review.[45]

Of the 86 instances of judicial review, there was a positive correlation between being a Democrat and exercising judicial restraint in 24 of the instances, a 0 correlation in 34, and a negative correlation in 27; and in one case (*Marbury* v. *Madison*) all the judges had the same party affiliation. These figures, however, are virtually meaningless until the cases are classified in various ways.[46] The most basic classification is in terms of the subject matter of the statute held unconstitutional. Of the 86 cases, 55 involved statutes that *authorized* governmental regulation or taxation. Statutes that *narrowed* civil liberties relating to the First Amendment, to criminal procedure, or to race relations were involved in 16 of the cases. The 15 remaining cases involved neither type of statute or involved both types simultaneously. Of these miscellaneous 15, 8 involved statutes designed to change the judicial process without affecting the civil liberty aspects of criminal procedure.[47]

In the 55 regulation-taxation cases, 22 involved a positive correlation between being a Democrat and exercising judicial restraint, whereas only 15 of the cases involved a negative correlation. On the other hand, in the 16 civil-liberty-narrowing cases, only 1 involved a positive correlation between being a Democrat and exercising judicial restraint, whereas 8 involved a negative correlation, as is shown in Table 20-4.

---

[44] *United States* v. *Cardiff,* 344 U.S. 174, 177 (1952) (Jackson); *Perry* v. *United States,* 294 U.S. 330, 358 (1935) (Stone); *Untermeyer* v. *Anderson,* 276 U.S. 440, 446 (1928) (Sanford); *Nichols* v. *Coolidge,* 274 U.S. 531, 543 (1927) (Holmes, Brandeis, Sanford, and Stone); *Newberry* v. *United States,* 256 U.S. 232, 258 (1921) (McKenna); *United States* v. *Railroad Co.,* 84 U.S. (17 Wall.) 322, 333 (1873) (Bradley).

[45] *Perry* v. *United States,* 294 U.S. 330, 361 (1935) (McReynolds, Van Devanter, Sutherland, and Butler); *Rassmussen* v. *United States,* 197 U.S. 516 (1905) (Harlan and Brown); *United States* v. *Klein,* 80 U.S. (13 Wall.) 128, 148 (1872) (Miller and Bradley).

[46] One method of classification not shown in the tables involves dividing the cases into those that are more important and those that are less important. The cases cited or excerpted in one or more designated treatises or casebooks can be considered more important, and the other cases can be considered less important. In this regard, the overall hypotheses of Tables 20-4 through 20-7 are substantially strengthened if only the cases important enough to be cited in PRITCHETT, THE AMERICAN CONSTITUTION (1959), are used in the tables. This strengthening is probably because the more important cases are more likely to be more controversial and, therefore, more likely to divide the judges along ideological and partisan lines.

[47] The cases were classified in basically the same manner as that used in Edgerton, *The Incidence of Judicial Control over Congress,* 22 CORNELL L. Q. 299 (1937). His 10 categories, however, were consolidated into 3 categories so that the categories would be larger.

TABLE 20–4

PARTY AFFILIATION AND JUDICIAL REVIEW
IN REGULATION CASES AND IN CIVIL LIBERTY CASES

Direction of Correlation*	Number of Instances	Percentage of All Instances	Percentage of Nonzero Instances
		A. In cases involving statutes that authorized governmental regulation or taxation:	
Positive	22	40%	59%
Zero	18	33	–
Negative	15	27	41
Totals	55	100%	100%
		B. In cases involving statutes that narrowed civil liberties:	
Positive	1	6%	11%
Zero	7	44	–
Negative	8	50	89
Totals	16	100%	100%
		C. There were 15 cases involving neither type of statute, and in these no pattern was discernible. Of the 15 cases, 9 were unanimous.	

* Correlation between being a Democratic judge and exercising judicial restraint.

In other words, in the regulation-taxation cases, the Democratic judges were more likely than the Republican judges to be found on the side upholding the legislation, and the Republican judges were more likely than the Democratic judges to be found on the side opposing legislation.[48] In the civil liberty-narrowing cases, however, the reverse situation was true in that the Republican judges were more likely to be found on the side upholding the legislation, and the Democratic judges were more likely to be found on the side opposing it.

These findings tend to conform to the difference between Democrats and Republicans in the general public. Thus, in a study made in 1954 the Survey Research Center found a substantially more *positive* attitude on the part of the average Democrat as contrasted to the average Republican toward whether "the national government should do more in trying to deal with such problems as unemployment, education, housing and

---

[48] This relationship is even stronger when the seven cases are excluded which involved statutes authorizing government regulation to protect freed Negroes. These seven cases were heard between 1876 and 1903. In only two of the seven cases (one of the seven was unanimous) did the Democrats show more restraint than the Republicans.

so on."[49] Likewise, the Survey Research Center found a substantially more *negative* attitude on the part of the average Democrat as contrasted to the average Republican toward Senator McCarthy, whose name has frequently been associated with a narrowing of civil liberties.[50]

It is interesting to note that the voting patterns shown in Table 20–4 have been particularly prominent since 1912. Thus, as is shown in Table 20–5, prior to 1912, 15 percent of the cases involving govern-

TABLE 20–5

PARTY AFFILIATION AND JUDICIAL REVIEW BEFORE 1912 AND AFTER 1912

Period	Direction of Correlation*	Number of Instances	Percentage of All Instances	Percentage of Nonzero Instances
	A. *In cases involving statutes that authorized governmental regulation or taxation:*			
	Positive	3	15%	21%
Before	Zero	6	30	—
1912	Negative	11	55	79
	Totals	20	100%	100%
1912	Positive	19	54%	83%
and	Zero	12	34	—
after	Negative	4	12	17
	Totals	35	100%	100%
	B. *In cases involving statutes that narrowed civil liberties:*			
	Positive	0	0%	0%
Before	Zero	4	67	—
1912	Negative	2	33	100
	Totals	6	100%	100%
1912	Positive	1	10%	14%
and	Zero	3	30	—
after	Negative	6	60	86
	Totals	10	100%	100%

* Correlation between being a Democratic judge and exercising judicial restraint.

mental regulation and taxation had a positive correlation; whereas from 1912 to 1960, 54 percent had a positive correlation. Likewise, prior to 1912, 33 percent of the cases involving a narrowing of civil liberties had a negative correlation; whereas from 1912 to 1960, 60 percent had a negative correlation. These trends can be explained at least partly by the fact that it was in 1912, approximately, when the Democratic

[49] CAMPBELL & COOPER, GROUP DIFFERENCES IN ATTITUDES AND VOTES 91 (1956).
[50] *Id.* at 91–93.

and Republican parties acquired much of their present-day image. In 1912, many progressives left the Republican party along with Theodore Roosevelt, never to return, and many urbanites joined the Democratic party.[51]

It is also interesting to note that the propensity of the Democratic judges to exercise judicial restraint in regulation-taxation matters is particularly prevalent in those cases that involved a regulation-taxation statute passed by a Democratic-controlled House and Senate. Thus, as shown in Table 20–6, in 22 cases a Democratic Congress passed the statute

TABLE 20–6

PARTY AFFILIATION AND JUDICIAL REVIEW
WITH DEMOCRATIC AND REPUBLICAN-PASSED STATUTES

Party Controlling Congress	Direction of Correlation*	Number of Instances	Percentage of All Instances	Percentage of Nonzero Instances
A. In cases involving statutes that authorized governmental regulation or taxation:				
Democratic	Positive	13	59%	81%
	Zero	6	27	—
	Negative	3	14	19
	Totals	22	100%	100%
Republican	Positive	8	27%	40%
	Zero	10	33	—
	Negative	12	40	60
	Totals	30	100%	100%
B. In cases involving statutes that narrowed civil liberties:				
Democratic	Positive	0	0%	0%
	Zero	2	29	—
	Negative	5	71	100
	Totals	7	100%	100%
Republican	Positive	1	17%	33%
	Zero	3	50	—
	Negative	2	33	67
	Totals	6	100%	100%

* Correlation between being a Democratic judge and exercising judicial restraint.

that was under scrutiny. Of these cases, 59 percent involved a positive correlation between being a Democrat and exercising judicial restraint. On the other hand, in 30 cases Republican-passed statutes were under scrutiny.[52] In these cases, the percentage involving a positive correlation

[51] BINKLEY, *op. cit. supra* note 29, at 344–48, 363–69.
[52] Five cases were excluded because they involved statutes passed by a split Congress in which one party controlled the House and the other party controlled the

between being a Democratic judge and exercising judicial restraint fell from 59 to 27 percent.[53] In the civil liberty-narrowing cases, there was no increase in judicial restraint on the part of the Democratic judges when they were faced with Democratic-passed legislation rather than Republican-passed legislation. The phenomenon in the regulation cases can possibly be explained by the fact that Democratic-passed legislation is probably more ideologically pleasing to a Democratic judge. Some of the phenomenon, however, may possibly be explained by partisan attitudes on the part of some judges independent of ideological considerations.

Finally, one might note that the voting patterns shown in Table 20-4 are slightly strengthened in Table 20-7 if one eliminates from the analysis judges who have been appointed across party lines to the Court or to the Chief Justiceship.[54] The percentage of the 55 regulation-taxation cases involving a positive correlation between being a Democratic judge and exercising judicial restraint then rises from 40 to 42, and the percentage of such cases involving a negative correlation falls from 27 to 20. The percentage of the 16 civil liberty-narrowing cases involving the hypothesized negative correlation, however, decreases from 50 in Table

---

Senate. One of the cases, *Bolling* v. *Sharpe*, 347 U.S. 497 (1954), also was excluded because it nullified a number of congressional acts dealing with school segregation in the District of Columbia passed at different times. Thus, the cases in Table 20-6 add up to only 65 rather than 71, as in Tables 20-4, 20-5, and 20-7. The year when each nullified statute was passed is given in Gilbert, Provisions of Federal Law Held Unconstitutional by the Supreme Court of the United States (1936), and Legislative Reference Service of the Library of Congress, Federal Acts Held Unconstitutional (1961). The party composition of Congress since 1789 is given in Legislative Reference Service, Political Classification of the Congress of the United States, 1798 to 1956 (1957). In determining which party dominated Congress when each statute was passed, one must bear in mind that prior to the lame duck amendment of 1933, the Congress that was elected in each even-numbered year did not begin its term until March 4 of the following odd-numbered year. Starting with the Congress elected in 1934, however, each Congress has begun its term on January 3 of the odd-numbered year. Swisher, American Constitutional Development 722-29 (1954).

[53] These relationships would probably be even stronger if the analysis confined itself to judicially reviewed statutes in which about 70 percent or more of the Democratic congressmen voted one way and about 70 percent or more of the Republican congressmen voted the opposite way.

[54] This would exclude: (1) Democrat Nelson who was appointed by Whig Tyler, (2) Democrat Field appointed by Republican Lincoln, (3) Democrat H. Jackson appointed by Republican Harrison, (4) Democrats Lurton and (5) J. Lamar appointed by Republican Taft to the Court, (6) Democrat White appointed by Taft to the Chief Justiceship, (7) Democrat Butler appointed by Harding, (8) Cardoza appointed by Hoover, (9) Stone appointed to the Chief Justiceship by Roosevelt, (10) Burton appointed by Truman, and (11) Brennan who was an Eisenhower appointee. Brandeis is generally considered to have been a Democrat at the time he was appointed by Wilson, although a Republican prior to 1912. Schubert, Constitutional Politics— The Political Behavior of Supreme Court Justices and the Constitutional Policies that They Make 37, 709-12 (1960).

20–4 to 31 in Table 20–7. Possibly, the explanation for the slightly strengthened relationship in regulation-taxation cases is that when a Democratic President appoints a Republican judge he is more likely to appoint a nontypical Republican (e.g., Roosevelt's appointment of Stone to the Chief Justiceship); and, likewise, when a Republican President appoints a Democratic judge, he is more likely to appoint a nontypical Democrat (e.g., Harding's appointment of Butler to the Court). In the civil liberty-narrowing cases, however, the Democratic-Republican labels seem to have less meaning than they do in the governmental regulation and taxation cases, although the nonconfirmation of some of the civil liberty hypotheses may be because, until recently, there have been relatively few civil liberty cases in the history of judicial review.

TABLE 20–7

PARTY AFFILIATION AND JUDICIAL REVIEW WITH CROSSOVER APPOINTEES ELIMINATED

Direction of Correlations*	Number of Instances	Percentage of All Instances	Percentage of Nonzero Instances
A. In governmental regulation or taxation cases with crossover appointees eliminated:			
Positive	23	42%	68%
Zero	21	38	—
Negative	11	20	32
Totals	55	100%	100%
B. In civil liberty-narrowing cases with crossover appointees eliminated:			
Positive	3	19%	38%
Zero	8	50	—
Negative	5	31	62
Totals	16	100%	100%

* Correlation between being a Democratic judge and exercising judicial restraint.

V. CONCLUSION

The United States Supreme Court in *Coleman* v. *Miller*[55] referred to the legislative and executive branches of government as the "political departments of the Government,"[56] implying that political factors do not play a significant role in the decision-making behavior of the members of the Court. A comparison between the splits in Congress in nonunanimous roll calls and the splits on the Court in nonunanimous cases would

---

[55] 307 U.S. 433 (1939).
[56] *Id.* at 449.

probably reveal, in support of the *Coleman* v. *Miller* implication, that party has been a more important variable in the legislative process than in the judicial process. Nevertheless, after examining the data of this paper one can possibly conclude that the Supreme Court's exercise of its important power of judicial review has been significantly shaped by such political considerations as the degree of party difference between Congress and the Court, the nature of the party in power in the national government, and the party affiliations of the individual judges deciding specific cases.[57]

---

[57] Three dittoed appendices are available on request from the writer which provide the raw data on the congressional terms, the cases, and the judges used in preparing the tables of this chapter.

CHAPTER 21

Curbing the Court: The Politics of Congressional Reaction

Due to its unavoidable involvement in the political process, the Supreme Court has often been an object of congressional attack. Excellent descriptive studies have been made of certain periods of conflict between Congress and the Court,[1] but there is a lack of writing that systematically analyzes relations between Congress and the Court throughout American history. It is the purpose of this chapter to analyze in a partially quantitative manner some of the factors that seem to account for the occurrence or nonoccurrence and for the success or failure of congressional attempts to curb the Court.

I. RESEARCH DESIGN

From a perusal of *The Congressional Record* and its forerunners and also from the previous literature in the field,[2] 165 instances of bills designed to curb the Supreme Court were compiled, along with information about their content, sponsor, and fate. In order to keep the data within manageable limits, resolutions and constitutional amend-

---

The author is very grateful to Nancy J. Fahrnkopf, a former graduate student at the University of Illinois, for the extensive research work she did for an early draft of this chapter.

[1] Walter F. Murphy concentrates on the problems of the Warren Court in his book, CONGRESS AND THE COURT (1962) as does PRITCHETT, CONGRESS VERSUS THE COURT (1960). Robert Jackson concentrates on the 1937 Court-packing plan in THE STRUGGLE FOR JUDICIAL SUPREMACY: A STUDY OF A CRISIS IN AMERICAN POWER POLITICS (1941). Walter Murphy's book was especially suggestive in writing some parts of this chapter.

[2] *Ibid.* See also Culp, *A Survey of Proposals to Limit or Destroy the Power of Judicial Review by the Supreme Court of the United States,* 4 IND. L. J. 386, 474 (1929); Warren, *The Early History of the Supreme Court of the United States in Connection with Modern Attacks on the Judiciary,* 8 MASS. L. Q. 1 (1922).

ments were not included, although they are introduced frequently and often contain proposals that would substantially reduce the powers of the Court.[3] Relatively narrow bills designed to reverse a single decision were also excluded. Relying on the distribution of bills as well as the consensus of historians, seven time periods, as shown in Table 21–1,

TABLE 21–1

HIGH- AND LOW-FREQUENCY PERIODS OF COURT-CURBING IN AMERICAN HISTORY

High-Frequency			Low-Frequency		
Years	# of Bills	% of 165	Years	# of Bills	% of 165
1. 1802–1804	2	1%	1. 1789–1801	0	0%
2. 1823–1831	12	7	2. 1805–1822	0	0
3. 1858–1869	22	13	3. 1832–1857	1	1
4. 1893–1897	9	5	4. 1870–1892	8	5
5. 1922–1924	11	7	5. 1898–1921	6	4
6. 1935–1937	37	22	6. 1925–1934	2	1
7. 1955–1959	53	32	7. 1939–1954	2	1
Total	146	87%		19	12%

were labeled high-frequency Court-curbing periods. This identification is both quantitative and qualitative. For example, the first period, covering the years from 1802 to 1804, had only two instances of overt congressional attempts to curb the Court, one of which was the unsuccessful impeachment of Justice Chase. While it may well be a quantitatively marginal period, most writers agree that this was a time of high friction between the Federalists on the bench and the Jeffersonians in Congress and the Administration.

A criterion by which to judge the relative success or failure of any one Court-curbing period is more difficult to establish. A total of only 9 out of the 165 bills regulating the Court have passed Congress. This group of "absolutely successful" bills, representing approximately 5 percent of the total instances, is too small to work with for the purposes of this study. Three criteria of "relative success" will therefore be used. First, *how many* anti-Court bills during each period were reported from committee, the lowest stage of the legislative process aside from introduction? Second, *what percent* of the bills introduced were reported

---

[3] Twenty-five joint resolutions were proposed in 1937, while thirty-three constitutional amendments were introduced during the two-year period from 1935 to 1937. Several attempts have been made—for example, in 1867 and 1871—to establish via Constitutional amendment a new court representing all the states, which would have jurisdiction over constitutional questions. A joint resolution in 1861 demanded the abolition of the federal judicial system.

out of committee? The third criterion of success, as shown in Table 21–2, is that of determining whether a congressional attack has had the effect of changing within the immediate future the pattern of voting

TABLE 21–2

RELATIVE SUCCESS OF SEVEN HIGH-FREQUENCY COURT-CURBING PERIODS

Years	Number of Bills out of Committee	Percent of Bills out of Committee	Judicial Retreat	Composite Success	Rank Order of Composite Success
1. 1802–04	1	50%	Yes	Yes	3
2. 1823–31	3	25	Yes	Yes	4
3. 1858–69	11	50	Yes	Yes	1
4. 1893–97	1	11	No	No	7
5. 1922–24	2	18	No	No	6
6. 1935–37	6	16	Yes	Yes	2
7. 1955–59	2	4	Partial	No	5
	Avg. = 3.7 (N = 26)	Avg. 25% per period	Usually Yes	Usually Yes	

behavior of the Court on the issues that originally provoked the attack. In four of the seven attacks, the Court did retreat from its previous controversial policy by executing a tactical abstention from further similar provocation (as was the case in the years following the 1804 conflict) or by effecting a reversal of policy (as was the case in 1937). At the climax of the seventh period, the Court drew back from its stand on one of the issues that antagonized Congress—namely, a broad interpretation of free speech—but remained firm on its policies toward segregation and criminal procedure, which were also under congressional fire.

The fourth column in Table 21–2 provides a composite index of overall success. Thus, a high-frequency period can be considered successful if it is above average on the number of bills that were reported out of committee (i.e., four or more); if it is above average on the percent of successful bills (i.e., 25 percent or above); and if it was climaxed by retreat of the Court on the majority of the issues involved. A period will be termed relatively successful if it is above average on at least two of these three criteria. Using this composite standard, four of the seven high-frequency periods have been classified as relative overall successes, and each period has been given a rough success ranking as shown in the last column of Table 21–2.

The variables influencing the occurrence and success of the seven Court-curbing periods seem to fit into a model like the psychological model of stimulus-organism-response. In the political phenomenon of Court-curbing, the stimulus is represented by judicial provocation. The organism is represented by the political system, which may contain certain catalytic or conditioning factors that shape the perception of the provocation and the response. The response manifests itself in certain types of Court-curbing bills and Presidential action. This response may feed back on the judiciary and thereby stimulate judicial counteraction. Having this overall model in mind helps one to see better the interrelations between the more specific variables discussed in this chapter.

II. JUDICIAL PROVOCATION

A. QUANTITY OF JUDICIAL REVIEW

To what extent does a high quantity of judicial review of legislative acts provoke Court-curbing, regardless of the type of interests involved? Table 21–3 shows that almost 50 of the total 86 instances of judicial

TABLE 21–3

OCCURRENCE OF JUDICIAL REVIEW DURING AND 3 YEARS PRIOR TO THE HIGH-FREQUENCY COURT-CURBING PERIODS

Years	Instances of Judicial Review of Federal Acts During or 3 Years Prior
1802–04	1
1823–31	0*
1858–69	5
1893–97	3
1922–24	13
1935–37	15
1955–59	5
Total	42

* Judicial review of state acts present.

nullification of federal statutes in American history have occurred during or within three years prior to the seven Court-curbing periods. Thus, over half of the instances of judicial nullification have occurred during a time span equaling less than one third of the history of the Supreme Court. The use of judicial review for the first time in *Marbury* v. *Madison*,[4] was certainly an irritant in the Federalist-Jeffersonian dispute over relative amounts of judicial and executive power in the early 1800's. The nullification of state bankruptcy and debtor laws as well as the

---

[4] 5 U.S. (1 Cranch) 137 (1803).

invalidation of a Maryland act taxing the Bank of the United States provoked the wrath of congressmen in the 1820's.[5] The 1858 *Dred Scott* case[6] nullified a federal statute, and congressional anticipation of judicial review of Reconstruction legislation led to the Court-packing and restrictions on habeas corpus in the 1860's. The 1890's attack was precipitated in part by the invalidation of a federal income tax law, and nullification of federal and state economic legislation led to another Progressive attack on the Court in the 1920's. The judicial review of 15 New Deal statutes was a prime causative factor in the 1930's conflict. In the 1950's, portions of federal and state laws were held unconstitutional, and proposed legislation, such as the Jenner bill, was clearly aimed at several decisions. In short, all the periods of intense Court-curbing have been provoked to some degree by the judicial review of legislative acts. Nullification of federal statutes, however, seems to provide a greater provocation than nullification of state statutes, since judicial review of state statutes seemed to be a prime factor only in the 1820's Court-curbing period and partially in the 1950's. Congress is apparently more protective of its own lawmaking than it is of the various state legislative bodies.

If the seven periods are divided into the relatively high and relatively low periods of judicial review of federal legislation, then, as Table 21–4 shows, a slightly greater proportion of the relatively high review periods

TABLE 21–4

THE RELATION BETWEEN INTENSITY OF JUDICIAL
REVIEW AND COURT-CURBING SUCCESS

Judicial Review of Federal Acts

	Relatively Low	Relatively High
Relatively Successful	1800's 1820's	1930's 1860's
Relatively Unsuccessful	1890's 1950's	1920's

involved relatively successful Court-curbing bills than did the relatively low review periods. Thus, the intensity of judicial review may be a partial determinant of the success of controversial Court-curbing bills as well as a determinant of the introduction of Court-curbing bills. There are, however, more important determinants of Court-curbing success, as is shown later.

---

[5] 17 U.S. (4 Wheat.) 316 (1819).
[6] 60 U.S. (19 How.) 393 (1857).

B. Subject of the Provoking Cases

The specific issues over which conflict has occurred whether from judicial review cases or other cases can be divided into four categories —economic regulation, civil liberties, federal–state relations, and general separation of powers. Table 21–5 indicates that, first, economic regulation

TABLE 21–5

Interests Involved in Court-Curbing during American History

Issues	Period	Overall Success
1. Economic interests		
a. Business regulation	1930's	Yes
	1890's	No
	1820's	Yes
b. Labor relations	1890's	No
	1920's	No
c. Taxes	1890's	No
2. Civil Liberties		
a. Segregation	1950's	No
b. First Amendment	1950's	Partial
	1860's	Yes
c. Criminal procedure	1950's	No
	1860's	Yes
3. Federal-state relations	1800's	Yes
	1820's	Yes
4. Separation of powers in the national government ...	1800's	Yes

has been involved to some extent in four of the seven high-frequency periods. Civil liberties and federal–state relations have each been at issue in two periods, while general separation of powers at the national level has been the main controversy in only the earliest period.

Trends in the frequency or occurrence of certain issues are apparent. For example, the attacks during the first half of the 19th century were largely concerned with federal–state relations and separation of powers, a fact that can be explained in part by the youth of the country. At this time, the power distribution between the parts of the newly established federal system was not at all clear; this question was a dividing point between the two political parties as well as a major public issue. From the latter half of the 19th century through 1937, the basic issue in Congress–Court relations was that of economic regulation. Conflict over civil liberties has occurred intermittently, but particularly in recent years.

From the data in Table 21–5, one might also be able to say that

Court-curbing bills are more likely to succeed where federal–state relations or separation of powers represent the prime subject matters involved. On the other hand, where intensely held economic interests or civil libertarian interests are involved, the likelihood of Court-curbing success is decreased.

C. Unanimity of Provoking Cases

Does the degree of conflict within the Supreme Court influence the occurrence of congressional Court-curbing? The degree of conflict within the Court can be measured by the degree of unanimity in key decisions at a given time. Using the statements of various writers and congressmen about what cases provoked the anti-Court bills, the voting split on these controversial decisions was determined. The average degree of unanimity for all the periods was 76 percent, which means that there was an average of two to three dissents in the cases provoking the attacks. This number contrasts with the higher degree of unanimity normally found in the totality of Supreme Court cases. The results of Table 21–6 support the hypothesis that during periods in which there

TABLE 21–6

Degree of Unanimity in the Supreme Court and the Effect on Occurrence and Success of Court-Curbing

Periods	Degree of Unanimity	Relative Success
1800's	100% relatively high	Yes
1820's	89 rel. high	Yes
1860's	59 rel. low	Yes
1890's	72 rel. low	No
1920's	69 rel. low	No
1930's	69 rel. low	Yes
1950's	76 rel. high	No
	Avg. = 76%	

is a relatively high (i.e., above average) degree of disagreement between members of the Court (and thus high controversy), congressional attack is more likely to occur.

Contrary to what one might expect, Table 21–6 shows that a slightly greater proportion of the high unanimity (rather than the low unanimity) periods involved relatively successful Court-curbing bills. However, the high unanimity in the 1800's and the 1820's does not necessarily indicate complete unity on the part of the Court. It may merely indicate that dissenting had not yet become an established practice.

III. CATALYTIC FACTORS

A. PARTIES AND FACTIONS IN CONGRESS

To what extent does party composition and the presence of factions in Congress during high-frequency time periods act as a catalytic or enabling factor influencing the occurrence and outcome of the attack? In five of the seven high-frequency periods, the Democratic party or its forerunners have dominated the Congress. A tabulation of the party affiliation of the individual sponsors of the bills also reveals that Democrats have sponsored over twice as much anti-Court legislation than have Republicans. This relationship, however, does not mean that having a Democratic Congress is sufficient to provoke Court-curbing bills, for many Democratic Congresses have enjoyed smooth relations with the Court. It does suggest that, when other factors have been present, the existence of a Democratic Congress may have stimulated the occurrence of Court-curbing. Thus, the pattern has been such that when the Court has been defending property rights, as in the 1930's and 1820's, the Democrats were more likely to attack it, and the Republicans were more likely to defend it. On the other hand, although to a lesser extent, when the Court has been defending civil liberties, as in the 1950's and 1860's, the Republicans were more likely to be attacking it, and the Democrats (at least the northern Democrats) were more likely to be defending it. This phenomenon can be explained by the socioeconomic bases of the two parties, and the frequent attacks of the Democrats point up the fact that the Supreme Court has more often defended property rights than civil liberties.

Perhaps a more adequate description of the groups attacking the Court would replace the party labels with conservative or liberal designations. Table 21–7 shows that liberal groups have attacked the Court in six of the seven periods, and conservative groups (representing a

TABLE 21–7

THE RELATION BETWEEN PARTY IN CONGRESS AND THE
OCCURRENCE OF COURT-CURBING BILLS

High-Frequency Period	Party or Faction Sponsoring Bills
1800's	Jeffersonians
1820's	Democrats
1860's	Radical Republicans
1890's	Democrats and Populists
1920's	Liberal Republicans
1930's	Democrats
1950's	Conservative Republicans and conservative Democrats

coalition between wings of the Republican and Democratic parties)
attacked the Court for the first time in the 1950's. Future attacks on
the Supreme Court will also probably come from conservative forces,
given the increased power of liberal urbanism in the United States—
a power that since 1932 has been increasingly making itself felt in
the electoral college system that chooses the President, and thus indirectly
in the President's choices for Supreme Court Justices.

The above discussion focused on the relation between party (or
faction) and the occurrence of a Court-curbing period. There is also
a relationship between the party sponsoring Court-curbing legislation
and the success of the attacks. Thus, when the percentage of Democrats
in Congress is high (over 65 percent), Democratic bills are more likely
to succeed, and they are less likely to succeed when the percentage
of Democrats in Congress is low.[7] Similarly, Republican bills are more
likely to succeed when the percentage of Republicans in Congress is
high, as is shown in Table 21–8. These relations, however, are much

TABLE 21–8

RELATIONS BETWEEN SPONSORING PARTY AND RELATIVE
SUCCESS OF COURT-CURBING BILLS
(where sponsor and party are known)

	Democratic Bills		Republican Bills	
	65% or less Dems. in Cong.	More than 65% Dems. in Cong.	65% or less Reps. in Cong.	More than 65% Reps. in Cong.
Relative Success	6 (9%)	7 (20%)	5 (20%)	7 (44%)
Relative Failure	60 (91%)	28 (80%)	20 (80%)	9 (56%)
	66 (100%)	35 (100%)	25 (100%)	16 (100%)

weaker than one would expect to find in a more disciplined two-party
system. A group's leadership in Congress may be as important as its
numerical strength and may strongly influence the cohesiveness of the
group. For example, the skillful leadership of Senators O'Mahoney and
Wheeler in 1937, and Lyndon Johnson in 1958, is credited by some
writers as being an important factor in the defeat of anti-Court legislation.[8]

---

[7] "Percent Democrats in Congress" equals

$$\tfrac{1}{2} \left(\frac{\text{House Dems.}}{\text{House Dems.} + \text{Reps.}} + \frac{\text{Senate Dems.}}{\text{Senate Dems.} + \text{Reps.}} \right)$$ and likewise with "percent Republicans in Congress."

[8] MURPHY, *op. cit. supra* note 1, at 249.

B. PARTY AND FACTIONAL DIFFERENCES BETWEEN CONGRESS AND THE COURT

Is there a relationship between (1) party or factional differences between Congress and the Court, and (2) the occurrence of Court-curbing bills? As Table 21–9 shows, a slightly greater proportion of Congresses having a dominant (i.e., majority) party different from the Court's dominant party were Congresses from the Court-curbing periods. It is also relevant to note that of 142 Court-curbing bills for which the Democratic or Republican affiliation of the sponsor was known, 39 were introduced by Congressmen of the party opposite to the party that dominated the Court when the bill was introduced. Congresses in which the same party did not dominate both houses of Congress were eliminated from Table 21–9 as were Congresses when the Court had an equal number of Democrats and Republicans.

The above analysis tends to show a weak causal relation between

TABLE 21–9

PARTY DIFFERENCES BETWEEN CONGRESS AND THE COURT
DURING THE HIGH AND LOW COURT-CURBING PERIODS

	Congresses Dominated by a Party Also Dominating the Court	Congresses Dominated by a Party Not Dominating the Court
Court-Curbing Periods	12 (21%)	9 (39%)
Non-Court-Curbing Periods	44 (79%)	14 (61%)
	56 (100%)	23 (100%)

Congress–Court party splits and an upsurge of Court-curbing bills. If, however, one hypothesizes that a party split between Congress and the Court is an important *condition* or *catalyst* rather than a cause, then Table 21–10, below, is more relevant. It shows that all seven high-frequency periods involved party or factional differences between Congress and the Court.

The degree of composite success of a congressional attack also correlates with the degree of party split between Congress and the Court. All three periods during which there was a sharp party split can be considered successful, whereas three out of the four periods during which there was not so sharp a split can be considered relatively unsuccessful, as is shown in Table 21–11. This table, like Table 21–9 but unlike Table 21–10, considers only party splits and not factional splits. The relation-

TABLE 21–10

THE RELATION BETWEEN CONGRESS-COURT PARTY OR
FACTIONAL SPLITS AND THE OCCURRENCE OF COURT-CURBING BILLS

High Occurrence Period	Party Sponsoring Majority of Bills	Party Dominating the Court
1800's	Jeffersonians	Federalists
1820's	States Rights Dems.	Nationalists
1860's	Republicans	Democrats
1890's	Democrats	Republicans
1920's	Liberal Reps.	Conservative Reps.
1930's	Democrats	Republicans
1950's	Conservative Reps. and Dems.	Liberal Dems.

TABLE 21–11

RELATION BETWEEN CONGRESS-COURT PARTY DIFFERENCES
AND THE RELATIVE SUCCESS OF COURT-CURBING BILLS

	Not so Sharp a Split	Sharp Split
Relatively Successful	1820's	1800's 1860's 1930's
Relatively Unsuccessful	1890's 1920's 1950's	

ship between relative success and party differences can be accounted for in part by the fact that when Congress represents a party different than the Court, then legislation introduced by members of that party, and particularly legislation directed against policies of the opposite party, will be more apt to get out of committee than will legislation introduced by the minority party. In addition, when there is a party split between Congress and the Court, public opinion is more apt to be on the side of Congress, since that body by virtue of its short terms is more responsive to changes in the public sentiment. It follows that when the public consensus is at odds with the policies of the Supreme Court, anti-Court legislation will not only increase in volume but also will have a better chance of being seriously considered.

C. CRISES

A third catalytic or enabling factor that may accelerate or decelerate congressional reaction to judicial provocation is the presence or absence of a crisis. Although the outbreak of war or depression may not directly cause attacks on the Court, one might hypothesize that when judicial provocation has first occurred, the presence or absence of a crisis may affect the speed and manner with which Congress reacts. Crisis may be defined as a period of depression, economic panic, war (including cold war), or postwar readjustment. In light of these definitions, during almost all the Court-curbing periods some degree of crisis has been present, as is shown in Table 21–12. The two classic examples of this

TABLE 21–12
RELATION BETWEEN CRISIS AND THE OCCURRENCE OF COURT-CURBING BILLS

High Occurrence Period	Type of Crisis
1800's	None, other than establishing a federal government
1820's	None
1860's	Civil War
1890's	Economic panic
1920's	Postwar readjustment
1930's	Depression
1950's	Cold war

relationship are the periods of the 1860's and 1930's. These attacks, which are perhaps the most famous and serious attempts to curb the Court, occurred during or just after two of the most serious crises this country has had to suffer—the Civil War and the Great Depression.

The relationship between crisis and the success of Court-curbing is more difficult to determine, but a positive correlation is suggested by the outcome of at least two of the high-frequency periods. The attacks of the 1860's and 1930's, which followed or accompanied great crises in American history, were both highly successful in relation to the other periods. The two most unsuccessful attacks, the 1890's and 1920's, occurred

TABLE 21–13
RELATION BETWEEN CRISIS AND THE SUCCESS OF COURT-CURBING BILLS

	Not So Severe Crisis	Severe Crisis
Relatively Successful	1800's 1820's	1860's 1930's
Relatively Unsuccessful	1890's 1920's	1950's

during periods of low degrees of crisis. The other three Court-curbing periods, however, fail to follow this pattern.

D. PUBLIC OPINION AND PRESSURE GROUPS

The element of public opinion should also be included in the discussion of catalytic or enabling factors that, through their presence or absence, accelerate or temper congressional attacks on the Supreme Court. The lack of extensive public opinion polls prior to recent years hinders scientific research and measurement of the impact of this factor on Court-curbing activity. An estimation of public support or disapproval for legislative policies toward the Court could be made through the rather crude method of analyzing the results of elections occurring immediately prior to or during periods of congressional attacks on the Court. An analysis of this sort would point, for example, to the landslide of 1936, which Roosevelt interpreted as a mandate for the New Deal and possibly for some kind of Court-curbing scheme. Public opinion polls taken at various stages of the fight over Roosevelt's Court-packing bill in the Senate indicate, however, that public opinion turned against his scheme after the election.[9] Another technique would involve the detailed analysis of newspaper comment, comments from the *Congressional Record*, and other contemporary publications, which tend to record the issues and sentiment of the time. This type of analysis would, however, primarily reflect the sentiments of the upper, more literate classes, just as election analysis would reflect the sentiment in respect to broad policy rather than the specific Court-curbing issue.

Pressure groups, representing certain segments of public opinion, have been active during legislative attacks on the Court. Again, their influence cannot be measured, but general comments about their probable roles can be made. In the 1930's, the American Bar Association, the National Association of Manufacturers, and the American Liberty League were the principal defenders of the Court, while the AFL-CIO was a principal attacker. In the 1950's, the NAACP and ACLU defended, and the White Citizens Councils and American Legion did some of the attacking. In both of these instances, the liberal pressure groups only partly won the battle, since the actual outcome was dependent on the operation of a number of variables. One can readily hypothesize, however, that when strong, prestigious groups are on the side of Congress, the attack is strengthened, and when such groups defend the Supreme Court, the attack is weakened.

---

[9] Murphy gives the results of Gallup polls taken during the Court fight in 1937, *op. cit. supra* note 1, at 61. Not only did the public increasingly disapprove of the Court-packing plan, but the President's personal popularity also fell during this period.

E. REGIONALISM

Regionalism is a catalytic factor like political party. When a judicial policy particularly affects one region of the country, the concerted efforts of that region's congressional representatives can strengthen the negative response of Congress. For example, 10 of the 12 anti-Court bills introduced during the 1820's were sponsored by Southerners in general and Kentuckians in particular who had been provoked by the Court's invalidation of land and debtor laws. Does one region of the country generally tend to be involved in Court-curbing more than others? Table 21–14 indicates that of the three main regions of the country—South,

TABLE 21–14

RELATIONSHIP OF REGIONALISM TO THE OCCURRENCE
AND SUCCESS OF COURT-CURBING

Period	Regional Sponsors	Success
1800's	Southern and western	Yes
1820's	Southern and western	Yes
1860's	Northern	Yes
1890's	Northern and western	No
1920's	Northern and western	No
1930's	Northern and western	Yes
1950's	Southerners and northern conservatives	No

West, and North—the West and North have been slightly more involved in Court-curbing than the South. This pattern is explained in part by considering the relationship between regionalism and issues. Economic issues, such as those at stake in the 1890's, 1920's, and 1930's, evoke a northern and western response, while the states' rights issues of the 1800's, 1820's, and 1950's evoke a southern reponse. This relationship is explained by the socioeconomic makeup of the various regions; the North and West are industrial and populist-wheat centers, while the South has been the locus of plantation agriculture and the Negro problem.

In terms of success, the South has enjoyed success in two thirds of its attempts to curb the Court, while the North and West have been successful in approximately half of their attempts. If the Court-curbing periods are ranked as in Table 21–2, however, two of the most successful periods, the 1860's and 1930's, were predominantly northern sponsored attacks. An explanation for this is that the northern states are more heavily represented in Congress, and the North enjoyed an additional advantage in the 1860's conflict, since the South and the Democratic Party were largely incapacitated. An analysis of regionalism points up that congressional attacks on the Supreme Court are often regional attacks, and that the Court has never really been faced with a united, national enemy, which along with public opinion and other factors may account in part for the generally low degree of success Court-curbing bills have had.

F. House and Senate Procedure

The House of Representatives has been almost twice as active as the Senate in Court-curbing, sponsoring 98 bills to the Senate's 57. What accounts for the greater volume of bills originating in the House? First, the difference may not be so great as it seems. Since the membership of the House is over four times as large as that of the Senate, one would expect the House to sponsor a greater amount of bills than the Senate on any issue. Second, House members, subject to biennial elections, might be more sensitive to short-run changes of sentiment than are Senate members. In addition, the smaller, more homogeneous constituencies of House members are possibly more conducive to sponsoring Court-curbing bills and other extreme legislation, which would be too divisive in a larger constituency. A third factor is that Senate members may sponsor bills jointly, whereas House bills can carry the name of only one sponsor—a practice tending to produce duplicate bills. Procedure, then, is a catalyst tending to affect the relative volume of bills generated in each house of Congress.

The Senate, in spite of its lower number of bills, has had a greater degree of success in getting its Court-curbing legislation out of committee. Almost one fourth of the Senate bills got out of committee, while only 13 percent of the House bills ever did. For reasons mentioned above, the House possibly tends to introduce harsher measures, which therefore have a smaller chance of success. In addition, the practice of introducing duplicate bills in the House lowers its average of success for individual bills.

IV.   CONGRESSIONAL AND PRESIDENTIAL RESPONSE

A. Congressional Response

Several courses of action are available to the congressman seeking to attack the policies of the Supreme Court. At the local level, he can participate in nullification movements to register disapproval of a particular decision. In Congress, he can attempt retaliation via the fiscal powers, introduce restrictive constitutional amendments, sponsor legislation to overturn a statutory interpretation, initiate joint resolutions or investigations, or, if a Senator, he can attempt to block a Presidential nominee for the bench. Although these methods account for a good share of the activity during congressional attacks on the Court, this chapter and Table 21–15 are concerned only with specific bills designed directly or indirectly to change some general policy of the Court.

After the congressman has decided to attack the power of the judges and to do it through legislative means, he still has a range of alternatives from which to choose. Table 21–15 indicates that about 30 percent of the Court-curbing bills dealt with regulating or abolishing judicial review, which particularly includes bills requiring special concurrences to declare statutes unconstitutional. Another 29 percent dealt with matters of Court personnel, particularly qualifications (like lengthy prior judicial experience) for holding a Supreme Court judgeship. Within this 29 percent are also included 13 bills designed to increase or decrease the size of the Court so as to allow a new President to make new appointments or to keep him from making new appointments. About 28 percent of the bills attempted to restrict the Court's appellate jurisdiction, and the relatively few remaining bills dealt with various procedural and miscellaneous matters.

Some measures have been peculiar to one time period. Bills curtailing the contempt and injunction powers were predominant, for example, during the period of the Progressives' attack on the Court, particularly before the enactment of the Clayton Act.[10] Bills pertaining to the appellate jurisdiction of the Court in respect to public schools, and bills abolishing the doctrine of preemptive federalism were characteristic of the 1955–1959 conflict. The broad historic trend has been away from bills that would remove or circumscribe a broad area of the Court's power and toward those bills that would limit a small, more specific part of the Court's functions. For example, the only serious attempt at impeachment occurred in 1804. Bills advocating the repeal of the 25th section of the Judiciary Act of 1789, which would be tantamount to removing the Court's appellate jurisdiction over state courts, were concentrated in the first half of the 19th century. Unsuccessful bills providing for equal representation of the states on the Court were proposed prior to 1870, and thus those groups favoring such a change have recently resorted to a constitutional amendment via a constitutional convention. In contrast, many bills proposed during the intense conflict in 1937 were designed to effect changes in the quorum, retirement of justices, and size of the Court. In the attack on the Warren Court, many bills prescribed limitation of jurisdiction in special cases dealing with subversion, public schools, and (after 1961) reapportionment. More extreme bills in the earlier years may be attributable to the fact that in the early 19th century the rule of the judicial branch of the government was not yet established,

---

[10] 64 Stat. 1125 (1950), 15 U.S.C. § 12 (1958).

TABLE 21–15

TYPES OF BILLS PROPOSED TO CURB THE SUPREME COURT

	Frequency		Relative Success	
	Number	% of 165	Number	% of Type
1. Judicial review				
a) Special concurrence needed	41	25%	5	12%
b) Miscellaneous regulate	5	3	0	0
c) Abolish	3	2	0	0
Total	49	30%	5	10% Avg.
2. Personnel				
a) Qualifications	24	15	0	0
b) Size of Court	13	8	5	38
c) Retirement	7	4	3	43
d) Appointing	4	2	1	25
e) Give states equal representation	1	½	0	0
Total	49	29½%	9	18% Avg.
3. Jurisdiction				
a) Regulate and define general appellate jurisdiction	23	14	3	13
b) Repeal Supreme Court jurisdiction over state	3	2	1	33
c) Limit jurisdiction in special cases				
(1) Habeas corpus appeals	3	2	2	67
(2) Reconstruction	1	½	0	0
(3) Public schools	7	4	0	0
(4) Other specific areas	8	5	1	12
Total	45	27½%	7	16% Avg.
4. Procedure				
a) General reorganization	6	4	3	50
b) Amend judicial code	4	2	2	50
c) Amend rules of practice and procedure	1	½	0	0
d) Facilitate decisions on constitutional questions	1	½	0	0
Total	12	7%	5	42% Avg.
5. Curtail contempt or injunction powers	4	2	3	75
6. Miscellaneous				
a) Let lower court ignore nonlegalistic Sup. Ct. decisions	2	1	0	0
b) Change doctrine of preemptive federalism	1	½	1	100
c) Postpone meeting of Court	1	½	1	100
d) Impeachment	1	½	1	100
e) Give some body direct review over Sup. Ct. decisions	1	½	0	0
Overall Total	165	100%	32	19% Avg.

and the obvious partisanship of some justices during the very early years was a hindrance to the growth of the judicial myth. In addition, history has shown that bills removing comparatively smaller amounts of the Court's power have the greatest prospect of success. Astute congressmen may well have taken note of this fact. One should note, however, that although the severity of bills during the Warren and Roosevelt Courts was lower than in prior periods, the quantity of bills was higher. This possibly indicated a more widespread discontent toward specific decisions and a lack of cohesive leadership by the anti-Court forces, which kept these forces from centering on one or a few bills.

With regard to success, 10 of the 23 categories of bills had a higher percentage of relative success (i.e., got out of committee) than the average of 19 percent. These 10 types of bills included repealing jurisdiction over state supreme courts, limiting jurisdiction in regard to habeas corpus appeals, changing the rules concerning retirement and the size of the Court, restricting the Court's procedure, and limiting the Court's contempt and injunction powers. Most of the 10 types could be considered as limited means of curbing the Court. The substantially higher rate of success for the relatively milder bills can be explained by the fact that during all the time periods there has been a sizable opposition in Congress to any attempts to curb the Supreme Court—a factor that necessitates compromise.

B. PRESIDENTIAL RESPONSE

To what extent have Presidents become involved in Court-curbing, and what effect has their participation had on the outcome of congressional court conflicts? Four Presidents have been openly critical of the Court during the high-frequency periods—i.e., Jefferson, Jackson, Lincoln, and Roosevelt, but not Eisenhower or the Presidents of the 1920's or 1890's. Presidents have been hesitant to openly initiate Court-curbing legislation. FDR's Court-packing plan of 1937 was an exception, but it was only one of numerous anti-Court bills introduced in the 1930's. This Presidential reluctance is possibly due to a fear of alienating the Court's numerous defenders in Congress and the public (as well as a respect for the independence of the judiciary), and in some instances to a favorable Presidential attitude toward the Court's policies.

With regard to the success of individual bills, Roosevelt's Court-packing bill was reported out of committee unfavorably. This is attributable to inadequate cultivation of support in Congress and among the public and to reversals by the Court itself. In view of the Court's retreat, however, the Roosevelt period can be considered a relative success. Presidents also have administrative weapons to either thwart or aid orders of the Supreme Court, and ultimately via his appointive power the

President can change the Court's policies. Nevertheless, with the astute use of his tools of leadership the President can be a powerful figure both in the initiation and successful outcome of Court-curbing bills. With his active support, Court-curbing legislation is probably more likely to pass; without it, such legislation is more likely to fail.

V. JUDICIAL COUNTERACTION

The behavior pattern of the Court-curbing process does not end with the action taken by Congress and the President. The Supreme Court can affect the outcome of legislative attacks by its reaction. First, the members of the Court can individually refute the charges made by congressmen. Prior to 1937, however, the judicial myth of aloofness from political disputes was generally followed by the Court. The only exceptions to this pattern were Marshall's criticism of Jefferson in *Marbury* v. *Madison*, Chase's partisan opinions, and Taney's criticism of Lincoln. The 1937 conflict involved the direct participation of members of the Court, and included Brandeis' testimony before the Judiciary Committee, Hughes' letter to the sympathetic congressional leaders in defense of the Court, and the timeliness of Van Deventer's retirement.

Second, the Court as a whole can counteract legislative attack by retreating from the policy stand that originally provoked the attack. In terms of frequency, this has happened in four of the seven high-frequency periods. The four periods involve the early 1800's conflict, the 1820's, the 1860's, and the 1930's. In 1959 the Court retreated in one of the three fields (free speech, segregation, and criminal procedure) that originally provoked the attack. In the 1890's and 1920's, on the other hand, a conservative Court protected by a Republican Congress easily withstood the disorganized attacks of the Democrats, Populists, and Progressives, without having to resort to a retreat. Since the composite index of success includes retreat as a major criterion, all four of the above-mentioned Court-curbing periods, by definition, can be called successful. In short, when the Court removes the provocation for the conflict, the attack dissipates but can be considered a success.

VI. CONCLUSIONS

Periods of intense Court-curbing bills have occurred only seven times during the 170-year history of the United States. Nevertheless, this mode of conflict between the legislative and judicial branches will no doubt recur when certain judicial provocations and catalytic factors are present.

The factors that have an affirmative correlation with the occurrence of Court-curbing bills are (in the order presented) as follows: (1) judicial review of federal and state statutes, (2) economic issues rather than other issues, (3) low degree of unanimity within the Supreme Court, (4) Democratic or liberal Congress when the Court is conservative, (5) Republican or conservative Congress when the Court is liberal, (6) crisis present, (7) public opinion and powerful pressure groups favor the attack, (8) the process for introducing bills in the House, and (9) the lack of cohesive Congressional leadership.

The factors that have an affirmative correlation with the success of Court-curbing bills (in the order presented) as as follows: (1) sponsored by the majority party in Congress, (2) party split between the Court and Congress, (3) crisis present and allegedly made more severe by the Court's decisions, (4) public and pressure group support, (5) northern sponsored attack, (6) introduced in Senate, (7) limited in purpose, and (8) has Presidential support and cohesive congressional leadership.

Although an accurate measurement of the relative importance of these factors to Court-curbing cannot be made, a behavior pattern that invariably occurs in such conflicts can be described. The sequence of events involves judicial provocation, the existence of circumstances that act as catalysts or as retarders, a set of congressional and Presidential responses, and judicial counteraction. This model, which is based on the psychological model of stimulus, organism, response, and feedback, can perhaps also be profitably applied to analyzing other legal and political phenomena.

Part Four

STUDIES THAT VIEW LAW MAKING AND ADJUDICATION AS STIMULI TO SUBSEQUENT RESPONSES

T he most important part of this book in terms of generality is Part One, since the conceptual and methodological orientation presented there has widespread applicability for future behavioral studies of the legal process. In terms of theoretical significance, Parts Two and Three are the most important, since they contain much data, verbalizing, and methodology relevant to explaining why the legal process operates the way it does. Part Four, however, is the most important in terms of social significance, because studies that deal scientifically with the effects of legal policies bring us closer to the long-sought goal of applying the scientific method to social and legal improvement rather than just to industrial and technological development.

In addition to their substantive content, each of the four chapters in this part introduces some new methodological techniques that were only casually mentioned, if at all, in the previous chapters. Chapter 22 applies the scalogramming technique to positioning newspapers with regard to their positive and negative attitudes toward the Supreme Court's decisions concerning separation of church and state in the realm of education. It then attempts to account for the differing attitudes of the newspapers in terms of their politics, religion, urbanism, and region by applying a form of correlation analysis which partials out or holds constant intervening variables which may be obscuring the relationship. The broader significance of the chapter lies in its potentiality for serving as a building block toward creating theories and planning policies that encourage attitudes and behaviors that comply with the constitutional law of the land.

Chapter 23 brings out many of the methodological problems involved in testing the effects of alternative legal policies. It discusses before-and-after designs, as contrasted to comparing entities all as of one point in time. It discusses working with a sample of gross entities like states as well as with individual entities, and also mixing gross statistical data like crime rates with individual attitudes. Comparing average scores of groups of entities rather than just tallying how often each entity falls into various categories is also discussed, as is the important problem of controlling for intervening variables by trying to randomize which entities will be subject to the new law or by trying to match the experimental and control entities in their similarity on the relevant intervening variables. The general significance of the chapter lies in showing that a retrospective questionnaire responded to by a variety of knowledgeable persons can produce some meaningful results with regard to the effects of a legal policy that is adopted in some states or areas and not in others.

Chapter 24 introduces the reader to computer programming and to some basic concepts of operations research. For ordinary statistical calculations, one does not need to know how to program or instruct a computer, because canned statistical programs are readily available. To use them, all one basically needs to know is how to punch a few numbers on a few IBM cards in order to indicate what options one wants to exercise that the canned program provides for. If, on the other hand, one is seeking to simulate on the computer what politicians do when they redistrict a state legislature or what residents of a city might do as a result of an urban renewal project, then this might require writing a new program or changing an old one to fit a new situation.

Likewise, for ordinary social science hypothesis-testing where one is merely seeking to determine the relation between variables, one does not need to know anything about operations research. If, however, one is interested in maximizing some variables, minimizing other variables, and optimizing still other variables at a point that is neither a maximum nor a minimum, then this might require a knowledge of operations research. O.R. (as it is usually abbreviated) can be defined as using quantitative techniques to determine the optimum combination of inputs in order to arrive at an optimum output.

Chapter 24 applies computer programming and operations research to determining what combinations of precincts, counties, or other political units will create a districting plan that will minimize deviations from equality, compactness, and certain optional political goals while preserving contiguity within districts. The specific application also uses basic principles of political science, which give this computer program a political realism lacking in other computer redistricting programs.[1]

Chapter 25 attempts to tie together the bivariable cross-tabulation methodology of Chapter 2, with the correlation and regression analysis of Chapters 10 through 13, with the causal analysis of Chapters 22 and 23, along with the computer programming and operations research concepts of Chapter 24. The resulting product is a methodological model for use in seeking to arrive at legal policies that will have optimum effects. The method is not one that can always be applied; but it can usefully shape one's thinking, and its application seems worth striving for in part or in total, even if some of the components have to be estimated rather than calculated precisely.

---

[1] R. Dixon, Democratic Representation: Reapportionment in Law and Politics 527–35, 15–22 (1968).

CHAPTER 22

Editorial Reaction to the Church
and State Cases

The purpose of this chapter is to present and analyze some data about the reaction in editorials in various newspapers to the major decisions of the Supreme Court dealing with the separation of church and state. The analysis is primarily directed toward accounting for the different reactions of the newspapers to the decisions.

I. THE STIMULI AND THE REACTIONS

The court decisions consist of: *Everson* v. *Board of Education,* 330 U.S. 1 (1947), which upheld the constitutionality of using public funds to provide bus transportation to parochial as well as public school children; *McCullom* v. *Board of Education,* 333 U.S. 203 (1948), which declared unconstitutional the conducting of voluntary doctrinal religious classes in the public schools during school hours; *Zorach* v. *Clausen,* 343 U.S. 306 (1952), which upheld the constitutionality of voluntary doctrinal religious classes for public school children during school hours but not on school property; and *Engel* v. *Vitale,* 370 U.S. 421 (1962), which declared unconstitutional unison recitation of religious prayers in public school classrooms, even when the prayers are considered nonsectarian and provision is made for objecting students to be excused.

The raw data for this study were obtained by analyzing the editorials for a two-week period subsequent to each of the four court decisions, for the large-circulation daily newspapers shown in Table 22–1.[1] The sample was confined to large-circulation newspapers available in the University

---

[1] The *Wall Street Journal* and the *Christian Science Monitor* were excluded because they differ substantially from the other newspapers with regard to having a metropolitan constituency. A few additional newspapers were excluded because no relevant editorials appeared in the periods available.

TABLE 22–1

Editorial Reaction and Characteristics of the Individual Newspapers

Newspapers	Everson	McCullom	Engel	Zorach	Relative Proseparation	% Dem. in City	% Dems. Endorsed	Population (in 1,000's)	% C and E	% J and P	Publisher Religion
St. Louis Post Dispatch	+	+	+	0	Yes	67%	80%	750	28%	6%	E
Atlanta Constitution	·	+	+	0	Yes	51	90	487	4	5	E
San Francisco Chronicle	0	+	+	0	Yes	58	20	740	28	4	C
Chicago Sun Times	0	0	+	0	Yes	64	40	3,550	37	8	P
Des Moines Register	0	·	+	·	Yes	46	20	209	12	6	·
Milwaukee Journal	·	·	+	·	Yes	62	80	741	35	5	·
Minneapolis Star	0	·	+	·	Yes	52	20	483	26	5	M
New Orleans Times	0	0	+	0	Yes	65	60	628	44	2	C
San Antonio Express	+	+	·	·	Yes	54	25	588	34	3	Ch
Washington Post	0	+	+	–	Yes	86	40	764	20	6	C
Chicago Daily News	0	+	+	–	Yes	64	20	3,550	37	8	P
Detroit Free Press	0	+	+	–	Yes	71	20	1,670	30	4	E
New York Times	0	0	+	·	Yes	63	40	7,782	34	22	J
New York Tribune	+	0	+	0	Yes	63	20	7,782	34	22	·
Chicago Tribune	0	+	–	0	No	64	0	3,550	37	8	·
Chicago American	0	0	–	·	No	64	10	3,550	37	8	·
Cincinnati Enquirer	·	·	–	·	No	50	0	503	31	6	E
Denver Rocky Mtn.	·	·	–	·	No	50	20	494	18	6	·
Indianapolis Star	·	·	–	0	No	42	10	476	13	4	M
Kansas City Star	0	0	–	·	No	56	20	476	14	5	·
Philadelphia Bulletin	·	·	–	·	No	68	20	2,003	33	11	P
Seattle Times	·	·	–	·	No	47	20	557	15	4	·
St. Louis Globe	0	–	·	·	No	67	13	750	28	6	P
Dallas Morning News	0	–	·	–	No	37	10	680	8	5	P

Symbols:
+ = favored the separation position; 0 = no editorial; – = opposed the separation position.
C = Catholic; Ch = Christian; E = Episcopalian; J = Jewish; M = Methodist; P = Presbyterian.
• = was unavailable.

of Illinois Library rather than to a randomly drawn sample of newspapers. The sample thus cannot be used to determine what proportion of the nation's newspapers reacted favorably or unfavorably to specific decisions. The sample, however, is diverse enough in some important respects to be useful for generating insights into variables that might account for why some groups of newspapers reacted differently from others.

Analysis of the editorials reveals that those taking a stand tended to favor separation of church and state in the case dealing with aid for parochial school bus transportation (3 favored, 0 opposed, 14 no editorial, 7 unavailable). They favored the decision nullifying religious classes on school time in the schools (8 favored, 2 opposed, 7 no editorial, 7 unavailable). They slightly favored the school prayer decision (13 favored, 9 opposed, 0 no editorial, 2 unavailable), and they opposed separation when it involved religious classes on school time but outside the schools (0 favored, 6 opposed, 8 no editorial, 10 unavailable). The reactions of the specific newspapers are shown in Table 22–1.[2]

With the exception of the *Zorach* case, the typical editorial reaction was to favor the separation of church and state. The seeming inconsistency toward *Zorach* might be explained by: (1) the mildness of the link between church and state in the *Zorach* case as compared to that in the other three cases; (2) the fact that the majority opinion was written by Justice Douglas, one of the most liberal, proseparation members of the Court; (3) the decreased tolerance toward civil liberties in 1952 as compared with the other years; and (4) the possible tendency of the newspapers to favor the Court's decisions, regardless of the direction of the decisions.

In accordance with Guttman scaling techniques,[3] the cases are arranged in Table 22–1 from the case that apparently was the easiest on which to take a proseparation position (*Everson*), to the next-to-easiest (*McCullom*), to the next-to-hardest (*Engel*), over to the case that apparently was the hardest on which to take a proseparation position (*Zorach*). By "hardest case" in this context is meant the case on which the fewest editorializing newspapers took a proseparation position. If a newspaper took a proseparation position on the hardest or the next-to-hardest cases, then it always took a proseparation position on the easier cases. Likewise, there is no instance in Table 22–1 of a newspaper taking both an antiseparation position on one of the easier cases and also a

---

[2] When a newspaper did not editorialize on the school prayer decision or was unavailable, its reaction to *Abington Township School District* v. *Schempp*, 374 U.S. 203 (1963) was used. The *Abington* case declared doctrinal Bible-reading exercises in the public schools to be unconstitutional.

[3] M. Hagood & D. Price, Statistics for Sociologists 138–59 (1952).

proseparation position on one of the harder cases. In other words, the responses form a perfect Guttman scale. The newspapers are arranged from those that were the most proseparation at the top down to those that were the most antiseparation at the bottom. In arranging the newspapers, a score of no editorial was considered to be between a plus or a minus. If two or more newspapers were equally proseparation or antiseparation on the scale, they are arranged alphabetically.

Although the typical reaction favored the separation of church and state, many of the newspapers were not typical. Fifteen of the newspapers favored the separation position in 50 percent or more of their editorials, and 9 favored separation less than 50 percent of the time. It is, however, more meaningful to note that 14 favored the separation position in all cases on which they editorialized up to the *Zorach* case, and 10 newspapers opposed separation in the *Engel* case or in a case to the left of *Engel* on the scale. In a sense, the 14 newspapers (or 58 percent) can be considered to be relatively proseparation newspapers, and the remaining 10 can be considered to be relatively anti- or less proseparation. What characteristics do the proseparation ones tend to have in common that might explain why they reacted differently from the anti separation ones?

II.   ACCOUNTING FOR DIFFERENCES IN THE REACTIONS

The authors suspected that perhaps the differences in the reactions to the Supreme Court decisions might be accounted for more by the politics of the newspapers than by geographical or religious factors. Tables 22–1 and 22–2 provide some data relevant to testing this general hypothesis. The correlation coefficients of Table 22–2 can, of course, range from −1.00 (complete inverse correlation between the variables being correlated) on up to +1.00 (complete direct correlation). All the correlations are based on 24 entities, except for the correlation with publisher's religion, which is based on 16 entities. As an alternative to the correlation approach of Table 22–2, one could dichotomize each characteristic into two categories, and then indicate what percentage of the affirmative category and what percentage of the negative category took proseparation positions. There is, however, no theoretically meaningful place to dichotomize these characteristics, and where the cutting line is drawn can substantially affect the findings when a small sample is involved.

Column 1 of Table 22–2 indicates that there is a +.34 correlation between the percentage of Democrats in the city of the newspaper and whether or not the newspaper took a relatively favorable position toward separation of church and state. The percentage of the two-party vote received by President Kennedy in 1960 was used to determine the city's

TABLE 22–2

NEWSPAPER CHARACTERISTICS AND EDITORIAL REACTION

Characteristics (Commonly Thought to Be Positively Correlated with Favorable Reaction)	Correlation with Favorable Reaction toward Separation (1)	Correlation with % Democrats in City (2)	Correlation with Favorable Reaction While Holding Constant % Dems. in City (3)
A. Politics			
1. % Democrats in city	+.34	+1.00	
2. % Democrats endorsed by the newspaper	+.59	+ .24	+.56
B. Geography			
3. Being North rather than South or border	−.11	− .08	−.09
4. Population in city	+.19	+ .31	+.09
C. Religion			
5. % Non-Catholic and non-Episcopalian in city	−.25	− .57	−.07
6. % Jewish or Presbyterian	+.13	+ .22	+.06
7. (% Catholic or Episcopalian) minus (% Jewish or Presbyterian)	−.20	− .48	−.04
8. Publisher being non-Catholic and non-Episcopalian	−.35	− .15	−.32

Democratic or Republican orientation.[4] The 1960 rather than 1964 figures were used because in 1964, more than in 1960, many people voted Democratic who normally vote Republican and consider themselves to be conservatives. Voting figures rather than registration figures were used because voting figures more clearly reflect behavior rather than intentions and because they are more accessible. Figures showing the liberal–conservative split in each city would probably have produced a higher correlation than figures showing the Democratic–Republican split. Figures prior to 1960 were not used because the reaction to the *Engel* case of 1962 was what mainly needed explanation.

The party correlation rises to a high of +.59 when one looks at the

---

[4] Voting statistics are available for most of the cities in R. SCAMMON, AMERICAN VOTER 4 (1962). For other cities, voting statistics were obtained from local governmental officials, although for Atlanta and Dallas the county figures had to be used. For Washington, D. C., the 1964 Presidential election was used, New York Times, December 13, 1964 at 85.

politics of the individual newspaper publishers as contrasted to the politics of their cities, although there is a +.24 correlation between these two measures of political orientation. With a sample size of 24, any correlation greater than plus or minus .40 could occur purely by chance less than 5 out of 100 times.[5] The +.59 correlation decreases only slightly to +.56 when Democrats in the city are statistically held constant by the technique of partial correlations.[6] The percentage of Democrats in the city is held constant in Table 22–2, because it can account for much of the correlation between the other characteristics and the editorial reaction of the newspapers. The endorsement characteristic is based on the percentage of times each newspaper endorsed the Democratic Presidential candidate in the Presidential elections from 1948 through 1964.[7] A neutral policy was counted as half a Democratic and half a Republican endorsement.

Common sense might expect to find a sharp divergence between the southern and northern newspapers on the church and state cases, with the southern newspapers being more opposed to the separation position. Such divergence might be found if all newspapers, regardless of size, were included in the sample. This study, however, in effect holds the urbanism variable constant when making regional comparisons, since all the newspapers are urban newspapers. Row 3, Table 22–2, shows that the southern and border newspapers were slightly *more* favorable to the separation position than the northern newspapers, as is indicated by the −.11 correlation between being northern and being favorable.[8] Using a larger sample of newspapers for a different purpose, Newland found that "contrary to common newspaper reports, more southern newspapers were neutral or favorable to the [prayer] opinion than opposed it."[9]

Although all the newspapers are large-circulation urban newspapers, some come from larger cities than others, as is shown in the population column of Table 22–1, where the cities range from 209,000 to 7,782,000.[10]

---

[5] J. P. GUILFORD, FUNDAMENTAL STATISTICS IN PSYCHOLOGY AND EDUCATION 181, 219, 538 (1956).

[6] H. BLALOCK, SOCIAL STATISTICS 333–36 (1960).

[7] Newspaper presidential endorsements are summarized in the journal EDITOR AND PUBLISHER at 11–15 (1948), at 9–10, 69–71 (1952), at 64–68 (1956), at 10–13 (1960), and at 9–13 (1964). If a newspaper was not listed for one of the five years, the denominator of its percentage was reduced below five.

[8] Southern states were defined as all states that were members of the Confederate States of America. Border states were defined as states that had legalized slavery as of 1860 plus the Oklahoma Territory but were not members of the Confederacy. THE WORLD ALMANAC, World-Telegram at 151 (1962). Northern states were defined as all the other states.

[9] Newland, *Press Coverage of the United States Supreme Court*, 17 W. POL. Q. 30 (1965).

[10] The population figures came from THE WORLD ALMANAC 259–79 (1962).

The correlation between the population variable and being proseparation is positive, as might be expected. This correlation, however, drops from +.19 to +.09 when percentage of Democrats is held constant, since percentage of Democrats has a correlation of +.31 with the population-urbanism variable.

What particularly seems to run contrary to conventional stereotypes are the religion findings for the next four rows of Table 22-2. Catholics and Episcopalians, or at least their priests and ministers, have been the two denominations most outspoken in opposing the separation position exemplified by the *Engel* v. *Vitale* case.[11] Yet, line 5, in effect, shows a correlation of +.25 between the percentage of Catholics and Episcopalians in the newspaper's city and being a proseparation newspaper. Although much of this correlation disappears when percentage of Democrats is held constant, the correlation does not change its direction.[12]

On the other side of the religious groupings (and the public positions of their leaders) are the Jews and Presbyterians.[13] There is, as hypothesized, a positive, although low, correlation between the percentage of adherents to these religions in the city and a proseparation editorial reaction, but more than half the correlation disappears when percentage of Democrats is held constant.

The percentages for all four religions are combined on row 7 by subtracting the percentage Jewish or Presbyterian from the percentage Catholic or Episcopalian. In every city, the latter pair of religions was numerically larger than the former pair of religions, with the exception of Atlanta, where the pairs are about equal in size. This partly explains why the negative results of line 7 look so much like the negative results of line 5.

Finally, the biggest negative correlation of all is produced in the last row, which correlates the publisher's being a non-Catholic and a non-Episcopalian with his being relatively favorable toward the separation position.[14] In other words, if the publisher is a Catholic or Episco-

---

[11] P. Blanshard, Religion and the Schools: The Great Controversy 50–75 (1963).

[12] Religious percentages for various areas are given in Churches and Church Membership in the United States Tables 136–39 (1956–57).

[13] Blanshard, *op. cit.* Universalists and Unitarians have also been highly proseparation, but (like avowed atheists) there are very few of them. D. Boles, in The Bible, Religion and the Public Schools at 218 (1963), says the Baptists seem to have a most consistent policy of proseparation. Blanshard, however (*op. cit.* at 64), quotes from Billy Graham, America's most noted Baptist minister, to the contrary, in contrast to "the strongest Protestant statement of all in support of the Supreme Court . . . from the General Assembly of the United Presbyterian Church" (*op. cit.* at 66). Nevertheless, the findings of this chapter are not significantly changed if Presbyterians and Baptists are considered equally proseparation.

[14] The religion of 15 of the 24 newspaper publishers was determined by checking Who's Who in America (1960).

palian in the sample, his newspaper is more likely rather than less likely to endorse the separation decisions of the Supreme Court, particularly the prayer decision on which the separation score hinges. The −.35 or −.32 of row 8 on publisher's religion contrasts strongly with the +.59 or +.56 of row 2 on publisher's politics.

Why did the political variables account for much more of the differences in the newspaper reactions than the religious variables? The explanation possibly lies in the fact that political party affiliation is, in general, a better predictor of attitudes on controversial public issues than is religion, and the issue of the desirability of the Supreme Court's church and state decisions does not seem to be an exception to this rule. Data compiled by the Survey Research Center, for instance, show that "There are significant differences between socio-economic groups [including religious groups] in their attitudes . . ., but the differences between party identifiers within each group tend to be greater than the differences between the groups themselves."[15] Likewise, data compiled by Nagel show that one can predict judicial behavior on controversial legal issues (possibly even in family law cases) substantially better by knowing a judge's party affiliation than by knowing a judge's religious affiliation.[16] Similar findings can also be offered with regard to legislative voting behavior.[17]

Political parties (at least, when region is held constant) seem to be more homogeneous attitudinal groups than are religions, with the possible exception of Jews. Thus, wealthy Catholics probably differ more sharply from working-class Catholics on most controversial public issues than is the case between wealthy Democrats and working-class Democrats. A political party affiliation seems to be more a matter of attitudinal choice than is a religious affiliation, whereas a religious affiliation seems more a matter of birth and inertia than is a political party affiliation. The church and state cases have important religious implications, but they do not involve issues of ceremonial propriety, which divide Protestant denominations, or issues like the infallability of the Pope, which separate Catholics from Protestants. The cases are more political controversies than religious controversies. They are possibly closely correlated attitudinally to opinions about freedom of speech, equality in race relations, and the welfare state, at least when class is held constant.

15 A. Campbell & H. Cooper, Group Differences in Attitudes and Votes: A Study of the 1954 Congressional Election 93 (1955).

16 Nagel, *Political Party Affiliation and Judges' Decisions,* 55 Am. Pol. Sci. Rev. 843–50 (1961) (partly in chap. 15 *supra*); and Nagel, *Ethnic Affiliations and Judicial Propensities,* 24 J. Pol. 92–110 (1962).

17 J. Turner, Party and Constituency: Pressures on Congress (1951); and Francis, *Voting Record of Catholics in Congress,* 49 Commonweal 342–45 (January 14, 1949).

Further studies of editorial and public attitudes toward controversial Supreme Court decisions can be useful for testing the above ideas and for generating further ideas about public opinion. Such studies can also provide insights into the intervening variables between legal stimuli and public and elite responses. An understanding of such variables can be useful to local and national governmental bodies in planning policies that will encourage attitudes and behavior that comply with the law of the land.

CHAPTER 23

Effects of Excluding Illegally
Seized Evidence

Much has been written about the need for more testing of the empirical effects of alternative legal policies.[1] Much has also been written about the desirability of adopting or not adopting the rule excluding illegally seized evidence from courtroom proceedings.[2] This chapter has two purposes. One is to illustrate some of the methodological problems involved in systematically testing legal effects. The other is to indicate the substantive findings of a study on the effects of the exclusionary rule.

The main data for this study were compiled through the use of questionnaires.[3] In November 1963, 250 questionnaires were mailed to a police chief, a prosecuting attorney, a judge, a defense attorney, and

---

The writer thanks Albert Wicks for his participation in an early phase of this study, and Robert Phares for compiling the data for Table 23–3. Both are former political science students at the University of Illinois.

[1] See, e.g., BEUTEL, SOME POTENTIALITIES OF EXPERIMENTAL JURISPRUDENCE AS A NEW BRANCH OF SOCIAL SCIENCE (1957); LASSWELL & LERNER, THE POLICY SCIENCES—RECENT DEVELOPMENTS IN SCOPE AND METHOD (1951); Cowan, *Experimental Jurisprudence—Science, Morality, Law*, 46 ARCHIV FUR RECHTS-UND SOZIALPHILOSOPHIE 57 (Supp. 1960).

[2] See, e.g., the four-article debate between Fred Inbau and Yale Kamisar: Inbau, *Public Safety v. Individual Civil Liberties: The Prosecutor's Stand*, 53 J. CRIM. L., C. & P.S. 85 (1962); Inbau, *More About P.S. v. I.C.L.*, 53 J. CRIM. L., C. & P.S. 329; Kamisar, *P.S. v. I. Liberties: Some "Facts" and "Theories*," 53 J. CRIM. L., C. & P.S. 171; Kamisar, *Some Reflections on Criticizing the Courts and "Policing the Police,"* 53 J. CRIM. L., C. & P.S. 453; and the debate among the Justices of the Supreme Court in *Wolf* v. *Colorado*, 338 U.S. 25 (1949 and *Mapp* v. *Ohio*, 367 U.S. 643 (1961).

[3] A copy of the questionnaire and the explanatory letter is included in the Appendix to this chapter. The items included in the questionnaire were chosen from a longer list in view of the criteria of (1) relevance to the exclusionary rule debate, (2) comparability of answers among respondents, (3) brevity of the question and likely answer, (4) meaningfulness of language, (5) interest to the respondent, and (6) avoidance of duplication.

an official of the American Civil Liberties Union in every state. These groups were chosen to provide diversity of relevant occupations. Questionnaires were sent to these occupations in each of the 50 states to supply a diversity of geographical areas. The police chief for each state was randomly drawn from the *Municipal Yearbook* for 1963. The prosecuting attorneys and defense attorneys were randomly drawn from the criminal cases in each state's published court reports for 1963. The court reports also supplied the names of 25 appellate judges and 25 trial court judges whose cases were being appealed. Recent annual reports of the American Civil Liberties Union provided a list of state chairmen and state correspondents.[4] Of the 250 questionnaire recipients, 113 or 45 percent sent back questionnaires in time to be processed. The 113 consisted of 22 police chiefs, 27 prosecuting attorneys, 17 judges, 24 defense attorneys, 19 ACLU officials, and 4 unknowns on occupations.[5] Relevant data were also obtained from the FBI's *Uniform Crime Reports,* the *Census of Population,* and from various court reports.

Prior to 1961, 23 states had voluntarily adopted the exclusionary rule, 24 had not, and 3 had partially adopted it.[6] In 1961, the United States Supreme Court declared in *Mapp* v. *Ohio* that the federal Constitution required all 50 states to adopt the rule.[7] The basic hypothesis of this

---

[4] The five recipients from each state were not selected from the same community because it was thought desirable to obtain a more representative sample from each state within the limits of the study's small budget. The random selection process from the sources used, however, occasionally produced two recipients from the same community. There was also no attempt made to control the size of the communities in the sample because it was thought desirable to provide communities of diverse populations for comparison purposes.

[5] Seven of the states had 4 respondents, 13 had 3 respondents, 19 had 2, 8 had 1, and 3 had none. This is too few respondents per individual state for providing a description of detailed conditions in an individual state. This chapter, however, is concerned only with types of states and only with general conditions. Respondents from states that had the exclusionary rule prior to 1961 consisted of 11 police chiefs, 10 prosecuting attorneys, 9 judges, 11 defense attorneys, 7 ACLU officials, and 1 unknown. Respondents from states that did not have the exclusionary rule prior to 1961 consisted of 10 police chiefs, 16 prosecuting attorneys, 8 judges, 12 defense attorneys, 12 ACLU officials, and 2 unknowns on occupation. A police chief, a prosecutor, and an unknown responded from the partial exclusionary states.

[6] See the appendix in *Elkins* v. *United States,* 364 U.S. 206, 224–32 (1960). The three partial exclusionary states were Alabama, Maryland, and Michigan. As of 1960, Alabama law allowed illegally seized evidence to be admitted except in some alcohol control cases; Michigan required exclusion except where narcotics or weapons were involved; and Maryland allowed admission except in some misdemeanor cases. In this study, South Dakota is considered to have been an exclusionary state, since its laws excluded all illegally obtained evidence regardless of the crime, except evidence obtained with a defective search warrant. If South Dakota were considered a partial exclusionary state (like Alabama, Michigan, and Maryland) and thereby removed from much of the analysis, then none of the findings of this chapter would have been significantly changed, mainly because there were only two respondents from South Dakota—a prosecuting attorney and a defense attorney.

[7] 367 U.S. 643 (1961). The rule of *Mapp* v. *Ohio* thus far applies only to criminal, not to civil proceedings. The *Mapp* case itself does not indicate what

study is that between 1960 and 1963 those twenty-four states forced
to initiate the rule have undergone more changes of various kinds relevant
to the rule than the twenty-three states that had the rule all along.[8]
This hypothesis was not made known to the questionnaire recipients.

I. EFFECTS ON POLICE BEHAVIOR

Table 23–1 illustrates the findings of the questionnaire with respect
to some effects on police behavior of requiring the initiation of the
exclusionary rule. However, it is necessary to discuss some general aspects
of the tables before turning to the substantive findings. For easier reading,
in each row the figure is underscored that seems most important for
comparing the initiating and noninitiating states. The percentages sometimes do not add up to exactly 100 percent because of rounding. And
the totals do not add up to 113 because respondents who did not answer
the specific question involved or who came from the three partial exclusionary states were excluded. The last column indicates the most common
response to the item from all the respondents.[9]

The findings of the first row of Table 23–1 indicate that there has
been an increase in police adherence to the requirements for legal search
and seizure in both the initiating and the noninitiating states. Of the
respondents from the initiating states, however, 75 percent reported increased adherence, whereas only 57 percent of the respondents from
the noninitiating states reported such increases.[10]

---

constitutes illegally (i.e., unconstitutionally) seized evidence, but only that such
evidence is not admissible in court unless the defendant waives his right to have it
excluded. For further discussion of the legal aspects of the *Mapp* case, see Wolf, *A
Survey of the Expanded Exclusionary Rule,* 32 Geo. Wash. L. Rev. 193 (1963).

[8] The tables in this chapter indicate that changes in relevant behavior are occurring in both the states newly initiating the exclusionary rule and in pre-1961
exclusionary states. Some of the changes in the prior exclusionary states may be due
to the spur of *Mapp* v. *Ohio,* but some of the changes may be due to social trends
irrespective of *Mapp.* The research design of this chapter is, however, primarily directed at comparing the differences in behavioral changes between the newly exclusionary and the former exclusionary states.

[9] The responses shown in Tables 23–1 and 23–2 could have been broken down
by the five types of occupations as well as by the two types of states. Such an additional breakdown, however, would involve five times the quantity of numbers now
present in Tables 23–1 and 23–2, and would not add very useful information. This
information would not be very useful because (1) this study is primarily concerned
with how the two types of states differ rather than how different types of occupations
differ; (2) the perceptions of the different occupations within each type of state
tend to balance each other; and, (3) the occupations did not differ so much in their
responses to parts one and two of the questionnaire (the empirical parts) as they
did to part three (the evaluative part). See note 27 *infra* and accompanying text.

[10] In addition to asking about increased police adherence to legality in searches,
it would have been useful if the questionnaire had also asked about increased police
adherence to legality in arrests. Edward Barrett has hypothesized that *Mapp* v.
Ohio may have encouraged the police to be more careful in making searches, but to

TABLE 23-1

EFFECTS ON POLICE BEHAVIOR OF ADOPTING THE EXCLUSIONARY RULE

Question Number	Change from 1960 to 1963	Respondents from States Not Initiating the Rule in 1961*				Respondents from States Initiating the Rule in 1961†				Most Common Response
		% Reporting Decrease	% Reporting No Change	% Reporting Increase	Total	% Reporting Decrease	% Reporting No Change	% Reporting Increase	Total	
7	Police adherence to legality in searches	9%	34%	57%	56	4%	21%	75%	48	Increase
6	Police education in re legality in searches	0	22	77	55	0	13	87	45	Increase
3	Police effectiveness in searches	9	65	26	54	43	39	17	46	No change
11	Police enthusiasm in searches	28	62	10	50	66	29	5	41	No change
8	Police friction with prosecution in searches	14	66	20	50	12	65	22	32	No change

* The term "noninitiating states" refers to those states that had voluntarily adopted the exclusionary rule prior to *Mapp v. Ohio.*
† The term "initiating states" refers to those states that were forced to adopt the exclusionary rule by *Mapp v. Ohio.*

298   *The Legal Process from a Behavioral Perspective*

An examination of newspapers or ACLU reports for mention of police illegality does not provide a meaningful alternative to the questionnaire approach used. Increased reference to police illegality in these sources may merely indicate increased societal sensitivity to the residue of police illegality that remains. For example, the annual reports of the ACLU during the early years of its existence contained almost no references at all to illegal searches and seizures. The reason for this seems to be that the earlier concern was with the far greater police abuses relating to flagrant brutality and mass arrests on insignificant evidence.

The second row indicates one reason why there has been an increased police adherence to legality. It shows that nearly everywhere in the United States there has been an increased emphasis given by police departments to educating their officers in legal requirements of search and seizure. This increase has especially occurred in the states required to initiate the exclusionary rule, as is indicated by the fact that 51 percent of the respondents from those states reported that the emphasis has "increased substantially" rather than just "increased a little," whereas only 27 percent of the respondents from the noninitiating states did so.[11]

Although no data were compiled in this study on the subject, there are other possible explanations for the increased police adherence to legality in both sets of states. Some of these may be a trickling down of the attitude of the United States Supreme Court, or the presence of increased local pressures by organizations like the ACLU and NAACP. More important, however, is that public and press opinion is probably demanding police adherence to proper procedures. Such a change in public attitudes may be due to the affluence in American society, which no longer makes civil liberties a luxury. It may also be due to greater educational opportunities, which bring a firmer commitment to the middle class values of procedural fairness.[12]

Increased adherence to legality and increased police education are desirable effects. Table 23–1, however, seems to indicate that the exclusionary rule may also have some undesirable effects on police behavior

---

be more prone to make repeated harassment arrests in view of their increased inability to gather admissible evidence unless the arrest is planned to be incident to a search. Barrett, *Personal Rights, Property Rights, and the Fourth Amendment,* 46 SUPREME COURT REVIEW 53–57 (Kurland ed. 1960).

[11] In order to avoid crowding, Table 23–1 does not show these degrees of increase and decrease, which the questionnaire allowed the respondents to indicate.

The increased emphasis on police education in search and seizure may also be confirmed by content analysis of the various professional police journals before and after *Mapp* v. *Ohio.*

[12] On the relationship between class, education, youth, urbanism and some aspects of civil libertarianism, see STOUFFER, COMMUNISM, CONFORMITY AND CIVIL LIBERTIES: A CROSS-SECTION OF THE NATION SPEAKS ITS MIND (1955).

in the short run, although possibly not in the long run. Row 3, for instance, indicates that 43 percent of the respondents in the initiating states said that the effectiveness of the police in obtaining evidence by making searches has decreased, whereas the figure was only 9 percent for the respondents from the noninitiating states. Likewise, the enthusiasm or morale of the police with respect to making searches seems to have decreased more in the initiating states than in the noninitiating states. However, one could argue that it is socially desirable for the police to shift their emphasis to other evidence-obtaining techniques because of the potential invasions of privacy involved in police searches. In this connection, it should be noted that the allegedly undesirable effects on police behavior have occurred to a lesser extent than the allegedly desirable effects. Much less change is indicated on rows 3 and 4 than is on rows 1 and 2, since most of the respondents gave "remained the same" as their response with regard to search effectiveness and police enthusiasm.

Even though one views the effects of the first two rows as socially desirable and the effects of the second two rows as socially undesirable, he still must go beyond the data of Table 23–1 to determine whether there is a net benefit or a net detriment from the adoption of the exclusionary rule. In other words, data like that in Table 23–1 can possibly indicate what the effects of a legal policy are, but a separate study that treats these effects as means to higher ends may be necessary to completely evaluate the legal policy. Ultimately, of course, one has to resort to pure value judgments that cannot be tested when there is no higher value to use as a criterion.

The last row in Table 23–1 illustrates a hypothesized effect that turned out to be irrelevant. In neither the initiating states nor the noninitiating states has there been a significant increase or decrease in friction between the prosecution and the police concerning police tactics in making searches. Indeed, many of the respondents commented that there was no friction to be increased or decreased.

II. EFFECTS ON JUDICIAL BEHAVIOR

The first row of Table 23–2 indicates that there has been a substantial increase in the raising of search and seizure issues in court by defense attorneys in both types of states. As one might suspect, however, the increase has been substantially greater in the states newly initiating the exclusionary rule. The increase in search and seizure cases, of course, cannot be interpreted as indicating decreased police legality. In fact, Table 23–1 indicated there has been a substantial increase in police legality. The increase in search and seizure cases merely reflects that

TABLE 23-2

Effects on Judicial Behavior of Adopting the Exclusionary Rule

Question Number	Change from 1960 to 1963	Respondents from States Not Initiating the Rule in 1961*				Respondents from States Initiating the Rule in 1961†				Most Common Response
		% Reporting Decrease	% Reporting No Change	% Reporting Increase	Total	% Reporting Decrease	% Reporting No Change	% Reporting Increase	Total	
10	Raising of search and seizure issues	2%	33%	65%	57	4%	10%	85%	49	Increase
1	Declaring searches illegal	13	53	35	55	6	36	57	47	No change
4	Broadening definition of legality in searches	20	55	25	55	29	24	47	45	No change
5	Releasing guilty persons	13	53	34	53	11	43	45	44	No change

* The term "noninitiating states" refers to those states that had voluntarily adopted the exclusionary rule prior to *Mapp v. Ohio.*
† The term "initiating states" refers to those states that were forced to adopt the exclusionary rule by *Mapp v. Ohio.*

the potential benefits to the defendant's case in raising the issue have now become greater.

Even though the search and seizure issue has been increasingly raised, the last column of the second row indicates that most of the respondents reported no change in the quantity of searches and seizures declared illegal by the courts. What increase there has been can probably be attributed mainly to the increased raising of the issue, especially in the newly initiating states, rather than to any increased negativism toward the police or to any increased police illegality.[13]

In order to determine partially and somewhat crudely the validity of the questionnaire responses relating to the raising of search and seizure issues and the declaring of searches to be illegal (the first two rows of Table 23–2), an analysis was made of the headnotes in *West's General Digest* dealing with search and seizure for the years prior to *Mapp v. Ohio*—1958, 1959, and 1960—and for the years after that decision— 1962, 1963, and 1964 up to May 1, 1964. Table 23–3 indicates that there were 285 search and seizure headnotes in the 2⅓ years subsequent to *Mapp* and only 244 headnotes for the full 3 years prior to *Mapp*.[14] If trial court records were available, the increase there might be even greater. Table 23–3 also indicates that 58 headnotes in the before period favored the defense, whereas 75 headnotes in the after period favored the defense. Nevertheless, the 58 pre-*Mapp* headnotes represented practically the same proportion of the 244 total as the 75 post-*Mapp* headnotes represented of the 285 total. Although the data were not compiled by states, if Table 23–3 were broken into two tables—one for initiating states and one for noninitiating states—then differences comparable to those shown in the first two rows of Table 23–2 might have appeared.

Row 3 of Table 23–2 is closely related to row 2, although row 2 deals with the decisions on search legality and row 3 deals with the definitional justification for the decisions. Some concern has been expressed in the debate on the exclusionary rule that the rule might cause judges to broaden their definitions of legality and reasonableness in search cases so as to avoid having to exclude otherwise reliable evidence.[15] Row 3 indicates that most of the respondents reported no

---

[13] The question might have been more meaningful if it had asked whether the proportion rather than the quantity of searches declared illegal has increased.

[14] The increase from 244 cases for the 3 years before *Mapp* to 285 cases for 2⅓ years after *Mapp* represents a 16 percent increase when no adjustment is made for the differences in the length of the two periods, and a 21 percent increase when such an adjustment is made. As a result of population trends and trends toward greater societal complexity and more legalistic dispute-settlement, there is a positive rate of increase in American cases in general, but not enough to account for the 21 percent increase in search and seizure cases. See ALLEN, BROOKS, & JAMES, AUTOMATIC RETRIEVAL OF LEGAL LITERATURE: WHY AND HOW 12–19 (1962), for growth curves of American court reports.

[15] Specter, *Mapp v. Ohio—Pandora's Problems for the Prosecutor*, 111 PA. L. REV. 4, 40 (1962).

TABLE 23–3

SEARCH AND SEIZURE CASES BEFORE AND AFTER *Mapp. v. Ohio*

	3 Years before	2⅓ Years after	
Favoring the Defense	58 (24%)	75 (26%)	133
Favoring the Prosecution	186	210	396
	244	285	529

change in this matter. The stimulus to stretch legality of police techniques because of the exclusionary rule is possibly counteracted by the stimulus to narrow the legality of police techniques caused by the changing public-opinion factors previously discussed. It is interesting to note, however, that with regard to what change there has been on the definitional issue the newly initiating states indicated both a bigger increase and a bigger decrease. This may be due to ambiguity in the question or to the fact that the same stimulus may have opposite effects on different judges, depending on their attitudes and decisional propensities. Thus, some prosecution-oriented judges in the newly initiating states may have been provoked by *Mapp* to broaden their definitions of legality, and some defense-oriented judges in the same set of states may have been inspired by *Mapp* to narrow their definitions of legality. However, both types of judges in the pre-1961 exclusionary states were more likely to keep their definitions unchanged.

The last row indicates that the release of guilty persons is the most unchanged of the four courtroom effects. Of the respondents from the newly initiating states, however, 45 percent did report an increase in such releases, but this was only 11 percentage points greater than the increase reported by the respondents from the other states. Such a difference is the smallest underscored change difference in either Table 23–2 or Table 23–1. Nevertheless, releasing guilty defendants because of an illegal search and seizure is clearly the most dramatic undesirable result of the exclusionary rule. The defendant, however, can sometimes be retried on other evidence, and, if not, he is still likely to be convicted later for some future crime, given the high rate of recidivism among guilty defendants. And such releases can possibly be justified by the socially desirable effects of the exclusionary rule on police behavior and by the lack of realistic alternatives to the exclusionary rule for achieving those effects.

III. EFFECTS ON CRIMINAL BEHAVIOR

Allegations have been made that excluding illegally seized evidence provides an impetus to criminality, because criminals feel that under the rule they are more likely to escape conviction.[16] Of the respondents to the questionnaire, 77 percent stated that the annual crime rate had increased in their community or area during the last 3 years, and only 7 percent indicated a decrease had occurred. These responses closely conformed to the FBI's crime report figures for the postmarked communities involved. There was no significant difference between the percentage reporting an increase in the initiating states (80 percent) and the percentage from the noninitiating states (74 percent).

A possibly better method of testing this effect would involve a systematic analysis of the FBI's crime statistics. The simplest, but not so reliable, way to analyze the data is to compare the crime rates of the states that had the exclusionary rule with the crime rates of the states that lacked the rule at a point in time before *Mapp* required all the states to adopt the rule. The first row of Table 23–4 does this. It shows that, based on data from the FBI's *Uniform Crime Reports*, 33 percent of the 24 nonexclusionary rule states had a total quantity of crimes per 100,000 population that was above the average state crime rate in 1960.[17] On the other hand, 57 percent of the 23 exclusionary rule states had a crime rate that was above the average. The states add up to 47 rather than 50 because the partial exclusionary states are excluded.

This type of analysis is unreliable because, standing alone, it does not match the exclusionary states and the nonexclusionary states on relevant social characteristics that might account for crime rate differences other than the adoption of the exclusionary rule. The theoretically ideal technique involves randomly picking some states to become exclusionary states and other states to become nonexclusionary states.[18] By virtue

[16] See, e.g., the references cited in the Inbau-Kamisar debate *supra* note 2. Also see row 5 of Table 23–6 *infra*. In a recent article, Kamisar suggests the exclusionary rule, by increasing police respect for the law of search and seizure, may increase public respect for law in general and thereby decrease criminality. Kamisar, *On the Tactics of Police–Prosecution Oriented Critics of the Courts,* 49 CORNELL L. Q. 436, 454–58 (1964).

[17] Perhaps somewhat different findings from those shown in Tables 23–4 and 23–5 would have been found if special crime rates like those for narcotics and gambling had just been used, since these crimes are disproportionately involved in illegal searches. Such crime rates, however, are not available in the FBI, UNIFORM CRIME REPORTS, and they are especially affected by cultural factors peculiar to certain parts of the country.

[18] For descriptions of other theoretically ideal and not-so-ideal research designs for compiling data to test effects, see Campbell & Stanley, *Experimental and Quasi-Experimental Designs for Research on Teaching,* in HANDBOOK OF RESEARCH ON TEACHING 171 (GAGE ed. 1963); GREENWOOD, EXPERIMENTAL SOCIOLOGY (1945).

TABLE 23–4

EFFECTS OF THE EXCLUSIONARY RULE ON CRIME RATES*

1st Group of States (Hypothesized to have lower crime rates)	2d Group of States (Hypothesized to have higher crime rates)	Number of States Group 1	Group 2	% in Group 1 Having above Avg. Crime Rate	% in Group 2 Having above Avg. Crime Rate	Difference
Nonexclusionary states, 1960	Exclusionary states, 1960	24	23	33%	57%	+24
Less urban (54% exclusionary)	More urban (43% exclusionary)	25	25	16	76	+64
East & Midwest states, 1960 (26% exclusionary)	West & South states, 1960 (64% exclusionary)	20	30	25	60	+35
West & South nonexclusionary states, 1960	West & South exclusionary states, 1960	10	18	60	61	+ 1

* One-point-in-time approach.

of the mathematical laws of probability, the two groups should then be better matched than any nonrandom method could provide. In addition, the likelihood of error can be meaningfully calculated. This is, of course, an impossible technique for testing the effects of most legal policies, although a few legal experiments have been made in which randomized application has been used. For example, Richard Schwartz, as part of a study relevant to improving legal compliance, divided a group of income taxpayers into three random groups. One was subjected to positive taxpaying appeals (for example, good citizenship), one to negative appeals (for example, conviction possibilities), and the third to no appeals.[19]

As an alternative, one can try to match the exclusionary and the nonexclusionary states on whatever other characteristics might be associated with having a high crime rate. Perhaps urbanism and its accompanying anomie might explain why the exclusionary states had higher crime rates than the nonexclusionary states. Table 23–4 divides the states into those in which 50 percent or more of the people lived in standard metropolitan areas in 1960 and those in which less than 50 percent did. It shows that 76 percent of the former group had above average crime rates, whereas only 16 percent of the latter group did. Urbanism, however, cannot be the explanatory variable because a greater proportion (54 percent) of the less urban states adopted the exclusionary rule than did the urban states (43 percent), using the above-mentioned dichotomous urbanism measure.

Another characteristic that might explain the higher crime rates of the exclusionary states, other than the adoption of the exclusionary rule, is regional culture. The United States can be meaningfully divided into four cultural regions: the East,[20] the Midwest,[21] the West,[22] and the states having legalized slavery in 1860—that is, the border and deep South.[23] As Table 23–4 indicates, 60 percent of the 30 western and southern states had above average crime rates, whereas only 25 percent of the 20 eastern and midwestern states did. This row, like the previous row, totals 50, since the three partial exclusionary states are included. Table 23–4 also notes that a much higher proportion of the western and southern states had adopted the exclusionary rule than had the

---

[19] Schwartz, *Field Experimentation in Socio-legal Research*, 13 J. LEGAL ED. 401 (1961); Schwartz, *On Legal Sanctions*, 34 U. CHI. L. REV. 274 (1967).

[20] Connecticut, Maine, Massachusetts, New Hampshire, New Jersey, New York, Pennsylvania, Rhode Island, and Vermont.

[21] Illinois, Indiana, Iowa, Kansas, Michigan, Minnesota, Nebraska, North Dakota, Ohio, South Dakota, and Wisconsin.

[22] Alaska, Arizona, California, Colorado, Hawaii, Idaho, Montana, Nevada, New Mexico, Oregon, Utah, Washington, and Wyoming.

[23] Alabama, Arkansas, Delaware, Florida, Georgia, Kentucky, Louisiana, Maryland, Mississippi, Missouri, North Carolina, Oklahoma, South Carolina, Tennessee, Texas, Virginia, and West Virginia.

eastern and midwestern states. This further strengthens the suspicion that elements of the western and southern way of life may have caused both the adoption of the exclusionary rule in the 1920's (when most of them adopted it) and the relatively high crime rates of 1960, instead of adoption causing the crime rates. Stronger proof of this is shown on the last row, where the crime rate differences disappear when non-exclusionary states are compared with exclusionary states, both of which are in the western–southern group. Unfortunately, too few eastern–midwestern states adopted the exclusionary rule to make a similar meaningful comparison among the eastern–midwestern group.

Although this chapter offers no data on the subject, perhaps one can explain the role of regionalism in the crime rate data by the fact that in the South and West a smaller proportion of people are in the white-collar middle class than are those in the East and Midwest, and by the fact that the South and West have a greater historical tradition of settling disputes through informal violence. Perhaps the disproportionate adoption of the exclusionary rule in the southern and western states can be explained by the relatively greater occurrence of police illegality in these regions or by their greater liberalism in matters like this during the 1920's. The general differences shown in Tables 23–1 and 23–2 between the exclusionary and nonexclusionary states with regard to police and judicial behavior, unlike crime rate behavior, were not significantly changed by making comparisons within the western–southern group and within the eastern–midwestern group.[24]

By analyzing one or N states or individuals before and after the adoption or application of the policy, one can make a more reliable test of the effects of a legal policy than can be made by analyzing two or twice N states or individuals at a single point in time, some of whom have adopted or have been subjected to the policy and some of whom have not. This is so because any differences found in the before-and-after (or longitudinal) approach of the same entities are less likely to be due to variables extraneous to the policy than is the

---

[24] As an example relevant to Table 23–1 on police behavior, 70 percent of the respondents from eastern and midwestern states newly initiating the exclusionary rule reported an increase in police adherence to legality in searches (item 7), whereas only 44 percent from the eastern and midwestern noninitiating states reported an increase. Likewise 83 percent of the respondents from the western–southern newly initiating states reported an increase, whereas only 58 percent from the western–southern non-initiating states reported an increase. As an example relevant to Table 23–2 on judicial behavior, 90 percent of the respondents from the newly initiating eastern–midwestern states reported an increase in the declaring of searches to be illegal, whereas only 40 percent from the noninitiating eastern–midwestern states reported an increase. Likewise, the analogous percentages for the initiating and noninitiating western–southern states are 90 percent and 82 percent, respectively. To simplify comparisons, the percentages in this footnote exclude the middle category of "no change" that was frequently used in the responses to the first part of the questionnaire.

case with the one-point-in-time (or latitudinal) approach using different entities. The previously described effects on police and judicial behavior were determined by a type of before-and-after approach using retrospective questionnaires sent to an experimental group (respondents from newly initiating states) and a control group (respondents from noninitiating states).

Table 23–5, like Table 23–3 on judicial behavior, illustrates a type of before-and-after approach using available data that were compiled by the FBI both in the before stage (pre-1961) and in the after stage (post-1961). Of course, this data were not compiled for the purpose of testing hypotheses about the effects of the exclusionary rule. Table 23–5 indicates the lack of effect of the exclusionary rule on crime rates more reliably than does row 1 of Table 23–4. The first two rows show that 46 percent of the newly initiating states were above the average increase in 1960–62 state crime rates, and almost 40 percent of the noninitiating states were also above the average increase. The small difference between the two groups of states can be readily attributed to regional or environmental differences like those mentioned in Table 23–4. The absence, as well as the presence, of a difference between two groups can sometimes be accounted for by lack of matching, but there does not seem to be any extraneous factor on which the two groups have not been matched that could explain the absence of a difference in crime rate increases.

The lower half of Table 23–5 leads to the same conclusion by comparing the average increase in crime rates for the newly initiating states with the average increase for the noninitiating states. Such an approach avoids dividing the states into the two categories of being above or

TABLE 23–5

EFFECTS OF THE EXCLUSIONARY RULE ON CRIME RATES*

Measure of Effect	Newly initiating States (N = 24)	Noninitiating States (N = 23)	Difference
I. Emphasizing Percentages			
% having above average increase in 1960–62 crime rates	46%	39%	+ 7
% having below average increase in 1960–62 crime rates	54%	61%	− 7
II. Emphasizing Averages			
Average 1960 crime rate per 100,000 population	770	879	−109
Average 1962 crime rate	819	921	−102
Increase from 1960 to 1962	49	42	+ 7
Percent increase	6%	5%	+ 1

* Before-and-after approach.

below the average increase of all the states. This solves the problem of throwing states with highly different crime rates into the same category, and states with similar crime rates (but near the cutting line) into different categories. The last line shows that both the newly initiating and noninitiating states underwent on the average an approximately 5 percent increase in crime rates.

Both Tables 23–4 and 23–5 were originally prepared with more categories on the crime rate variable, but doing so did not affect the general findings. Likewise, nothing significantly different was learned by analyzing crime rate data over three points in time (1958, 1960, and 1962) instead of two in order to get at longer term changes. An additional option for Tables 23–4 and 23–5 involved using the communities of the respondents or random communities instead of states, but the general findings still remained approximately the same.[25]

IV.   ATTITUDES AND ATTITUDINAL EFFECTS

The ultimate attitudinal objective of the exclusionary rule is to increase the public's feeling of security from illegal police searches. The questionnaire item relating to this effect produced the highest quantity of nonresponses. And it is clear that a public opinion poll would be a more meaningful way to determine shifts in public opinion. Nevertheless, of the 84 who did respond, 61 respondents or 73 percent indicated that in their community or area, feelings of public security from illegal searches have remained about the same over the last three years.[26] Of the 23 respondents reporting a change, 7 of the 11 respondents from the nonintiating states reported an increase in feelings of public security from illegal searches, whereas 10 of the 11 respondents from the newly initiating states reported an increase. One respondent reporting a change was from a partial exclusionary state.

What about the attitudes of the police chiefs, prosecutors, judges, defense attorneys, and ACLU officials? Their attitudes, as of November 1963, are indicated in Table 23–6. The percentages represent the percent of each group who agreed either strongly or less strongly with the statements made in the last part of the questionnaire. The base of each percentage excludes those individuals who indicated they were undecided

---

[25] For further details on alternative ways to manipulate experimental data including three-variable analysis of variance, see CHAPIN, EXPERIMENTAL DESIGN IN SOCIOLOGICAL RESEARCH (1955); EDWARDS, EXPERIMENTAL DESIGN IN PSYCHOLOGICAL RESEARCH (1960). Technically speaking, Table 23–4 and the upper half of Table 23–5 use what is known as contingency table analysis, and the lower half of Table 23–5 uses analysis of variance.

[26] A similarly high percentage might be found from a public opinion poll, since only a small percentage of the public is likely to be aware of the existence of *Mapp v. Ohio* or the exclusionary rule. In addition, it will take time for the changes in police behavior to become perceptible to the general public, especially if the public is becoming increasingly sensitive to given quantities of police illegality.

TABLE 23-6

ATTITUDES TOWARD VARIOUS ASPECTS OF THE EXCLUSIONARY RULE†

Questionnaire Number & Statement (See Appendix)	Police Chiefs	Prose-cutors	Judges	Defense Attor-neys	ACLU Officials	All Re-spond-ents	Direction of Change
3 Have same rules for federal and state police	80%	70%	88%	92%	95%	84%	Agree
5 Exclusion reduces illegal searches	82	73	88	87	82	81	None
4 Admit reliable evidence regardless	50*	32	12	5	5	21	Disagree
8 Exclusion is socially desirable	71	62	82	83	88	76	None
6 Exclusion increases crime	61	41	40	24	20	38	None
7 Criminal & civil remedies are adequate	89	57*	64	39	44*	59	None
9 Should broaden legality of search	73	60	69	48*	17	57	Agree
1 Exclusion hinders police	73	62	56	42	39	56	None
10 Need flexible search warrants	68	69	60	38	27	55	Agree
2 Emphasize safety more & liberty less	91	60	53*	33	11	51	Agree

† Percent who agreed with each questionnaire item.
* = lowest uniformity in the occupation column.
Underscore = highest uniformity in the occupation column.

on the item involved. Thus, by subtracting the percentages shown from 100 percent, one can obtain the percent of each group that disagreed with each questionnaire statement. The 113 respondents averaged only 8 undecided responses per statement for each of the 10 statements, meaning an average of less than 2 undecided responses per occupation per statement.

It is interesting to note that the percentages generally ascend (items 3, 5, and 8) or descend (other items) in neat staircase fashion from one occupational group to another with the judges almost always occupying a middle position consistent with their judicial role. A similar, although considerably reduced, staircase phenomenon also occurred with regard to the perceptions of police and judicial behavior, which the questionnaire elicited.[27] The most interesting column, however, is prob-

---

[27] To be more exact, the average absolute (irrespective of the plus or minus sign) correlation between occupation and response in part one of the questionnaire was .20. The average for the middle part, excluding the question on occupation, was .16, and it was .34 for the last part. In making these correlations, each occupation was assigned

ably the one giving the percentages for all 113 respondents. This is particularly true since each occupational group is about equally counter-balanced by its opposite group in terms of the number of respondents. The number of respondents, as earlier mentioned, are 22, 27, 17, 24, and 19, respectively, and 4 unknowns. By subtracting these percentages from 0 or 100, whichever is nearer, one can get a measure of uniformity among the respondents. This is the order in which the rows are arranged.

The highest uniformity was reached on the statement that the federal and state governments ought to have the same search and seizure rules. However, the statement does not indicate whether this identity of rules should be achieved by having all jurisdictions adopt or reject the exclusionary rule. A surprisingly high uniformity of respondents agreed with item 5 that the exclusionary rule was a relatively effective method of reducing illegal searches, and a similarly high percentage agreed with closely related item 8. Very few of the respondents agreed that reliable evidence should be admitted into state criminal proceedings, regardless of the methods used in obtaining it, although 50 percent of the police chiefs endorsed the statement. Also, 61 percent of the police chiefs believed that the exclusionary rule increased crime rates, although the consensus of those indicating an attitude was to the contrary. However, an unusually high 19 respondents were undecided on this item.

The remaining five items all involved a relatively low degree of uniformity. Although the respondents had previously indicated that the exclusionary rule is relatively effective, a majority of them indicated that adequate protection can be secured by available criminal and civil remedies if presumably they are applied. A narrow majority agreed that the definition of what constitutes a reasonable search should be broadened, although the agreement was 69 percent among the judges, who are in the best position to bring about such a broadening. A narrow majority also had the attitude that across the country in general the exclusionary rule hinders the police, but (as can be calculated from Table 23–1 on police behavior) 75 percent reported no change or an increase in their *own* community or area in police effectiveness in making searches and seizures.[28] That the procedure for obtaining search warrants should be made more flexible was indicated by 55 percent, although this question like some others might have been improved by also asking

---

a category number from police chief, prosecutor, judge, defense atorney, to ACLU official. The occupational correlations for the first 27 items in the questionnaire are -.18, -.19, .24, .01, -.30, -.35, -.45, .12, .05, -.11, .23, .11, .28, .10, .15, .18, 1.00, -.32, -.58, .31, -.45, .11, -.33, -.31, .26, -.34, and -.39, respectively. For the meaning of correlation coefficients, see note 37 *infra* and accompanying text.

[28] The 75 percent is derived from the data in row 3 of Table 23–1 by dividing the sum $(.65)(54) + (.26)(54) + (.39)(46) + (.17)(46)$ by $54 + 46$.

for recommendations of specific changes. The last row indicates the most divisive question: 91 percent of the police agreed that as regards searches and seizures too much emphasis is being given to individual liberty and not enough to public safety, whereas only 11 percent of the ACLU officials agreed with that statement.

It might be noted that respondents from the noninitiating states had more favorable attitudes toward the exclusionary rule than did the respondents from the initiating states, especially as shown by their relative responses to items 8 and 4.[29] This phenomenon, of course, may indicate that the more favorable attitudes were responsible for their adoption of the exclusionary rule rather than that the adoption of the exclusionary rule was responsible for their more favorable attitudes. The causal relation is probably a reciprocal one, although social forces more important than adoption of the exclusionary rule promote more favorable attitudes toward civil liberties.[30]

The last column of Table 23–6 represents an analysis of the responses to the instruction at the end of the questionnaire asking the respondents to "please circle the numbers of the attitudinal items immediately above on which your attitude has been at least partially reversed over the last five years." An average of only seven respondents per question circled the questions involved, indicating very little attitudinal reversal over the last five years.[31] The direction of the attitudinal change was considered nonexistent in the last column if less than four respondents indicated a change, or if the quantity of respondents indicating a change in one direction was less than twice the quantity of respondents indicating a change in the opposite direction. Given this standard, a rough direction of change is indicated for 5 of the 10 items.

For instance, on item 3 (row 1 of Table 23–6), five respondents indicated they formerly disagreed but now agree that federal-state uniformity was needed in search and seizure rules, whereas two respondents indicated an opposite reversal. On item 4, six of the eight respondents

---

[29] Of the respondents who took a position and came from the pre-1961 exclusionary states, 87 percent agreed that the exclusionary rule is a socially desirable method of enforcing the Fourth Amendment, whereas just 65 percent of the respondents from the states lacking the exclusionary rule prior to 1961 agreed. Likewise, 30 percent of the latter respondents agreed that reliable evidence should be admitted, regardless of the methods used in obtaining it, whereas just 14 percent of the former respondents agreed.

[30] For a technique useful in determining causal direction where a before-and-after approach is not available, see Blalock, *Spuriousness versus Intervening Variables—The Problem of Temporal Sequences,* 40 Soc. Forces 330 (1962.)

[31] The instruction should have said "To the left of the number for each attitudinal item immediately above, put a + for those items on which you agree more or disagree less now than you did five years ago, a - for those items on which you agree less or disagree more now than you did five years ago, and a 0 for those items on which you agree or disagree about the same now as you did five years ago."

indicated they no longer agreed that reliable evidence should be admitted, regardless of the methods used in obtaining it.[32] On item 9, all nine relevant respondents indicated they now felt that what constitutes a reasonable search should be broadened, but they formerly did not hold such a view. This shift, like all five of the shifts indicated in the last column, particularly occurred in the newly initiating states in that seven of the nine relevant respondents were from such states. Of the 12 relevant respondents to item 10, 10 indicated a shift toward favoring more flexible search warrant procedures. Finally, 12 of the 14 relevant respondents indicated current agreement but past disagreement with the statement that "as regards searches and seizures, too much emphasis is being given to individual liberty and not enough to public safety." This shift, however, like the shifts on items 9 and 10, was indicated mainly by police chiefs and prosecutors in that 8 of the 12 respondents who now feel individual liberty is being overemphasized were police chiefs and prosecutors.

V. EXCLUSIONARY ALTERNATIVES AND KNOWLEDGEABILITY

The first part of the questionnaire investigates retrospective effects of the exclusionary rule on police, judicial, and other behavior. The third part deals with police, prosecution, judicial, defense, and ACLU attitudes and to a lesser extent with attitudinal changes. The middle part of the questionnaire considers some miscellaneous matters, which will now be discussed.

Question 4 in the middle part of the questionnaire asked: "To your knowledge how many times have law enforcement officials in your area been subjected to criminal prosecution for committing an illegal search and seizure during the past 5 years." Of the 113 respondents, 92 answered none, 8 answered more than none but not more than 5, and 13 said they did not know. Thus, of the 100 who answered, 92 percent said none and only 8 percent said more than none. Question 5 asked the same question but substituted being sued in a civil action for being subjected to a criminal prosecution. Of the 113 respondents, 76 answered none, 21 answered more than none but not more than 5, and 3 answered more than 5. Thus, of the 97 who answered, 74 percent said none and 26 percent said more than none.

The lack of criminal and civil actions probably cannot be attributed to strict police adherence to the law of search and seizure over the

---

[32] This opinion shift is the one most relevant to the change in attitude of the Supreme Court from *Wolf* v. *Colorado* to *Mapp* v. *Ohio*. It is relevant because some of this shift in respondent opinion might be due to seeing the exclusionary rule in operation, or to increased respectability given to the rule by the Supreme Court. If this type of shift in informed opinion had been occurring prior to *Mapp*, and if it had been perceived by the Supreme Court, then it might also be relevant as a partial explanation of the shift by the court itself.

last five years. This statement seems to be supported by the data in row 1 of Table 23–1. One can readily calculate from this data that 66 percent of the respondents indicated that in the past 3 years police adherence to legality had increased, implying that there was some nonadherence to be improved on, 6 percent indicated a decrease in adherence, and the remaining 27 percent indicated police adherence or nonadherence to legality had remained the same. In a statistical study of the Chicago Racket Court records for 1950, motions to suppress evidence obtained by illegal search and seizure were granted in 4,593 of the 6,649 cases heard.[33] It is possible that a better explanation for the lack of criminal action is the refusal of the prosecutor to generate friction with the police over police tactics. This conclusion is supported by the last row of Table 23–1 and in the comments some respondents made concerning question 8.

There were substantially more civil actions in relation to criminal ones. Yet, the total number of these suits is also negligible. The reasons for this may be the cost of an action, the unlikelihood of a favorable decision (given the law and the general nature of the complainant), and the fact that rarely are there assets that a successful plaintiff may reach.

The reports of criminal and civil action against the police correlated meaningfully with some other variables. For instance, the respondents from the more urban communities reported more criminal and civil actions than the respondents from the less urban communities. This is probably mainly because the more urban communities have more cases of all types, and because of the less personal relation between the police and the public, which generates more formal complaint settlement. The ACLU officials also reported more instances of criminal and civil action than the police chiefs did. This may be partially because a higher proportion of the ACLU officials are from urban areas, but another partial explanation may be that this is a manifestation of personal values influencing perceptions.

The most interesting relation, however, was the almost complete zero correlation between reports of occasional criminal or civil action against the police and the reports via question 7 of increased police adherence to legality in making searches and seizures. Apparently, an occasional lawsuit that is generally unsuccessful has little effect on the attitudes of the police force.[34]

Questions 1, 2, and 3 in the middle part were designed to provide a test of the technical, strictly legalistic knowledge of the police chiefs,

---

[33] Note, 47 Nw. U. L. Rev. 493 (1952).

[34] A higher than zero correlation might have been achieved, however, if the question had asked whether criminal and civil actions had increased over the last three years instead of asking how many times had the police been subjected to criminal or civil actions.

prosecutors, judges, defense attorneys, and ACLU officials. The postmark of the return letter was used to determine the state law of each respondent. The main hypothesis was that the incorrect responses would correlate with the activities and values of the respondents. The numerical findings, however, are not too meaningful because of serious ambiguities revealed in the questions.[35] A methodological conclusion that could be derived from this experience is that questions relating to legal knowledge are of considerably less value than empirical questions (as in the first part of the questionnaire) or evaluation questions (as in the last part) unless they are very precisely worded and extensively pretested.[36]

For what it is worth, it might be noted that of the few apparent errors that were made with regard to the presence of the exclusionary rule (which was the most objective of the three questions), a greater proportion of errors was made by the police (who possibly have relatively little legal training) and by the defense attorneys (some of whom were only occasional defense attorneys). The errors of the police chiefs tended to be in the direction of thinking the exclusionary rule did not exist in their states prior to 1961 when it did, whereas most of the errors of the other groups were in the direction of thinking that the exclusionary rule had always existed. If most people tend to think the past was more like the present than it really was, then the changes in police and judicial behavior mentioned earlier in this chapter may be even greater than the respondents indicated. An analysis of the answers and comments to questions 2 and 3 in the middle part indicates that both the police chiefs and ACLU officials perceive the law of search and seizure as being more restrictive than the other groups do.

VI.   CONCLUSIONS, VALIDITY, AND UTILITY

Figure 23–1 shows most of the more important relations discussed in this chapter with regard to the effects of excluding illegally seized evidence from courtroom proceedings. The arrows indicate the hypothe-

---

[35] For instance, some respondents interpreted one or more of the three questions as asking for information concerning police and trial court *practice* as contrasted to information concerning constitutional or statutory *law*. The correct answer to question 3 was supposed to be "no," but the question did not consider that searches and seizures may be made without a search warrant and not incident to an arrest if consent is present, if a noncriminal inspection is involved, if open grounds are involved, or if there is probable cause based on observation to indicate the search or seizure is likely to reveal stolen property or other incriminating evidence. Question 2 was apparently ambiguous with regard to what was meant by exploratory and what was meant by general, and one respondent to question 1 perceptively indicated that even the exclusionary states do not require exclusion of illegally seized evidence unless there has been a timely motion to suppress, and then only in criminal cases.

[36] Ambiguities in the wording of the first part of the questionnaire would tend to result in responses that would make the differences in changes between the newly initiating and noninitiating states appear to be somewhat less than they really are. See WALKER & LEV, STATISTICAL INFERENCE 299–301 (1953).

FIGURE 23–1

CORRELATES OF INITIATING THE EXCLUSIONARY RULE

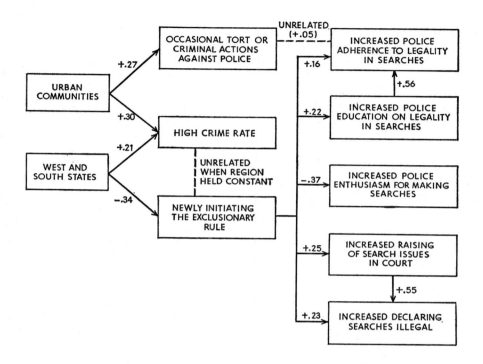

sized causal direction, and the numbers on the arrows indicate the degree of correlation between the variables connected by the arrows. The correlation coefficients can range from −1.00 (complete inverse correlation) to 0 (no correlation) to +1.00 (complete direct correlation).[37] The coefficients were calculated using the respondents and their communities as entities except for the two correlations involving regionalism, which used states as entities. The data for the variables were obtained

[37] An inverse correlation between two variables means that if an entity (i.e., a community or state) is in an affirmative or high category on one variable, it will tend to be in a negative or low category on the other variable. A direct correlation means that entities will tend to be in affirmative categories or in negative categories on both variables. The higher the absolute value of a correlation coefficient, irrespective of its minus or plus sign, the closer the relationship is between the variables.

The correlations between the 27 items of the questionnaire and whether the respondents came from noninitiating states or initiating states are .23, .07, -.32, .10, .16, .22, .16, 0, .22, .25, -.37, -.70, .09, .18, .12, -.04, -.06, .09, .22, -.09, .23, -.04, .08, .06, -.20, .34, and .06, respectively.

For further information on correlation coefficients, see GUILFORD, FUNDAMENTAL STATISTICS IN PSYCHOLOGY AND EDUCATION 133–53 (1956).

from the questionnaires, with the exception of the urbanism, regionalism, crime rate, and exclusionary variables, which were obtained from the census, FBI, and court report data for 1960, respectively. In calculating the coefficients, the retrospective-effect variables were divided into the five categories provided for in the questionnaire. The other variables were either dichotomized (regionalism, exclusionary, and suits against police) or were divided into 10 numerical categories (urbanism and crime rate). A correlation coefficient is a gross summarizing device, and as such it loses much of the detail provided by the percentages in Tables 23–1 through 23–5. A correlation diagram like Figure 23–1, however, does graphically integrate the separate findings into a theoretical model from which one can roughly deduce various characteristics of a given community, if one knows that it did or did not newly initiate the exclusionary rule in 1961.

Those skeptical of the reliability of questionnaire data might question the validity of the findings. Surely, specific coefficients and percentages might differ substantially from the true coefficients and percentages knowable by an omniscient being, but one can feel reasonably confident in the validity of the overall relations found for a number of reasons. There were 113 respondents widely distributed throughout the country, thereby offsetting the distortions that might result from a smaller or more geographically narrow sample. The respondents consisted of a balanced sample of police chiefs, prosecutors, judges, defense attorneys, and ACLU officials, thereby offsetting the distortions that might result from using respondents unduly biased in one direction. There is considerable internal consistency in the comparisons between the newly initiating states and the noninitiating states, as shown in Tables 23–1 and 23–2. There is also considerable internal consistency in the comparisons between the occupational groups, as shown in Table 23–6. In addition, the questionnaire responses were in close accordance with empirical data gathered from available statistics shown in Tables 23–3, 23–4, and 23–5. Where differences were alleged to exist in Tables 23–1, through 23–6, the differences were generally large enough so that they could not be readily attributed to chance sampling or measurement error.[38] All the findings are reasonable, although not commonsensical or uncontroversial. Thus, the sample size, geographical distribution, occupational distribution, internal consistency, external congruence, percentage differences, and reasonableness should enable one to have confidence in this type of approach to testing the effects of alternative legal policies.

One might, however, question the utility of such a venture, since

---

[38] With a random sample size of approximately 100, a correlation coefficient greater than .10 in the direction hypothesized can occur by chance sampling error less than 5 times in 100. *Id.* at 181, 209, 539.

the exclusionary rule has already been adopted by the Supreme Court for the country as a whole. There are a number of points that can be made in reply. One, a systematic analysis of the effects of an adopted policy can conceivably be useful in providing information relevant to repealing or modifying the policy. Such an analysis can also be useful in making the policy more respectable if the analysis reveals the effects considered beneficial are greater than the effects considered detrimental. In addition, such an analysis could conceivably be useful to other countries that are still debating the desirability of the policy. It can also be relevant to debates on analogous policies. It should especially be noted that every effect tested in this chapter could have been tested prior to *Wolf* v. *Colorado* in 1949 when the Supreme Court refused to make the exclusionary rule binding on the states. Between 1922 and 1949, 17 states had adopted the exclusionary rule. One could have easily made a one-point-in-time comparison with questionnaires and available data using these 17 states and the other 31 states. One could also have made a comparison before and after adoption for each of the 17 states and a control comparison on a random or matched sample of 17 out of the other 31 states for the same before-and-after time periods. For certain types of legal policies, like alternative jury instructions, one can even test the potential effects before any jurisdiction has adopted the policy by artificially simulating the behavior of the participants involved.[39]

In conclusion, it might be stated that the methodological tools are available for some worthwhile testing of alternative legal policies. What is primarily needed is the personnel, among legal scholars, who are willing and able to apply those tools. It is heartening to read of the exciting research being conducted in Chicago's Law and Behavioral Sciences Program under the direction of Harry Kalven,[40] in Columbia's Project for Effective Justice under Maurice Rosenberg,[41] and in California's Center for the Study of Law and Society under Philip Selznick.[42] The future is looking brighter for a lessening of the cultural lag between the application of the scientific method to building better medicines, washing machines, and bombs and its application to building a little better legal system than might otherwise be the case.[43]

---

[39] Broeder, *The University of Chicago Jury Project*, 38 NEB. L. REV. 744 (1959).

[40] See for example, ZEISEL, KALVEN & BUCHOLZ, DELAY IN THE COURT—AN ANALYSIS OF THE REMEDIES FOR DELAYED JUSTICE (1959); and note 39 *supra*.

[41] See for example, Greenbaum & Schwartz, *The Columbia Project for Effective Justice*, 14 RECORD N.Y.C.B.A. (1959); Rosenberg, *Comparative Negligences in Arkansas—A "Before and After" Survey*, 13 ARK. L. REV. 89 (1959).

[42] See for example, CARLIN, ETHICS AND THE LEGAL PROFESSION—A STUDY OF SOCIAL CONTROL IN THE NEW YORK CITY BAR (1965); CENTER FOR THE STUDY OF LAW AND SOCIETY, ANNUAL REPORT (1963).

[43] For a more general discussion than this chapter provides of the application of statistical techniques to the evaluation of legal policies, see Nagel, *Optimizing Legal Policy* (chap. 25 *infra*).

APPENDIX

THE EXPLANATORY LETTER

Mr. John Doe, (title)
Street Address
City, State

DEAR MR. DOE:

As you are probably aware, constitutional law research often fails to consider the effects of Supreme Court decisions on the behavior and attitudes of prosecuting attorneys, police officers, defense attorneys, interest group officials, and lower court judges. As a step in the direction of determining these effects, I have undertaken a study of the effects of the rule excluding illegally seized evidence from courtroom proceedings.

Your name and the names of 249 other prosecuting attorneys, police officers, defense attorneys, judges, and American Civil Liberties Union officials have been randomly drawn from various directories.

I shall greatly appreciate your filling out the enclosed questionnaire. It has no identifying marks and you are guaranteed total anonymity in any publication which results from the study. It will only take about five minutes to complete, although you may make any comments you wish between the lines of the questionnaire or on a separate sheet. A stamped self-addressed envelope is enclosed for your convenience in mailing it back. Whether or not you fill out the questionnaire, I shall be happy to send you a summary of the results of the project when the study is completed.

I am hoping for the widest possible response because a large sample of opinions is needed if the study is to have scientific validity.

Sincerely yours,
STUART S. NAGEL
Assistant Professor

THE QUESTIONNAIRE

For each of the following statements, please indicate your opinion of the situation in *your community or area* during the *last three years* using the following symbols:

++ Increased substantially; + Increased a little; O Remained the same;
− Decreased a little; − − Decreased substantially; U Unknown.

1. Searches and seizures declared illegal by the courts have .. ———
2. The annual crime rate has .... ———
3. The effectiveness of the police in obtaining evidence by making searches has .... ———
4. Any tendency on the part of the courts to broaden their interpretation as to what constitutes a legal search and seizure has .... ———
5. The number of persons which the evidence indicates should be convicted that are ultimately released because law enforcement officials have seized evidence illegally has ...... ———
6. Emphasis given by police departments to educating their officers as to the legal requirements of search and seizure has ———
7. The adherence of police officials to the requirements for legal search and seizures has .... ———
8. Friction between the prosecution and the police concerning police tactics in making searches has .... ———
9. Feelings of public security from illegal police searches has ———
10. The raising of search and seizure issues in court by defense attorneys has .... ———
11. The enthusiasm or morale of the police with respect to making searches has .... ———

The following questions can be answered with "yes" or "no" responses or by giving appropriate figures.

1. Did your state require the exclusion of illegally seized evidence from court proceedings prior to 1961 ———Yes ———No
2. Are general exploratory searches permissible in your state provided the official performing the search has first secured a search warrant? ———Yes ———No
3. Is a search and seizure legal in your state if made prior to arrest without a warrant where evidence found justifies subsequent arrest? ———Yes ———No
4. To your knowledge how many times have law enforcement officials in your area been subjected to criminal prosecution

for committing an illegal search and seizure during the last
5 years?   _____

5. To your knowledge how many times have law enforcement
officials in your area been sued in a civil action for committing an illegal search and seizure during the last 5 years?   _____

6. How many years have you served in each of the following
professions? (Please circle your present profession)
Defense attorney——— Police officer——— ACLU official——— Judge——— Prosecuting attorney———

Please indicate your attitude toward the following statements regarding
the country in general using the following symbols:

++ Agree strongly; + Agree, but not strongly; O Undecided; — Disagree, but not strongly; — — Disagree strongly.

1. The exclusion of illegally seized evidence from state court
proceedings hinders police officials in securing evidence
necessary for the successful prosecution of lawbreakers. ..   _____

2. As regards searches and seizures, too much emphasis is being given to individual liberty and not enough to public
safety. ....   _____

3. The same legal requirements regarding searches and seizures should apply to both federal and state law enforcement officers. ....   _____

4. Reliable evidence should be admitted into state criminal
prosecutions regardless of the methods used in obtaining it.   _____

5. Exclusion of illegally seized evidence in court proceedings is
a relatively effective method of reducing the number of illegal searches and seizures by police officers. ....   _____

6. The exclusion of illegally seized evidence causes an increase
in crime rates. ....   _____

7. Adequate protection from illegal searches and seizures can
be secured by available criminal and civil remedies. ......   _____

8. The exclusion of illegally seized evidence from court proceedings is a socially desirable method of enforcing the
guarantee against unreasonable searches and seizures. ....   _____

9. The definition of what constitutes a reasonable search and
seizure without a search warrant should be broadened. ....   _____

10. The procedure for obtaining search warrants should be made
more flexible. ....   _____

Please circle the numbers of the attitudinal items immediately above on
which your attitude has been at least partially reversed over the last five
years.

CHAPTER 24

Simplified Bipartisan Computer Redistricting

The purpose of this chapter is twofold. The primary purpose is to describe a simple and politically feasible computer program that can reapportion a legislature or other body of people who represent geographical districts. Its secondary aim is to describe some basic computer programming techniques that can help solve some policy problems that cannot be adequately handled either by traditional noncomputer techniques or by existing computer programs.

The redistricting program proposed is designed to implement the value judgments of those responsible for reapportionment. Not only can it transfer a set of agreed-on values into a concrete plan, it can also provide alternative redistricting plans predicated on conflicting values and thereby facilitate compromise. In addition, the program can provide useful information concerning equality, compactness, and politics for an agreed-on redistricting pattern.

The program enables its user to adjust the relative weight to be given to three significant considerations: first, the relative equality of population among the districts—the one man–one vote requirement;[1]

The writer is especially grateful to Henry F. Kaiser, Professor of Educational Psychology at the University of Wisconsin, for creating the essence of the moving and revising sections of the computer program, and for providing inspiration on many other points. The writer is also especially grateful for the many helpful insights of John Gilbert, the statistical consultant to the Center for Advanced Study in the Behavioral Sciences. Thanks for helpful comments are also owed to Samuel Gove of the Institute of Government, and Public Affairs at the University of Illinois; William Day of the Illinois Legislative Council; James Weaver of Atlas Chemical Industries; John Whelan of the DuPont Company; Henri Semarne, staff consultant to the California Assembly; Miriam Gallaher, Editorial Consultant to the Behavioral Sciences Center; Lyle Jones, Director of the Psychometric Laboratory at the University of North Carolina; David Couts and Charles Zartman, both of the Arthur D. Little operations research firm, and James Bell of the Stanford Computation Center.

[1] See *Reynolds* v. *Sims*, 377 U.S. 533, 558 (1964).

second, the contiguity and degree of compactness of the districts;[2] third, the impact of redistricting on the political balance of power.[3]

The program can be used by nonpartisan entities, such as a court or a civic association; it can be used by partisan entities, such as a Democratic or Republican state central committee; or it can be used by politically divergent entities, such as a legislative committee or a reapportionment commission composed of both Republicans and Democrats. Its main advantage over traditional techniques is its ability to produce in a matter of seconds districting patterns that accurately reflect whatever political value judgments are fed to the computer and simultaneously to meet the legally imposed requirements of one man–one vote and compact, contiguous districts.

The program also permits the user to maintain certain political units intact. The political units from which the districts are to be formed are predetermined by the user. This permits the user to maintain the status quo as much as possible, as does the fact that the status quo is used as the starting pattern to build on. Entire districts can be kept intact if they meet certain minimal legal requirements. After the initial choice of political units has been made, the computer will group the units into districts that meet the legal requirements and yield the politically desired result. This grouping is accomplished either by moving one unit at a time from one district to an adjoining district or by trading on a one-for-one basis between two districts.

A computer is used for this task because the number of possible transfers is likely to result in a large number of possible combinations. Computing all reasonable combinations and then examining them to determine whether they meet the legal requirements and the politically desired result by traditional means is so time-consuming and expensive that it can be accomplished much more satisfactorily through the use of a computer. The computer program bears a relation to traditional redistricting techniques that is similar to the relation between voting machines and traditional paper ballots. The machine is a useful tool that has no voting power. The program described in this chapter has been applied to some extent in such states as California, Illinois, New York, and Pennsylvania.

I.   THE INPUT AND THE OUTPUT

A. THE INPUT CARDS

In order to illustrate the program a simple, though realistic example will be used. In December 1963, one of the issues that deadlocked the commission attempting to redistrict the Illinois lower house was

---

[2] See *id.* at 578–79.

[3] THE POLITICS OF REAPPORTIONMENT (JEWELL ed. 1962).

whether Mercer County should be combined with Rock Island County to form a district (the Republican proposal) or combined with another group of seven counties (the Democratic proposal). When taken out of the political context, this is basically a problem of making two districts out of three units. It is then almost too simple for a computer, but it serves well to illustrate the method. The political results of this three-unit redistricting, however, might require complex adjustments elsewhere in the state, which the computer is particularly capable of handling.

1. The Parameter Card. Figures 24–1 and 24–2 show the input and output involved in applying the program to this problem. The input consists of four IBM cards. The first card, called a parameter card, Figure 24–1a, informs the computer of eight things.

NUA—there are *3* indivisible units out of which the districts are to be made.

NDA—there are *2* districts.

AVGPOP—the total 1960 Illinois population divided by the 59 districts of the state equals *171*.[4]

MAXCUT—according to the state constitution, no district may be more than *20* percent under the average population per district.

MINCUT—the program should stop redistricting if the most deviant district is *0* percent under or over the average population per district.

W—the weight of compactness relative to equality should be *1*; i.e., they should be weighted equally.[5]

TRADE—the seventh parameter is set to *1* to indicate that redistricting should be done by simultaneously trading pairs of units from adjacent districts as well as by moving one unit at a time from one district to its adjacent districts.

PR—the eighth parameter is set to *0* to indicate that no proportional representation or gerrymandering should be attempted.[6] The term "gerrymandering" in this chapter refers to deliberately drawing district lines in such a way as to enable one party to win a percentage of the districts in the state that is substantially greater than its percentage of voters in the state. More will be said about these parameters when the program is explained in further detail.

By setting the maxcut parameter to 20, the program will try to prevent any district from being more than 20 percent *under or over* the average population per district. The program could be changed slightly so as to provide two parameters, one for a floor (as the Illinois constitution

---

[4] To further simplify this example, population and voting figures have been rounded to the nearest 100,000 and the last three zeros dropped.

[5] Punched as a decimal because the redistricter usually wants this weight to be a decimal less than 1.

[6] In the revised program, a ninth parameter relevant to PR should be punched on each parameter card. See note 19 *infra* and accompanying text.

FIGURE 24-1a

THE PARAMETER CARD FOR THE ROCK ISLAND-MERCER EXAMPLE

The Numbers Punched

3	2	171	20	0	1.0	1	0

The Corresponding Symbols

NUA	NDA	AVGPOP	MAXCUT	MINCUT	W	TRADE	PR

does) and one for a ceiling (as the Illinois constitution does not). It may, however, violate the federal Constitution to provide a floor (which keeps rural areas from being overrepresented) without providing a ceiling (which keeps urban areas from being underrepresented as in northeastern Illinois and in the East St. Louis area). A tolerance of as much as a 20 percent deviation does not seem constitutionally unreasonable.[7] The program, however, is capable of working with a much smaller tolerance, although keeping within this tolerance may require that at least some units be smaller in population than counties tend to be.

All eight parameters are determined by whoever is responsible for the computer redistricting. Thus, the quantity of units and districts depends on what area within a state one wants to redistrict and what different kinds of geographical places one wants to consider as indivisible units. Likewise, the average population per district in the state depends on how many districts the residents want to have in the legislature and what year is used for determining the state's population. The maximum cutoff and the minimum cutoff can be set at any percentage. The weight of compactness relative to equality can be adjusted upward or downward on different computer runs until the ratio producing the most desirable districting pattern is found. If the trade parameter is 0, rather than 1, fewer changes are made and less computer time is used, but the result may still be sufficient for the purposes desired. If PR is set to 1 rather than 0, the computer will strive to bring all the districts within the maximum cutoff percentage, and then strive to make the Democrats and Republicans win the same proportion of districts as the proportion of Democrats and Republicans in the state.

---

[7] A bill proposed in the United States House of Representatives by the House Judiciary Committee, H. R. 5505, 89th Cong., 1st Sess. (1965), provides with regard to congressional districts for a maximum deviation of 15 percent from the average population per district in each state. This bill passed the House, March 16, 1965. 111 CONG. REC. 4939 (daily ed. March 16, 1965).

A three-judge federal district court has ruled that the Georgia Legislature must apportion its districts to within 15 percent of the average. N.Y. Times, April 3, 1965, § 1, p. 30, col. 2.

If PR is set to 2 or 3, the computer will try to bring the number of districts exceeding maxcut down to 0, and then show the maximum number of districts the Democrats (PR = 2) or Republicans (PR = 3) can expect to win.[8]

2. *The Data Cards.* Figure 24–1b shows the contents of the three data cards. The first data card represents Rock Island County; the next, Mercer County; and the third, the seven counties taken collectively as a unit. The first number on each card corresponds to the identification number (I) of each unit. The identification numbers do not have to begin with 1 or be consecutive, but the numbers 1, 2, and 3 are used here to simplify the example. A good way to number the units for ease in finding them is to number them on a map from west to east, starting in the northern part of the state and moving down the way a page is read. The next number on each card (151, 17, and 160, respectively) corresponds to the population (P) of each unit. Here, the population figures consist of raw population, although they could have been the population of citizens, eligible voters, or whatever is desired for the legislative house being districted. The next two numbers on each card represent the longitude (X) and latitude (Y) of the geographical center of each unit. These figures will be used in the computation of compactness.[9]

The fifth number on each data card (the 1, 2, and 2 respectively) corresponds to the district (D) in which the unit is located before the redistricting is done. The districts should be numbered in ascending order from 1 up to the total number of districts. Rock Island and Mercer were actually in the same district before the redistricting, but the input data show them to be in different districts in order to better illustrate the program. The next number indicates the number of units making contact (NK) with the first unit, the second unit, and the third unit, respectively. Then, the touchlist for each unit is given. It indicates the identification numbers of the touching units. Thus, unit 1 (Rock Island) and unit 3 (the outer 7 counties) are each touched by only one unit— namely, unit 2. On the other hand, unit 2 (Mercer) being in the middle is touched by units 1 and 3. For two units to touch or be contiguous, they must share part of a common line, not merely a common point.

---

[8] The numbers *0, 1, 2,* and *3* have no significance other than indicating which political criteria the redistricter wishes to achieve.

[9] These longitudes and latitudes should be expressed as distances from some baseline on a map. In this case, they represent 10ths of inches from the bottom and left side of an 8½ by 11-inch map of the Illinois counties, which was made available to the author by William Day of the Illinois Legislative Council. The center of a unit can be determined visually, as was done for this illustration, or, better yet, by having the computer make some arithmetic calculations on data available on magnetic tape from the United States Census Bureau, as will be explained in the economic feasibility part of this chapter.

FIGURE 24-1b

The Data Cards for the Example

The Numbers Punched

1	151	38	80	1	1	2		99	90
2	17	36	76	2	2	1	3	10	16
3	160	41	68	2	1	2		89	138

The Corresponding Symbols

IU(1)	PU(1)	XU(1)	YU(1)	DU(1)	NKU(1)	TOUCHLISTU(1,1)		DEMSU(1)	REPSU(1)
IU(2)	PU(2)	XU(2)	YU(2)	DU(2)	NKU(2)	TOUCHLISTU(2,1)	TOUCHLISTU(2,2)	DEMSU(2)	REPSU(2)
IU(3)	PU(3)	XU(3)	YU(3)	DU(3)	NKU(3)	TOUCHLISTU(3,1)		DEMSU(3)	REPSU(3)

In reality, there are other units in the state of Illinois touching these three units, but they are excluded from the touchlists to simplify the illustration.

The last two numbers on each card represent the number of votes cast for Democratic (DEMS) and Republican (REPS) candidates in each unit in the 1960 election for the Illinois Assembly. More recent figures could be used, but they were not available when this study was written. Even projections of future figures can be used, although obtaining accurate projections of population or voting figures is a computer program in itself. The total number of votes cast in each unit is greater than the population figure because the voters in each district elect three representatives.[10]

B. THE OUTPUT PRINTING

1. Analysis of Data before Redistricting. Figure 24–2 shows the computer output that the program produces. The first part of the output, Figure 24–2a, shows some of the characteristics of the units, the districts, and the area before redistricting. The second part of the output, Figure 24–2b shows the characteristics after redistricting. It is possible for the initial picture to be the same as the final picture only if the initial picture cannot be improved. The way the program is written, it is impossible for Rock Island to be combined with the outer seven counties, since that would not involve creating a contiguous district (i.e., a district all of whose units are linked together). Thus, in this simplified example there is only one change possible if contiguity is to be preserved; and that change, as will be seen, promotes both equality and compactness.

In the initial picture, district 1 consisted of just unit 1, and district 2 consisted of units 2 and 3. The population of district 1 was 151, which was 88 percent of the average population per district in the state or 12 percent under the average. Likewise, the population for district 2 was 177, which was 104 percent of the average or 4 percent over. District 1 had a number of units equal to 1, and the average distance from the population center of the unit to the population center of the district was 0, since it was a one-unit district. District 2 had two units, and the average distance from their population centers to the center of population gravity in the district (with each person having a weight of 1) was about three tenths of an inch, which can be translated

---

[10] In light of the program language used, the numbers on the parameter card and the data cards can be punched on any IBM card columns, as long as the numbers are given in the order shown and as long as there is at least one blank column between each number. If the information for a unit goes beyond the 80 columns available on an IBM card, then a second or third card can be used for the unit without changing the program.

into miles given the scale of the map. The next set of lines provides the voting information, and it shows a slight preponderance of Democrats in the first district and a substantial preponderance of Republicans in the second district.

The last section of Figure 24–2a shows the values that were assigned to the eight parameters. It also shows that the average deviation from equality was 8 percent, computed by adding the 12 percent to the 4 percent and dividing by the number of districts. Likewise, it shows that the average deviation from compactness is 1.4 10ths of an inch, which is equal to the sum of the 2.8 and the 0 divided by 2. In the area, there were 452 votes cast (46 percent of which were Democratic votes), and the Democrats had a preponderance of votes in 50 percent of the 2 districts.

FIGURE 24–2a

THE INITIAL OUTPUT FOR THE MERCER–ROCK ISLAND EXAMPLE

```
INITIAL DISTRICTING

FOR DISTRICT   1,   UNITS =    1,.
FOR DISTRICT   2,   UNITS =    2;   3,.

FOR DISTRICT   1,   POP. =   151.   POP./AVG. =  88.PCT.   100-(POP./AVG.1 =  12.PCT.
FOR DISTRICT   2,   POP. =   177.   POP./AVG. = 104.PCT.   100-(POP./AVG.1 =   4.PCT.

FOR DISTRICT   1,   NU =   1   AVG. DISTANCE FROM UNIT CENTERS TO THE DISTRICT CENTER =   .0.
FOR DISTRICT   2,   NU =   2   AVG. DISTANCE FROM UNIT CENTERS TO THE DISTRICT CENTER =  2.8.

FOR DISTRICT   1,   DEMOCRATIC VOTES =   99.   REPUBLICAN VOTES =    90.   DEM. PERCENT = 52..
FOR DISTRICT   2,   DEMOCRATIC VOTES =   99.   REPUBLICAN VOTES =   154.   DEM. PERCENT = 39.

FOR THIS AREA,       NU =   3.   NO =   2.   AVG. POP. =   171.;   MAXCUT =. 20 PCT.

   MINCUT =  0 PCT.    WEIGHT = 1.00   TRADE = 1   PR = 0

   AVG. DEVIATION FROM EQUALITY =  8. PCT.    AVG. DEVIATION FROM COMPACTNESS =  1.4

   TOTAL VOTES =    442.   DEM. VOTES = 45. PCT.   DEM. WINS =  50. PCT.
```

2. Analysis of Data after Redistricting. The second half of the output, "Redistricting at the End of the Program," Figure 24–2b, shows that the computer has redrawn the district lines so that district 1 now includes units 1 and 2 instead of just unit 1, and district 2 includes just unit 3. All the other relevant numbers have been changed accordingly, though the parameters, of course, are still the same. As can be seen, the average deviation from equality is now only 4 percent, and the average deviation from compactness has also been reduced. The total votes and the Democratic portion of the total votes cannot be changed by the computer, but the percent of Democratic wins can change, although by coincidence it did not. The margin of Democratic victory in district 1 has, however, been reduced to 50.7 percent, which the program instructs the computer to round off to 51 percent.

FIGURE 24–2b

THE END OUTPUT FOR THE EXAMPLE

```
REDISTRICTING AT THE END OF THE PROGRAM
FOR DISTRICT   1,   UNITS =    1,  2,,
FOR DISTRICT   2,   UNITS =    3,,

FOR DISTRICT   1,   POP. =    168.    POP./AVG. =  98.PCT.    100-(POP./AVG.) =   2.PCT.
FOR DISTRICT   2,   POP. =    160.    POP./AVG. =  94.PCT.    100-(POP./AVG.) =   6.PCT.

FOR DISTRICT   1,   NU =   2    AVG. DISTANCE FROM UNIT CENTERS TO THE DISTRICT CENTER =   1.3.
FOR DISTRICT   2,   NU =   1    AVG. DISTANCE FROM UNIT CENTERS TO THE DISTRICT CENTER =    .0.

FOR DISTRICT   1,   DEMOCRATIC VOTES =    109.    REPUBLICAN VOTES =    106.    DEM. PERCENT = 51.
FOR DISTRICT   2,   DEMOCRATIC VOTES =     89.    REPUBLICAN VOTES =    138.    DEM. PERCENT = 39.

FOR THIS AREA,    NU =   3.    ND =   2.    AVG. POP. =    171.    MAXCUT.= 20 PCT.

   MINCUT =   0 PCT.    WEIGHT = 1.00    TRADE = 1    PR = 0

   AVG. DEVIATION FROM EQUALITY =  4. PCT.    AVG. DEVIATION FROM COMPACTNESS =  .7

   TOTAL VOTES =    442.    DEM. VOTES = 45. PCT.    DEM. WINS = 50. PCT.
```

If more recent voting figures had been used, the switch of Mercer County to the Rock Island district might have caused Republican dominance over that district. Such a result would have required the computer to make a switch elsewhere to favor the Democrats if those responsible for the redistricting wanted to preserve the statewide balance of power. How the program does this will be shown in the proportionality part of this chapter. Here, though, it should be emphasized that the program is not immoral or even amoral. It has built-in implicit values in favor of the notions that (1) the Supreme Court decisions on reapportionment should be followed unless they are reversed by amendments or by the Court itself, and (2) those responsible for redistricting should not become so bogged down with desk calculators and pencil-paper figuring that they run out of time or become paralyzed and have to hold an at-large election (as in Illinois), call for a national constitutional convention (as in California), or consume tens of thousands of dollars (as in New York) on a redistricting that a computer could have done for a few hundred dollars.

II. THE PROGRAM

Figures 24–3 through 24–9 show the program exactly as it has been run on the IBM 7090 computer at Stanford University. Although the program was written for that computer, it can easily be adapted to any high-speed computer, as will be explained in the economic feasibility part of this chapter. Each line in Figures 24–3 through 24–9 represents the punched contents of one IBM card. The numbers at the far right serve to identify the cards and, thus, the lines. In order for legislators, judges, administrators, and civic leaders to make use of the program (as well as political scientists, legal scholars, and programmers) it is helpful for them to have a general notion of what it does and how it does it. Each type of potential user, however, does not need to have an equally detailed knowledge of the program. Portions of the program that may seem unclear at first will probably become clearer after the entire chapter has been read or skimmed.

A. SYMBOLS

To understand the program, certain symbols need to be defined for future reference. Prefixes used in the program are as follows: N = number of; S = sum of; AVG = average of; V = variation from; Q = questionable (i.e., it is questionable whether the quantity that follows will result in improving the districting pattern). Root symbols are: E = equality of; C = compactness of; P = population of; X = longitude of; Y = latitude of. Suffixes are: A = area being redistricted; D = district; U = unit; 2 = squared.

Identification symbols are: IU = the identification number of a unit, punched on each data card; I = the position number of a unit in the deck of input data cards (i.e., the I of the third card in the pile is 3 regardless what its IU is); J = the identification number of any district; F = the identification number of the district from which it is proposed that a unit be moved; T = the identification number of the district to which it is proposed that a unit be moved; DU = the district of a unit.

Symbols representing program operations are as follows: $\$$ = end of a program instruction; $*$ = the next quantity is an exponent of the preceding quantity; NEQ = not equal to; ABS = the absolute value irrespective of the plus or minus sign; $(1, 1, N)$ = start with one and move up in steps of one at a time until coming to N; an equals sign $(=)$ in the program means replace the contents of the phrase on the left with the contents of the phrase on the right. The words "begin" and "end" bracket sets of instructions that relate to the same condition, clause, or phrase. Frequently, a 1 is used to indicate that the preceding expression is true, rather than to indicate that it is arithmetically equal to 1. Likewise, a 0 is frequently used to indicate that an expression is false, as can be seen by the context. Expressions are assumed to be false until shown to be true.

All other important symbols in the program are combinations or slight variations of the above symbols, are self-explanatory, or are defined by formulas given in the program. Symbols are deliberately chosen to avoid duplication and to be easy to recall. In the programming language, all single quantities must be referred to by a single word rather than a phrase. This accounts for the frequent use of telescoped acronyms in the program. There are some minor exceptions to the definitions given above, but these exceptions will be indicated in the discussion that follows.

B. THE STARTING PART

As can be seen by scanning Figures 24–3 through 24–9, the program basically consists of seven parts—namely, the starting, moving, revising, proportionality, trading, residual contiguity, and output parts. The first part consists of a section of input operations and a section of initial calculations. Section 1A tells the computer that symbols starting with certain letters need decimal points (i.e., are "real" numbers) and that symbols starting with certain other letters are whole numbers (i.e., integers). Section 1A also indicates which symbols can refer to many

FIGURE 24–3a

THE STARTING PART OF THE PROGRAM

```
COMMENT,  (SECTION 1) INPUT OPERATIONS                                    1
COMMENT,  (1A) DECLARING SOME SYMBOLS   $                                 2
REAL W, Q...., N...., S...., DE...., R...., CR....,-PC...., A...., MOS...,  3
   E...., DI...., TE...  S                                               4
INTEGER QB...., QCO....,-NUC, TEST  S  INTEGER OTHERWISE  S               5
INTEGER ARRAY IU(1000), DU(0..1000), DISU(1000), NKU(1000),              6
   TOUCHLISTU(1000, 10), NUD(200), CLUSTER(50)  S                        7
REAL ARRAY PU(1000), XU(1000), YU(1000), DEMSU(1000), REPSU(1000),       8
   PD(200), VED(200), SXD(200), SYD(200), SX2D(200), SY2D(200),          9
   VXCD(200), VYCD(200), VCD(200), DEMSD(200), REPSD(200),              10
   PCTDEMSD(200), MARGIN(200)  S                                        11
                                                                        12
COMMENT,  (1B) READING THE PARAMETER CARD  $                            13
STARTING..  BEGIN                                                       14
CARDREAD (S PARAMETER1, PARAMETER2, PARAMETER3, MAXCUT, MINCUT, W,      15
   TRADE, PR)  $                                                        16
NUA = PARAMETER1  S  NDA = PARAMETER2  S  AVGPOP = PARAMETER3  S        17
                                                                        18
COMMENT,  (1C) READING THE DATA CARDS  $                                19
FOR I = (1, 1, NJA)  S  BEGIN                                           20
   CARDREAD ( IU(I), DATA2, DATA3, DATA4, DU(I), NKU(I)),                21
      FOR K = (1, 1, NKU(I))  S  TOUCHLISTU(I,K), DATA8, DATA9 )  S     22
   PU(I) = DATA2  S  XU(I) = DATA3  S  YU(I) = DATA4  S  DISU( IU(I) )   23
      DU(I)  S  DEMSU(I) = DATA8  S- REPSU(I) = DATA9  S  END  S        24
```

units or many districts. It currently provides for a *maximum* of 1,000 units and 200 districts per area, but these numbers can be increased by punching new maxima on cards 6 through 11. Similarly, Section 1A says 50 is the maximum number of units per district, and 10 is the maximum number of units on a touchlist (i.e., that can be touched by a single unit).

Section 1B tells the computer to read the parameter card (which provides the eight parameters mentioned in connection with Figure 24–1). Line 17 has the effect of placing decimal points at the end of some of the parameters, even though they were not punched with decimal points on the parameter card. Section 1C tells the computer to read the data cards, starting with the first one and moving up in steps of one at a time until it gets to the number of units in the area (i.e., the last card). It also indicates that on each card corresponding to each unit will be found IU, PU, XU, YU, DU, NKU, touchlist, DEMSU, and REPSU for each unit (as was also mentioned in connection with Figure 24–1). Some of these numbers are then given decimal points. Numbers that are involved in division particularly need decimal points. DU for a unit always equals DISU, but DU uses I (the unit's position number) as a subscript, and DISU uses IU (the unit's punched identification number) as a subscript. These two ways of designating the district of a unit are needed whenever the I and IU of a unit differ, a will become clearer later.[11]

The second portion of the starting part, Figure 24–3b, makes the initial calculation of the variation from equality and compactness. Section 2A calculates the characteristics of the districts. Some symbols that are repeatedly incremented are initially set equal to 0 the way one would clear a desk calculator. The I loop (i.e., FOR I = 1, 1, NUA) calculates eight different sums needed to determine the variation from equality and compactness for each district. Note that the longitude and latitude of each unit are multiplied by the population of each unit. This is done because the population center of a district can easily be calculated by averaging the population centers of the units, whereas the geographical center of a district cannot be determined by averaging the geographical centers of the units. Working with population centers of districts rather than with geographical centers also tends to cluster people of similar economic and social interests.[12]

Line 44 indicates that the measure of equality involves determining the deviation between the population of each district and the average

---

[11] The word COMMENT is an instruction to ignore what follows until a dollar sign is reached.

[12] This method of measuring compactness is similar to that used in Weaver & Hess, *A Procedure for Non-Partisan Districting: Development of Computer Techniques*, 73 YALE L. J. 288 (1963). They do not, however, calculate an average compactness. Thus, by their measure, no matter how jagged a district of a few units might be, it will generally show more compactness than a district shaped like a perfect circle but composed of many units. Much more serious is that their program as of April 1965 does not consider equality and compactness simultaneously, it does not guarantee contiguity, and it has no political features. The Weaver-Hess program is thus nonpartisan only in the sense that it is unpredictable on which party it will favor. It consists of about 1,200 hard-to-read Fortran IV program statements rather than the simplified, versatile language of ALGOL, a variant of which is used in Figures 24–3 through 24–9. For further information on this language, see BURROUGHS CORP., BURROUGHS ALGEBRAIC COMPILER (rev. ed. 1963); Stanford University Computation Center, Subalgol: The Stanford University Algorithmic Language (1963).

FIGURE 24–3b

THE STARTING PART OF THE PROGRAM
(continued)

```
COMMENT, (SECTION 2) CALCULATING THE CHARACTERISTICS OF THE INITIAL    25
   DISTRICTING  $                                                      26
COMMENT, (2A) CALCULATING THE CHARACTERISTICS OF THE DISTRICTS  S       27
BADCOUNT = SVEA = SVCA = DEMSA = REPSA = O  S                           28
FOR J = (1, 1, NDA)  S  BEGIN                                           29
   NUD(J) = PD(J) = SXD(J) = SYD(J) = SX2D(J) = SY2D(J) =               30
   DEMSD(J) = REPSD(J) = O  S                                           31
   FOR I = (1, 1, NUA)  S  IF DU(I) EQL J  S  BEGIN                     32
   NUD(J) = NUD(J) + 1  S                                               33
   PD(J) = PD(J) + PU(I)  S                                             34
   SXD(J) = SXD(J) + XU(I).PU(I)  S                                     35
   SYD(J) = SYD(J) + YU(I).PU(I)  S                                     36
   SX2D(J) = SX2D(J) + (XU(I)*2).PU(I)  S                               37
   SY2D(J) = SY2D(J) + (YU(I)*2).PU(I)  S                               38
   DEMSD(J) = DEMSD(J) + DEMSU(I)  S                                    39
   REPSD(J) = REPSD(J) + REPSU(I)  S                                    40
   END  S                                                              41
   VXCD(J) = ( SX2D(J) / PD(J) ) - ( SXD(J) / PD(J) )*2  S              42
   VYCD(J) = ( SY2D(J) / PD(J) ) - ( SYD(J) / PD(J) )*2  S              43
   VED(J) = (PD(J) - AVGPOP)*2  S                                       44
   VCD(J) = VXCD(J) + VYCD(J)  S                                        45
                                                                       46
COMMENT, (2B) CALCULATING THE CHARACTERISTICS OF THE AREA  S            47
   IF 1-0.ABS(1 - PD(J)/AVGPOP) GTR MAXCUT  S  BADCOUNT = BADCOUNT + 1 S 48
   SVEA = SVEA + VED(J)  S                                             49
   SVCA = SVCA + VCD(J)  S                                             50
END  S                                                                 51
AVGVEA = SVEA / NDA  S                                                 52
AVGVCA = SVCA / NDA  S                                                 53
FOR I = (1, 1, NUA)  S                                                 54
   ( DEMSA = DEMSA + DEMSU(I)  S  REPSA = REPSA + REPSU(I) )  S         55
PCTDEMSA = 100.DEMSA / (DEMSA + REPSA)  S                              56
                                                                       57
CRITERION = (BADCOUNT + 1)*2 . AVGVEA . AVGVCA*W  S                    58
END STARTING  S                                                        59
COMPLETION = O  S  ENTER PRINTING  S                                   60
```

population per district in the state. These deviations are then squared to get rid of possible minus signs, since underpopulation of a district is as much inequality as is overpopulation. The negative signs could also be eliminated by determining the absolute deviation (i.e., ignoring the minus sign), rather than the squared deviation. Squared deviations, however, must be used for the compactness measure because the change in compactness of a district when a unit is moved out of it or into it can be calcualted from the raw scores of the unit (i.e., PU, XU, and YU) only if the squaring method is used.

Determining the average variation from equality for the area logically involves summing the variation from equality for each district and dividing by NDA. Compactness is calculated similarly, as is shown in Section 2B. Other measures of equality and compactness could be used, such as the maximum deviation or the standard deviation (which merely involves taking the square root of AVGVEA and of AVGVCA), but they either produce less equality and less compactness or they involve unnecessary additional calculations to achieve the same equality.[13] Section 2B also counts the number of districts whose populations deviate from the state average by more than the percent specified in the maxcut parameter. In addition, the section determines the percentage of Democrats or Republicans in the area, a figure that will be used if it is desired that the parties should win a fraction of the districts approximately equal to their percentage of votes.

Finally, the program informs the computer of the criterion it is initially to minimize. This criterion is basically equal to the product of badcount (i.e., the number of districts exceeding maxcut) times the average variation from equality times the average variation from compactness. The integer 1 is added to badcount so that when badcount gets down to 0 the criterion will not equal 0. Badcount plus 1 is given a weight of 2, so that no changes can be made that will increase badcount. Average VCA is given a weight equal to the value of the parameter W. After calculating the initial value of the criterion, the initial characteristics of the units, districts, and area are printed out, as was done for Figure 24–2.

C. The Moving Part

Figure 24–4 shows the moving part of the program. It attempts to move each unit from the district it is in to each other district, one unit and one district at a time. Line 67 identifies this part of the program to the computer as looptype number 1 in order to distinguish it from the trading part of the program, which is looptype number 2. Before even a tentative move can be made, four conditions on lines 73 to 77 must be met.

---

13 On diverse measures of equality, see Schubert & Press, *Measuring Malapportionment*, 58 Am. Pol. Sci. Rev. 302 (1964). And see Alker & Russett, *On Measuring Inequality*, 9 Behavorial Sci. 207 (1964). On diverse measures of compactness, see Weaver & Hess, *supra* note 12. And see Reock, *Measuring Compactness as a Requirement of Legislative Apportionment*, 5 Midwest J. Pol. Sci. 70 (1961). On measuring variation in general, see Hagood & Price, Statistics for Sociologists 115–37 (1952). And see Guilford, Fundamental Statistics in Psychology and Education 78–103 (3d ed. 1956).

Neither the measure of equality used here (i.e., the variance) nor the standard deviation nor the coefficient of variation—see Schubert, *supra*, or Guilford, *op. cit. supra* at 101—should be used to compare different states as to the equality present in their respective districting patterns. This is so because it can be proved algebraically that these measures of equality vary with the number of districts provided. For an interstate measure of equality that is independent of the number of districts, one could use the geometric mean of the product of the ratios for each district's population to the average population. It is calculated by multiplying PD/AVGPOP for each successive district, and then taking this product to the Nth root where N is the number of districts. See Guilford, *op. cit. supra* at 72. This measure was suggested by Henry Kaiser.

FIGURE 24–4

THE MOVING PART OF THE PROGRAM

```
COMMENT,  (SECTION 3) MOVING UNIT I FROM DISTRICT F TO DISTRICT T  $      61
MOVING..                                                                  62
MOVES = 0  $                                                              63
FOR I = (1, 1, NUA)  $   BEGIN                                            64
   FOR T = (1, 1, NDA)  $   BEGIN                                         65
   F = DU(I)  $                                                           66
   LOOPTYPE = 1  $                                                        67
                                                                         .68
   COMMENT,  (3A) TESTING TO SEE IF UNIT I IS ELIGIBLE TO BE MOVED  $     69
   TCONTIGUITY = 0  $                                                     70
   FOR K = (1, 1, NKU(I))  $                                             71
   IF DISU( TOUCHLISTU(I,K) ) EQL T  $  TCONTIGUITY = 1  $               72
   IF (TCONTIGUITY EQL 1)                                                73
     AND (F NEQ T)                                                       74
     AND (NUD(F) GTR 1)  $   BEGIN                                       75
   ENTER JCONTIGUITY  $                                                  76
   IF FCONTIGUITY EQL 1  $   BEGIN                                       77
                                                                         78
   COMMENT,  (3B) EFFECT OF THE MOVE ON DISTRICT F  $                    79
   QNUDF = NUD(F) - 1  $                                                 80
   QPDF = PD(F) - PU(I)  $                                               81
   QSXDF = SXD(F) - XU(I).PU(I)   $                                      82
   QSYDF = SYD(F) - YU(I).PU(I)   $                                      83
   QSX2DF = SX2D(F) - (XU(I)*2).PU(I)   $                                84
   QSY2DF = SY2D(F) - (YU(I)*2).PU(I)   $                                85
   QDEMSDF = DEMSD(F) - DEMSU(I)  $                                      86
   QREPSDF = REPSD(F) - REPSU(I)  $                                      87
                                                                         88
   COMMENT,  (3C) EFFECT OF THE MOVE ON DISTRICT T  $                    89
   QNUDT = NUD(T) + 1  $                                                 90
   QPDT = PD(T) + PU(I)  $                                               91
   QSXDT = SXD(T) + XU(I).PU(I)   $                                      92
   QSYDT = SYD(T) + YU(I).PU(I)   $                                      93
   QSX2DT = SX2D(T) + (XU(I)*2).PU(I)   $                                94
   QSY2DT = SY2D(T) + (YU(I)*2).PU(I)   $                                95
   QDEMSDT = DEMSD(T) + DEMSU(I)  $                                      96
   QREPSDT = REPSD(T) + REPSU(I)  $                                      97
                                                                         98
   ENTER REVISING  $  END  $  END  $                                    99
  END  $                                                                100
 END  $                                                                 101
 IF MOVES GTR 0   $   GO TO MOVING  $                                   102
 IF TRADE EQL 0   $   ( COMPLETION = 1  $  ENTER PRINTING )  $          103
```

(1) The district of at least one unit on the touchlist of unit I (the unit proposed to be moved) must be district T (the district to which the unit is proposed to be moved) so as to preserve the contiguity of district T.

(2) The district from which it is proposed to move the unit must not be the same as the district to which it is proposed to move the unit.

(3) The number of units in the district from which it is proposed to move the unit must be greater than one so that the district will not be destroyed by the move.

(4) It must be determined whether pulling unit I out of district F will result in a hole that will destroy the contiguity of district F. How this type of contiguity is checked will be discussed in the residual contiguity (or J contiguity) part of the chapter.

The quantity of F's should equal the quantity of T's. Therefore, if the number of districts in an area is to be reduced, one should give the same DU in the input data to the units from some neighboring, smaller districts. Such an adjustment is used in the larger example described later in the chapter. Likewise, if the number of districts is to be expanded one should put some of the units from any of the larger districts into new DU's in the input data. These adjustments of the input data will not significantly affect the quality of the output so long as all input districts are contiguous.

If the four conditions are met, then the characteristics of unit I are taken from district F and added to district T, as shown in Sections 3B and 3C. After each such tentative move, the revising section is entered to determine whether the move further minimized the criterion; and if it did, the district lines are redrawn and the number of consummated moves is counted. Line 102 indicates that after an attempt to move every unit to every district has been made, if the number of consummated moves is greater than 0, the computer goes back to line 62 and starts over again because the most recent moves may have improved some potential moves that formerly looked bad. This reiteration process is repeated until no more improvement moves can be made. Then, if the trade parameter has been set to 1, the computer goes to the trading section of the program, since that is the next part of the program that does not require an "enter" command. On the other hand, if the trade parameter has been set to 0, line 103 indicates that completion is true and the printing section should be entered.

D. THE REVISING PART

Sections 4A and 4B recalculate the characteristics of districts F and T, respectively, in light of the preceding move (or trade, since the trading section also feeds into the revising part). The calculations are analogous to those made in the initial calculation section. Likewise, the tentative or questionable badcount is calculated (4C), as is the average VEA and average VCA. The word TEMP stands for temporary storage location. Line 138 indicates that if badcount equals 0, and the proportional representation parameter has been given a value other then 0, then the proportionality section should be entered. In that section, some value other than 1 will be given to a new criterion factor that is called disprop, which is short for disproportion.

Then, at the start of section 5, Figure 24–5b, comes the most important instruction in the program. In essence, it says that if the newly calculated criterion is less than the previously calculated criterion, then the questionable changes are firmly recorded by the computer's bookkeeping apparatus as is indicated on lines 146 through 171. These changes then

FIGURE 24–5a

THE REVISING PART OF THE PROGRAM

```
COMMENT,  (SECTION 4) CALCULATING THE CHARACTERISTICS OF THE TENTATIVE   104
    REDISTRICTING  $                                                      105
    SUBROUTINE REVISING  $  BEGIN                                         106
                                                                          107
    COMMENT,  (4A) RECALCULATING THE CHARACTERISTICS OF DISTRICT .F  $    108
    QVXCDF = (QSX2DF / QPDF) - (QSXDF / QPDF)*2  $                        109
    QVYCDF = (QSY2DF / QPDF) - (QSYDF / QPDF)*2  $                        110
    QVEDF = (QPDF - AVGPOP)*2  $                                          111
    QVCDF = QVXCDF + QVYCDF  $                                            112
                                                                          113
    COMMENT,  (4B) RECALCULATING THE CHARACTERISTICS  OF DISTRICT T  $    114
    QVXCDT = (QSX2DT / QPDT) - (QSXDT /. QPDT)*2  $                       115
    QVYCDT = (QSY2DT /. QPDT) - (QSYDT /. QPDT)*2  $                      116
    QVEDT = (QPDT - AVGPOP)*2  $                                          117
    QVCDT = QVXCDT + QVYCDT  $                                            118
                                                                          119
    COMMENT,  (4C) RECOUNTING THE DISTRICTS THAT EXCEED THE MAXIMUM       120
        DEVIATION DESIRED  $                                              121
    TEMP1 = PD(F)  $  TEMP2 = PD(T)  $                                    122
    PD(F) = QPDF  $  PD(T) = QPDT  $                                      123
    QBADCOUNT = 0  $                                                      124
    FOR J = (1, 1, NDA)  $                                                125
        IF 100.ABS(1 - PD(J)/AVGPOP) GTR MAXCUT  $                        126
        QBADCOUNT = QBADCOUNT + 1  $                                      127
    PD(F) = TEMP1  $  PD(T) = TEMP2  $                                    128
                                                                          129
    COMMENT,  (4D)  RECALCULATING THE OTHER CHARACTERISTICS OF THE        130
        AREA  $                                                           131
    QSVEA = SVEA - VED(F) - VED(T) + QVEDF + QVEDT  $                     132
    QSVCA = SVCA - VCD(F) - VCD(T) + QVCDF + QVCDT  $                     133
    QAVGVEA = QSVEA / NDA  $                                              134
    QAVGVCA = QSVCA / NDA  $                                              135
                                                                          136
    DISPROP = 1  $                                                        137
    IF (BADCOUNT EQL 0) AND (PR NEQ 0)  $  ENTER PROPORTIONALITY  $       138
    QCRITERION = (QBADCOUNT + 1)*2 . QAVGVEA . QAVGVCA*W . DISPROP  $     139
```

become the new districting pattern to be improved on. Lines 142 to 144 indicate that in order for a move to be considered desirable, Q criterion must be less than criterion, and either (1) badcount must be greater than 0 or (2) badcount and Q badcount must both be equal to 0. In other words, once badcount gets down to 0, no moves can be made that will increase it, even if disprop is the new criterion.[14] The com-

---

[14] In a revised version of the program, the condition on lines 144 and 145 is simplified and made more powerful by rewording it to read, "AND (QBADCOUNT LEQ BADCOUNT)." LEQ stands for less than or equal to. By analogy, one could add a pro-Republican condition to say, "AND (QDEMWINS LEQ DEMWINS)" or a pro-Democratic condition to say, "AND (QDEMWINS GEQ DEMWINS)," where Demwins is the number of districts in which the Democrats have a majority and GEQ stands for greater than or equal to. Slight changes would then be needed in section 7A of the program to determine the value of QDemwins and Demwins. These political conditions can also be guaranteed by giving Demwins a high weight in section 7B, although a weight of 2 seems high enough. It produced the same results as a weight of 10 in the 18-district Illinois example described later. The weighting encourages good moves in addition to preventing bad ones. If, however, badcount or Demwins is reduced to zero, it will have no influence on the value of the criterion no matter how heavily it is weighted.

puter then reads line 182, which tells it to return to the moving section (or trading section depending on where it came from) to attempt more moves. Each successive loop will involve fewer moves. When no further improvement moves can be made, then the relooping stops, and the computer goes to the trading or output sections.

FIGURE 24–5b

THE REVISING PART OF THE PROGRAM
(continued)

```
COMMENT,  (SECTION 5) REPLACING THE FORMER DISTRICTING PATTERN WITH THE      140
IMPROVED DISTRICTING PATTERN  $                                             141
      IF (QCRITERION LSS CRITERION)                                          142
        AND ( (BADCOUNT GTR 0)                                               143
          OR ((BADCOUNT EQL 0) AND (QBADCOUNT EQL 0)) )  $  BEGIN            144
                                                                             145
          COMMENT,  (5A) CHANGE THE DISTRICTS OF UNIT I AND UNIT L  $        146
          IF LOOPTYPE EQL 1  $  BEGIN                                        147
            MOVES = MOVES + 1  $                                             148.
            DU(I) = DISU( IU(I) ) = T  $  END  $                             149
          IF LOOPTYPE EQL 2  $  BEGIN                                        150
            TRADES = TRADES + 1  $                                           151
            DU(I) = DISU( IU(I) ) = T  $                                     152
            DU(L) = DISU( IU(L) ) = F  $  END  S                             153
                                                                             154
          COMMENT,  (5B) CHANGE DISTRICT F AND DISTRICT T  $                 155
          NUD(F) = QNUDF  $                  NUD(T) = QNUDT  $                156
          PD(F) = QPDF  $                    PD(T) = QPDT  $                 157
          SXD(F) = QSXDF  $                  SXD(T) = QSXDT  $                158
          SYD(F) = QSYDF  $                  SYD(T) = QSYDT  $                159
          SX2D(F) = QSX2DF  $                SX2D(T) = QSX2DT  $              160
          SY2D(F) = QSY2DF  $                SY2D(T) = QSY2DT  $              161
          VXCD(F) = QVXCDF  $                VXCD(T) = QVXCDT  $              162
          VYCD(F) = QVYCDF  $                VYCD(T) = QVYCDT  $              163
          VED(F) = QVEDF  $                  VED(T) = QVEDT  $                164
          VCD(F) = QVCDF  $                  VCD(T) = QVCDT'  $               165
          DEMSD(F) = QDEMSDF  $              DEMSD(T) = QDEMSDT  $            166
          REPSD(F) = QREPSDF  $              REPSD(T) = QREPSDT  $            167
                                                                             168
          COMMENT,  (5C) CHANGE CHARACTERISTICS OF THE AREA  $               169
          SVEA = QSVEA  S                    SVCA = QSVCA  $                  170
          BADCOUNT = QBADCOUNT  $            CRITERION = QCRITERION  $        171
                                                                             172
COMMENT,  (SECTION 6) CUTTING OFF THE MOVING OR TRADING BEFORE ALL           173
MOVES AND TRADES ARE MADE  $                                                 174
      IF BADCOUNT EQL 0  $  BEGIN                                            175
        MOSTDEV = 0  $                                                       176
        FOR  J = (1, 1, NDA)  $                                              176
          IF 100.ABS(1 - PD(J)/AVGPOP) GTR MOSTDEV  $                        177
          MOSTDEV = 100.ABS(1 - PD(J)/AVGPOP)  $                             178
        IF MOSTDEV LSS MINCUT  $                                            178
        ( COMPLETION = 1  $  ENTER PRINTING )  $                             179
      END  S                                                                 179
                                                                             180
    END  $                                                                   181
  RETURN                                                                    -182
  END REVISING  $                                                           183'
```

Section 6 is the last portion of the revising part. It is designed to cut off the moving or trading as soon as the most deviant district falls below whatever value the parameter called mincut has been given. This section, like much of the program, has been designed with realistic politics in mind. It is naïve to think that incumbent politicians are likely to want to upset the status quo any more than the minimum extent required by the state constitution and courts or by the federal Constitution and courts. In Illinois, for instance, it is conceivable that the incumbent legislators might want to set both maxcut and mincut to 20 percent for at least one of the outputs they might desire to see the computer produce. One who is greedy for perfection might object to such a parameter, but he would fail to recognize what tremendous reform would be achieved if none of the legislative districts in any of the states had more than a 20 percent deviation from the average population per district. Someday, however, the United States Supreme Court may end its vagueness on reapportionment standards and say something to the effect that maxcut must not be greater than 20 percent and mincut must not be greater than 0. This would be somewhat analogous to the Court's statements that in picking a jury there can be accidental Negro exclusion but not deliberate exclusion.[15]

E. The Proportionality Part

Section 7A counts the number of districts in which the Democrats had a preponderance of the vote in the last election or will have in the next election if forecasted figures are used on the input cards. By subtracting the number of Democratic wins from the number of districts, one can determine the number of Republican wins, assuming there are only two major parties. This section also calculates the margin of victory or defeat in each district by determining the absolute difference between the percentage of Democrats and 51 percent. If badcount has gone to 0 and PR is equal to 1, 2, or 3, then section 7B sets the questionable average VEA and VCA equal to 1, thereby making the value of disprop the new criterion to be minimized.

If PR has been set to 1 for the computer run, then disprop equals the product of (1) the difference between the percentage of Democratic victories in the area and the percentage of Democrats in the area times (2) the average Democratic margin (if the percentage of Demwins is less than the percentage of Democrats) or the reciprocal of the average margin (if the percentage of Demwins is greater than the percentage of Democrats). The program can thus provide a kind of proportional representation without the complicated voting procedures that are usually associated with proportional representation. If PR has been set to 2, disprop equals the product of the reciprocal of the Demwins times the average margin. On the other hand, if PR has been set to 3, disprop equals Demwins times the reciprocal of the average margin.

---

[15] *Brown* v. *Allen*, 344 U.S. 443, 471 (1953). Ulmer, *Supreme Court Behavior in Racial Exclusion Cases: 1935–1960*, 56 Am. Pol. Sci. Rev. 325 (1962).

FIGURE 24–6

The Proportionality Part of the Program

```
COMMENT, (SECTION 7) PROVIDING PROPORTIONAL REPRESENTATION OR INDICAT-    184
  ING HOW MANY DISTRICTS THE DEMOCRATS OR REPUBLICANS CAN WIN  $          185
SUBROUTINE PROPORTIONALITY  $  BEGIN                                      186
                           o                                             187
  COMMENT,  (7A) COUNTING THE NUMBER OF DISTRICTS THAT THE DEMOCRATS      188
   ARE LIKELY TO WIN AND THE AVERAGE MARGIN  $                           189
     TEMP1 = DEMSD(F)  $  TEMP2 = REPSD(F)  $                            190
      TEMP3 = DEMSD(T)  $  TEMP4 = REPSD(T)  $                           191
     DEMSD(F) = QDEMSDF  $  REPSD(F) = QREPSDF  $                        192
      DEMSD(T) = QDEMSDT  $  REPSD(T) = QREPSDT  $                       193
     DEMWINS = SMARGIN = 0  $                                           194
     FOR J = (1, 1, NDA)  $  BEGIN                                       195
       IF DEMSD(J) GTR REPSD(J)  $  DEMWINS = DEMWINS + 1  $             196
       PCTDEMSD(J) = 100.DEMSD(J) / (DEMSD(J) + REPSD(J))  $             197
       MARGIN(J) = ABS( PCTDEMSD(J) - 51.0 )  $                         198
       SMARGIN = SMARGIN + MARGIN(J)  $                                 199
     END  $                                                             200
     AVGMARGIN = SMARGIN / NDA  $                                        201
     DEMSD(F) = TEMP1  $  REPSD(F) = TEMP2  $                           202
     DEMSD(T) = TEMP3  $  REPSD(T) = TEMP4  $                           203
                                                                        204
  COMMENT,  (7B) DETERMINING THE NUMERICAL VALUE OF THE DISPROPORTION    205
   AND THUS THE NEW CRITERION  $                                         206
     QAVGVEA = 1  $  QAVGVCA = 1  $                                      207
     IF PR.EQL 1  $  BEGIN                                               209
       IF 100.DEMWINS/NDA LSS PCTDEMSA  $                               210
         EQUALIZER = AVGMARGIN  $                                        211
       IF 100.DEMWINS/NDA GTR PCTDEMSA  $                               212
         EQUALIZER = 1 / AVGMARGIN  $                                    213
       DISPROP = (100.DEMWINS/NDA - PCTDEMSA)*2 . EQUALIZER  $  END  $   214
     IF PR EQL 2  $                                                      215
       DISPROP = (1 / (DEMWINS+1))*2 . AVGMARGIN  $                     216
     IF PR EQL 3  $                                                      217
       DISPROP = (DEMWINS+1)*2 . (1 / AVGMARGIN)  $                     218
                                                                        219
RETURN                                                                  220
END PROPORTIONALITY  $                                                  221
```

The first factor in these three products is always given a weight of 2 so that no move can be made that will change Demwins contrary to the setting of the PR parameter. The integer 1 is added to Demwins in case Demwins becomes 0, in order that the average margin or its reciprocal can still be minimized. Demwins or its reciprocal alone, like badcount alone, cannot be a criterion because few single moves will change Demwins, although there might be many possible moves in that direction as indicated by changes in the average margin. The absolute value of the average margin of victory or defeat is used on the theory that it is equally as bad to have a surplus of one's party in a district as it is to have a shortage. Certain districts near the average in population but in which one's party has only a small percentage of the votes can be excluded from the computer run. The 51 percent figure can be raised if one wants his party to win fewer districts with a safer margin.[16] In special situations if

_____

[16] For example, when PR was set to 2 and the 51 percent figure was used in the 18-district Illinois run described later, the Democrats obtained a majority in 7 of the 18 districts, but the Democrats had an average percentage in these 7 districts

minimizing disprop is consistent with minimizing badcount, then the program can be changed slightly to make disprop a factor in the criterion before badcount reaches 0. This, however, is unnecessary if there are many units per district and maxcut has not been set too low, thereby increasing the flexibility to move after badcount reaches 0.

One reason for allowng PR to be set to 2 or 3 is to let the Democratic leaders and Republican leaders see at once just how far they can gerrymander within the confines of a maxcut of 20 percent. If such information had been available to the five partisan Democrats and five partisan Republicans who constituted the Illinois Reapportionment Commission of 1963, they might have been able to compromise before their time expired and an at-large election had to be held. Unfortunately, they consumed considerable time with pencils and paper and desk calculators, trying to out-gerrymander each other. An additional purpose for section 7B is to indicate that computer redistricting can be gerrymandered redistricting despite statements to the contrary.[17]

Another setting of PR that could be added is a set of statements that say if PR equals 4, disprop equals the product of (1) the difference between the percentage of Demwins after badcount reaches 0 and the percentage of Demwins at the last election times (2) an equalizer analogous to the one used when PR was set to 1. Such a setting would tend to preserve the party balance of power if that is what is needed to facilitate a redistricting compromise. A couple of instructions would then have to be added in Section 2, enabling the computer to calculate the initial percentage of Demwins in the area.[18] Likewise, one can add a parameter to the program called something like "desired Demwins," so

---

of only 51 percent. When a 55 percent figure was used, the Democrats obtained a majority in only 6 of the 18 districts, but the average majority rose slightly to 52 percent. Specific safe districts can be guaranteed by having as an indivisible unity any geographical space in which one's party has a high percentage of the votes and in which the population is close to the average population per district.

[17] Edward Forrest, for instance, states: "Since the computer doesn't know how to gerrymander—because two plus two always equals four—the electronically generated map can't be anything but unbiased." Forrest, *Apportionment by Computer*, Am. Behav. Sci. 23 (December 1964). Mr. Forrest has, however, indicated in a telephone conversation with this writer that he is aware that the program he recommends is capable of some gerrymandering. The exact nature of his program is a commercial secret.

[18] Such an addition involves inserting the word OLDEMWINS followed by an equals sign after the last equals sign on card 28; adding a card after card 50 to say IF DEMSD(J) GTR REPSD(J) $ OLDEMWINS = OLDEMWINS + 1 $; and then adding the following program statements after card 218:

```
IF PR EQL 4 $ BEGIN
    IF DEMWINS LSS OLDEMWINS $
        EQUALIZER = AVGMARGIN $
    IF DEMWINS GTR OLDEMWINS $
        EQUALIZER = 1 / AVGMARGIN $
    DISPROP = (DEMWINS − OLDEMWINS)*2 . EQUALIZER $ END $
```

that if PR is set to 2 or 3 and desired Demwins is reached, completion will be considered true.[19] Such a parameter might be needed to convert a compromise between the political parties into a redistricting pattern.[20] Instead of or in addition to using voting figures in the input, other attitudes or background characteristics of the population might be used to achieve an optional pattern.[21]

If PR is set to 0, this means that there will be no deliberate favoring of one party over the other. It does not mean that the output will make both parties happy or even that the output will minimize unhappiness. In general, the only way to arrive at such a neutral solution is to manipulate the parameters and the data in light of the value judgments of the Democrats and Republicans. In this sense, the solution that produces the least total protest from both sides and is within the legal requirements should perhaps be considered the best solution.[22]

F. The Trading Part

Because of the nature of the data or the parameters, merely moving one unit at a time may not provide what those responsible for redistricting consider an optimum solution, whereas the simultaneous trading of two or more units may. For instance, suppose that a state consists of just two districts, F and T. Suppose further that district F consists of 2 units

---

[19] Such an addition involves changing DE... to DEM... on card 3; adding a comma and the word DESWINS after the word PR on card 16; adding after card 203 the instruction IF ((PR EQL 2) OR (PR EQL 3)) AND (DEMWINS EQL DESWINS) $ (COMPLETION = 1 $ ENTER PRINTING) $; adding the word DESWINS and a comma after the word PR on card 365; and adding the phrase ' DESWINS = ', 14, before the W4 on card 371. PR should be set at 2 or 3 depending on the direction Demwins should move in order for Demwins to equal desired wins after badcount equals 0. PR can be set to 2 and then 3 on successive runs if the proper setting is not obvious beforehand. When PR is set to 0, 1, or 4, deswins can be arbitrarily set to 0 since its value is only used when PR is 2 or 3. The above method for achieving a given deswins level is more effective than minimizing the product of (1) the difference between Demwins and deswins times (2) an equalizer analogous to that used when PR equals 1.

[20] The program could, of course, be perverted in states where the party in power is so overwhelming in votes (e.g., the Democrats in Mississippi) that it does not have to make any concessions to the minority party and can thus legislate a complete gerrymander, assuming the courts would uphold such a districting pattern. In such states, though, gerrymandering is a minor factor in perpetuating a one-party system. The Supreme Court has declared racial gerrymandering to be unconstitutional. *Gomillion* v. *Lightfoot*, 364 U.S. 339 (1960).

[21] In redistricting California, for example, the input can consist of voting returns from certain statewide referenda or presidential primaries in order to provide Southern California with additional districts (thereby making many Southern Californians happy), while drawing the district lines in such a way as to hold constant the liberal or conservative influence in the legislature (thereby making many Northern Californians happy).

[22] Along related lines, see Appel, *A Note Concerning Apportionment by Computer,* Am. Behav. Sci. 36 (March 1965).

with populations of 10 and 5, and district T also consists of 2 units with populations of 6 and 11. The total population in this state is thus 32, and the average population per district is 16. No single move, however, will bring the populations of each district any closer to the average. On the other hand, a trade of the 5-man unit from F for the 6-man unit from T will result in both districts having 16 people. One can easily draw a map of this two-district state so that such a trade will not disrupt contiguity.

The trading part of the program is designed to provide for trades between unit I of district F and unit L of district T. Each unit gets an opportunity to be an I and an L, and each district (as in the moving section) gets an opportunity to be an F and a T. The conditions of

FIGURE 24–7

THE TRADING PART OF THE PROGRAM

```
COMMENT,  (SECTION 8) TRADING UNIT I OF DISTRICT F FOR UNIT L OF DIS-    222
    TRICT T  S                                                          223
TRADING..                                                               224
TRADES = 0  S                                                           225
FOR I = (1, 1, NUA)  S  BEGIN                                           226
  FOR L = (1, 1, NUF)  S  BEGIN                                         227
    F = DU(I)  S  T = DU(L)  S                                          228
    LOOPTYPE = 2  S                                                     229
                                                                        230
    COMMENT,  (8A) TESTING TO SEE IF UNITS I AND L ARE ELIGIBLE TO BE   231
      TRADED  S                                                         232
    CONDITION1 = CONDITION2 = 0  S                                      233
    FOR K = (1, 1, NKU(I))  S  BEGIN                                    234
    IF ( DISU( TOUCHLISTU(I,K) ) EQL T )                                235
    AND ( TOUCHLISTU(I,K) NEQ IU(L) )  S  CONDITION1 = 1  S             236
    IF ( DISU( TOUCHLISTU(L,K) ) EQL F )                                237
      AND ( TOUCHLISTU(L,K) NEQ IU(I) )  S  CONDITION2 = 1  S  END  S   238
    IF (CONDITION1 EQL 1)                                               239
      AND (CONDITION2 EQL 1)                                            240
      AND (F NEQ T) - S  BEGIN                                          241
    ENTER JCONTIGUITY  S                                                242
    IF (FCONTIGUITY EQL 1)                                              243
      AND (TCONTIGUITY EQL 1)  S  BEGIN                                 244
                                                                        245
    COMMENT,  (8B) EFFECT OF THE TRADE ON DISTRICT F  S                 246
    QNUDF = NUD(F)  S                                                   247
    QPDF = PD(F) - PU(I) + PU(L)  S                                     248
    QSXDF = SXD(F) - XU(I).PU(I) + XU(L).PU(L)  S                       249
    QSYDF = SYD(F) - YU(I).PU(I) + YU(L).PU(L)  S                       250
    QSX2DF = SX2D(F) - (XU(I)*2).PU(I) + (XU(L)*2).PU(L)  S             251
    QSY2DF = SY2D(F) - (YU(I)*2).PU(I) + (YU(L)*2).PU(L)  S             252
    QDEMSDF = DEMSD(F) - DEMSU(I) + DEMSU(L)  S                         253
    QREPSDF = REPSD(F) - REPSU(I) + REPSU(L)  S                         254
                                                                        255
    COMMENT,  (8C) EFFECT OF THE TRADE ON DISTRICT T  S                 256
    QNUDT = NUD(T)  S                                                   257
    QPDT = PD(T) + PU(I) - PU(L)  S                                     258
    QSXDT = SXD(T) + XU(I).PU(I) - XU(L).PU(L)  S                       259
    QSYDT = SYD(T) + YU(I).PU(I) - YU(L).PU(L)  S                       260
    QSX2DT = SX2D(T) + (XU(I)*2).PU(I) - (XU(L)*2).PU(L)  S             261
    QSY2DT = SY2D(T) + (YU(I)*2).PU(I) - (YU(L)*2).PU(L)  S             262
    QDEMSDT = DEMSD(T) + DEMSU(I) - DEMSU(L)  S                         263
    QREPSDT = REPSD(T) + REPSU(I) - REPSU(L)  S                         264
                                                                        265
    ENTER REVISING  S  END  S  END  S                                  266
  END  S                                                                267
END  S                                                                  268
IF TRADES GTR 0  S  GO TO TRADING  S                                    269
COMPLETION = 1  S  ENTER PRINTING  S                                    270
```

eligibility are only slightly more complicated than those involved in moving. Simply stated, I must touch T at some unit other than L, and likewise L must touch F at some unit other than I in order to preserve the contiguity of the recipient district. This type of contiguity might be called recipient contiguity. In addition, F must not be equal to T, and the residual contiguity (or J contiguity) of the two districts left behind by I and L respectively must be satisfied.

If these conditions are met, then the characteristics of the I unit are taken out of district F and put into district T, and the characteristics of the L unit are taken out of district T and put into district F. The revising part of the program is then entered and the criterion is recalculated. The trade is consummated if the newly calculated criterion is less than the previously calculated criterion and badcount is not increased. Line 269 indicates the trading process is repeated until no more improvement trades can be made, at which time completion is true and the printing section is entered.

Even the trading section, however, will not guarantee that the criterion is as low as mathematically possible, though it should be low enough to satisfy the political and judicial powers that be. To make the program do more work, one could replace line 270 with the statement, "Traded = 1, go to moving," since the trading may have made desirable some moves that were formerly undesirable. This statement, though, should be preceded by a statement, "If traded equals 1, completion = 1, enter printing," so that the cycle will end the next time around. One could, however, write some statements designed to send the computer from trading back to moving again and again as long as some trading occurred, and designed to end the program if no moving occurred.

Ideally, if the program were to reach the mathematician's dream of being able to minimize any hypothetical situation, regardless how unrealistic, then additional sections would have to be added to provide for 2-for-1 trades, 2-for-2 trades, 3-for-1 trades, and so on up to 25 units traded for 25 units, where 50 is the maximum number of units that a district can have. Perhaps, in some unknown hypothetical situation, a trade might even have to involve more than two districts simultaneously. By means of what is known as nonlinear integer mathematical programming, one can probably determine whether the criterion is at the true minimum and then stop the larger scale trading before computer time is wasted.[23]

---

[23] For an introduction to that kind of programming or optimizing see VAJDA, MATHEMATICAL PROGRAMMING (1961); HADLEY, NONLINEAR AND DYNAMIC PROGRAMMING (1964). If the criterion in this program had been stated as the sum of the variables multiplied by their weights (instead of being stated as the product of the variables with their weights as exponents), then linear optimizing techniques might be applicable. See HADLEY, LINEAR PROGRAMMING (1962). The weights in the summed criterion (as contrasted to the multiplied criterion) have to take into consideration the differences in the scales on which the variables are measured as well as their relative importance.

A simple way of trying to reach the true minimum is to run the same set of data cards a few times, with the cards arranged in a different random order each time. Each run on the computer will probably cost only a few dollars, as will be indicated more clearly later. The program in this way might make some early moves that will prevent it from getting coincidentally stuck at a point close to but not quite at the true minimum—e.g., where a trade of 3 units from F for 2 units from T might be needed. It has been the writer's experience, however, that the average deviation from equality never changed by more than five percentage points on repeated runs of different orders of the same data when both moving and one-for-one trading were employed. This is especially true if the average quantity of units per district is over 5 and there are more than 10 districts, thereby increasing the flexibility of movement. There does not seem to be any consistent rule on what is the best order of the data cards, although arranging them in identification number order is convenient, enables the computer to operate faster, and seems to increase flexibility if the identification number order is in geographical sequence.

It might also be mentioned that setting maxcut too low decreases the flexibility of movement and becomes self-defeating. Thus, if maxcut were set at 5 percent when one might really be satisfied with 15 percent, then no district under 5 percent will be changed, even though some of its population might be needed by a district that is over 15 percent in order to bring them both to about 12 percent. In other words, one can experiment with different maxcuts, including a maxcut of 500 percent, which is really no maxcut, since badcount presumably will then start out at 0. Normally, a maxcut is needed, otherwise the average variation from equality might be low, but some districts might be excessively deviant. Under the equal protection clause of the Constitution, one excessively deviant district may invalidate an entire districting scheme, no matter how good the average is.

G. The Residual Contiguity Part

Section 9 shows how the contiguity of district J is tested after one of its units has been temporarily removed. First, a position number of one of the remaining units in district J is determined. This number is placed on a list called the cluster list. In Section 9, the symbol II has the same meaning as I but is used to avoid changing the value of I in the large I loop of which the J contiguity test is a part. C in this section is a suffix meaning cluster rather than compactness.

Section 9b determines whether the remaining units form an unbroken cluster by adding to the cluster list each unit that (1) touches the first unit in the cluster list and (2) is in district J. Then, each unit that (1) touches the second unit in the cluster list and (2) is in district J is also added to the cluster. This goes on until there are no more units to add to

FIGURE 24–8

THE RESIDUAL CONTIGUITY PART OF THE PROGRAM

```
COMMENT,  (SECTION 9) TESTING THE CONTIGUITY OF DISTRICT J WHEN ONE OF     271
   ITS UNITS IS REMOVED  $                                                  272
SUBROUTINE JCONTIGUITY  $  BEGIN                                            273
FCONTIGUITY = DU(I) = 0  $                                                  274
J = F  $  TEST = 1  $                                                       275
                                                                           276
COMMENT,  (9A) DETERMINING THE NUMBER OF A REMAINING UNIT IN DIS-          277
   TRICT J  $                                                              278
SECTION9A..                                                                279
FOR II = (1, 1, NUA)  $  IF DU(II) EQL J  $  BEGIN                          280
   IJ = II  $  GO TO SECTION9B  $                                           281
END  $                                                                      282
                                                                           283
COMMENT,  (9B) DETERMINING WHETHER THE REMAINING UNITS IN DISTRICT J       284
   FORM AN UNBROKEN CLUSTER  $                                              285
SECTION9B..                                                                286
FOR IC = (1, 1, 50)  $  CLUSTER(IC) = 0  $                                  287
CLUSTER(1) = IJ  $  NUC = 1  $  IC = 1  $                                   288
BUILDCLUSTER..                                                             289
FOR K = (1, 1, NKU( CLUSTER(IC) ))  $  BEGIN                                290
   QCOMPONENT = TOUCHLISTU( CLUSTER(IC),K )  $                              291
   IQ = 0  $  TRANSLATE..  IQ = IQ + 1  $                                   292
      IF IU(IQ) NEQ QCOMPONENT  $  GO TO TRANSLATE  $                       293
   FOR IIC = (1, 1, NUC)  $  IF IQ EQL CLUSTER(IIC)  $                      294
      GO TO NOWCLUSTERED  $                                                 295
   IF DU(IQ) EQL J  $  BEGIN                                                296
      NUC = NUC + 1  $                                                      297
      CLUSTER(NUC) = IQ  $                                                  298
      NOWCLUSTERED..  END  $                                                299
END  $                                                                      300
IC = IC + 1  $                                                              301
IF CLUSTER(IC) NEQ 0  $  GO TO BUILDCLUSTER  $                             302
                                                                           303
COMMENT,  (9C) INDICATING THE DIFFERENT HANDLING OF MOVING AND TRAD-       304
   ING  $                                                                   305
IF (TEST EQL 1) AND (NUC EQL NUD(J)-1)  $  FCONTIGUITY = 1  $              306
IF TEST EQL 1  $  DU(I) = F  $                                              307
IF (TEST EQL 1) AND (LOOPTYPE EQL 2)  $  BEGIN                              308
   TCONTIGUITY = DU(L) = 0  $                                               309
   J = T  $  TEST = 2  $                                                    310
   GO TO SECTION9A  $  END  $                                               311
IF (TEST EQL 2) AND (NUC EQL NUD(J)-1)  $  TCONTIGUITY = 1  $              312
IF TEST EQL 2  $  DU(L) = T  $                                              313
RETURN                                                                     314
END JCONTIGUITY  $                                                          315
```

the cluster. If at that point the number of units in the cluster equals the number of units in district J minus 1, then J is a contiguous district.

Lines 292 and 293 merely translate the identification numbers taken from the touchlist into position numbers. Thus, Q component and IQ refer to the same unit, but Q component is its identification number and IQ its position number. To become an addition to the cluster list, Q component must not already be on the cluster list, and its district must be J. Section 9C and the beginning of Section 9 indicate that when the moving section feeds into the J contiguity section, J equals F, and when the trading section feeds into the J contiguity section, J first equals F and then T. I and L are temporarily taken out of F and T simply by saying DU(I) and DU(L) equal 0 and then later saying DU(I) and DU(L) equal F and T respectively.

H. The Output Part

The first portion of the output part indicates what headings are to be printed. The B10 means 10 blank spaces should precede the heading. The W3, W2 means start the heading on a new page with a blank line before and after the heading. Sections 10B through 10E all indicate that a line of information should be written for each district from the first to the last. For Section 10B, the line of information is the identification numbers of the units in the district. The I4 on line 331 indicates allowance should be made for a 4-digit integer. Anything within quotes is printed out as quoted. The W0 means single space the line.

The one line per district in Section 10C consists of three items of information concerning equality of population in addition to the district number. The X7.0 means allow for a 7-digit decimal number with 0

FIGURE 24–9a

The Output Part of the Program

```
COMMENT,  (SECTION 10) OUTPUT OPERATIONS  $                              316
SUBROUTINE PRINTING  $  BEGIN                                            317
                                                                        318
COMMENT,  (10A) HEADINGS                                                 319
IF COMPLETION EQL 0  S   WRITE (SS HEADING1)  $                          320
   FORMAT HEADING1 (B10,  'INITIAL DISTRICTING', W3, W2)  $              321
IF COMPLETION EQL 1  S   WRITE (SS HEADING2)  S                          322
   FORMAT HEADING2 (B10,  'REDISTRICTING AT THE END OF THE PROGRAM',     323
   W3, W2)  S                                                            324
                                                                        325
COMMENT,  (10B) ALLOCATION OF UNITS PER DISTRICT  $                      326
FOR J = (1, 1, NDA)  S   WRITE (SS UNITS, FORM1)  $                      327
   OUTPUT UNITS ( J, FOR I = (1, 1, NUA)  S                              328
   ( IF DU(I) EQL J  S  IU(I) ) )  S                                     329
   FORMAT FORM1 ('FOR DISTRICT', I4, ',     UNITS = ',  S  NUD(J)  $     330
   (I4, ',',), '.', W0)  S                                              331
WRITE (SS BLANKLINE)  $   FORMAT BLANKLINE (W0)  S                       332
                                                                        333
COMMENT,  (10C) EQUALITY INFORMATION PER DISTRICT  $                     334
FOR J = (1, 1, NDA)  S   WRITE (SS EQUALITY, FORM2)  $                   335
   OUTPUT EQUALITY (J, PD(J), 100.PD(J)/AVGPOP, 100.ABS(1 - PD(J)/       336
   AVGPOP) )  S                                                          337
   FORMAT FORM2 ('FOR DISTRICT', I4, ',  POP. = ', X7.0,                 338
   '    POP./AVG. = ', X4.0, 'PCT.                                       339
   'PCT.',  W0)  S            100-(POP./AVG.) = ', X4.0,                 340
WRITE (SS BLANKLINE)  S                                                  341
                                                                        342
COMMENT,  (10D) COMPACTNESS INFORMATION PER DISTRICT  $                  343
FOR J = (1, 1, NDA)  S   WRITE (SS COMPACTNESS, FORM3)  S                344
   OUTPUT COMPACTNESS ( J, NUD(J), SQRT(VCD(J)) )  S                     345
   FORMAT FORM3 ('FOR DISTRICT', I4, ',    NU = ', I3,                   346
   '    AVG. DISTANCE FROM UNIT CENTERS TO THE DISTRICT CENTER = ',      347
   X4.1, '.', W0)  S                                                    348
WRITE (SS BLANKLINE)  S                                                  349
                                                                        350
COMMENT,  (10E) PARTIES INFORMATION PER DISTRICT  S.                     351
FOR J = (1, 1, NDA)  S   WRITE (SS PARTIES, FORM4)  S                    352
   OUTPUT PARTIES ( J, DEMSD(J), REPSD(J), 100.DEMSD(J)/                 353
   (DEMSD(J) + REPSD(J)) )  S                                           354
   FORMAT FORM4 ('FOR DISTRICT', I4, ',    DEMOCRATIC VOTES = ',         355
   X7.0, '    REPUBLICAN VOTES = ', X7.0, '    DEM.',                    356
   'PERCENT = ', X3.0, W0)  S                                           357
```

numbers to the right of the decimal point. Section 10D produces two items of compactness information per district. It might be noted that the square root of the variation from compactness for a district is equal to a measure of distance because of the Pythagorean theorem—i.e., the diagonal side of a right triangle equals the square root of the sum of the squares of the other two sides. Section 10E provides three items of information per district about political party strength. Finally, Section 10F makes some simple calculations and then prints out, appropriately labeled, the values of the eight parameters, two averages, and some overall voting information. W4 means double space the preceding line.

FIGURE 24–9b

The Output Part of the Program
(continued)

```
COMMENT,  (10F) GENERAL INFORMATION ABOUT THE AREA BEING REDISTRICTED $      358
SUMRATIO = SUMDISTANCE = DEMWINS = 0  $                                      359
FOR J = (1, 1, NDA)  $  BEGIN                                                360
   IF DEMSD(J) GTR REPSD(J)  $  DEMWINS = DEMWINS + 1  '$                    361
   SUMRATIO = SUMRATIO + 100*ABS(1 - PD(J)/AVGPOP)  $                        362
   SUMDISTANCE = SUMDISTANCE + SQRT(VCD(J))  $  END  $                       363
WRITE ($$ AREA, FORM5)  $                                                    364
   OUTPUT AREA (NUA, NDA, AVGPOP, MAXCUT, MINCUT, W, TRADE, PR,              365
   SUMRATIO/NDA, SUMDISTANCE/NDA, DEMSA + REPSA, PCTDEMSA,                   366
   100*DEMWINS / NDA)  $                                                     367
   FORMAT FORM5 (W0, 'FOR THIS AREA,          NU = ', X5.0, '      ND = ',   368
   X4.0, '      AVG. POP. = ', X7.0, '    MAXCUT = ', I2, '.PCT.', W4,       369
   '    MINCUT = ', I2, ' PCT.    WEIGHT = ', X4.2, '    TRADE = ',          370
   I1, '    PR = ', I1, W4, '    AVG. DEVIATION FROM EQUALITY = ',           371
   X3.0, ' PCT.    AVG. DEVIATION FROM COMPACTNESS = ', X4.1, W4,            372
   '    TOTAL VOTES = ', X8.0, '    DEM. VOTES = ', X3.0,                    373
   ' PCT.    DEM. WINS = ', X4.0, ' PCT.', W4)  $                            374
                                                                            375
IF COMPLETION EQL 1  $  GO TO STARTING  $                                    376
RETURN                                                                      377
END PRINTING  $                                                             378
FINISH  $                                                                   379
```

Line 376 instructs the computer that if completion equals 1, it is to go to the starting section, where it will see if there is a new parameter card and more data to be processed. If completion does not equal 1, the computer returns to the instruction on line 61, which is the one immediately after the instruction to enter printing. Immediately after the finish card (line 379), the user of the program should place as many sets of data cards as he wants. Each set of data cards should be preceded by a parameter card as shown in Figure 24–1. The same data can be processed with different parameter cards, or else both the data cards and parameter cards can be different on successive runs.

Figure 24–10 summarizes the flow of operations between the parts of the program. In order to simplify the figure, the trading part is omitted, but its relations to the other parts of the program are almost identical to

FIGURE 24–10

THE FLOW OF OPERATIONS

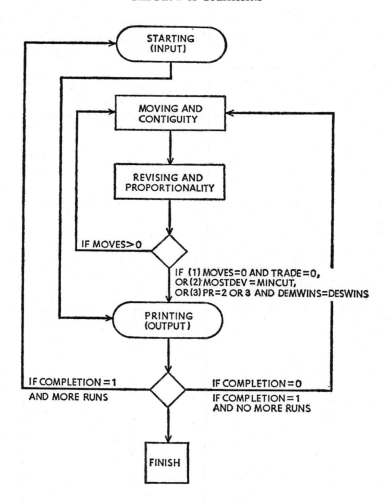

those of the moving part of the program. Also, for the sake of simplicity, the moving and contiguity parts have been grouped together, as have the revising and proportionality parts. In a flow diagram like that shown in Figure 24–10, ovals represent input and output parts, rectangles represent major internal processes, diamonds represent decision points or if-type instructions (not all the if instructions are shown), and squares represent termination points.

III.   A LARGER EXAMPLE

In order to illustrate what is involved in applying the program to a large set of realistic data, the writer undertook to redistrict 90 of the 102 Illinois counties. Of the 12 excluded counties, 10 came from northeastern Illinois, and 2 came from the East St. Louis area. These two areas were excluded because they contained counties that by themselves had more than 120 percent of the average population per district. Such large population counties must be split up if all the districts in the state are to be within 20 percent of the average population. In other words, for these two areas to be satisfactorily redistricted at least some of the basic units will have to be parts of counties. All the basic units, however, need not be of the same type. Some can be townships, wards, cities, census tracts, or arbitrary portions of counties. It is of no importance to the computer what label is applied to the basic units. The Illinois constitution does require that counties be used as districting units whenever doing so will not result in a district's having more than 150 percent of the average population.

In redistricting the lower Illinois House, the Republican and Democratic leaders were agreed that Chicago must be redistricted separately from the Cook County suburbs, and the suburbs must be redistricted separately from downstate Illinois. The program can handle such a value judgment by redistricting these areas on separate runs, and then no units from one area will be in the same district as a unit from another of the areas. If one wants to prevent two units present in the same run from being joined in the same district, one can change their touchlists so as to remove their common linkage.

As of 1963, the 90 Illinois counties used were grouped into 21 districts. The population figures for these 21 districts are shown in the upper half of Figure 24–11, which contains the relevant portion of the initial printout. As can be seen, 8 of the 21 districts deviated by more than 20 percent from the average population. All 8 were more than 20 percent *under* the average. None of the 21 was more than 11 percent *over* the average. These 8 districts were thus clearly illegal in light of the state constitution and possibly the federal Constitution as well, although the Illinois constitution is more explicit than the Supreme Court's reapportionment decisions. The district numbers shown in the first half of Figure 24–11 start with 1 and end with 21. The same districts in Illinois start with numbers 34 and end with 59. Districts 35, 36, 37, 53, and 54 were excluded from the computer run because they are part of the northeastern and East St. Louis areas.

The lower half of Figure 24–11 shows the redistricted populations. The 21 districts have been reduced to 18 because the 90 counties have a total

FIGURE 24-11

REDISTRICTING 90 COUNTIES FROM 21 DISTRICTS INTO 18 DISTRICTS

INITIAL POPULATIONS

```
FOR DISTRICT  1,   POP. = 147422.   POP./AVG. =  86.PCT.   100-(POP./AVG.) = 14.PCT.
FOR DISTRICT  2,   POP. = 150690.   POP./AVG. =  88.PCT.   100-(POP./AVG.) = 12.PCT.
FOR DISTRICT  3,   POP. = 168140.   POP./AVG. =  98.PCT.   100-(POP./AVG.) =  2.PCT.
FOR DISTRICT  4,   POP. = 133812.   POP./AVG. = .78.PCT.   100-(POP./AVG.) = 22.PCT.
FOR DISTRICT  5,   POP. = 149010.   POP./AVG. =  87.PCT.   100-(POP./AVG.) = 13.PCT.
FOR DISTRICT  6,   POP. = 143613.   POP./AVG. =  84.PCT.   100-(POP./AVG.) = 16.PCT.
FOR DISTRICT  7,   POP. = 189044.   POP./AVG. = 111.PCT.   100-(POP./AVG.) = 11.PCT.
FOR DISTRICT  8,   POP. = 161031.   POP./AVG. =  94.PCT.   100-(POP./AVG.) =  6.PCT.
FOR DISTRICT  9,   POP. = 129738.   POP./AVG. =  76.PCT.   100-(POP./AVG.) = 24.PCT.
FOR DISTRICT 10,   POP. = 171475.   POP./AVG. = 100.PCT.   100-(POP./AVG.) =  .PCT.
FOR DISTRICT 11,   POP. = 161161.   POP./AVG. =  94.PCT.   100-(POP./AVG.) =  6.PCT.
FOR DISTRICT 12,   POP. = 146539.   POP./AVG. =  86.PCT.   100-(POP./AVG.) = 14.PCT.
FOR DISTRICT 13,   POP. = 155360.   POP./AVG. =  91.PCT.   100-(POP./AVG.) =  9.PCT.
FOR DISTRICT 14,   POP. = 159562.   POP./AVG. =  93.PCT.   100-(POP./AVG.) =  7.PCT.
FOR DISTRICT 15,   POP. = 131886.   POP./AVG. =  77.PCT.   100-(POP./AVG.) = 23.PCT.
FOR DISTRICT 16,   POP. = 152402.   POP./AVG. =  89.PCT.   100-(POP./AVG.) = 11.PCT.
FOR DISTRICT 17,   POP. = 122491.   POP./AVG. =  72.PCT.   100-(POP./AVG.) = 28.PCT.
FOR DISTRICT 18,   POP. = 122368.   POP./AVG. =  72.PCT.   100-(POP./AVG.) = 28.PCT.
FOR DISTRICT 19,   POP. = 104349.   POP./AVG. =  61.PCT.   100-(POP./AVG.) = 39.PCT.
FOR DISTRICT 20,   POP. = 131842.   POP./AVG. =  77.PCT.   100-(POP./AVG.) = 23.PCT.
FOR DISTRICT 21,   POP. = 121201.   POP./AVG. =  71.PCT.   100-(POP./AVG.) = 29.PCT.
```

REDISTRICTED POPULATIONS

```
FOR DISTRICT  1,   POP. = 163768.   POP./AVG. =  96.PCT.   100-(POP./AVG.) =  4.PCT.
FOR DISTRICT  2,   POP. = 147422.   POP./AVG. =  86.PCT.   100-(POP./AVG.) = 14.PCT.
FOR DISTRICT  3,   POP. = 164024.   POP./AVG. =  96.PCT.   100-(POP./AVG.) =  4.PCT.
FOR DISTRICT  4,   POP. = 150991.   POP./AVG. =  88.PCT.   100-(POP./AVG.) = 12.PCT.
FOR DISTRICT  5,   POP. = 157275.   POP./AVG. =  92.PCT.   100-(POP./AVG.) =  8.PCT.
FOR DISTRICT  6,   POP. = 165966.   POP./AVG. =  97.PCT.   100-(POP./AVG.) =  3.PCT.
FOR DISTRICT  7,   POP. = 189044.   POP./AVG. = 111.PCT.   100-(POP./AVG.) = 11.PCT.
FOR DISTRICT  8,   POP. = 165314.   POP./AVG. =  97.PCT.   100-(POP./AVG.) =  3.PCT.
FOR DISTRICT  9,   POP. = 200412.   POP./AVG. = 117.PCT.   100-(POP./AVG.) = 17.PCT.
FOR DISTRICT 10,   POP. = 156936.   POP./AVG. =  92.PCT.   100-(POP./AVG.) =  8.PCT.
FOR DISTRICT 11,   POP. = 161161.   POP./AVG. =  94.PCT.   100-(POP./AVG.) =  6.PCT.
FOR DISTRICT 12,   POP. = 161078.   POP./AVG. =  94.PCT.   100-(POP./AVG.) =  6.PCT.
FOR DISTRICT 13,   POP. = 172383.   POP./AVG. = 101.PCT.   100-(POP./AVG.) =  1.PCT.
FOR DISTRICT 14,   POP. = 151325.   POP./AVG. =  89.PCT.   100-(POP./AVG.) = 11.PCT.
FOR DISTRICT 15,   POP. = 192299.   POP./AVG. = 113.PCT.   100-(POP./AVG.) = 13.PCT.
FOR DISTRICT 16,   POP. = 196346.   POP./AVG. = 115.PCT.   100-(POP./AVG.) = 15.PCT.
FOR DISTRICT 17,   POP. = 176356.   POP./AVG. = 103.PCT.   100-(POP./AVG.) =  3.PCT.
FOR DISTRICT 18,   POP. = 181036.   POP./AVG. = 106.PCT.   100-(POP./AVG.) =  6.PCT.
```

population of 3,053,136, according to the 1960 census. The state's total population of 10,081,158, when divided by the 59 districts of the lower house, gives an average of 170,867 per district. The number 3,053,136 divided by 170,867 is 17.9 or 18 districts. Since the number of initial districts is different from the number of final districts, the first half of Figure 24–11 was produced on a computer run with the parameter NDA set to 21, and completion considered true (i.e., set to 1) after the starting part. The second half was produced on a second run with NDA set to 18, and completion considered true after the moving part. In the second run, the units of three pairs of small adjacent districts were assigned the same district number for reasons mentioned in discussing the moving part of the program. The renumbering of the districts can be accomplished almost automatically by blanking out the old punched numbers with an

IBM reproducer and putting in the new numbers with a programmed key punch. The other characteristics of the units, including their identification numbers, never have to be changed unless one wants to change the population or voting figures to use different time periods.

The most interesting thing about the lower half of Figure 24–11 is that after the computer redistricting none of the districts exceeds the average population by more than 17 percent. It is also of interest that after the program was read into the computer (which took 16 seconds) it then took only 81 seconds to complete the redistricting. At $4.17 a minute for IBM 7090 computer time ($250 an hour), an 81-second run costs only $5.63. The 16 seconds for reading the program need be consumed only once in order to cover many runs backed up behind the program cards.

The parameters for the results shown in the lower half of Figure 24–2 were an NUA of 90, an NDA of 18, an average population of 170,867, a maxcut of 20 percent, a mincut of 0 percent, a weight of 0, and both trade and PR were set to 0. The weight of compactness relative to equality was set to 0 for three reasons. First, using counties as units means there will be few units per district, and few units per district means the contiguity constraint by itself will cause the units in a district generally to be almost as close to the population center of the district as the compactness factor can get them. Second, having a few large units per district makes it difficult to obtain a high degree of equality unless compactness is given a low weight relative to equality. Third, the latitude and longitude data the writer used during this study were based on his visual centering rather than on the more accurate measurements available from the Census Bureau.

Trade was set to 0, thereby preventing the trading of units, because it was suspected that single moves alone could get all the districts below the 20 percent deviation figure. If trading had been used, an even greater degree of equality would have been achieved, although adding the trading requires three to four times as much computer time. PR was set to 0, thus preventing deliberate proportional representation or gerrymandering, because a PR of 0 is a setting that would frequently be used. PR was also set to 0 because after the badcount of excessively deviant districts reaches 0, having only a few units per district leaves little flexibility for further movement. Nevertheless, by changing PR from 0 to 2, the Democratic wins were raised from 28 to 39 percent, a figure substantially closer to the percentage of Democrats in the area's population.[24] The

---

[24] In nearly all states, winning a district (i.e., having a majority of the votes) results in capturing all the legislative seats allocated to that district—usually one seat. However, given the cumulative voting system of Illinois and the distribution of Democrats and Republicans, if the Democrats (or Republicans) win a district in Illinois, two out of the three seats allocated to the district are captured.

number of excessively deviant districts still remained at 0, as required by lines 137 through 144.[25]

Other before-and-after numbers show that the average deviation from equality dropped from 16 percent to 8 percent, although the average deviation from compactness rose slightly from 4½ tenths of map inches to 5½ tenths. In view of the scale to which the map was drawn, 5½ tenths of inches means that if the legislator from each district were to have an office at the population center of his district he would have on the average only about 25 miles to travel in order to be at the population center of any of the counties in his district. With PR set to 0, the Democrats got shuffled out of one district in southern Illinois, so that their percentage of wins was reduced from an initial 33 percent (7 out of 21 districts) to a final 28 percent (5 out of 18), although the 3-district reduction will benefit the northeastern and East St. Louis areas, where the Democrats are relatively strong. Incidentally, the map drawn from the full output had the perfect contiguity required by the program, but contiguity could, if desired, be made an optional feature, as are compactness and trading.

IV. FURTHER ASPECTS OF POLITICAL AND ECONOMIC FEASIBILITY

A. POLITICAL FEASIBILITY

Many of the political aspects of the program have already been discussed in connection with the proportionality, minimum cut, input, and other program sections. One important concern of incumbent legislators that has been only tangentially discussed is what effect the program will have on their districts. The most reassuring answer is to point out that it has various features for minimizing change (in addition to the mincut and PR settings) while still reducing the number of excessively deviant districts to 0. First, if the incumbents do not want to split a given district, which consists of, say, three counties, then these three counties can be fed

---

[25] When PR was set to 1, the Democrats also won 39 percent of the districts, though they have 47 percent of the population in the 90 counties. Many Democratic votes are wasted because they are not spread out so evenly as Republican votes. When PR was set to 3 and desired wins to 0, the Democrats won only 17 percent of the districts. Demwins can sometimes be brought to a higer maximum or lower minimum by taking the reciprocal of the second factor on lines 214, 216, or 218. This is what was done to reduce Demwins to 17 percent since the regular card 218 made Demwins 22 percent. When PR was set to 4, the Democrats won 33 percent of the 18 districts, as they had when the 90 counties were divided into 21 districts. To achieve this 33 percent, a temporary card was inserted at the end of section 2 saying OLDEMWINS = 6, because the initial districting of the redistricting run involved 18 rearranged districts, not the original 21 districts.

into the computer as a single unit. The program as written will not split the districting units, which are fed into the computer whether they be counties, combination of counties, or other units. Moreover, if the hypothetical combination of three counties has a collective population above or close to the mean population of the districts, then the computer is not likely to add an outside county or unit to it. To guarantee completely the wholeness and separateness of a combination of counties, they can simply be omitted from the redistricting input, and the number of districts to be created by the computer reduced accordingly. What geographical spaces are to be treated as combination units, as regular units, or are to be broken into subunits can be decided in the political negotiations preceding or concurrent with the computer redistricting.[26]

The program also tends to preserve incumbents in office, since the starting point is the districting pattern of the status quo. Use of random districting patterns as starting points might result in the same average deviation from equality, but the final districting pattern would differ more from the status quo than where the status quo is the only starting point. Randomizing the starting patterns, like randomizing the order of data input, will not produce a lower average deviation from equality if all possible simultaneous trades are provided for, and will not produce a substantially lower average deviation even if only moves and one-for-one trades are used.

The program also minimizes change by not moving a unit if doing so will destroy the existence or the contiguity of a district. It will also refuse to move a unit if the move will result in a districting pattern merely as good as the prior pattern rather than an improvement on it. Nor will any move be made that will increase the count of excessively deviant districts or change the quantity of either party's wins in a direction opposite to the setting of the PR parameter once badcount equals 0.

An important aspect of political feasibility is the problem of how many districts to assign to an area or even to a whole state. The major issue that deadlocked the Illinois Reapportionment Commission, for instance, was whether the 30 districts allocated to Cook County should be split by allocating 23 districts to Chicago and 7 to the suburbs, or 22 to Chicago and 8 to the suburbs, or 21 to Chicago and 9 to the suburbs. Any one of the 3 splits could have resulted in districting patterns that would satisfy the 20 percent deviation allowed by the Illinois constitution. Likewise, in California there is a controversy over what percentage of the districts in the state senate should be allocated to northern California and what percentage to southern California. This controversy has even threatened

---

[26] This predetermination by the user of what the redistricting units and areas are also prevents, for example, the possibility of dividing a city into three districts each of which is dominated by rural voters, or of distributing the city voters outward so that the rural voters will be diluted and made powerless.

to split California into two states. How can the program handle such problems?

Since the number of districts for an area (NDA) is an input parameter and not an output result, the program cannot directly decide what NDA should be, but it can help the political decision makers to decide. It could possibly have done so in Illinois by generating various districting patterns for the 23-to-7 split, for the 22-to-8 split, and for the 21-to-9 split. The members of the Reapportionment Commission could have looked over these patterns and perhaps arrived at a compromise that would, for instance, have given Chicago only 21 districts (thereby pleasing the Republicans), but drawn in such a way as to provide for a greater or equal number of Democratic wins obtainable from 22 or even 23 districts (thereby pleasing the Democrats). Similarly, the program can generate numerous districting patterns for a variety of northern versus southern California allocations (say, 46 percent versus 54 percent, 39 percent versus 61 percent, and so on), one or a combination of which might strike a responsive chord among those responsible for the redistricting.

But, one might argue, why could not the Illinois and California politicians draw up their own sets of trial districting patterns with some maps and a crayon without a computer? The answer for Illinois is that this is exactly what they did attempt from before the beginning of the 1963 legislative session until their legal time ran out, and an extremely expensive, cumbersome, embarrassing, and unrepresentative at-large election was required, in which each voter could vote to fill 177 legislative seats simultaneously. If a computer can generate districting patterns for the perusal of the decision makers at the rate of 1 every 81 seconds, as was done for the 90 counties in Figure 24–11, it can produce 1,066 different districting patterns in a day. Presumably, however, only a fraction of a day's computing time would be needed.

Another aspect of political feasibility is that of keeping people of similar economic and social interests together so that their interests will be better represented in the legislature. As previously mentioned, the population compactness factor in the criterion tends to provide for this on the assumption that people who live near one another tend to have similar interests. If ethnic neighborhoods or economic regions are considered input units, this will even more effectively achieve that purpose. The population compactness factor also helps guarantee that legislators will not have to travel such long distances in visiting their constituents as they would in the absence of such a factor. It also helps to increase the confidence of the opposition party that the redistricting pattern is not gerrymandered in favor of the party in power.[27]

---

[27] Compactness, however, does not necessarily prevent gerrymandering. It can be demonstrated that even if a high weight is given to compactness relative to equal-

B. ECONOMIC FEASIBILITY

The most important aspect of economic feasibility has already been mentioned—namely, that a redistricting as large as 90 counties into 18 districts can be done for $5.63 in computer running time charges. Other important cost aspects are those of assembling the data cards and of adapting the program to one's local computer.

The cost of assembling the data cards is amazingly low. For $112, William Fay of the Geography Division of the Census Bureau will supply a 2,400-foot IBM tape, containing basic information for every census tract and other minute place in the entire United States. For the same or a lower price, he will supply punched cards for any state. The tape provides for each place the standardized location serial number, the place name, whether it is urban or rural, the latitude and longitude expressed in degrees, the latitude and longitude expressed as distances in hundreds of meters from specified baselines, and the 1960 population.

Since the places on the Census Bureau tape are quite small, it may be necessary to combine specified census places to make districting units. An additional program section can be written that will average the population centers of such subunits to determine the latitude and longitude of the center of population of the input units. If longitudes and latitudes weighted by population are used as input to the program, rather than the unweighted longitudes and latitudes used in generating Figures 24–2 and 24–11, then the population symbols can be omitted from the compactness instructions in the program. If the tape is used in generating some of the input, then the card-reading instructions in Section 1 should be supplemented with tape-reading instructions. Some cards will still have to be punched to provide the initial districts, the touchlists, and the voting information for each unit. The voting information, however, can be dispensed with if it is not wanted, provided that the words DEMSU and REPSU are taken out of the card reading instruction. The latitude and longitude information can also be omitted if it is felt that the contiguity constraint by itself gives sufficient compactness.

The quantity of input units is the most important item in determining the number of cards to punch as well as the amount of computer running time. The more units there are for a state, the higher the costs become, though flexibility of movement also increases. Many states, like Illinois, tend to keep the number of units low by prohibiting the splitting of counties or other political entities unless the entity has a population substantially larger than the average district. Furthermore, local politi-

---

ity on the parameter card, and AVGVCA is not set to 1 on line 207, there is still plenty of room to gerrymander when the units are small and maxcut is not set too low.

cians would prefer to see various political entities remain whole because the jurisdiction of party committees and governmental bodies is often determined by the boundaries of these political entities.[28]

Suppose a judge, legislative committee, or party leader wanted to put the program to use, how would he go about doing so? He can take a copy of this chapter to a programmer who works for the state university, or other state or federal agency, or commercial computer firm (such as the Service Bureau Corporation), and ask him to adapt it to whatever high-speed local computer is available. As a better alternative, he can obtain on magnetic tape from Stanford University for $35 what is known as a Balgol compiler, which will enable the program to be run on any IBM 7090 computer when some simple instructions accompanying the compiler are followed. A copy of the program deck can be obtained (for the cost of the postage involved in mailing about 400 IBM cards) by writing to this author or to the Inter-University Consortium for Political Research at Ann Arbor, Michigan.[29]

Some clerical help must be hired to write out and punch the initial district, touchlist, and possibly the voting data and the other figures if the census tape is not used. All the mechanics plus forecasting research and intelligent advice can be handled by an experienced operations research or simulation firm (such as the Simulmatics Corporation of New York City or C-E-I-R, Inc., of Washington, D.C.).[30] A competent programmer can also make changes in the program to cover special situations. Those financing the redistricting research should indicate the parameters they want to use for various runs. All the parameters and runs need not be planned in advance. A few quick runs can be made and the results examined so as to generate ideas about what the next set of partmeters and runs should be.

If desired, optical scanners to read maps as part of the input data and cathode ray tubes to generate maps as part of the output data can be added at greater expense. These are standard techniques in the program recommended by Edward Forrest.[31] Given the Census Bureau tape, however, electronic map readers seem wasteful. Unless the quantity of units is extremely large, one can quickly draw on a map a line around the

---

[28] One of the redistricting issues in some states is whether or not county lines should be crossed in creating districts. The computer program can generate various districting patterns using either alternative. These outputs could then be helpful to the politicians in deciding the issue.

[29] The program deck received from either of these sources will provide for the PR setting of 4 referred to in note 18 *supra,* and will provide for the DESWINS parameter referred to in note 19 *supra.* Other revisions will be described in an addendum accompanying the program deck.

[30] Commercial computer firms are listed in the yellow pages of large telephone directories under "data processing services." Operations research firms can be found under "management consultants" or "city and regional planners."

[31] Forrest, *supra* note 17.

units in each district from the lists given by the program output. One need not draw a map for every run, especially those runs whose output characteristics are considered relatively undesirable.

It should also be noted that, unlike commercially developed programs, no costs are charged for the use of this program, although many months of intensive research went into developing it. The writer welcomes comments, and he will be pleased to answer questions that potential and actual users might have. Such feedback will aid him in improving the program.

V. SOME BROADER IMPLICATIONS

This study was conducted primarily to help resolve some of the deadlocks that have occurred in legislative redistricting, such as the deadlock that led to the at-large election of the lower house of the Illinois Legislature. It was also stimulated by the high costs and poorer quality output resulting from the use of noncomputer methods to redistrict—e.g., the approximately $100,000 spent by New York for one redistricting. It might also be considered an attempt to provide a way of making more precise the one man–one vote principle of the United States Supreme Court.

It is hoped, moreover, that this chapter might take some of the mystery out of computer programming and thereby stimulate those interested in other policy problems to investigate the applicability of computer processing. Many standard statistical programs already are available at most computing centers to take a set of data cards (each one describing a person, place, or thing) and produce a variety of percentages, averages, correlation coefficients, probabilities, and other numbers. Frequently, however, these canned programs try to anticipate everybody's needs, and thus produce unnecessary output and consume excessive computer time. More serious is that frequently no canned program is available to do what one wants to have done.

Since the early 1950's when computers first began to be widely used for scholarly research, it is possible that many research projects have been shaped by the availability of canned computer programs. It is almost an abuse of a computer not to take advantage of its great versatility. Further, with the advent of simple programming languages, like the version of the ALGOL language shown in Figures 24–3 through 24–9, it is no excuse to say that one needs to be a mathematician or an engineer to program a computer, or to say that the language is so foreign that one has constantly to use it to avoid forgetting it.[32] In addition to being useful

---

[32] For an introduction to ALGOL in general, see McCracken, A Guide to ALGOL Programming (1962). For an introduction to the mathematical formulation of policy problems, see Miller & Starr, Executive Decisions and Operations Research (1960).

for testing some policy proposals—e.g., alternative districting patterns or the relationship between releasing suspects without bail and their subsequent appearances in court[33]—successfully writing a program can be an exciting experience, and the precision required does help to sharpen thinking about the substantive problems involved.

---

[33] See Ares, Rankin & Sturz, *The Manhattan Bail Project: An Interim Report on the Use of Pre-Trial Parole,* 38 N.Y.U. L. REV. 67 (1963). Other legal policy studies that have made use of computers include ZEISEL, KALVEN, & BUCHOLZ, DELAY IN THE COURT (1959); SILVERSTEIN, DEFENSE OF THE POOR IN CRIMINAL CASES IN AMERICAN STATE COURTS (1964); Nagel, *Testing the Effects of Excluding Illegally Seized Evidence,* 1965 WIS L. REV. 283 (1965) (chap. 23 *supra*).

CHAPTER 25

Optimizing Legal Policy

Various scholars have written in recent years about the quantitative optimization of managerial decisions,[1] and a few have dealt with social decisions.[2] It is the purpose of this chapter to offer an alternative quantitative method to the approaches given in those materials. This alternative method is designed to be particularly applicable to proposed legislation and, to a lesser extent, to judge-made law. It emphasizes estimated correlation coefficients to determine the relation of policies to goals and paired comparisons to weight goals, and to determine the likelihood that a policy will be adopted. In order to make the method simpler for the reader to perceive, elementary algebraic symbols and dichotomous variables will be used throughout the chapter. No knowledge beyond high school algebra will be presumed. Two previous studies provide lengthy specific applications of many of the broader methods and concepts presented here.[3]

The author gratefully acknowledges the perceptive critique of this chapter, which was offered by Mary Ellen Caldwell, Layman Allen, and Myres McDougal of the Yale Law School and Thomas Cowan of the Rutgers Law School.

[1] See, e.g., CHURCHMAN, ACKOFF, & ARNOFF, INTRODUCTION TO OPERATIONS RESEARCH (1957); MILLER & STARR, EXECUTIVE DECISIONS AND OPERATIONS RESEARCH (1960); SCIENTIFIC DECISION MAKING IN BUSINESS—READINGS IN OPERATIONS RESEARCH FOR NON-MATHEMATICIANS (SHUCHMAN ed. 1963). Thomas Cowan has recently called the attention of legal theorists to operations research materials. Cowan, *Decision Theory in Law, Science, and Technology,* 17 RUTGERS L. REV. 499 (1963).

[2] ARROW, SOCIAL CHOICE AND INDIVIDUAL VALUES (2d ed. 1963); BRAITHWAITE, THEORY OF GAMES AS A TOOL FOR THE MORAL PHILOSOPHER (1955); BRAYBROOKE & LINDBLOM, A STRATEGY OF DECISION—POLICY EVALUATION AS A SOCIAL PROCESS (1963). Although the Braybrooke & Lindblom book is not quantitative, the authors do recognize "the boundary between problems that can be solved by calculation and those that must be treated by a strategy of multiple adjustment has thus shifted. With the development of more and more sophisticated computer techniques, the boundary may be expected to go on shifting." *Id.* at 247. The policymaking scheme of this article mainly involves policies that promote a medium degree of change and are based on a medium degree of understanding. *Id.* at 78.

[3] Nagel, *Testing the Effects of Excluding Illegally Seized Evidence,* 1965 WIS. L. REV. 283 (particularly Figure 1) (chap. 23 *supra*); Nagel, *Simplified Bipartisan Computer Redistricting,* 17 STAN L. REV. 863 (1965) (chap. 24 *supra*).

I. ONE POLICY AND ONE GOAL

A. CORRELATION COEFFICIENTS

The simplest policy problem merely involves attempting to determine whether a given policy or means to an end will increase or decrease the presence of a given intermediate or ultimate goal. An X can be used as a symbol for a policy, and a Y can be used as a symbol for a goal. In terms of correlation coefficients, this problem involves determining whether there is a positive (direct), negative (inverse), or zero correlation between X and Y.

To determine the direction of the correlation between X and Y, one can compare a group of geographical units or individuals who have been subjected to X with a group of geographical units or individuals who have not been subjected to X or who have been subjected to less X. The first group can be referred to as group E for experimental, and the second group as group C for control. The geographical units can be communities, states, countries, or other units, and the individuals can be businessmen, school children, taxpayers, or other individuals, depending on whom the policy is supposed to affect. The entities may also be time periods or events, some of which had X present and some of which had X absent. If the proportion of group E that is high on Y is a greater proportion than the proportion of group C that is high on Y, then there is a positive correlation between X and Y; and if all other things are temporarily held equal or constant for the sake of discussion, then X should be adopted. If the relative size of these proportions (that is, P_E and P_C) is reversed, then there is a negative correlation between X and Y; and X should be rejected.[4] The difference between these two proportions represents an approximate measure of the degree of correlation between X and Y. It is symbolized r and can range from -1.00 to 0 to $+1.00$. The relationships discussed in this paragraph can be shown in a four-cell table like Table 25–1.[5]

In correlating X and Y, one should try to have entities in group E that are like the entities in group C with regard to any Z characteristics (that is, region, prosperity, or industrialism) that cause X and also cause Y so as to eliminate the possibility of spurious correlation between X and Y. E and C, of course, should be unlike on X, and the choosing of entities should be unrelated to how they are positioned on Y. One can also apply

---

[4] If Y can be measured in degrees rather than merely as high and low, then one would determine whether the entities in the E group had a higher average Y than the entities in the C group.

[5] For further detail on gathering empirical data and correlating variables in legal research, see Nagel, *Testing Empirical Generalizations in Legal Research*, 15 J. LEGAL ED. 365 (1963) (chap. 2 *supra*) and the references cited therein.

TABLE 25–1

CORRELATING POLICY X WITH GOAL Y
(dichotomous variables)

	Group C $-X$	Group E $+X$	
$+Y$	N_1	N_3	$N_1 + N_3$
$-Y$	N_2	N_4	$N_2 + N_4$

$$N_1 + N_2 \quad + \quad N_3 + N_4 \quad\quad = N \text{ entities}$$

$P_C = N_1/(N_1 + N_2)$ 　　　　　　 $r = P_E - P_C$

$P_E = N_3/(N_3 + N_4)$ 　　　　　　 $\text{chi}^2 = r^2 N$

$M_Y = (N_1 + N_3)/N$ 　　　　　　 $S_Y = \sqrt{(M_Y)(1 - M_Y)}$

$M_X = (N_3 + N_4)/N$ 　　　　　　 $S_X = \sqrt{(M_X)(1 - M_X)}$

(1) a chi-square test to determine whether the r is big enough given the N to be considered not due to chance and (2) a test of reasonableness in light of known relationships. A correlation coefficient can be thought of as being related to the probability that X will achieve Y. It would, however, be erroneous to substitute P_E alone for r, because P_E merely indicates the probability of $+Y$ occurring if $+X$ occurs. P_E does not indicate the probability of $+Y$ occurring, even if $-X$ occurs. The r takes both P_E and P_C into consideration. As an alternative to determining at one point in time whether each entity in group E and group C was high or low on Y, one can determine whether each entity in group E and group C underwent a big or a little increase in Y after the entities in E were subjected to X.

Relevant data can frequently be obtained from available records or from questionnaires. Most X's and most Y's, though, cannot be measured like physical or even monetary things can, but entities can at least be positioned as having X or Y present or absent, as high or low, or as more or less than some entity that is used as a standard. It may, however, sometimes be impractical to calculate r because of lack of available data, lack of time or money to obtain or simulate data, or because of the presence of an X variable that cannot be simulated and is practically unique in world history. In such a situation, one will still gain insights into the relation between X and Y by attempting to roughly estimate what P_E and P_C might be or by attempting to have others make such an estimation. The estimate may be based on analogies, known relationships between other variables, knowledge of human nature, or an informed imagination. In making such an estimate, one can simplify the arithmetic by taking an N of 20 and estimating what quantity of the 20 are likely to be $+X$ and what quantity are likely to be $+Y$, and then estimating what quantity of the $+X$ entities are also likely to be $+Y$. Once these three estimates are made, all the other values shown in Table 25–1 can be calculated by simple arithmetic. One can assume that $N_1 + N_2 = N_3 + N_4$ and that $N_1 + N_3 = N_2 + N_4$ if no better estimate can be made. Where policy decisions must be made, a rough estimate of the relation between X and Y may be better than no estimate and no decision.

Although an X having a calculated or estimated negative correlation with Y should generally be rejected, it may be wise to adopt X if only a small negative correlation is involved and if more is to be lost by an error of rejecting an X that really had a positive correlation with Y than by an error of adopting an X that really had a negative correlation.

B. Regression Equations

Suppose one finds or estimates a positive correlation between policy X_1 and Y, and also a positive correlation between policy X_2 and Y, and one has the resources to adopt both X_1 and X_2, should he then adopt both policies? Not necessarily. Such a pair of correlations merely indicates X_1 alone will increase Y, and X_2 alone will increase Y. If the combined effect of X_1 and X_2 does not produce sufficient Y, then a policy of X_3 may have to be sought. On the other hand, if policy X_1 alone or policy X_2 alone can produce sufficient Y, then it might be wasteful to adopt both policies. This problem involves finding an equation that indicates how many units of X are needed to produce a given quantity of Y.

Such an equation (called a regression equation) can be symbolized as follows: $Y = a + bX$, where a is referred to as the a-coefficient and b is referred to as the b-weight. The a can be calculated by the formula, $a = M_Y - M_X b$, where M_Y is the mean of Y and M_X is the mean of X. The b can be calculated by the formula, $b = r(S_Y/S_X)$, where S_Y is the standard deviation of Y and S_X is the standard deviation of X. Simple formulas for calculating M's and S's for a four-cell table are given in Table 25–1. Standard statistics textbooks give more complex formulas for calculating M's, S's, and r where X and Y have not both been dichotomized. In using the regression equation where Y has been dichotomized, simply substitute a 1 for $+Y$ and solve for X. If X is also dichotomized, then an X value equal to or greater than .5 equals $+X$ and an X value less than .5 equals $-X$. Likewise one could solve for Y by substituting a 1 or 0 for X in the equation. If r is positive, then $+X$ will yield $+Y$; and if r is negative, $-X$ will yield $+Y$. Where X or Y are continuum variables rather than dichotomies, more precise values than 1's or 0's can be substituted for X and Y, and the regression analysis becomes more worthwhile.

The regression equation given presupposes a roughly linear relationship between X and Y. In other words, the more X one adopts, the more Y one will get, although additional units of X may not produce proportionately additional units of Y. In a completely curvilinear relationship, the more X one adopts, the more Y one will get up to a maximum point, and then additional units of X take away units of Y rather than merely add smaller units of Y. At least a six-cell table like Table 25–2 is needed to reveal such a curvilinear correlation. If P_2 is greater than P_1 and greater than P_3, a curvilinear relation is present. The regression formula for such a hill-shaped relation is $Y = a + b_1 X + b_2 X^2$. To calculate a, b_1, and b_2 requires solving a system of three simultaneous equations. In a three-by-two table like Table 25–2, however, when an entity is in the first category on X, one can predict P_1 on Y; when an entity is in the second category on X, one can predict P_2 on Y; and when an entity is in the third category, one can predict P_3 on Y. One can make similar predictions on Y for each category of X, regardless of the number of X categories, as long as Y is dichotomized. This gives the same predictions as the regression equation does.[6]

Interpretation of the data in a table like Table 25–1 or 25–2 will in-

TABLE 25–2

A Curvilinear Relation between X and Y
(P_2 greater than P_1 or P_3)

	low X	middle X	high X
+Y	N_1	N_3	N_5
−Y	N_2	N_4	N_6

$$P_1 = N_1/(N_1 + N_2) \quad P_2 = N_3/(N_3 + N_4) \quad P_3 = N_5/(N_5 + N_6)$$

form the policymaker whether adopting or adding to X will increase or decrease Y. That would be an inductive approach. A deductive approach, on the other hand, involves deducing from a regression or other equation whether or not X should be adopted. The equation itself may be derived by induction from the analysis of data or by deduction from related empirically tested formulas, intuitively accepted axioms, or from definitions. If the regression equation involves a hill-shaped relation and both X and Y can be numerically measured, then one can use simple calculus to determine the number of units of X needed to reach a peak on Y before diminishing total returns set in. To do so, one determines the derivative of

---

[6] For further detail on linear and curvilinear regression with one or multiple X's, see Blalock, Social Statistics 273–358 (1960); Peters & Van Voorhis, Statistical Procedures and Their Mathematical Bases 425–35 (1960).

Y with respect to X given the regression equation, replaces the derivative sign with a zero, and then solves the resulting equation for X. This would be one of the rare instances in which calculus, as contrasted to algebra or statistical analysis, has any direct value to legal research.[7]

II. MORE THAN ONE POLICY OR GOAL

A. MULTIPLE POLICIES AND ONE GOAL

Suppose one wants to compare two or more policies (X_1, X_2, X_3, et cetera) that have been proposed for achieving desired goal Y. In terms of correlation coefficients, the logical thing to do is to compare the correlation coefficient (r) between X_1 and Y with the coefficient between X_2 and Y, and so on down to the coefficient between X_n and Y, where X_n is the last X. If other considerations are held constant, then the X with the highest r is best, the X with the next highest r is next best, and so on. X's with positive r's are worthy of adoption, assuming the X's are not mutually exclusive, and X's with negative r's are not. As previously mentioned, if a certain correlation coefficient cannot be calculated because of lack of data, it may be better to estimate it or have others who are knowledgeable estimate it than to abandon the correlation approach. Regression equations can be calculated for multiple X's by a method analogous to the method described where one X was involved. The general regression formula is $Y = a + (b_1X_1) + (b_2X_2) + \ldots + (b_nX_n)$. Standard computer programs make such calculations relatively easy after the individuals, geographical units, or other entities involved have been categorized on the X and Y variables.

When there are a great many mutually exclusive X's, a computer can also quickly determine the Y that all or many of the X's will produce. Such a situation is involved in determining the optimum policy for assigning counties or other geographical units to legislative districts. The Y or Y's in redistricting are mainly equality and compactness.[8]

B. ONE POLICY AND MULTIPLE GOALS

The problem is a little more complicated if one has many Y's in mind and one wants to know whether or not to adopt policy X. If all the Y's are equally worthy and nonduplicative, then in terms of correlation coefficients one would logically add the correlation coefficient between X

---

[7] The derivative of a hill-shaped equation $Y = a + b_1 X + b_2X^2$ equals $b_1 + 2b_2X$. PROTTER & MORREY, COLLEGE CALCULUS WITH ANALYTIC GEOMETRY 126–127, 160 (1964). Thus, when the derivative sign is replaced with a zero, the X that will give a maximum Y equals $-b_1/2b_2$.

[8] Nagel, *Simplified Bipartisan Computer Redistricting*, note 3 *supra*.

and Y_1 (symbolized r_{Y_1X}) to r_{Y_2X} to r_{Y_3X} and so on. If the sum of the r's is plus or positive and the other considerations are held constant, then X should be adopted because a positive sum indicates that X correlates positively with the desired goals more than it correlates negatively. If the sum of the r's is minus or negative, then X should be rejected for the converse reason.

If, however, all the Y's are not equally valuable, as is more likely to be the case, then each r_{YX} should be multiplied by the weight (symbolized w) or relative worth of the X in the r_{YX} before summing the r_{YX}'s. How can one assign weights to each goal? A simple and meaningful method is the method of paired comparisons. To apply this method, one pairs each goal with each other goal. If there are N goals, then there are $N(N - 1)/2$ comparisons. In preparing the list of pairs, every goal should appear sometimes on the left and sometimes on the right, and no goal should be involved in two successive pairs. The list of pairs is then given to a group of legislators, philosophers, public opinion experts, or some segment of the public, depending on whose values one is interested in. Each person in this group should indicate which goal he prefers in each pair or which goal he thinks the public would prefer. A matrix is then prepared in which one lists each goal along both the top and the side. The cells in the matrix indicate the proportion of times the goal at the top was chosen in preference to the goal at the side. The sum of these proportions downward for each goal can represent the value points or weight for each goal, or one can mathematically manipulate the matrix to determine more precise value points and intervals between goals. Paired comparison programs, as well as correlation and regression programs, are now available in various computer program libraries.[9]

The number of comparisons becomes unwieldy if the number of goals exceeds 10, but that is unlikely to occur in most policy problems. If it does occur, then as an alternative to the paired comparisons method one can use the method of successive categories to weight the goals. This method involves asking the evaluators to place a goal in one of five or more categories, such as (1) highly undesirable, (2) mildly undesirable, (3) neither desirable nor undesirable, (4) mildly desirable, (5) highly desirable. A matrix is then prepared with the goals on the side and the successive categories on the top. The cells in the matrix indicate the proportion of times the goal at the side was placed in the category at the top. The matrix is then mathematically manipulated to assign each goal a definite weight.

Neither the paired comparisons method of weighting nor the successive categories method adequately indicates the degree of difference

---

9 STATISTICAL SERVICE UNIT OF THE UNIVERSITY OF ILLINOIS, MANUAL OF COMPUTER PROGRAMS FOR STATISTICAL ANALYSIS (1964) [hereinafter cited as SSU MANUAL].

between the Y's if all the evaluators always prefer a certain Y or always reject a certain Y, or if the evaluators always put a certain Y in the highest category or always in the lowest category. This problem can be handled by increasing the number of categories or by providing a thermometer-type rating scale on which the evaluators can attempt to position the goals. Such ratings, however, can be checked by each evaluator for consistency by seeing whether the combined weights of various preferred combinations total more than the combined weights of various nonpreferred combinations. The only such comparisons worth making are those where the outcome is not obvious on the basis of the ranks alone. For example, where there are four separate, compatible goals rated in descending order Y_1, Y_2, Y_3, and Y_4, which combination is more valued: Y_1 or $(Y_2 + Y_3 + Y_4)$; $(Y_1 + Y_4)$ or $(Y_2 + Y_3)$; Y_1 or $(Y_2 + Y_3)$; Y_1 or $(Y_2 + Y_4)$; or Y_1 or $(Y_3 + Y_4)$; Y_2 or $(Y_3 + Y_4)$? If the sums of the weights are inconsistent with any of these value judgments, then the evaluator can adjust the weights to conform with the judgments. The weights assigned by the evaluators to each Y can then be averaged to give average weights for the group of evaluators.[10]

C. Multiple Policies and Multiple Goals

Suppose one wants to compare two or more policies, and he has many goals in mind. This is the problem of multiple X's and multiple Y's simultaneously. The general formula for the relative utility (symbolized U) of X_1 or any X given any number of Y's is:

$$U_{X_1} = (r_1 w_1) + (r_2 w_2) + \ldots + (r_n w_n),$$

where r_n is a shortened way of writing $r_{Y_n X_1}$ (that is, the correlation between X_1 and Y_n), and w_n is a shortened way of writing w_{Y_n} (that is, the weight of Y_n). Thus, if other considerations are held constant, then the X with the highest U is best, the X with the next highest U is next best, and so on. X's with positive U's are worthy of adoption, and X's with negative U's are not. For example, if one is attempting to decide between X_1 (which produces $+Y_1$ and $-Y_2$) as contrasted to X_2 (which produces $-Y_1$ and $+Y_2$), then one should logically choose the X that produces the Y with the greater w, unless the correlations offset the difference in w's. In other words, if only one X can be chosen, choose the X with the greater U. If, however, the U_{X_1} is only Q times the value of U_{X_2} but one can obtain more than Q times as much X_2 than he can obtain X_1,

---

[10] For further detail on the method of paired comparisons, successive categories, and other methods for preparing an evaluation or prediction scale, see Guilford, Psychometric Methods 154–301 (2d ed. 1954). For alternative methods not covered in Guilford, see Churchman, Ackoff, & Arnoff, *op. cit. supra* note 1, at 136–54.

then one should choose the maximum X_2 obtainable, all other things held constant.

X_1 may have a higher U than X_2 if the future is a period of $+Z$, but a lower U than X_2 if the future is a period of $-Z$. If it is practically certain that the future will be $+Z$, then X_1 is clearly better than Y_2. If, however, the estimated probability that $+Z$ will occur is P and the ratio $(1 - P)/P$ is more than the ratio U_{X_1}/U_{X_2}, then X_2 should be preferred. In other words, where the U of an X is contingent on the occurrence of some future condition, the U should be multiplied by the probability of the condition occurring when comparing the U with the U's of other X's. If it is impossible to arrive at a roughly meaningful probability that a crucial Z will occur, then it is traditional to assume that Z has a 0.50 chance of occurring.[11]

The utility score in the above formula is only a relative score. It enables one to rank policy proposals in light of the goals of the policymaker or interest group concerned. To determine the quantity of goal achievement that a given set of policies will achieve when one has a number of goals in mind, one can calculate the a-coefficient and b-weights for a regression equation for each goal, using the general regression formula previously given. Then, substitute the quantity or category of $X_1, X_2, \ldots,$ and X_n to be adopted into each regression equation, and solve for Y in each equation. The set of Y values obtained represents the total quantity of goal achievement predicted. The separate Y values, however, cannot be added together, since that would involve adding different kinds of things together. On the other hand, one can talk about maximizing the overall goal (G) where G equals the product of the Y values with each Y value raised to the power of its weight.[12] In other words, $G = (Y_1{}^{w_1})(Y_2{}^{w_n})$. A correlation coefficient between a set of X's on the one hand and a set of Y's on the other hand can be determined by a technique known as canonical correlation.[13]

To maximize Y (rather than obtain a specific Y) where there is a linear relationship between X and Y, choose the maximum X available. To maximize Y where there is a hill-shaped relationship between X and Y, choose the X equal to $-b_1/2b_2$, as previously mentioned in note 7 *supra*. Where there is more than one X, the optimum value for each X depends on the cost of one unit of X and on the maximum amount of money available to achieve Y. Suppose X_1 costs \$10,000 per unit, X_2 costs \$20,000 per unit, and there is a maximum of approximately \$500,000 to

---

[11] MILLER & STARR, *op. cit. supra* note 1, at 79–100.

[12] *Id.* at 161–65. Where the weights are decimals, large numbers, or negative numbers, one can calculate such a G easier by the formula: $\text{Log } G = (w_1 \text{ Log } Y_1) + (w_2 \text{ Log } Y_2) + \ldots + (w_n \text{ Log } Y_n)$. RICHARDSON, COLLEGE ALGEBRA 391–404 (1958).

[13] TINTNER, ECONOMETRICS 114–21 (1952); SSU MANUAL.

spend in order to achieve Y. In such a situation, the optimizing problem becomes one of maximizing Y where $Y = a + b_1X_1 + b_2X_2$ and where $10X_1 + 20X_2$ is less than or equal to 500. If one has the data to solve a, b_1, and b_2 in the regression equation, then this regression equation and the above cost equation can be put into a programming routine that will indicate the appropriate units of X_1 and the appropriate units of X_2 in order to maximize Y in light of these two equations.[14] One might also wish to add an equation that X_2 be less than or equal to $-b_1/2b_2$. The regression equation would then be $Y = a + (b_1X_1) + (b_2X_2) + (b_3X_2^2)$, where the third and fourth terms indicate X_2 and Y have a hill-shaped relation.

D. LISTING POLICIES AND GOALS

In order to make the analysis more meaningful when one is working with more than one X, he should be careful to eliminate from consideration those X's that are duplicative. A duplicative X is one that represents basically the same thing as another X, although the two X's are described in different words. Likewise, duplicative Y's should be eliminated when one is working with more than one Y. In instances when one can obtain or estimate a meaningful correlation coefficient for every X with every other X from tables like Table 25–1, one can put these coefficients into a correlation matrix and factor the matrix, thereby giving a set of nonoverlapping X factors smaller in quantity than the original X's. These X factors can then be correlated with the Y's. Likewise, one could conceivably reduce the number of Y's and eliminate overlapping Y's by intercorrelating each Y with each other Y and then factoring the resulting correlation matrix.[15] It is, however, generally easier and more meaningful to reduce the X's and Y's by doing some hard thinking and rewording with regard to the distinctiveness of each X from each other X and each Y from each other Y. Careful thinking will also help to eliminate impractical X's. It might also be noted that where there are multiple X's the b-weight for each X is generally computed in such a way as to hold constant statistically the other X's. Thus, where such b-weights are available they can be substituted for the r's, and then the proper U formula requires multiplication of powers rather than the addition of products, since the b's are not pure numbers like the r's.[16] The U formula in such circumstances becomes

---

[14] See the linear programming routine described in the SSU MANUAL and in KEMENY, SNELL, & THOMPSON, INTRODUCTION TO FINITE MATHEMATICS 249–65 (1957).

[15] Factor analysis is discussed in FRUCHTER, INTRODUCTION TO FACTOR ANALYSIS (1954) and is programmed in the SSU MANUAL.

[16] See the references cited in note 12 *supra*.

$$U_{x_1} = (b_1^{w_1})(b_2^{w_2}) \ldots (b_n^{w_n}).$$

In order to do a factor analysis or calculate a multiple regression equation with b-weights that hold other X's constant, it is necessary to correlate each X with each other X. Such correlations may also be helpful by themselves in eliminating duplicate X's or Y's, since duplicates will have a correlation of approximately $+1.00$ with each other, although a perfect correlation may be due to causes other than duplication. The correlation between two X's or two Y's that are mutually exclusive is -1.00. The correlation between two X's or two Y's that are not duplicative or mutually exclusive can be calculated by gathering or estimating data for a table like Table 25–1. If this is impractical, it may be reasonable to say there is a zero correlation between the X's or the Y's, in which case P_1 equals P_2.

In listing the goals involved, one should include possible side effects, both desired and undesired, as well as intended goals. In the calculations, however, side effects need not include effects of effects of the policies; otherwise, the evaluation process might become unwieldy. One of the Y goals should generally be low monetary cost, and the relation between the X's and such a Y can be determined by accounting and budgeting techniques rather than by the gathering of behavioral data. For ease in handling, all goals should generally be stated in an affirmative way so that $+Y$ is what is desired and $-Y$ is what is not desired, and all w's are thus positive. In wording the goals, one should try to be as explicit as possible. A well-stated set of goals should possibly consider the intensity sought, the coverage over persons, and the coverage over time. There is, however, no quantitative system for making a best list of goals as contrasted to weighting the goals within a list or as contrasted to optimizing a set of policies for achieving goals. One can, though, determine whether a goal should be adopted if the goal is a policy toward a higher goal. Ultimately, however, one has to resort to pure value judgments that cannot be correlated with a higher goal when there is no higher goal to use as a criterion. Likewise, although policies can be quantitatively tested and ranked, there is no quantitative method for generating policy ideas. Such ideas are largely dependent on awareness of the relevant literature, on imaginative creativity, and on trial and error.

III. THE PROBABILITY OF POLICY ADOPTION

Determining the probability (symbolized P) that a given policy will be adopted is important because, regardless whether the utility of a given policy is positive, it would generally be wasteful of resources for an interest group outside or inside the membership of a legislature or a judicial body to push the adoption of a policy that has a low probability of being adopted, unless something is to be gained (such as publicity) even if the policy does not pass, or unless the policy is being pushed with the intention of compromising on a milder passable policy.[17] Likewise, it is wasteful of the time, money, and friendship resources of an interest group to push policy X, thinking this is the best they could hope for, when with just a little extra effort they could have gained the adoption of both X_1 and X_2, unless there is something to be gained by passing a weak policy by a large majority (such as significantly increased enforcement and compliance) rather than a stronger policy by a narrower majority. In this context, P equals the proportion of the policymakers that are likely to vote in favor of the X under consideration. If P is considerably less than 51 percent, it may as well be 0.

The logical ideal strategy for a policymaker or interest group seems to be to push the policy or combination of policies that has the greatest relative utility (U) or goal achievement (Y or G) to the policymaker or the interest group involved, provided the policy has at least a 0.51 probability of being adopted. In practice, a policymaker may rationally push a desired policy for nonpublicity, nonbargaining motives, even though it appears to have only a 0.40 probability of adoption, in order to avoid an error of underestimation that would result in a bill's not being pushed when it would have been adopted. Likewise, a policymaker may rationally push X_1 and not X_1 plus X_2 combined, even though X_1 plus X_2 appears to have a 0.60 probability (and both X's are desired by the policymaker) in order to avoid an error of overestimation, which could result in the loss of both X_1 and X_2.

How does one calculate the probability that a policy will be adopted? A policy or policies can be given a probability score by first putting it or them on a list along with policies that have been recently adopted or rejected by the current legislature or court involved. The list can then be submitted in the form of paired comparisons (pairing each policy with each other policy) to a group of persons who have some knowledge of the attitudes of the policymaking body. Each person should indicate which policy in each pair would be more likely to be passed. Using the method of analysis previously mentioned for paired comparisons, each policy can be given an adoption score. To give the proposed policy a specific probability, calculate the average of the percent of favorable votes for the policy immediately below and immediately above the proposed policy on the adoption scale. If the number of paired comparisons becomes unwieldy, the method of successive categories of adoption-probability, previously mentioned, can be used. If one believes that he

---

[17] The U of an X does not equal Y times w times P because such a formula falsely assumes that if Y_{X_1}/Y_{X_2} is greater than P_{X_2}/P_{X_1}, then X_1, which has a highly unlikely chance of being adopted, should be pushed in Congress or the Supreme Court in preference to X_2, which has a good chance of being adopted. Clearly, a small Y achievement is better than none at all.

is an adequate legislative predictor or goal evaluator, then he can assign rough adoption probabilities to the proposals and weights or ranks to the goals without using the pairing or categories method and without using other persons' judgments.

For example, if X has a paired comparison adoption score of 4.9 and a bill with an adoption score of 4.4 was approved by the United States Senate by a 55-to-45 vote (55 percent favorable), and a bill with an adoption score of 5.7 was approved by the United States Senate by a 70 to 20 vote (79 percent favorable), then one can say that the probability of X passing is 0.67. Instead of simply averaging 0.55 and 0.79, one could solve for P by interpolation where $(P - 0.55)/(0.79 - 0.55) = (4.9 - 4.4)/5.7 - 4.4)$. A probability could be similarly calculated for the House of Representatives, and then the two probabilities could be averaged to give an overall probability of congressional adoption.

It would be less meaningful to attempt to arrive at a probability of adoption by analyzing the correlation coefficients between the presence or absence of certain factual elements surrounding the policy and the occurrence or nonoccurrence of adoption using past policy proposals as entities. Such an approach, although possibly useful in predicting adjudication outcomes, does not adequately consider (1) the significant effects of changes in policymaking personnel as contrasted to policy-applying personnel, (2) the relative uniqueness of policymaking proposals as contrasted to case adjudications, and (3) the insights of knowledgeable persons. Likewise, any method that attempts to position the attitude of each individual policymaker in a 535-man legislature would probably be too unfeasible to be useful, although sometimes an inside political leader can make an accurate prevote survey of nearly all the members of a legislature.

There is no necessary relation between the utility of a policy and its probability of adoption if utility is determined in terms of the values of specific policymakers or interest groups. If, however, a policy has a high utility in terms of the values of the general public, and the policymakers are aware of this utility, then, in a democratic society, in the long run the policy will probably be adopted. In the short run, though, there may be a big difference between general utility and adoption probability given such institutions as the gerrymander, filibuster, rules committee veto, and Negro voter deprivation, as well as lack of accurate information on relations between policies and goals.

IV.   CONCLUSIONS

The key principles in this optimizing scheme in abbreviated form are: (1) the relative utility of a policy proposal equals the sum of the correlation weights for each goal relevant to the policy; (2) the goal achievement of a set of policy proposals equals the sum of the *a*-coefficient and the *b*-weights times the X values for each policy; and (3) the policy or combination of policies that should be pushed is the one that has the greatest relative utility or goal achievement, with the general proviso that the policy have approximately a 0.51 probability of being adopted. The most important formulas are thus:

$$U_{x_1} = (r_1 w_1) + (r_2 w_2) + \ldots + (r_n w_n);$$

and

$$Y = a + (b_1 X_1) + (b_2 X_2) + \ldots + (b_n X_n).$$

The method presented for optimizing legal policy is definitely not meant to be one that can always be applied. It is meant to be a method of thinking whose application is possibly worth striving for wherever it can be applied in part or in whole, even if some of the components have to be estimated rather than calculated precisely. The method presented is also hopefully meant to stimulate further analysis of the applications of operations research and statistical analysis to optimizing legal policy.

Epilogue

Epilogue

The purpose of this epilogue is to provide an overall evaluation of the role of political science as a contributor to a social science of law. It also particularly examines the role of the public law field within political science as a contributor to a policy science that deals with the effects of alternative legal policies.

I. POLITICAL SCIENCE AND A SOCIAL SCIENCE OF LAW

As the perspective of this book has emphasized, a social science of law should view legal policies both as responses to prior stimuli and as stimuli to subsequent responses. To use an alternative terminology, law making and adjudication are viewed as both effects or outputs and as causes or inputs. Chapter 3 discussed the contributions of a social science of law to the practicing lawyer, the legal policymaker, and to the legal scholar. But what can political science contribute to a social science of law?

A. Causes of Legal Policies and Decisions

With regard to the causes of legal policies and decisions, political science can possibly make both a methodological and a substantive contribution. As concerns methodology, in a recent article Professor Harry Jones of the Columbia Law School somewhat downgrades the judicial prediction studies of political scientists.[1] Professor David Cavers of the Harvard Law School, however, perceptively states that judicial prediction studies of political scientists "may be a useful tool for a social scientist investigating the relative importance of different types of recurrent factors in the decision of related cases."[2] In other words, the determination of the relative importance of types of facts in legal decision making is aided by quantitative analysis. Regression and discriminant techniques that have been borrowed by political scientists from other social scientists do provide useful tools for such an analysis.[3]

---

[1] Jones, *A View from the Bridge*, LAW AND SOCIETY 39 (summer 1965 supplement to SOC. PROBS.).

[2] Cavers, *Science and the Law Symposium: Introduction*, MICH. L. REV. 1333 (1965).

[3] Kort, *Content Analysis of Judicial Opinions and Rules of Law* in G. SCHUBERT (ed.), JUDICIAL DECISION MAKING 133 (1963); Tanenhaus *et al.*, *The Supreme Court's Certiorari Jurisdiction: Cue Theory* in G. SCHUBERT, *ibid.* 111; and Nagel, *Judicial Prediction and Analysis from Empirical Probability Tables*, 41 IND. L. J. 403 (1966) (chap. 13 *supra*).

In his evaluative article, Professor Jones also advocates more concern with the legislative process. This is surely a field in which political scientists have something substantial to contribute. Indeed, nearly all the social science literature on legislative law making comes from political scientists such as John Wahlke and David Truman.[4] Much of this work borrows theory and method from other social sciences, such as the role theory and the questionnaire techniques used in Wahlke's studies. Some of the theory and method, however, originated years ago with political scientists, such as the interest group approach used by Truman, which stems from Arthur Bentley, or the analysis of cohesion, which Truman gets in part from Stuart Rice.[5] For material on the process of administrative law making and adjudication, one might also do well to look to the work of such political scientists as Marver Bernstein and Peter Woll.[6]

Also with regard to the causes of legal policies and decisions, some political scientists have made extensive studies of the role of backgrounds and ideologies of various participants in the legal process. Much of this work stems from the current behavioral emphasis in political science on studying the correlates of policymaking behavior.[7] In the legislative realm, one might look to the work of Julius Turner on the relations between the backgrounds of legislators and their voting behavior, and to Duncan MacRae on the relations between ideologies and votes.[8] In the judicial realm, there is John Schmidhauser on the role of judicial backgrounds and Glendon Schubert on judicial ideologies.[9] Some political scientists have also studied the effects of the backgrounds of lawyers, litigants, and lobbyists on the legal process.[10]

---

[4] J. WAHLKE *et al.*, THE LEGISLATIVE SYSTEM: EXPLORATIONS IN LEGISLATIVE BEHAVIOR (1962); D. TRUMAN, THE CONGRESSIONAL PARTY: A CASE STUDY (1959).

[5] A. BENTLEY, THE PROCESS OF GOVERNMENT (1908); S. RICE, QUANTITATIVE METHODS IN POLITICS (1928).

[6] M. BERNSTEIN, REGULATING BUSINESS BY INDEPENDENT COMMISSION (1955); P. WOLL, ADMINISTRATIVE LAW: THE INFORMAL PROCESS (1963). On the need for sociology of law to concern itself more with the legislative and administrative process as well as other aspects of political science, see Auerbach, *Legal Tasks for the Sociologist*, 1 LAW & SOC'Y 91 (1966).

[7] H. EULAU *et al.* (eds.), POLITICAL BEHAVIOR: A READER IN THEORY AND RESEARCH (1956); S. ULMER (ed.), INTRODUCTORY READINGS IN POLITICAL BEHAVIOR (1961); N. POLSBY *et al.* (eds.), POLITICS AND SOCIAL LIFE: AN INTRODUCTION TO POLITICAL BEHAVIOR (1963).

[8] J. TURNER, PARTY AND CONSTITUENCY: PRESSURES ON CONGRESS (1951); D. MACRAE, THE DIMENSIONS OF CONGRESSIONAL VOTING (1958).

[9] Schmidhauser & Gold, *Backgrounds and Decisions*, in J. SCHMIDHAUSER (ed.), CONSTITUTIONAL LAW IN THE POLITICAL PROCESS 483 (1963); SCHUBERT, THE JUDICIAL MIND: THE ATTITUDES AND IDEOLOGIES OF SUPREME COURT JUSTICES 1946–1963 (1965).

[10] Nagel, *Attorney Characteristics and Courtroom Results*, 44 NEB. L. REV. 599 (1965) (chap. 9, *supra*); Nagel, *Disparities in Criminal Procedure* (a mimeographed paper presented at the 1965 annual meeting of the American Sociological Association) (chap. 8, *supra*); MILBRATH, THE WASHINGTON LOBBYIST (1963).

B. EFFECTS OF LEGAL POLICIES AND DECISIONS

In the realm of policy effects and impact studies, political scientists have had less to contribute because they have been more concerned with the policymaking and decision-making processes. Nevertheless, in a relatively recent survey of empirical legal research Ernest Jones of the Florida Law School particularly mentions work by various political scientists as key examples of impact studies.[11] Jack Peltason's name has become especially associated with studies of the grass-roots application of important constitutional law decisions.[12] Such studies do relate to the problem mentioned in Harry Jones' article with regard to the need for studies of the social efficacy of law in action.

Closely related to impact studies are theoretical studies designed to indicate the problems involved in maximizing the goals of a policymaker or policy applier. In this field, the work of such political scientists as Herbert Simon and Harold Lasswell particularly comes to mind.[13] They and other political scientists are frequently referred to in an excellent recent article on optimizing policy decisions by Louis Mayo of the George Washington University Law School.[14]

C. THE MAIN CONTRIBUTIONS OF SOCIOLOGY AND LAW

Now that I have said something about what political science can contribute to a social science of law, allow me briefly to suggest what I think the field of sociology and the field of law might best contribute. The greatest potential contribution from sociology may well be methodological in nature. The two most useful sociology textbooks I would recommend to legal scholars interested in doing creative empirical legal research are the Selltiz book on *Research Methods in Social Relations* and Blalock's *Social Statistics*.[15] I know these are elementary undergraduate textbooks, but if the ideas contained in them were prevalent in the law schools, imagine all the sociology of law research we would

---

[11] E. Jones, *Some Current Trends in Legal Research*, 15 J. LEGAL ED. 121 (1962).

[12] J. PELTASON, FIFTY EIGHT LONELY MEN: SOUTHERN FEDERAL JUDGES AND SCHOOL DESEGRATION (1961); J. PELTASON, FEDERAL COURTS IN THE POLITICAL PROCESS (1955). Other impact studies partly inspired by Peltason's work include: Patric, *The Impact of a Court Decision: Aftermath of the McCollum Case*, 6 J. PUB. L. 455 (1957); and Nagel, *Testing the Effects of Excluding Illegally Seized Evidence*, WIS. L. REV. 283 (1965) (chap. 23, *supra*).

[13] H. SIMON, THE NEW SCIENCE OF MANAGEMENT DECISION (1960); R. ARENS & H. LASSWELL, THE EMERGING FIELD OF SANCTION LAW (1961).

[14] Mayo & Jones, *Legal Policy Decision Process: Alternative Thinking and the Predictive Function*, 33 GEO. WASH. L. REV. 318 (1964).

[15] C. SELLTIZ *et al.*, RESEARCH METHODS IN SOCIAL RELATIONS (1959); H. BLALOCK, SOCIAL STATISTICS (1960).

now have. I also know that sociologists are proudest of their broad-gauged theories of society, but these general theories are not necessarily applicable to describing how a court or a legislature or a police force operates. Lower level theories of political bureaucracy being experimented with at the Berkeley Law and Society Center may be much more relevant.[16]

As for the contribution of legal scholarship, let me indicate my agreement with Harry Jones that jurisprudence has a good deal to offer the social scientists, particularly the social science-oriented jurisprudence of men like Jerome Frank, Julius Stone, and Thomas Cowan.[17] Perhaps, however, what the sociologist needs most to obtain from the law school people is not the content of the third-year seminar in jurisprudence but, rather, the content of some first-year courses in elementary legal research techniques and in basic legal principles, supplemented possibly by a legal process course that uses a textbook such as Auerbach's or the Hart and Sacks materials.[18] I know this is elementary stuff for law professors, but in talking with nonlawyer sociologists interested in law I have sometimes been surprised at their admitted lack of knowledge concerning how one finds what the law on a given subject is and how the formal legal process operates.

In other words, what seem to be especially needed are more lawyers with modern social science research training and more social scientists with some law training. It is heartening to see curriculum developments moving in both these directions, particularly at such schools as Wisconsin and Northwestern. As many are aware, both those schools have law and social science programs that are jointly administered by sociologists, law professors, and political scientists. Perhaps in the near future other universities will follow their leads. Indeed, we may be on the threshold of establishment of a new field of study that in time will become partially independent of its three core disciplines of law, sociology, and political science.

II. PUBLIC LAW RESEARCH AS POLICY SCIENCE

A. THE PROBLEM OF THE LACK OF POLICY SCIENCE STUDIES

Public law research within political science has traditionally emphasized three types of research—namely, case analysis, judicial biography,

---

[16] ANNUAL REPORT OF THE CENTER FOR THE STUDY OF LAW AND SOCIETY 1962–1963 (1963).

[17] J. FRANK, COURTS ON TRIAL: MYTH AND REALITY IN AMERICAN JUSTICE (1948); J. STONE, SOCIAL DIMENSIONS OF LAW AND JUSTICE (1965); T. COWAN, *Decision Theory in Law, Science and Technology*, 17 RUTGERS L. REV. 499 (1963).

[18] C. AUERBACH, THE LEGAL PROCESS: AN INTRODUCTION TO DECISION-MAKING BY JUDICIAL, LEGISLATIVE, EXECUTIVE, AND ADMINISTRATIVE AGENCIES (1961); H. HART & SACKS, THE LEGAL PROCESS: BASIC PROBLEMS IN THE MAKING AND APPLICATION OF LAW (1958) (mimeographed materials).

and law evaluation. C. Herman Pritchett's *The American Constitution* represents an outstanding example of case analysis by a political scientist.[19] Likewise, Swisher and Mason are among the top judicial biographers and constitutional historians.[20] Good examples of traditional evaluations of existing or proposed decisions or laws are included in McCloskey's book of essay on constitutional law and Shapiro's more recent book of readings on constitutional rights.[21]

In recent years, the traditional analysis of cases to determine what they collectively stand for has been supplemented by the quantitative analysis of Kort, Lawlor, and others.[22] Likewise some judicial biographical and attitudinal data have been quantitatively synthesized to arrive at generalizations concerning the significance of the characteristics of judges.[23] The evaluation of decisions and laws, however, is the area of traditional public law research on which behavioral methodology has thus far had the smallest impact.

In the past, attacks have been made on the alleged lack of concern in judicial behavior research for means–ends evaluation. The attackers have included Julius Stone,[24] Walter Berns,[25] Hans Baade,[26] and others. As recently as April, 1968, James Davies of the University of Oregon in a paper presented at a Claremont College conference said:

> If judicial behavior with its new and already indispensable research techniques . . . continues to ignore or depreciate such basic research [as clarifying the concept of justice], it will become increasingly futile, inconsequential, and dull. Or as lawyers put it, irrelevant, incompetent and immaterial.[27]

My purpose in this part of the epilogue is to summarize some of the recent scientific legal research that has had substantial policy significance as well as theoretical significance, and to say something about

---

[19] C. H. PRITCHETT, THE AMERICAN CONSTITUTION (1968).

[20] C. SWISHER, ROGER B. TANEY (1935) and A. MASON, BRANDEIS—A FREE MAN'S LIFE (1946).

[21] R. McCLOSKEY (ed.), ESSAYS IN CONSTITUTIONAL LAW (1957); and M. SHAPIRO (ed.), THE SUPREME COURT AND CONSTITUTIONAL RIGHTS (1967).

[22] G. SCHUBERT (ed.), *Mathematical Models of the Decision Function* in JUDICIAL BEHAVIOR: A READER IN THEORY AND RESEARCH 477 (1964); G. SCHUBERT (ed.), *Statistical Prediction and Decisions* in JUDICIAL DECISION-MAKING 111 (1963); and Nagel, *Judicial Prediction and Analysis from Empirical Probability Tables,* 41 IND. L. J. 403 (1966) (chap. 13, *supra*).

[23] G. SCHUBERT (ed.), *Political Socialization* in JUDICIAL BEHAVIOR: A READER IN THEORY AND RESEARCH 187 (1964); and G. SCHUBERT, THE JUDICIAL MIND: THE ATTITUDES AND IDEOLOGIES OF SUPREME COURT JUSTICES (1965).

[24] Stone, *Man and Machine in the Search for Justice,* 16 STAN. L. REV. 515 (1964).

[25] Berns, *Law and Behavioral Science,* 28 LAW & CONTEMP. PROB. 185 (1963); and Berns, *Behavioral Science and Equal Justice Under Law,* a paper presented at the Claremont Conference on "The U.S. Supreme Court: Usurper or Trustee?" April 28–30, 1968.

[26] Baade, *The Judicial Process: A Law Professor's View,* a paper presented at the 1967 annual meeting of the Southern Political Science Association.

[27] Davies, *The Study of Justice and the Study of Judicial Behavior: The Computer Confronts the Courts,* a paper presented at the Claremont Conference on "The U.S. Supreme Court: Usurper or Trustee?" April 28–30, 1968.

the future of such research. By policy significance is meant relevance to improving legal procedure or legal substance in light of given ends. By theoretical significance is meant relevance to explaining why things behave the way they do. By scientific is meant the quantitative testing of generalizations on a sample of entities, usually with a control group and an experimental group. Thus, policy science can be defined as the quantitative testing of generalizations relevant to improving legal procedure or substance and to explaining why things behave the way they do.

B. Past Policy Science Studies

As concerns the past, it is easy to agree with critics like Jim Davies that quantitative legal research has paid insufficient attention to important policy problems. It is, however, hard to agree with critics like Walter Berns who say that the value judgments involved in policymaking make scientific legal research inherently incapable of playing a substantial or desirable policy role. Numerous scientific studies can be cited that have resulted in important legal changes, although most of these studies have been made by law professors or sociologists rather than by political scientists.

With regard to improving the judicial process, the scientific bail studies of the Vera Foundation have clearly shown that one can release a high percentage of defendants pending trial on their own recognizance, and yet still obtain an equal or better rate of appearances in court by using scientific screening and notices than by using the traditional bail bond system.[28] Before the increase in pretrial release promoted by these studies, a greater number of innocent jailed defendants were damaged by loss of their jobs, imprisonment with hardened criminals, and decreased ability to prepare their defenses. The jury project studies of the University of Chicago have provided considerable quantitative data on the important policy issue of the relative merits of jury trials versus bench trials.[29] They have also provided data of high theoretical significance with regard to why jurors behave the way they do. The policy problem of delay in civil, criminal, and administrative procedure has benefited from the scientific studies of such people as Zeisel, Rosenberg, and Navarro.[30] Herb Jacob's forthcoming book, *Debtors in Court,* may

---

[28] Ares, Rankin, & Sturz, *The Manhattan Bail Project: An Interim Report on the Use of Pre-Trial Parole,* 38 N.Y.U. L. Rev. 67 (1963); and Wald & Rankin, *Pretrial Detention and Ultimate Freedom: A Statistical Study,* 39 N.Y.U. L. Rev. 631 (1964).
[29] H. Kalven & H. Zeisel, The American Jury (1966). See especially the project bibliography on pages 541–45.
[30] H. Zeisel, H. Kalven & B. Buchholz, Delay in the Court (1959); M. Rosenberg, The Pretrial Conference and Effective Justice (1964); J. Navarro, Data Analyses and Simulation of a Court System for the Processing of Criminal Cases (1967); and Nagel, Evaluation Charts and Questionnaire Survey on Delay in Administrative Proceedings (1966).

be instrumental in improving judicial procedures relating to bankruptcy and debt collection; and the forthcoming book by Watson, Downing, and Spiegel, *Judicial Selection under the Nonpartisan Plan,* may have a significant impact on legislation concerning judicial recruitment.[31]

With regard to improving legal substance, one can cite scientific studies that have led to proposed or adopted reforms in laws covering automobile accident liability, capital punishment, the transmission of property at death, and other matters of who gets what, when, and how.[32] The study of Negro voter registration by Don Matthews and Jim Prothro played a significant part in shaping the 1965 Voting Rights Act by way of their roles as consultants to the Civil Rights Commission.[33] Their study used a sophisticated regression analysis, which showed how influential the repeal of poll taxes and literacy tests would be on Negro voter registration. Their study also showed that these legal changes would be much more important than changes in the party structure, pressure group organizations, or antilynching laws. Don Campbell, the experimental social psychologist, has recently written a paper for presentation at the American Sociological Association Convention that provides useful insights on how to measure the effects of legal changes and that may have significant bearing on the policy controversy over the relevance of harsher sanctions as a means of securing compliance with the law.[34]

Policy studies can be classified in ways other than procedural versus substantive. They may also be classified as dealing with proposed policies or adopted policies. Studies dealing with adopted policies may cover general effects or merely deal with whether the law is being complied with. Policy studies can be verbal or quantitative, although some measurement and tallying of entities is necessary to make a policy study scientific. Policy studies can also be classified as broad in the variables

---

[31] H. Jacob, Debtors in Court (forthcoming) (The material from one of Jacob's chapters was reported in *Judicial and Political Efficacy of Litigants,* a paper presented at the U. of Iowa Shambaugh Conference on Judicial Research, 1967); R. Watson, R. Downing, & F. Spiegel, The Politics of the Bench and The Bar: Judicial Selection Under the Non-Partisan Court Plan (forthcoming). Both these books are authored by political scientists.

[32] A. Conard et al., Automobile Accident Costs and Payment Studies in the Economics of Injury Reparation (1964); T. Sellin, The Death Penalty (1959); and Dunham, *Method, Process and Frequency of Wealth Transmission at Death,* 30 U. Chi. L. Rev. 1 (1963).

[33] Matthews & Prothro, *Political Factors and Negro Voter Registration in the South,* 57 Am. Pol. Sci. Rev. 355 (1963).

[34] Ross & Campbell, *The Connecticut Speed Crackdown: A Study of the Effects of Legal Change,* 3 Law & Soc'y Rev. 33 (1968). For a potentially influential experimental study of the effect of positive appeals and negative sanctions in which the researcher was able to determine who would be in the experimental group, see Schwartz & Orleans, *On Legal Sanctions,* 34 U. Chi. L. Rev. 274 (1967). Those interested in a more extensive bibliography of legal policy science studies can write to Stuart Nagel at the University of Illinois for a copy of the 1969 bibliographic syllabus he uses in his "Law, Policy, and Social Science" seminar.

or entities covered, thereby increasing the likelihood of having theoretical significance, or they can be more narrow policy studies, like those associated with applied commercial research. Procedural studies can be judicial, legislative, or administrative. Likewise, substantive studies can cover any field of public or private law. There have been legal policy studies in the past, fitting into each of these general categories.

C. The Future of Policy Science Studies

What does the future hold for policy studies? There are signs to indicate that in the future there will be a substantial increase in policy science studies by political scientists, including those within public law. A sudden increase in concern for policy problems manifested itself at the 1967 APSA Convention when "The Caucus for a New Political Science" was able to draw an audience of approximately 500 to a hurriedly called meeting at the same time as the APSA awards ceremonies, which drew only a few dozen. The 1968 APSA meetings for the first time devoted approximately 30 panels to public policy topics and the APSA constitution was amended to provide that "the association . . . actively encourages in its membership and its journal research in and concern for significant contemporary political and social problems and policies, however controversial and subject to partisan discourse in the community at large these may be."

Foundations such as Ford, Russell Sage, and NSF are increasing their grants for legal policy-oriented studies. A number of book publishers have recently published or agreed to publish books specifically dealing with scientific policy evaluation, such as Yehezkel Dror's recent book, *Public Policymaking Re-examined,* and Austin Ranney's forthcoming book, *Political Science and Public Policy.*[35] Specifically within the public law field are such publications as those previously cited, plus a recent upsurge in articles calling for increased legal policy science research by such people as Arthur Miller, Ernest Jones, and others.[36]

These signs of increased interest in policy science studies are mainly symptoms rather than causes of the new concern. Four factors seem

---

[35] Y. Dror, Public Policymaking Reexamined (1968). Also see Governing Urban Society: New Scientific Approaches (S. Sweeney & J. Charlesworth ed. 1967); E. Suchman, Evaluative Research (1967); and G. Fairweather, Methods for Experimental Social Innovation (1967). Forthcoming books include Ranney (ed.), Political Science and Public Policy (1968); and Jones, An Introduction to the Study of Policy-Making (1969).

[36] A. Miller, *On the Need for Impact Analysis of Supreme Court Decisions,* 53 Geo. L. J. 365 (1965); C. Jones, *Impact Research and Sociology of Law: Some Tentative Proposals,* 1966, Wis. L. Rev. 1 (1966); Lempert, *Strategies of Research Design in the Legal Impact Study: The Control of Plausible Rival Hypotheses,* 1 L. & Soc'y Rev. 111 (1966); and Nagel, *Optimizing Legal Policy,* 18 Fla. L. Rev. 577 (1966) (chap. 24, *supra*).

to be particularly important in explaining why this increase has occurred. First, the methodological tools in social research have now become more sophisticated and more known to social scientists. This has given social scientists more confidence in being able to make a contribution to policy analysis that does not duplicate the approach of the philosopher, the journalist, or the man on the street. Second, the Vietnam war, civil rights, and the problems of poverty have aroused many people, including social scientists, to much greater involvement in doing something to alleviate these problems. Third, interdisciplinary activities, such as the establishment of the Law and Society Association and various research centers, have helped to promote collaboration between law and the social sciences, which is important in legal policy research. Fourth, a saturation point is almost being reached with regard to the statistical analysis of judges' characteristics and the contents of cases. These were the relatively easy topics on which to apply behavioral research methods, and it is understandable that they were the first topics researched when the behavioral movement began in public law in the 1950's.

In spite of the trends toward more policy science research and the causal forces behind the trends, a number of things still will always limit how policy science-oriented public law can become. First, some subject matter areas are more appropriate for political science, and others are more appropriate for other social or natural sciences. Thus, the evaluation of laws governing judicial, legislative, or administrative procedure is very appropriate to political science, as is the evaluation of substantive law in such fields as civil liberties, international law, and government regulation of the economy. On the other hand, divorce problems may be best left mainly to the sociologists, and mental health problems to the psychologists. Most public policy problems, however, do come within the scope of such political science textbooks as Peltason's *Function and Policies of American Government.*[37] A substantial portion of the nation's most significant domestic problems concern civil liberties and poverty, and these come heavily within the jurisdiction of public law and judicial policymaking.

In addition to subject matter, there are also methodological restrictions on policy science. It is usually more difficult to measure the dependent variables in a means–end study than in a voting behavior or case prediction study. It may also be more difficult to obtain a meaningful sample of persons, places, or things on which policy hypotheses can be systematically tested. More expensive financing may also be needed. These methodological problems have been imaginatively overcome in

[37] J. PELTASON & J. BURNS, FUNCTIONS AND POLICIES OF AMERICAN GOVERNMENT (1962); L. GREENE & G. STEVENS, AMERICAN GOVERNMENT: POLICIES AND FUNCTIONS (1967); and W. SWARTZ, AMERICAN GOVERNMENTAL PROBLEMS (1961). All provide relevant text material rather than original research studies.

the legal policy studies that were previously mentioned, and it should be emphasized that an imperfect policy study is more likely to offer more social and theoretical benefits than no policy study at all.

The main restriction on the expansion of policy studies, however, is simply the matter of personal tastes that cannot be dictated by any national organization or individual. Some public law people, whether they are traditional or behavioral in their methodology, are just not interested in doing research that has social significance. At the other extreme are the political scientists who prefer to do narrowly defined applied research of no theoretical significance on such topics as whether some specific city ought to adopt a city manager system. Most political scientists, however, prefer to do broad research that has both social and theoretical significance.

Tastes in research vary over time as well as among researchers. Thus, prior to the 1940's political science was heavily policy-oriented but highly impressionistic and nonquantitative. Subsequent to the 1940's, partly as a reaction to the unscientific nature of political science the discipline went to the other extreme of emphasizing quantification at the expense of policy significance and often theoretical significance. We may now be entering on a new era when we shall be applying the scientific methods of the behavioral movement to important problems that will result in findings beneficial toward building better theories and explanation systems, and also toward building better social and political systems. Political science and public law research within political science may yet become both truly political and a science.

Index of Names

A

Ackoff, R., 360
Adamany, David, 191
Adams, 151
Alker, H., 334
Allen, Layman, 31, 301
Allinsmith, B., 233
Appel, John, 342
Arens, Richard, 33, 379
Ares, Charles, 31, 83, 105, 359, 382
Arnoff, E., 360, 367
Arrow, K., 360, 367
Auerbach, C., 380

B

Baade, Hans, 381
Ball, Harry, 33
Banks, A., 67
Barrett, Edward, 298
Barton, A., 12
Barton, Roy, 70
Beardsley, Arthur, 60
Beattie, Ronald, 81, 82
Becker, Theodore, 158, 175, 209
Beiser, Edward, 141
Bell, W., 209
Bentley, Arthur, 378
Berman, Harold, 71
Berns, Walter, 381, 382
Bernstein, Marver, 237, 241, 378
Beutel, Fred, 294
Binkley, W., 250, 256
Bishop, Donald, 158
Black, Hugo, 228
Blalock, Hubert, 122, 142, 144, 149, 164, 167, 290, 311, 364, 379
Blanshard, P., 291
Boles, D., 291
Bone, Hugh, 225, 247
Bonham, Jerry, 12
Borgotta, Edgar, 59
Borko, H., 20
Bowen, Don, 185
Braithwaite, K., 360
Brandeis, Louis, 257
Braybrooke, D., 360
Break, George, 32

B (continued)

Brennan, William, 233, 257
Broeder, Dale, 30, 86, 315
Buchholz, Bernard, 12, 31, 54, 105, 317, 359, 382
Bullock, Robert, 81, 83, 124
Burdick, William, 71
Burns, James, 385
Buros, O., 16, 181, 201
Burton, Harold, 228, 257
Byars, Robert, 81

C

Cairns, H., 12
Callahan, Thomas, 31
Campbell, Angus, 191, 223, 235, 255, 292
Campbell, Donald, 303, 383
Cardozo, Benjamin, 257
Carlin, Jerome, 85, 113, 119, 317
Carr, R., 178, 208
Cavers, D., 377
Centers, Richard, 209
Chapin, S., 308
Charlesworth, C., 384
Chase, Stuart, 261
Chatlain, Lois, 81
Churchman, W., 360, 367
Clark, Thomas, 228, 241
Cohen, Felix, 12
Cohen, Morris, 199
Coleman, James, 170
Conard, Alfred, 383
Cooley, William, 143, 144
Cooper, H., 255, 292
Cowan, Thomas, 168, 294, 360, 379, 380
Cramer, Harold, 152, 167
Culp, M., 260
Curris, Constantine, ix, 12

D

Dahl, Robert, 177
Danelski, David, 175
Dauer, Manning, 137
David, Rene, 71
Davies, James, 381, 382
Davis, James F., 29
Dawson, William, 46

Day, W., 321
Dennis, Sally, 135
Dickinson, Marsha, ix
Dixon, Robert, 141, 283
Dolbeare, Kenneth, 175
Douglas, William O., 228
Douty, Harry, 32
Downing, Rondal, 383
Dror, Yehezkel, 384
Dull, C., 62
Dunham, Allison, 32, 383

E

Edgerton, D., 253
Edwards, Allen, 114, 308
Eisenhower, Dwight D., 257
Eldridge, William, 135
Erikson, Robert, ix
Eulau, Heinz, 214, 378
Evan, William, 29, 246
Evans, 246
Ewing, Cortez, 178
Eysenck, Hans, 201, 212, 234

F

Fagen, Richard, 133
Fahrnkopf, Nancy, 260
Fairweather, G., 384
Fay, William, 356
Fellman, David, 86
Fisher, F., 143
Fishman, 33
Forgie, George, ix
Forrest, Edward, 341, 357
Francis, Dale, 292
Francis, Roy, 12
Franck, T., 37
Frank, Jerome, 178, 179, 210, 216, 217, 218, 379
Frankfurter, Felix, 178, 252
Freund, Paul, 246
Friedman, B., 19
Fruchter, Benjamin, 147, 369
Fuller, Lon, 138

G

Gagliano, Felix, ix
Gallaher, M., 321
Gaudet, F., 178
Gilbert, John, 81, 144, 157, 321
Glueck, Eleanor, 151, 159
Glueck, Sheldon, 143, 151, 159
Gold, David, 378
Goldfarb, R., 105
Goldfield, E., 61, 62
Goldman, Sheldon, 185
Goode, William, 12, 181

Goodman, Martin, 157
Gove, Sam, 321
Green, Edward, 81, 83, 91, 93
Greenbaum, 317
Greenberg, Jack, 29
Greene, L., 385
Greenwood, E., 303
Grossman, Joel, 68, 175
Groves, H., 37
Grunbaum, Werner, 68
Guetzkow, Harold, ix, 59
Guilford, J. P., 17, 19, 114, 128, 136, 137, 139, 142, 143, 144, 154, 155, 162, 172, 185, 188, 189, 194, 290, 315, 334, 367
Gurin, G., 191, 223, 235
Gurr, Ted, 31
Guttman, L., 17

H

Hadley, G., 344
Hagood, M., 209, 287, 334
Haines, C., 378
Hakman, Nathan, 68
Hale, 120
Hall, A., 178
Harding, Warren G., 257, 258
Harlan, John, 228
Hart, H., 380
Hatt, Paul, 12, 181
Heller, Francis, 59
Herring, Pendleton, 237
Hess, Sid, 332, 334
Hicks, J., 250
Hoebel, Adamson, 32, 70, 71
Holmes, Oliver Wendell, 125
Horn, Robert, 246
Howard, Jan, 85
Hudson, G. F., 158
Hughes, Charles Evans, 278
Hunting, Roger, 33
Hyneman, Charles, 209

I

Inbau, Fred, 294, 303

J

Jackson, H., 257
Jackson, Robert, 210, 260
Jacob, Herbert, 383
Jacobs, Bruce, 171
Jefferson, Thomas, 278
Jewell, Malcolm, 214, 322
Johnson, D., 251
Johnson, Lyndon B., 42, 251, 268
Jones, Charles, 384
Jones, Ernest, 12, 379, 384

Index of Subjects

A

Abington Township School District v. *Schempp*, 32, 287
Administrative agencies, 46–58, 237–44
  adjudication procedure, 50
  congestion and delay, 52, 54
  Dawson Committee, 46, 55
  fairness of proceedings, 51
  hearing examiners to decrease delay, 52
  prehearing conferences and agreements, 54
  public participation, 46, 47
  rulemaking, 47
Administrative Conference, 55
Administrative Office of the United States Courts, 82, 87, 105
Administrative Procedure Act, 46, 47, 50
Administrators, 199–218
Afro-Asian countries, 9, 11
Age
  attorneys, 115–16
  defendants, 96
  judges, 211, 231
Alabama, 139, 221
ALGOL programming language, 358
American Association of Law Schools, 117
American Bar Association, 105, 117, 123, 124, 179, 210, 228
  Committee on Electronic Data Retrieval, 131
American Bar Foundation, 82, 85, 88, 96
American Civil Liberties Union, 153, 210, 295, 296, 298, 311–14, 316
American governmental structures, relationship with formation of public policy, 39–45
American Law Institute, 217
  Code of Criminal Procedure, 85
American Law Reports, 113, 114
American Legion, 210, 228
American national government, 39–45
  cold-war foreign policy, 41
  democracy, 39
  federalism, 39, 40
  judicial review, 41
  regulatory and welfare functions, 41, 42

American national government (*cont.*)
  separation of powers, 39, 42, 43
  two-party system, 39, 42, 44
American Political Science Association, 384
American Sociological Association, 383
American Veterans Committee, 210
Americans for Democratic Action, 210
Analysis of variance, 307–8
Anthropologists, 32, 69
Appointment of judges, 174, 193–98, 211, 220–21, 258
Asbury Park Press, Inc. v. *Woolley*, 134
Ashanti, 70
Assault, 82–84, 86, 90, 92–96, 99, 100, 102
Attitudes, 199–218
  civil liberties, 310
  criminal lawyers, 84, 89, 93, 99, 105, 106–12, 121, 300–302, 309
  judges, 9, 199, 234–35, 309
  police, 308
Attitudinal characteristics, Supreme Court justices, 9
Attorneys
  backgrounds
    age, 115, 116, 118, 122–23
    associations, 115, 118, 122–23
    education, 115, 117, 118, 122–23
    evaluation, 115, 118, 122–23
    interrelations among characteristics, 122–24
    nationality, 115, 118, 122–23
    related to courtroom results, 68, 113–24
  benefits from behavioral perspective, vii
  cross-cultural, 69–80
  defense attorneys, 82, 229, 309
  prosecutors, 229, 309
Avery v. *Midland County*, 141

B

Background characteristics, 378
  attorneys, 113–24
  defendants, 81–112
  judges
    backgrounds described, 199–226
    backgrounds related to decisions, 227–44
Bail, 83, 84, 88, 89, 93, 97, 98, 101, 382

393

D

Data cards, 325, 330, 349
Dawson Committee questionnaire, 46, 55, 56, 57, 58
Decisional variation among judges, 174, 227–44
Delay, 52–55, 85, 89, 93, 99, 105, 382
Democracy, 41–45, 75–77, 205
Democrats, 42, 191, 196, 221, 288, 290, 291, 292, 322, 324, 328, 339, 341, 342, 352
Dependent variables, 14, 22, 24
Desegregation, 10, 153
Dichotomizing variables, 150, 157, 360
Dictatorship, 75–77
Directory of American Judges, 181, 189, 194, 195, 200, 204, 208, 209, 219, 221, 227, 228, 233
Discretion, 46–58, 69–80; *see also* Decisional variation among judges
Discriminant analysis, 142, 149, 167
  assigning weights to the variables, 149
  determining the cutoff level, 150
  distinguished from correlation and regression analysis, 147–50
Dissenting, 242–44, 266
District, population center, 332
District of Columbia, 83, 85
Domestic policy, 41–43
Dred Scott decision, 249, 264
Dyer v. *Abe,* 134

E

East St. Louis, 324, 350, 353
East-West Center, ix
Education
  attorneys, 115, 117
  defendants, 97
  judges, 211, 231
  police, 298
Effects of court decisions, 379
  on criminals, 303–8
  on judges, 299–302
  on newspaper opinions, 285–93
  on police, 296–98
Egypt, 71–78
Election of judges, 174, 193–98, 211, 220–21
Elkins v. *United States,* 295
Empirical facts, 6
Empirical probability tables, 157–72
  for analytic purposes, 162
  broader implications, 168–69
  how to produce, 164–67
  for prediction purposes, 159
Empirically testing generalizations, 12–28
  choosing a topic, 13

Empirically testing generalizations (*cont.*)
  compiling the data, 20
  drawing conclusions, 13, 20
  explaining the conclusion, 13, 21
  formulating the hypotheses, 14
  measuring the variables, 16
  planning the analysis, 17, 25, 69, 113
  reviewing prior literature, 13, 23
  sampling the entities, 15
England, 42
Engel v. *Vitale,* 285, 287, 288, 289, 290
Episcopalian, 291, 292
Equal protection under the law, 145, 153
Erie v. *Tompkins,* 63, 64
Eskimo, 70, 72, 74, 76, 78
Ethnic groups, 205; *see also* Nationality, ancestral; Race; *and* Religion
Everson v. *Board of Education,* 285, 287
Every-combination prediction method, 170
Exclusionary rule, 294, 296–316
Experimental design, 303, 308
Explaining conclusions; *see* Causal explanation
Extroversion of courts, 62

F

Factor analysis, 142, 147, 172, 370
Factual stimuli to adjudication and law making, 67, 69–172
  competing contestants, 67, 81–124
  cultural context, 67–68, 69–80
  evidentiary facts, 68, 125–72
Family law, 205
Fay v. *New York,* 31
Federal Bureau of Investigation, 307, 316
Federal Communications Commission, 47, 237
Federal Power Commission, 47, 49, 237
Federal-state relations and comparisons, 41, 64, 134, 146, 220–21, 311
Federal Trade Commission, 47, 237
Ford Foundation, 384
Foreign policy, 43–45
Fourfold tables, 17, 18, 25, 361
Fourteenth Amendment, 134
Freedom of religion, 145, 153, 205
Freedom of speech, 145, 153, 205
French Fourth Republic, 71, 72, 74, 78

G

Girard College case, 10
Goal achievement, predicting, 363, 365
Gomillion v. *Lightfoot,* 342
Grand jury, 85, 89

Theoretical significance, 382
Thurstone judgmental scale, 17, 172, 366
Traditional legal research, vii–viii, 28, 69,
    178, 380–81
Trend analysis, 171
Trial courts, 81, 184, 195
Trial technique, 30
Trobriand Islanders, 70, 71, 72, 74, 76,
    78
Two-party system, 41–45

U

United Nations, 44
United States as a party in litigation,
    158–63
Urbanism, 98–104
Utility formula, 367

V

Validity of an attitude test, 201
Variables
    correlating, 126
    defining, 14, 22, 24
    dichotomizing, 150
    measuring, 16, 181–83

Variables (*cont.*)
    weighting, 147–49, 162, 366
Vera Foundation, 105, 382
Vietnam war, 385
Voting rights, 383

W

Watson v. *City of Memphis,* 11
Weighting variables
    for evaluating policies, 366
    for predicting outcomes, 147–49, 162
Wesberry v. *Sanders,* 135, 141
West Publishing Company, 60
West's General Digest, 301
Whites, 93, 94, 95, 102, 104
Who's Who in America, 181, 219, 228,
    238, 242
Wisconsin, University of, 380
W.M.C.A., Inc. v. *Simon,* 134
Wolf v. *Colorado,* 317
World War I, 43, 44

Z

Zorach v. *Clausen,* 285, 287, 288

This book has been set in 10 and 9 point Caledonia, leaded 2 points. Part numbers are in 36 point Bernhard Modern Bold; part titles are in 18 point Bernhard Modern Bold. Section numbers and titles are in 24 point Bernhard Modern Bold. Chapter numbers are in 14 point Bernhard Modern Bold; chapter titles are in 18 point Bernhard Modern Bold. The size of the type page is 27 by 45½ picas.